PARLIAMENTARY POLITICS AND THE HOME RULE CRISIS

Parliamentary Politics and the Home Rule Crisis

THE BRITISH HOUSE OF COMMONS IN 1886

W. C. LUBENOW

CLARENDON PRESS · OXFORD

1988

Oxford University Press, Walton Street, Oxford OX2 6DP
Oxford New York Toronto
Delhi Bombay Calcutta Madras Karachi
Petaling Jaya Singapore Hong Kong Tokyo
Nairobi Dar es Salaam Cape Town
Melbourne Auckland
and associated companies in
Beirut Berlin Ibadan Nicosia

Oxford is a trade mark of Oxford University Press

Published in the United States
by Oxford University Press, New York

British Library Cataloguing in Publication Data
Lubenow, W. C.
Parliamentary politics and the Home Rule
crisis: the British House of Commons in 1886.
1. Great Britain — Politics and government —
1837–1901
I. Title
320.941   DA550
ISBN 0-19-822966-6

Library of Congress Cataloging-in-Publication Data
Lubenow, William C.
Parliamentary politics and the home rule crisis.
Bibliography: p.
Includes index.
1. Great Britain. Parliament. House of Commons —
Voting — History — 19th century.   2. Great Britain.
Parliament — Elections, 1886.   3. Great Britain —
Politics and government — 19th century.   I. Title.
JN673.L83 1988   941.081   87-12288
ISBN 0-19-822966-6

Phototypeset by Dobbie Typesetting Service,
Plymouth, Devon
Printed in Great Britain
at the University Printing House, Oxford
by David Stanford
Printer to the University

PREFACE

Meanwhile we have probably the most interesting and difficult political situation to face which this country has seen. The Parliament will be big with the fates of the Ministries and the reputations of statesmen.

Edward Hamilton, 19 December 1886[1]

THIS book returns to a lost moment, to the time when Gladstone failed to solve the Irish problem. On the face of it, the chances were with him. He was the undisputed head of his party; he had great experience with the social, ecclesiastical, and economic problems of Ireland; he had a parliamentary majority, once the Conservatives declared themselves for coercion, at his back. And yet Gladstone failed to square the circle, and, in failing, split his party. The Corn Laws crisis of 1846 and the Home Rule crisis of 1886 mark two of those great occasions which transformed the parliamentary system in the nineteenth century. The Corn Laws question divided the Conservative party, sending the Tories into the wilderness and the Peelites into a season of coalition with the Liberals. The Home Rule question had the same consequences for the Liberals. Gladstone and his followers, after seizing the nettle of Irish government, were defeated in the House of Commons and in the country during the general election of 1886. With Gladstone and the Liberals in the wilderness, the Liberal Unionists found themselves engaged in voting coalitions with the Conservatives in the period from 1886 to 1892.

The subject of this study is the political behaviour of the Members of the House of Commons in 1886 at the time of the Irish Home Rule crisis. The study consists of a detailed analysis of the various voting patterns which can be established for this House of Commons, and compares these, as systematically as the evidence will permit, with the partisan, social, and constituency backgrounds of these Members. Strictly speaking, this book is not about policy itself, though it is deeply concerned with the political responses to policy formation. Neither is it about the House of Lords. It seems unwise to burden a subject such as this with issues which would require books in themselves.

It is extremely difficult to generalize about legislatures, since explanations of them are so frequently specific to time and place; but the problems special to this House of Commons—the crisis in the regime, the realignment of parties, and the reformulation of

[1] Edward Hamilton Diary, 19 Dec. 1885, BL Add. MS 48642, f. 56.

v

policy — are precisely the matters which make it a stimulating topic for investigation. To produce, for a specific House of Commons, detailed findings on general intellectual issues may make a useful contribution to what is known about parliamentary behaviour. Though it is sobering to find the evidence sometimes pointing in more directions than one, or to have findings which run contrary to what others have found, this research provides an opportunity to reconsider received opinion, and to re-evaluate significant questions.

One necessarily obtains the assistance and friendship of many in the course of a project such as this, and to all those, named and unnamed, I wish to extend my gratitude. My thanks are due particularly to Professor D. E. D. Beales, Dr Peter Clarke, Dr David Cannadine, Dr H. C. G. Matthew, Dr Roland Quinault, Dr M. S. Marsh, President D. G. T. Williams and the Fellows of Wolfson College, Cambridge, Mr Robert Faber, Mr James Brandl, Mr Bernard Lorence, Mr Chong Lee, Miss Susan Bennett, P. D. G. Ahlsted, L. A. Tullio, A. E. Lubenow, and E. V. Burkeley. Dr Richard Gerber and Dr F. C. Mench provided resources for the typing of this manuscript. The American Philosophical Society and the Trustees of the Huntington Library and Art Gallery encouraged this research with grants and fellowships. Some preliminary findings were published in the *Proceedings of the American Philosophical Society, Victorian Studies, The Historical Journal, Histoire sociale–Social History*, and *Parliaments, Estates, and Representation*, and I wish to thank the editors of those journals. Mrs Patricia Bradford and Miss Marion Stewart, at Churchill College, Cambridge, Mr R. H. Harcourt Williams, at Hatfield House, Herts., Dr B. S. Benedikz, at the University of Birmingham Library, Mr Paul Woudhuysen, at the Fitzwilliam Museum, and the staffs of the manuscript room at the British Library and the Bodleian Library were exceptionally helpful to me. Sir William Gladstone, Bt., Sir Richard A. P. Temple, Bt., the Marquess of Salisbury, the Duke of Argyll, the Viscount Esher, Earl Balfour, the Earl of Iddlesleigh, the Earl of Carnarvon, Mr Peregrine Churchill, and the Syndics of the Fitzwilliam Museum made available to me manuscript materials in their keeping or over which they hold copyright. My special thanks to M. S. Marsh, who encouraged this research in many ways, and to Professor W. O. Aydelotte. The mistakes in what follows, of course, are mine alone.

Naskeag Point, Maine   W. C. L.
St Swithin's Day, 1986

CONTENTS

INTRODUCTION

The House is a funny place, rather like a grown up school; with plenty of jokes and fun under the upper current of serious business. Many of the new Members seem possessed with an earnestness and a dullness which is quite appalling but we must hope that the former, if not the latter, will wear off in time . . . We are not so busy tonight as it is not a Government night, but as a rule we all squash about the Lobby to prevent sleepy or hungry men going home to bed or to dinner. It is like the demons who get no rest themselves but make up for it by letting no one else get any.

George Leveson-Gower, 23 February 1886[1]

The fatal day at length arrived, and with it the division in the House of Commons, which was the outward and visible sign of the cleavage of the Liberal Party. Those of us who took part in the memorable scene will, I imagine, never forget the poignant sensations it evoked as long as memory lasts. The moment was intensely exciting. I have many times thought that the greatest artist of the day could not have found a subject more impressive or dramatic than was presented when Mr. Gladstone walked to the desk where the division clerks were ticking off the names of members as they passed through the lobbies. With a marvelous firmness of step, and his mobile features set in an extraordinary expression of gravity and fixed determination, the statesman who all England learned to call the Grand Old Man might have been an early Christian martyr marching to his doom. From a point of vantage I was enabled to see him full in the face as he approached, and to me at least the sight was most sublime—the look of fixed, almost agonized resolve of a great leader to sacrifice his proud position at the head of a great and powerful party to satisfy the claims of justice and to bestow the blessings of peace and prosperity upon a sorely vexed country.

Henry Broadhurst[2]

LEVESON-GOWER'S and Broadhurst's descriptions of behaviour in the House of Commons could not differ more. Namier once spoke of the House as 'a club', and Leveson-Gower called attention to its convivial atmosphere and the earnest, even dull qualities of its Members under normal conditions shortly before the Home Rule question came to dominate action there. Broadhurst recognized the excitement of the decisive moment in which Gladstone's Government, having failed to achieve a solution to the Irish government problem, fell. What follows places the drama of the Home Rule crisis in its proper place in British parliamentary politics. This is a perfectly

[1] George Leveson-Gower to a friend (written from the House of Commons), 23 Feb. 1886, in *Years of Content, 1856–1886* (London: 1940), p. 242.
[2] Henry Broadhurst, *Henry Broadhurst, M.P., The Story of His Life* (London: 1901), p. 198.

1

appropriate thing to do. Legislatures and representative assemblies have long been regarded as avenues to an understanding of public attitudes and political behaviour. The types of representatives selected in different times and places, their policies, and their actions serve as indicators of the values, shared as well as disputed, in public life. The remarkable thing about the House of Commons in 1886 is that its Members were elected under a new franchise and a new electoral distribution. With new parliamentary cadres everywhere, the House faced the deepest and most intense constitutional crisis of the century. One new Member, the Quaker coal-mine owner John Edward Ellis, revealed his uncertainty in this political world. 'The more I learn of this place the less hasty do I become in forming conclusions. It has its hidden currents and shoals like all such bodies.'[3]

The House of Commons which sat from 1880 to 1885 died a quiet death. The Liberal Government which had presided over it had been frustrated by a foreign and imperial policy which had brought the dishonour of General Gordon's death at Khartoum, by the depression in trade, and by the reminder, as a result of Charles Booth's investigations of life and labour of the London poor, that the Industrial Revolution had failed to produce social justice. Above all, it was the claims of justice by the Irish, expressed in the twistings and tragedy of the Phoenix Park murders, the land war, and the Irish Nationalist Party's disruption of parliamentary business which brought home to Gladstone's party all that they had not done. Lord Salisbury's Conservative party might be grateful that the Liberal party had been unable to accomplish radical work, and after the fall of Gladstone's second administration on 9 June 1885, Salisbury formed a caretaker government. All sides, however, awaited the electoral consequences of the legislation of 1884–5 which extended the franchise and reorganized the political system. The old Parliament was dissolved on 18 November 1885, and the first nomination occurred on 23 November. The first contest took place on 24 November, and, except for the university seats and Orkney and Shetland, the polling was complete by 9 December. The result looked like a hung House. The Liberals enjoyed a majority over the Conservatives, but the Conservatives and the Irish Nationalists together exactly equalled the Liberals.

The Queen opened Parliament on 21 January. The Government of Lord Salisbury, for the time, remained in office, but that time was not long. Immediately, back-benchers in both parties set upon

    [3] Ellis to his brother-in-law, 9 April 1886, quoted in Arthur Tilney Bassett, *The Life of the Rt. Hon. John Edward Ellis, M.P.* (London: 1914), p. 73.

their leaders. Salisbury received some advice, but not much, recommending reconciliation with the Irish.[4] Anti-nationalist pressure came when Edward Clarke and twenty-eight other Tories sent Salisbury a petition demanding the suppression of the National League and the restoration of law and order in Ireland.[5] Amongst the Liberals, Arthur Elliot and Albert Grey, the latter 'thirsting for the blood of the Irish and all who sympathise with them',[6] tried to force Gladstone's hand, and, in insulting tones, demanded Liberal support for the legislative union. Such behaviour went down badly with Liberal leaders and rank and file. When Elliot rose to speak in the House he 'was wildly cheered by the Tories but had not support on our side'.[7] 'The Party appears to care as little for A. Eliot [*sic*] as for Grey', Herbert Gladstone said to Labouchere.[8]

The first Liberal opportunity to run Salisbury's Government to ground came on James Barclay's amendment to the Address to the Queen's Speech on behalf of the agricultural labourers. Not all Liberals, however, wished for the fall of Salisbury's Government and Lewis Harcourt regarded Barclay's amendment as insufficient. 'It would have looked like a surprise', he wrote, 'and would not be nearly so good a card in the counties as Jesse Collings's.'[9] Collings's 'three acres and a cow' amendment provided a second opportunity to dish the Tories, but even here the Liberals were in some disarray. Lewis Harcourt wanted to settle internal differences before casting the Conservatives out; Ferdinand de Rothschild and Arnold Morley, who would be a new whip in the next administration, planned to abstain; Francis Mildmay came to town, but abstained under the influence of some preliminary Liberal Unionist plotting; Lord Richard Grosvenor, the then Liberal whip who was not abreast of the situation, 'took no pains to get people up and is said not to have sent a single telegram'.[10] The Conservatives were not exactly arrayed on this occasion either. Edward Norris, a retired leather merchant and a Member sitting for the first time in 1886, had been assigned

[4] John Henniker Heaton to Salisbury, 9 Dec. 1885, Third Marquess of Salisbury MSS Class E.

[5] Clarke to Salisbury, 25 Jan. 1886, Third Marquess of Salisbury MSS Class E.

[6] Lewis Harcourt Journal, 12 Jan. 1886, Bodleian Library Harcourt deposit, 376, ff. 51–2.

[7] Hansard, 302: 142–4, 256–60; Harcourt Journal, 22 Jan. 1886, Harcourt dep. 376, f. 118.

[8] Herbert Gladstone to Labouchere, 23 Jan. 1886, BL Add. MS 46105, f. 165.

[9] Harcourt Journal, 26 Jan. 1886, Harcourt dep. 377, ff. 16–17.

[10] Harcourt Journal, 22, 23, and 28 Jan. 1886, Harcourt dep. 376, ff. 116–17, 123; 377, ff. 48–9; Labouchere to Chamberlain, 22 Jan. 1886, Chamberlain Papers JC5/50/67.

the task of avoiding a division by interpolating an amendment which was not on the agenda paper. Showing his inexperience, he failed to rise when the Speaker looked at him.[11] The Speaker then turned to Collings, who moved his amendment, and the Government fell on 27 January at one o'clock in the morning.

Everyone knew, however, about the borrowed time the Tories had been living on, and Salisbury allowed it to run out. After his Cabinet had been divided on a policy of coercion for some weeks, he dragooned it to order[12] behind a policy of coercion. In the process, he delivered the Irish Nationalist votes to the Liberals. The division on the Collings amendment, Salisbury knew, would end in a decision 'adverse to the Government; and an adverse division on the address is equivalent to a vote of censure'.[13] 'I have every hope that we will be out of office before the end of January — and what a blessing that will be for us all.'[14] For the Liberals, this meant the taking up of new constitutional responsibilities, and they were not all prepared for it. The Irish Nationalists greeted the defeat of the Conservative Government with wild cheering and waving of their hats. But it 'was received with almost complete silence by our own men', Lewis Harcourt wrote. 'Never were victors less triumphant or [the] vanquished less depressed.'[15] Salisbury's Government resigned on 27 January and the resignations were taken to the Queen at Osborne on 28 January. According to Reginald Brett, 'the Queen cried all yesterday at the prospect of losing her Ministers. She thinks Mr. Gladstone's Government will be the worst ever constructed, even by him.'[16] Both Houses adjourned until 1 February.

On 30 January, at about 12.15 a.m., Sir Henry Ponsonby, the Queen's private secretary, called on Gladstone and offered him the seals of office. Gladstone accepted, and on 1 February he went to Osborne to kiss hands. Immediately he sought to form a government, and he approached his former colleagues with 'an invitation to "examine" the question of Home Rule'. 'Upon this phrase, and the idea it contains,' Brett wrote, 'Mr. G. laid great

[11] Labouchere to Herbert Gladstone, 11 Feb. 1886, BL Add. MS 46016, f. 8–8ᵛ.
[12] Salisbury to the Queen, 15, 16 or 17, 21, 24, 26 Jan. 1886, Third Marquess of Salisbury MSS Class D/87/307, 318, 321, 287, 331.
[13] Salisbury to the Queen, 26 Jan. 1886, Third Marquess of Salisbury MSS Class D/87/331.
[14] Salisbury to Lady John Manners, 25 Dec. 1885, Third Marquess of Salisbury MSS Class D/48/269.
[15] Harcourt Journal, 26 Jan. 1886, Harcourt dep. 377, ff. 23–4; Brett Journal, 27 Jan. 1886, Esher Papers 2/7.
[16] Memorandum of Reginald Brett, 29 Jan. 1886, Esher Papers 2/7.

stress.'[17] Lord Hartington and Sir Henry James, suspecting the worst, could not be drawn; nor, as Gladstone noted later, could fully half of the former Liberal ministers.[18] Joseph Chamberlain and Sir George Trevelyan, Bt., however joined him, the former as President of the Local Government Board and the latter as Secretary for Scotland. Even Gladstone did not fully understand their motivations in joining, but, in retrospect, he thought they were prepared to seek 'some method of dealing with the Irish case other than coercion'.[19] According to some speculations, Chamberlain had been turned and would support Home Rule; but when John Morley was asked, ' "What is Joe playing at"?', he responded, ' "Fast and Loose".'[20] Getting Chamberlain into the Cabinet was not accomplished easily. Gladstone further bruised Chamberlain's prickly nature, already roused by his suspicions of Gladstone's Irish government plans and his own ambitions, when he asked Jesse Collings, who was closely associated with Chamberlain, to join the Government as Secretary to the Local Government Board, but at a reduced salary. Collings regarded this as a low estimate of his abilities and responsibilities. 'Damn! Damn! Damn!', Chamberlain wrote to Harcourt, who was trying to resolve this dispute.[21] Patience smoothed over these difficulties.

Other disputes marred the formation of Gladstone's third administration. These were quarrels about the places working men and young aristocrats would occupy in the new Government. Henry Broadhurst had been intended to serve as Under-Secretary of the Board of Trade, but Anthony Mundella, the President of the Board, 'protested against him as it is thought that the Manufacturers etc. would object to a Trades Unionist being put in that position'. 'Broadhurst might retort that the Working men would object to a manufacturer like Mundella being head of the dept.', Lewis Harcourt responded. Hugh Childers wanted Thomas Burt as his

---

[17] Memorandum of Reginald Brett, 3 Feb. 1886, Esher Papers 2/7.

[18] Mr Gladstone's recollections of the formation of his third Government is dated 28 Sept. 1897 and is published in *The Prime Minister's Papers, W. E. Gladstone, I, Autobiographica*, ed. John Brooke and Mary Sorenson (London, HMSO: 1971), p. 111.

[19] Gladstone's recollections, *The Prime Minister's Papers, W. E. Gladstone, I, Autobiographica*, p. 111.

[20] Brett Journal, 28 and 29 Jan. 1886, Esher Papers 2/7.

[21] For this dispute, see: Gladstone to Collings and Collings to Gladstone, 5 Feb. 1886; Gladstone to Collings, 6 Feb. 1886; Collings to Gladstone, 7 Feb. 1886, BL Add. MS 44494, ff. 164, 165–6, 178, 185–7; Chamberlain to Harcourt, 5, 8, 9 Feb. 1886, Harcourt to Chamberlain, 7 Feb. 1886, Chamberlain Papers JC5/38/43, 153, 154–5.

Under-Secretary at the Home Office, but Gladstone would not have it and sent Broadhurst there.[22] Since Arnold Morley, Edward Marjoribanks, and George Leveson-Gower had been appointed whips with junior ministerial positions, the fourth, Sir William Harcourt, said, ' "must be a cad" as two of the three already settled on are honourables'. Though it would 'make too aristocratic a gang to please our Radical wing', Arnold Morley wanted, and got, Cyril Flower as the last whip.[23] When the new ministers went to the Queen to receive the seals of office, Sir William Harcourt, the Chancellor of the Exchequer, 'being absent minded', nearly shook the Queen's hand, instead of kissing it.[24]

Even on its formation this Government had its critics. It was remarkable, Lord Cranbrook observed, for the absence in it of important names. Campbell-Bannerman and Mundella would be 'workers but will not add to the influence of the body and will be echoes of their Chief'. Morley's 'is the ominous name for Ireland'.[25] Labouchere, always looking to radicalism's main chance, did not favour the appointment of experienced men. This, and the Cabinet reshuffling after Chamberlain's and Trevelyan's resignations, were opportunities for reshaping the leadership of the Liberal party in a more radical image. If men such as Arch and Spensley were appointed to places, 'every new Member could hope for something at once, and would be kept sweet for the divisions.'[26] For others, the composition of the Government made little difference. Gladstone, according to Brett, was 'more completely master of the country and of his Cabinet than he has ever yet been'. He could form a Government out of 'ragtag and bobtail'.[27] As Lord Wolverton said, '12 broomsticks would do as well as 12 men'.[28] But Brett and Wolverton were not quite fair. If one compares the pool of talent from which Gladstone recruited his colleagues in 1886 with the Conservative front bench, one finds little difference. Both groups were highly experienced. Only one of the fifteen Liberals sitting in the House of Commons who held, or had held, Cabinet rank had entered the House between 1880 and

[22] Harcourt Journal, 5 Feb. 1886, Harcourt dep. 377, ff. 112–13.

[23] Ibid., 2 and 3 Feb. 1886, Harcourt dep. 377, ff. 89–90, 97.

[24] Ibid., 6 Feb. 1886, Harcourt dep. 377, f. 119.

[25] Cranbrook Diary, 5 Feb. 1886, *The Diary of Gathorne-Hardy, Later Lord Cranbrook, 1886–1892: Political Selections*, ed. Nancy E. Johnson (Oxford: 1981), p. 596.

[26] Labouchere to Herbert Gladstone, 10 Apr. 1886, BL Add. MS 46016, ff. 28ᵛ–29.

[27] Brett to Chamberlain, 9 Feb. 1886, Brett Journal, 27 Jan. 1886, Esher Papers 2/7.

[28] Harcourt Journal, 24 Jan. 1886, Harcourt dep. 376, ff. 124–5.

1885, and only two had entered between 1874 and 1885. Two entered the House between 1868 and 1874, and nine had entered before 1868. All members of Gladstone's Cabinet, with the exceptions of Lord Herschell at the Woolsack and John Morley at the Irish Office, had held positions in previous Liberal Governments. Of the members of Lord Salisbury's late Cabinet, only Lord Randolph Churchill and Lord Halsbury had not had previous government offices. Of the nine Conservatives who had such previous experience and who were sitting in the House of Commons in 1886, three entered the House between 1874 and 1880, two entered between 1868 and 1874, and four entered before 1868. The formative parliamentary experiences of both front benches came from the period before the second reform bill.

While Gladstone and his Cabinet formed their Home Rule policy, normal legislative life went on in the House of Commons, Gladstone leading his party 'from its left centre, rather than from its extreme left'.[29] For their part, the Tories sought to avoid parliamentary divisions which would drive potential Unionist allies in the Liberal party into the same lobby with Gladstone. It was an advantage for the Tories, Major Saunderson observed, when the Liberals accepted the Address to the Queen's Speech as they found it on taking office. It avoided a division in which the 'Whigs would find themselves opposed to us which undoubtedly would be a great disaster'. When Childers's proposal for the indemnification of businessmen who had suffered damages during the February riots came before Parliament, Salisbury wrote, 'I doubt the wisdom in the next few weeks of pushing Hartington & Co., unnecessarily into the Ministerial lobby'.[30] This policy of partisan restraint, however, became broken-backed when Hugh Holmes advanced a motion on 4 March, encouraged by Lord Randolph Churchill, to force Gladstone's Irish hand. The hand Gladstone produced brought all branches of his party into the same division lobby, and he was rewarded with a straight-party Liberal vote over the Conservatives.[31]

There was neither peace in the Cabinet nor in the division lobbies when the Government brought in its supply estimates for the various departments. The Inland Revenue predicted a 'deficiency in customs receipts' of £1 million and Campbell-Bannerman at the War Office and Lord Ripon at the Admiralty put forward requests of £2 million

[29] Brett to Chamberlain, 9 Feb. 1886, Esher Papers 2/7.
[30] Salisbury to Cranbrook, 15 Feb. 1886, Saunderson to Salisbury, 17 Feb. 1886, Third Marquess of Salisbury MSS Class D/29/183, and Class E.
[31] Churchill to Salisbury, 9 Mar. 1886, Third Marquess of Salisbury MSS Class E.

over the previous year's request. In this row between Campbell-Bannerman, Ripon, and Sir William Harcourt, Gladstone supported his Chancellor of the Exchequer. Part of his policy was grounded in Irish necessities. 'I am morally certain that it is only by exerting ourselves *to the uttermost* our financial strength (not mainly by expenditure but as credit) on behalf of Ireland, that we can hope to sustain the burden of an adequate Land measure; while, without an adequate Land measure, we cannot either establish social order, or face the question of Irish Government.' Other parts of his policy were grounded in deeper sentiments of a retrenching nature. Gladstone said to Thomas Burt: 'there is one thing wanting in all of you — none of you are economists. I am sorry there is such a dearth of sound economists in the House, the Liberals seem as indifferent to expense as the Conservatives. As for me I glory in the appellation of skin flint.'[32] In the House of Commons, radicals hung amendments on the estimates as protests against Government policy in Egypt and Burma, and against aggressive military and imperial policies.

The political and social order in Ireland came under parliamentary scrutiny in the Belfast Main Drainage Bill, and in legislation for the amendment of the Irish Labourers Acts. The motion to repeal the Contagious Diseases Acts raised a long-standing question of State intervention for moral purposes. In late March and early April, Liberal attempts to regulate the liquor traffic proceeded cheek by jowl with legislation on behalf of the Scottish crofters. In April and May, legislation to limit the carrying of arms in Ireland came before the House, along with measures for the further reform of Irish electoral conditions. At the end of the session, a coal-mines bill and a bill regulating shop hours received parliamentary attention. All the while the Home Rule crisis gathered force. Edward Hamilton, a close observer of these events, thought the new House of Commons was 'curiously constituted', having a character quite unlike its predecessor. 'It votes wildly and has no scruples about supporting individual crotchets in the Lobby.'[33] At Grillions, Lord Derby and Sir Richard Assheton Cross discussed the behaviour of this House of Commons. 'Its ways are peculiar', Derby recorded. 'Very few go away to dine: they sit like hens: sit through the whole evening: no chance

[32] Harcourt Journal, 10, 11, 13, 18, 19, 20 Feb. 1886, Harcourt dep. 377, ff. 132, 133–4, 143, 159, 162–3, 163–4; Gladstone to Harcourt, Harcourt to Gladstone, Harcourt to Ripon and Campbell-Bannerman, all on 12 Feb. 1886, BL Add. MS 44200, ff. 44–5, 40–2, 46–7, 48–9. Lady Dorothy Stanley's Diary, 3 Feb. 1886, Chamberlain Papers JC/8/2/2.

[33] Edward Hamilton Diary, 20 Mar. 1886, BL Add. MS 48643, f. 48.

of a count-out.' Cross described these Members as 'very rough' and there was widespread agreement that 'they are quite unmanageable by the whips'.[34] The House sat long hours. The strain put on the Conservatives, according to Lord Frederic Hamilton, 'was very severe. . . . Our constant attendance was demanded, and we spent practically our whole lives in the precincts of the House. However much we longed for a little relaxation and a little change, it was really impossible to resist the blandishments of the Assistant Whip.' Hamilton and his younger brother amused themselves by renting tricycles from the House dining-room attendants and racing up and down the river terrace.[35]

Gladstone began his progress towards Home Rule during the summer of 1885, and his diary records his reading, writing, and brooding on the subject until he was able to conclude that the Act of Union was 'a gigantic though excusable mistake'.[36] He treated his guests at Hawarden to discussions of estate management, theology, Genesis, and science, and, of course, Ireland.[37] To some, he made his intentions pretty clear. 'Pitt had assigned no sufficient justification for destroying the national life of Ireland', he told Lord Derby.[38] To others, he made his intentions less clear. 'He is very full of the Irish question, but I do not gather that he has any plan of dealing with it', Chamberlain wrote.[39] Gladstone had a plan, however, and one which was fully formulated even before the general election of 1885. There is a secret memorandum in the Gladstone papers which contains all of the essential elements of the Home Rule scheme which emerged the next spring.[40]

With the general election over, there was a new sense of urgency. Strong Parnellite majorities produced some of it. Other pressures

[34] Derby Diary, 15 Mar. 1886, *The Later Derby Diaries: Home Rule, Liberal Unionism, and Aristocratic Life in Late Victorian England*, Selected Passages, ed. John Vincent (printed and published by the author at the University of Bristol: 1981), p. 63.

[35] Lord Frederic Hamilton, *The Days Before Yesterday* (London: 1920), pp. 214–15.

[36] Gladstone Diaries, 19 Sept. and 9 Oct. 1885. I am grateful to Dr H. C. G. Matthew for making these references available to me.

[37] Sir Thomas Dyke Acland, Bt. to his wife, 11–12 Dec. 1885, in Arthur H. D. Acland (ed.), *Memoirs and Letters of the Right Honourable Sir Thomas Dyke Acland, Bt.* (printed for private circulation, London: 1902), pp. 355–6.

[38] Derby to Granville, 2 Oct. 1885, Lord Edward Fitzmaurice, *The Life of Granville George Leveson-Gower, Second Earl Granville, K.G., 1851–1891* (London, New York, and Bombay: 1905), vol. 2, p. 465. Derby gave a more extended account of this discussion in his diary, 1 Oct. 1885, *The Later Derby Diaries*, pp. 30–3.

[39] Chamberlain to Harcourt, 9 Oct. 1885, Chamberlain Papers, JC5/38/151.

[40] Memorandum marked secret, 14 Nov. 1885, BL Add. MS 56446, unbound and unfoliated.

came from Gladstone's entourage. Whether Gladstone considered himself an old man in a hurry cannot be judged, but others were in a hurry for him. Henry Neville Gladstone believed the Home Rule question had to be forced at once because his father was the only man who could handle it: 'With him is it not a case of now or never?'[41] Herbert Gladstone, apparently acting alone, lofted the Hawarden kite as an expression of his father's intentions. This produced 'fearful excitement' at Chatsworth, where Harcourt was visiting Hartington, and 'people are hoping against hope and trying to believe that it is not true'.[42] Rumours spread, even one about a visit by Parnell to Hawarden.[43] What others believed Gladstone to be thinking and doing was as important in these circumstances as what he in fact thought or did. For Liberals to believe that Gladstone was negotiating with the Parnellites meant that their leader was trafficking with disloyalty.

Meanwhile, a further sense of emergency arrived from Ireland when Sir Robert Hamilton wrote describing the dangers of 'the dreadful policy of drift'. 'We are in the throes of a revolution', Hamilton wrote. 'We are now face to face with the serious alternatives either of letting Ireland govern herself with all the dangers attending this course, or of ruling her with a rod of iron involving disenfranchisement in one shape or other, and coercive legislation.'[44] During this time the Irish Nationalists had not yet renounced the support they had given to the Conservatives in the previous election, and the word went out from the Gladstone household asking for intelligence about their actions. 'If the Irish split from the Tories', H. N. Gladstone wrote to Edward Hamilton, 'are (say) 335 men to allow 250 to guide Parliament and the country at the opening of the session? This seems altogether unconstitutional and impractical.'[45]

The Conservatives settled the matter themselves when they declared themselves for coercion, delivering the Nationalists to Gladstone. But, before this, Gladstone embarked on a cross-party solution to the Irish question modelled on Peel's repeal of the Corn Laws with

---

[41] Henry Neville Gladstone to Edward Hamilton, 10 Dec. 1885, BL Add. MS 48611, ff. 197–197ᵛ.

[42] Harcourt Journal, 16 Dec. 1885, Harcourt dep. 375, ff. 7–8.

[43] Minnie Pollen to W. S. Blunt, 16 Dec. 1885?, Blunt MS 21-1977, unfoliated.

[44] Sir Robert Hamilton to Edward Hamilton, 12 Jan. 1886, BL Add. MS 48525, ff. 1–2ᵛ. Edward Hamilton immediately dispatched the gist of this letter to Gladstone. Edward Hamilton to Herbert Gladstone, 14 Jan. 1886, BL Add. MS 56447, unbound and unfoliated.

[45] Henry Neville Gladstone to Edward Hamilton, 7 and 10 Dec. 1885, BL Add. MS 48611, ff. 195ᵛ, 196–196ᵛ.

the assistance of the Liberals forty years earlier. Just before Christmas Gladstone approached Arthur Balfour at Eaton, the country home of the Duke of Westminster, and 'walked him up and down the library for an hour trying to impress on him that it was the absolute duty of the Tories to deal with Home Rule at once'.[46] Gladstone pledged his support if the Conservatives would settle 'the whole question of the future Government of Ireland'.[47] His strategy proved to be impossible. Gladstone received only 'a curt and barely courteous acknowledgement' from 'Artful Arthur', as Churchill called him.[48] Such a scheme was unacceptable to the broad body of Conservative back-benchers represented by the likes of Sir Walter Barttelot-Barttelot, Bt., who wanted only a firm position from his leaders against 'Home Rule and a Parliament on College Green'.[49] It was also unacceptable to Salisbury, for whom order, not nationalism, was the solution to the Irish question. Other solutions would have to come from other hands. 'Arthur has another letter from G. O. M.', Salisbury wrote to Churchill. If 'we don't bring forward a plan for the Govt. of Ireland, he will, which is as it should be'.[50] 'It is not possible', Salisbury declared simply, 'for the Conservative party to tamper with the question of Home Rule.'[51] Both Conservatives and Liberals derided Gladstone's effort. 'His hypocrisy makes me sick', Salisbury declared.[52] 'What a simple minded old man', Lewis Harcourt wrote.[53]

Thus passed the initiative to Gladstone. Grasping for support on all flanks of his party, yet going his own way, he framed a policy consisting of two parts: a Home Rule Bill, creating a parliament in Dublin for the conduct of affairs strictly Irish; and a Purchase Bill, giving landlords the option of selling at a price fixed by a land commission, and giving tenants the option of buying at 20 per cent below the rental with Treasury loans of £50 million.[54] This was not

[46] Harcourt Journal, 23 Dec. 1885, Harcourt dep. 375, f. 49.
[47] Gladstone to Balfour, 20 Dec. 1885, Balfour to Gladstone, 22 Dec. 1885, Gladstone to Balfour, 23 Dec. 1885, BL Add. MS 44493, ff. 254–5, 263–4, 265–6.
[48] Churchill to Salisbury, 8 Jan. 1886, Lord Randolph Churchill Letters 1/11/1261b.
[49] Barttelot to Salisbury, 26 Jan. 1886, Third Marquess of Salisbury MSS Class E.
[50] Salisbury to Churchill, the second of two letters on 24 Dec. 1885, Third Marquess of Salisbury MSS Class D/15/158.
[51] Salisbury to the Queen, 14 Dec. 1885, Third Marquess of Salisbury MSS Class D/87/295.
[52] Salisbury to Churchill, the first of two letters on 24 Dec. 1885, Third Marquess of Salisbury MSS Class D/15/157.
[53] Harcourt Journal, 23 Dec. 1885, Harcourt dep. 375, f. 49.
[54] *Parliamentary Papers*, 1886, vol. 5, pp. 383–413.

a revolutionary proposal. It was not, according to Edward Hamilton, a 'repeal of the Union'. 'Indeed, the object which Mr. G. has in view is exactly the reverse: he seeks to render the countries better united; to establish a new union—a federal union.'[55] Even Carnarvon, though he could not accept it himself, said that Gladstone's plan could not be 'said to be a revolutionary measure'.[56] Others were not so sanguine, and Sir William Harcourt considered it 'utterly impracticable' and called Gladstone a 'criminal lunatic'.[57]

After Gladstone brought his plan before the Cabinet on 13 March, fierce disputes broke out. At one point Gladstone 'flew into an ungovernable temper and abused [Chamberlain] without mercy. Joe retaliated and Chex [Lewis Harcourt's manner of referring to his father] says they almost came to blows.'[58] Chamberlain's time in the Cabinet was not long. Neither was Trevelyan's. 'Gotto', as Sir William Harcourt called him, 'is in a very lugubrious mood and blubbering like a big baby when he was in his (Chex's) room in the H of C this afternoon. He has quite made up his mind to go.'[59] Directly, Chamberlain and Trevelyan went, taking a few minor ministerialists with them. In the Cabinet discussions leading to the introduction of the Home Rule Bill, Gladstone remained unforthcoming. They would only learn something about the bill, Harcourt complained to his colleagues, when the Prime Minister introduced it.[60] Suspense grew. 'Everyone is holding their breadth till the 8th', Minnie Pollen wrote to W. S. Blunt, then in Ireland.[61] On April 8 Gladstone introduced the Home Rule Bill in a House so far crowded that, for the first time, chairs were arranged along the floor in double rows. The Prince of Wales and his entourage were in the Peer's Gallery. Gladstone spoke for four hours, aided by his mixture of raw egg and sherry, in the greatest speech of his career. Passions, already excited, grew even more. 'The state of feeling in London is frightful', Campbell-Bannerman reported. 'It is lucky that Easter will take all our M.P.s into the country to wash the poison of Pall Mall out of them.'[62]

[55] Hamilton Diary, 6 Feb. 1886, printed in *The Prime Minister's Papers, W. E. Gladstone, I Autobiographica*, p. 116.

[56] Carnarvon Diary, 11 Apr. 1886, BL Add. MS 60926, f. 54.

[57] Harcourt Journal, 8 Mar. 1886, Harcourt dep. 378, f. 4.

[58] Ibid., 26 Mar. 1886; Harcourt dep. 378, f. 41.

[59] Ibid., 16 and 24 Mar. 1886, Harcourt dep. 378, ff. 21–2, 37–8.

[60] Ibid., 6 Apr. 1886, Harcourt dep. 378, f. 65.

[61] Minnie Pollen to W. S. Blunt, n.d., Blunt MS 29-1977, no foliation.

[62] Campbell-Bannerman to George W. T. Ormond, 14 Apr. 1886, Duke University Library, Ormond Papers.

The Easter recess and the by-elections to replace the twice-returned, the resigned, the expelled, and the dead provided opportunities for testing the country's sentiment on Home Rule. Local Liberal associations, even the one in Birmingham, rallied behind Gladstone. Chamberlain's 'letter bag is empty and Birmingham is in revolt', Lewis Harcourt said.[63] By-election results are difficult to interpret, and the mood of the country was not easily seen in them. In the earliest of these contests, before the details of Gladstone's Irish policy could be known, Ireland was not much discussed, though some observers noted a switch of Irish electors from Conservative to Liberal candidates. A pattern began to emerge in the Altrincham division of Cheshire, where Sir William Cunliffe Brooks, Bt. contested the seat vacated by his nephew's death. Brooks described the polling.

The total number of voters was fewer; but, the party-spirit is very strong in that Division, yet the abstentions were almost exclusively on the Liberal side: — so many declared that, though they had never yet voted *for* a Conservative, they would not vote against me, because of my advocacy of the Trade policy, which I thought it my duty to express.

Then the Irish went *solid* for my opponent — orders were given in the Chapels, that the flocks were to vote for him — the priests personally led them to the polls.

The transference of these Irish votes made many hundreds against us; so, I must have received very many votes from sound-thinking Liberals, who naturally are frightened at being led by Mr. Gladstone.[64]

At Ipswich, Charles Dalrymple, the Tory candidate who would win one of the seats there, objected to the 'wild and novel projects in reference to Ireland' and called for the 'preservation of the Union with Ireland as well as the restoration of law and order there'.[65] At Barrow-in-Furness, a Tory and a candidate put up by the Irish Nationalists opposed W. S. Caine, the Liberal who was suspected, correctly as it turned out, of being unsound on Home Rule.[66] Lewis Harcourt interpreted Caine's victory, with a majority larger than David Duncan's, who had been unseated for bribery, as a rebuke to Gladstone.[67] The smell of Home Rule hung over the by-election at Bradford when Shaw-Lefevre sought to fill the seat vacated by the death of W. E. Forster. As Chamberlain described the result, the

[63] P. C. Griffiths, 'The Caucus and the Liberal Party in 1886', *History*, 61.202 (June 1976), pp. 183–97; Harcourt Journal, 5 Apr. 1886, Harcourt dep. 378, f. 62.

[64] William Cunliffe Brooks, Bt. to Salisbury, 1 Apr. 1886, Third Marquess of Salisbury MSS Class E.

[65] *The Times*, 5 Apr. 1886, p. 7; 7 Apr. 1886, p. 10.

[66] Ibid., 30 Mar. 1886, p. 10; 5 Apr. 1886, p. 7; 6 Apr. 1886, p. 11.

[67] Harcourt Journal, 8 Apr. 1886, Harcourt dep. 378, f. 68.

'Bradford Election shows what will be the end of it all. In spite of
the large Irish vote now transferred to the Liberal candidate
the majority of 1500 has dwindled to half that number'.[68] Though
the only seats to pass to the Conservatives were in Ipswich, the
Liberal majorities, save in Barrow, declined in these contests.

Back at Westminster, the controversy turned on clause 24 of the
Home Rule Bill, the clause excluding Irish representatives from
Westminster. From the beginning this was for Gladstone incidental
rather than essential.[69] For John Bright, with his intense dislike of the
Irish, this was the only good feature of the Bill.[70] For Chamberlain
it was the essence of the question: imperial unity as opposed to
separation. And, if it was incidental, Chamberlain said, there 'is no
excuse for his not publicly giving way'.[71] When Gladstone, in the
Cabinet deliberations on the Bill, appeared prepared to drop the
clause he faced a mutiny by his colleagues. Harcourt, shocked, made
a scene; he, Morley, and Herschell threatened to resign.[72] Harcourt
and Labouchere negotiated with Chamberlain in an effort to bring
him into the Home Rule lobby.[73] However, as Harcourt said to
him, 'dictating to [Gladstone] publicly terms of surrender is quite
out of the question'.[74] Chamberlain wished 'the matter could have
been squared but it is hopeless and we shall have to take the gloves
off very soon'.[75] The gloves, of course, had never been on. For a
moment the opportunity for compromise opened. Labouchere told
Chamberlain that Gladstone would agree to have Irish MPs at
Westminster to vote on imperial questions and Irish taxation.
Chamberlain closed the opportunity when he wrote to Collings and
other comrades, 'I am assured that there is a complete surrender to
me'.[76] Captain O'Shea, whose dealings were always double, got a
copy of one of these communications and showed it to Parnell, who

---

[68] *The Times*, 16 Apr. 1886, p. 8; 17 Apr. 1886, p. 12; 22 Apr. 1886, p. 5;
Chamberlain to Labouchere, 22 Apr. 1886, Chamberlain Papers JC5/50/80.

[69] Gladstone to Granville, 31 Dec. 1885, BL Add. MS 56446, unbound and
unfoliated.

[70] Harcourt Journal, 12 Apr. 1886, Harcourt dep. 378, f. 79. Harcourt had
dined with Gladstone and Bright.

[71] Chamberlain to Labouchere, 4 May 1886, Chamberlain Papers JC5/50/
90.

[72] Harcourt Journal, 13 and 14 Apr. 1886, Harcourt dep. 378, ff. 88, 90–1.

[73] See two letters from Arnold Morley to Gladstone on 9 May 1886 describing
Labouchere's negotiations with Chamberlain, BL Add. MS 56447, unbound and
unfoliated.

[74] Harcourt to Chamberlain, 19 Apr. 1886, Chamberlain Papers JC5/38/48.

[75] Chamberlain to Harcourt, 22 Apr. 1886, Chamberlain Papers JC5/38/157.

[76] Chamberlain to Collings, 10 May 1886, Chamberlain Papers JC5/16/116.

sent it to Gladstone, who backed out.[77] More than one observer detected a sharp difference between Chamberlain's and Hartington's attitude toward Gladstone. 'Chamberlain's mind', Brett wrote, 'is tinged with bitterness against individuals; and revenge for slights unjudiciously put upon him.'[78] And this in contrast to Hartington, 'who laments his quarrel with Gladstone for whom he still had a deep affection'.[79]

It is not necessary to stoop to theories of authoritarian personalities to understand Chamberlain. A self-made man with the tendencies of an amalgamator and a monopolizer, suspicious and lacking an easy confidence, he was also proud and obstinate.[80] Never a part of the high politics tradition, this wrecker of parties differed in substance and approach from even other Liberal Unionists. Where Hartington and Bright thought their function was limited to criticizing Gladstone's policy, Chamberlain wished to frame an alternative, a positive Liberal Unionist policy.[81] A consistent thread ran through it: devolution might be accomplished, but without the restoration of an Irish Parliament. Chamberlain's detailed proposals, as he explained them to Hartington, were for a federated system, protecting the imperial Government, modelled somewhat after the Canadian example.[82] As he expressed it to his brother, the policy of the Radical Unionist Committee was 'to secure the extension of Local Govt. on similar principles to all parts of the United Kingdom under the supreme authority of the Imperial Parlt.'.[83]

Chamberlain masked whatever concessions toward Ireland there were in this in a truculent hardness. Reginald Brett discussed Irish policy with Chamberlain in January, just before Salisbury's Government fell, and Chamberlain revealed his rigidity. Chamberlain would

[77] Henry W. Lucy, *Later Peeps at Parliaments from Behind the Speaker's Chair* (London: 1905), pp. 184–5.

[78] Journal of Reginald Brett, 15 Dec. 1885, Memorandum of a conversation with Chamberlain, 16 Jan. 1886, Journal of Reginald Brett, 20 May 1886, Esher Papers 2/7, 8.

[79] Blunt Diary, 15 June 1886, Blunt MS 335-1975, ff. 105–6.

[80] Michael Hurst, *Joseph Chamberlain and Liberal Reunion, The Round Table Conference of 1887* (London: 1967), pp. 28 ff.

[81] See the exchange of letters amongst these individuals immediately after the defeat of the Home Rule Bill: Chamberlain to Bright, 8 June 1886; Hartington to Bright, 8 June 1886; Bright to Chamberlain, 9 June 1886; Chamberlain Papers JC5/7/49–50, 52.

[82] Memorandum to Hartington, dated Mar. 1886, Memorandum from Harcourt to Gladstone describing negotiations with Chamberlain, 20 Mar. 1886, Chamberlain Papers JC5/22/110 and JC5/38/45.

[83] Chamberlain to Arthur Chamberlain, 7 June 1886, Chamberlain Papers JC5/11/12.

turn out the Tories once they demonstrated no positive policy toward Ireland; he would approach Parnell and describe the lengths to which he would go to settle the land question and to give the Irish self-government along municipal lines; if Parnell refused, Chamberlain would govern the country, putting 'down any outbreak by the sword'; if the Irish MPs disrupted the public's business, he would suspend the constitution and put them out of the House after 'rousing strongly public opinion against them'. What then? 'Well, it is impossible to look further ahead', Chamberlain said.[84] Salisbury came to understand the thread of authority in Chamberlain's position. 'I am glad to see Chamberlain coming to the idea that a representative body interfering with every detail of executive government is incompatible with strong government', he told Balfour.[85] Chamberlain's position, W. S. Blunt noted in one of his shrewdest observations, arose from the fact that he was a democrat in whose democracy there was no room for nationalism.[86] At the very end, even some of his associates found it impossible to follow Chamberlain. Fletcher Moulton and T. H. Bolton advised him to take what he had, and call it a victory for his principles and leadership.[87] J. Powell Williams wanted to abstain in the division on the Home Rule Bill, but finally voted with Chamberlain because of friendship and because he 'would not be guilty, whatever may be my own opinion upon the particular point at issue, of the meanness of standing aloof from you in the critical moment'.[88]

In the last days, with all sides hardening, leaders summoned their followers into conclaves. On 14 May, Hartington presided over a meeting of the Liberal Unionist Committee at Devonshire House. Chamberlain, Trevelyan, and sixty-three additional Liberals who attended resolved to oppose the second reading of the Home Rule Bill.[89] The next day, at St James's Hall, Lord Salisbury gave his Manacles and Manitoba speech, declaring Hottentots to be unworthy of representative institutions. 'The Irish', he said, 'had become habituated to the use of knives and slugs.' On 27 May, Gladstone

---

[84] Memorandum of Brett's conversation with Chamberlain, 16 Jan. 1886, Esher Papers 2/7.

[85] Salisbury to Balfour, 29 Mar. 1886, Third Marquess of Salisbury MSS Class D/4/90.

[86] Blunt Diary, 24 Mar. 1886, Blunt MS 334-1975. f. 84.

[87] Fletcher Moulton to Chamberlain, 27 May 1886; T. H. Bolton to Chamberlain, 27 May 1886, Chamberlain Papers JC8/5/3, 34–5.

[88] J. Powell Williams to Chamberlain, 3 June 1886. Chamberlain Papers JC5/72/6.

[89] Harcourt Journal, 14 May 1886, Harcourt dep. 378, f. 133.

called to the Foreign Office all Liberals 'who are desirous, while retaining full freedom in all particulars of the Irish Government Bill, to vote in favour of the establishment of a Legislative Body in Dublin, for the management of the affairs specifically and exclusively Irish'.[90] Two hundred Liberals attended. Gladstone asserted the supremacy of the imperial Parliament, and promised to frame a plan which would allow Irish MPs to sit and vote in Westminster on imperial questions and Irish taxation. 'Wrapped in a speech an hour long', as one observer commented, these ideas 'still had about them a disquieting mistiness'. Then Samuel Whitbread rose, and said, 'then we understand that the Irish will sit at Westminster'. Gladstone 'positively glared at him', and read what he was prepared to do. It was 'turned so that it might appear that, whilst conceding the demands of Chamberlain and his party, he was really doing nothing more than what he had contemplated from the first, the alterations being quite immaterial. In short, having been right in proposing that Irish Members should not sit at Westminster, he was equally right in now proposing that they should.'[91] This was not satisfactory. George Pitt Lewis failed 'to understand their nature or effect'. 'I cannot accept the concessions made', he wrote to Chamberlain, 'as enough to justify me in supporting the Irish Government Bill.'[92] On 31 May, in committee room 15 of the House of Commons, Chamberlain met with his followers. At a dramatic moment he read a letter from John Bright advising Chamberlain and his followers to abstain in the second reading division, but declaring his intention to oppose the Bill. Bright's letter 'braced & encouraged the meeting on Thursday to take a bold course'. Only four decided to abstain, and forty-six decided to vote against the Bill. As Chamberlain explained to Bright later, 'the meeting admired your example even more than your advice, and perhaps they were emboldened by the first to disregard the second'.[93] The next day Hartington urged sixty Liberals he had gathered together to vote against the Bill; fifty-eight pledged so to do.

In the last hours of the debate on Home Rule, the drama heightened even further. Parnell, in his closing speech, shocked the House when

---

[90] This is quoted from the copy of the summons to the Foreign Office found amongst Sir John Lubbock's materials in the Avebury Papers, BL Add. MS 49649, f. 54.

[91] These quotations are from a Liberal who was present at the Foreign Office, who reported them to Henry Lucy who published them in *Later Peeps at Parliament from Behind the Speaker's Chair*, pp. 188-9.

[92] Pitt Lewis to Chamberlain, 31 May 1886, Chamberlain Papers JC8/5/3/38.

[93] Bright to Chamberlain, 31 May 1886, Chamberlain to Bright, 2 June 1886, Chamberlain to Bright, 6 June 1886, Chamberlain Papers JC5/7/46.

he declared that a minister in the late Conservative Government had given him every reason to suppose that a Tory Government would confer a statutory parliament, with the power to protect Irish industries, upon Ireland. When challenged by Sir Michael Hicks Beach, Parnell would go no further; he would not name the minister.[94] Then, in this emotionally charged atmosphere, Gladstone rose to deliver his final appeal. Gladstone hoped to make more of Tory ministers consorting with Parnell, and T. M. Healy had the task of getting Parnell to make a further statement. Healy was to signal Gladstone by dropping a sheet of paper if Parnell would respond to a further question. Parnell refused. 'Limp and irresolute', his mind and heart were on Mrs O'Shea rather than Nationalist business at Westminster.[95] Gladstone wound up the debate. 'The oldest member had heard nothing equal to this; the youngest cannot hope that it will ever be heard again.'[96] In the early morning of 8 June, the House divided on the second reading of the Home Rule Bill. Gladstone was defeated, and his Government fell. Labouchere paid gambling debts totalling £700 to Churchill, Henry Chaplin, Balfour, and Albert Grey for wagering on the passage of the Bill.[97] After the business of the session was cleared away, the Queen, on 26 June, dissolved Parliament. The House had sat on eighty-nine days for a total of 694 hours and five minutes. One hundred and fifty-eight Bills had been introduced, and eighty-three received Royal Assent. The first nomination in the general election of 1886 occurred on 30 June; the first seat was contested on 1 July; the last contest was held, save for those in Orkney and Shetland and in the universities, on 17 July.

[94] Hansard, 306: 1199–1200. The minister, of course, was Lord Carnarvon, who had made contact with Parnell, with Salisbury's knowledge, during the period of the Conservative caretaker Government. To the comfort of his colleagues, Carnarvon spent much of the following spring at Portofino. Troubled by his colleagues' coolness, and wishing to make his position clear, he returned to England and consulted with Salisbury and his family. He held his peace publicly, but allowed the word to circulate in private that he favoured a solution to the Irish question which would include 'some extension of local self-government'. Tory Leaders watched the situation nervously. 'I should certainly keep away from the H. of Lords & London at the moment', Harrowby wrote, 'as awkward questions might be put'. Carnarvon Diary, 24 April, 6 and 7 May 1886, BL Add. MS 60926, ff. 60, 66ᵛ, 67; Harrowby to Carnarvon, 9 May 1886, BL Add. MS 60863, unbound and unfoliated. See Hansard, 306: 1256–60 for Carnarvon's statement in the House of Lords on 10 June 1886.

[95] T. M. Healy, *Letters and Leaders of My Day* (London: 1928), vol. 1, pp. 255–7.

[96] For a description of the fall of Gladstone's third Administration, see George W. Smally, 'A Great Night in the House of Commons', in *London Letters and Some Others* (London: 1890), vol. 2, pp. 227–56.

[97] Labouchere to Herbert Gladstone, 8 June 1886, BL Add. MS 46016, f. 85.

In these events there lurk some questions of the utmost stimulation and interest. This House of Commons began and ended with two great elections. How did they affect the behaviour of Members and events in the House? The period was characterized by the great play of highly emotional issues. Was this the mere mischief of politicians scrambling for power and place? What was the role of ideology in these events, and to what extent did it guide political action? What was the place of Home Rule in the parliamentary agenda? Did these questions have substantive importance? This was the great age of political parties. Were parties in the process of decomposition and reconstruction? What was the relationship between leaders and led? What was the structure of the Liberal party in 1886? What were the motivations of MPs as they struggled with the issues before them? To what extent were they subject to cross-pressures produced by their social backgrounds and constituencies? Numerous answers have been proposed to these questions, and these answers may be summarized under three heads: the high politics school of historical research; interpretations resting on theories of social class and class conflict; and interpretations resting on critical election and realignment theory.

The high politics school of historical research[98] holds the field in the study of politics at the end of the nineteenth and the beginning of the twentieth centuries. Through the combined luminosity of their work, they have made a stunning contribution to the field. Their scepticism, their astringency, their unwillingness to be gulled by what politicians say has led them to expose the nature of political motivation, the way in which policy is moulded, and the way decisions are taken at the highest level of government. One of their particular contributions has been to show how great the gap is between policy formation and public opinion; the intellectual gap between the attitudes of the ruling élite and the ruled. Their detailed mastery of manuscript sources is daunting. It is as difficult as it is unfair to try to summarize their views as if they share a common interpretation of political life. They share an approach, not conclusions. Yet the general approach they share conforms to an

---

[98] For this school, see: Andrew Jones, 'Where "Governing is the Use of Words" ', *The Historical Journal*, 19.1 (1976), pp. 251–6; A. B. Cooke and J. R. Vincent, *The Governing Passion: Cabinet Government and Party Politics in Britain, 1885–1886* (Hassocks, Sussex: 1974): Andrew Jones, *The Politics of Reform: 1884* (Cambridge: 1972); Maurice Cowling, *1867: Disraeli, Gladstone, and Revolution* (Cambridge: 1967), *The Impact of Labour* (Cambridge: 1971), *The Impact of Hitler* (Cambridge: 1975), *Religion and Public Doctrine in Modern England* (Cambridge: 1980); Roy Foster, *Lord Randolph Churchill, A Political Life* (Oxford: 1981).

aristocratic notion of politics.[99] For them, parliamentary politics, like all politics, is about people rather than ideas; people in politics are forced to take positions, and in taking them they present reasons, sometimes expressed as principles, in order to account for their actions; politics is a gamble, and frequently that fickle bitch fortune goes against them; compromise is necessary; consistency is impossible; the great thing is to survive. For the high politics school, as for Machiavelli and Castiglione, *virtù* and *sprezzatura*, rather than fidelity to principle, are the political virtues.

The debate over the high politics approach sticks on this matter of the importance of principles and ideas in political action. As one of the most important of the exponents of this approach, Maurice Cowling, has written,

[the actions of politicians] follow from the solipsisms in which they are located. . . . The political system consisted of fifty or sixty politicians in conscious tension with one another whose accepted authority constituted political leadership. . . . High politics was primarily a matter of rhetoric and maneuver. . . . Politics was conceived as touching the hem of the garment of truth. It was an area of Right illuminated by Faith.

Directly, Cowling speaks of the role of the politician as 'corporate monarch, witch-doctor and bard' dealing in incantations.[1] The reader has difficulty in failing to conclude that, for the high politics scholar, politics is a matter of conspiracy and intrigue. Politics, it would seem, commands the actions of those at the top of the greasy pole as they scramble for power and place. Support from the rank and file and their policies in this collusive way of looking at things is not terribly important, so long as leaders can dupe the led. Now this reading of their work has not gone down well with the high politics school, and to be fair, they do not speak with a uniform voice on the question of ideological motivation.[2] Their aphorisms frequently get the best of them, and their protestations fail to carry absolute conviction when one is faced with the following:

Concentrating on the primacy of politicians' positions within party hierarchies inevitably breeds a historical doctrine in which ultramontane cardinals

---

[99] Noel Lord Annan, 'Hons and Huns', *The New York Review of Books*, 12 May 1977, p. 3.

[1] These quotations are found in Cowling, *The Impact of Hitler*, p. ix, and *The Impact of Labour*, pp. 3, 4, 5, 6, 8–9.

[2] J. P. Parry, 'Religion and the Collapse of Gladstone's First Government, 1870–1874', *The Historical Journal*, 25 (1981), p. 72 n. 7; Michael Bentley, 'Party Doctrine and Thought', *High and Low Politics in Modern Britain: Ten Studies*, ed. Michael Bentley and John Stevenson (Oxford: 1983), pp. 130–1.

consume their own church and exchange jokes behind the altar. At this height ideas, principles, and doctrines remain only as a form of self-realization (every man should have a hobby) at the end of a hard day's work.[3]

These criticisms, in consequence, have not been set to rest. As one scholar concludes, the common denominator of the high politics school 'is an impatience with interpretations that hinge on ideology, which they invariably subordinate to forces of ambition'.[4]

There is something baroque about the high politics school. In the first place, they are blind-sided by power. Power is the subject of their research. Power is a very serious business, of course, but their treatment of it is highly playful. For them politics is a game. There are winners; there are losers; but it really matters not who is who. Politics has velocity, but not mass. It has action and movement, but no substance. It is like reading Hobbes. Secondly, politics is about words, their elaborations, and their embellishments, the meanings of which are only partially obvious. This is the politics of mystery, and its analysis is gnosticism. As one of its practitioners puts it, the 'recognition of the mystery of political language' is fundamental.[5] Professor Vincent has represented this view as neatly and concisely as anyone.

Unfortunately Victorian society never generated a historian trained in its traditions. Unlike Lord Acton, most historians are not related to the Foreign Secretary. They are lower-middle-class professionals uncertain of themselves in the unfamiliar world of power, confidence, and leisure responsibly used. The professional man cannot interpret the nuances of this world, he needs to have it interpreted for him by someone like Lord Stanley.[6]

Political analysis, in consequence, is both an analysis of conspiracy and a conspiracy itself; only insiders truly know what is going on. In the long term this is an approach which cannot fully satisfy, because it fails to consider the nature of the support leaders require from the led, and it ignores that which binds the front benches and the back benches together. This is a matter of policy and the debate over

---

[3] Bentley, 'Party, Doctrine, and Thought', pp. 129–30.

[4] Stephen Koss, 'The Whirling Tory Dervish', *The Times Literary Supplement*, 20 Nov. 1981, p. 1343. See also Joseph Lee, 'Gladstone and the Landlords', *TLS*, 9 May 1975, p. 505. For a sharp criticism of the high politics school and especially of Cooke and Vincent's *The Governing Passion*, an examination of cabinet politics in the period under study, see R. E. Quinault, 'Lord Randolph Churchill and Home Rule', *Irish Historical Studies*, 21.83 (Mar. 1979), esp. pp. 400–3.

[5] Jones, 'Where "Governing is the Use of Words" ', p. 254.

[6] John R. Vincent, 'Introduction', *Disraeli, Derby, and the Conservative Party: Journals and Memoirs of Edward Henry, Lord Stanley, 1849–1869* (Hassocks, Sussex: 1978), p. xiii.

policy, which is only another way of talking about ideology. The unimportance of back-benchers was not an impression contemporaries had. James Stuart, a former Fellow of Trinity College, Cambridge and a Professor of Mechanism and Applied Mathematics in that university, a radical sitting for the Hoxton division of Shoreditch, had entered the House of Commons in a by-election during 1884. In his memoirs, Stuart contrasted his early experience there with more recent times. 'I think it cannot be doubted that at the earlier date of which I am speaking it was possible for individuals who were not on the Treasury Bench to influence legislation considerably more than it is now their power to do so.'[7]

Theories of social class, class conflict, and political behaviour abound. They come from all political directions: the left, the right, the centre; no one can claim a monopoly. Theories based upon social class share with the high politics school a disdain of ideology. Instead of replacing it in their motivational hierarchy with the quest for power, historians fond of theories of social class subordinate ideology to motivations based upon economic or social interest. The Home Rule crisis and the transfer of power in 1886 from Liberals to Conservatives, consequently, are regarded by both as little more than a coup, a palace revolution, because, according to this view of things, neither is concerned with policy and both are preoccupied with personnel. In the social sciences and social science history there has long been a crypto-Marxist tradition which, unlike the high politics school, has some considerable interest in the rank and file, but which, like those concerned with Cabinet politics, treats belief systems as inferior phenomena, as functions and results of other motivations rather than as motivations themselves. Though he would be shocked to be included in this tradition, and though he held to a very different political and intellectual position, Sir Lewis Namier believed the history of England could be written in terms of the social composition of the House of Commons. '[The] idea of representation and the nature of the body politic vary from age to age, and with them varies the social structure of the House of Commons.'[8] Scholars in the nineteenth century became fascinated by parliamentary history. For them, dominated by a teleology which did not see how representative institutions could serve as instruments for resisting social and political change, parliaments advanced liberty democracy and equality at the

---

[7] James Stuart, *Reminiscences* (Printed for private circulation at the Chiswick Press, London: 1911), p. 240.

[8] Sir Lewis Namier, *England in the Age of the American Revolution* (London: 1930), p. 3.

expense of traditional élites. This is the Whig interpretation of history. Monarchial power, in this way of looking at things, is incompatible with the interests represented by parliaments. These last serve as agencies for the defeat of social anacronisms by rising social forces. In the English-speaking world, William Stubbs provided the classic statement of this position in *The Constitutional History of England in its Origin and Development*, which began appearing in 1874. Its very title, with the tell-tale expressions 'origin' and 'development', reveals the teleology of one for whom, according to Helen M. Cam, 'parliament stood for democracy, and its representative element was its essential feature'.[9]

R. C. K. Ensor made, for British politics in the 1880s, what has become one of the most influential applications of social class theories.[10] In this manner he explains three interrrelated events: in England, the shift in political power from the Liberals to the Conservatives; in Ireland, the rise of violent nationalism; and, throughout the United Kingdom, the displacement of old élites by new political forces. I have expressed myself elsewhere[11] on the degree to which Ensor's ideas can be confirmed by formal methods, and here, therefore, I wish merely to point to the more general implications of his work. For Ensor, new prairie wheat, acting 'as a bolt from the blue', undermined Irish and English agriculture. Tenants, unable to pay their rents, resorted to agrarian violence which aroused English hostility toward the Irish. 'The result throughout English society was a Conservative reaction' which became 'Conservative in the party sense'. What turned the Liberal business class of 1886 really was the Irish agrarian revolution. Ensor is careful to avoid attributing social and political change to a rising proletariat—it was Irish, not English; it was agricultural, not industrial—but at a single stroke he accounts for ideological changes and for changes in the ruling élite by calling attention to prior changes in the economic and social structure. Historians have taken up this point of view, and have argued that class voting emerged in 1886, when upper- and

---

[9] Helen M. Cam, *Law-Finders and Law Makers in Medieval England, Collected Studies in Legal and Constitutional History* (New York: 1963), p. 195, quoted in John Bell Henneman, 'Introduction: Studies in the History of Parliaments', *Legislative Studies Quarterly*, 8.2 (May 1982), p. 268.

[10] R. C. K. Ensor, 'Some Political and Economic Interactions in Later Victorian England', *Transactions of the Royal Historical Society*, 4th series, 31 (1949), pp. 17–28, reprinted in Robert Livingston Schuyler and Herman Ausubel (eds.), *The Making of English History* (New York: 1952), pp. 534–42.

[11] W. C. Lubenow, 'Ireland, the Great Depression, and the Railway Rates: Political Issues and Backbench Opinion in the House of Commons of 1886', *Proceedings of the American Philosophical Society*, 122.4 (Aug. 1978), pp. 204–13.

middle-class Liberals, taking Home Rule as a mere excuse, departed to the Conservatives from a party whose social radicalism had sore disturbed them.[12]

Theories of social class and social conflict have made an enormous contribution to historical understanding, and historical consciousness. However, social class is not for nothing one of the most disputed concepts in the social sciences. One is torn dreadfully as one begins to explore the social history of politics. Studies of legislative politics have shown little relationship between voting and the social background of Members.[13] More recently, the severest criticism of class interpretations of behaviour have come from students of electoral politics who find religion, rather than social position, to be the best predictor of political cleavages in the period from 1885 to 1914.[14] The evidence for social conflict in the House of Commons of 1886 is, as this study shows, extremely recalcitrant.

Another approach to the study of British politics at the end of the nineteenth century is to adopt critical election and realignment theories, an important field in the study of American electoral politics, and one thought sufficiently fertile for transport to Britain.[15] This body of ideas may be summarized in the following manner. Partisan transformation is a process which begins in 'surges of electoral movement', powered by increased turn-out, and which gives

---

[12] Neal Blewett, *The Peers, the Parties, and the People: The General Elections of 1910* (London: 1972), pp. 4, 10, 75; O. F. Christie, *The Transition to Democracy, 1867–1914* (London: 1934), p. 198; Ivor Jennings, *Party Politics* (London: 1961), vol. 2, p. 184; Stephen Koss, *Sir John Brunner, Radical Plutocrat* (Cambridge: 1970), pp. 113–14; P. F. Clarke, *Lancashire and the New Liberalism* (Cambridge: 1971), *passim*.

[13] W. O. Aydelotte, 'The Country Gentlemen and the Repeal of the Corn Laws', *English Historical Review*, 82, (Jan. 1967), pp. 47–60.

[14] Kenneth Wald, 'The Rise of Class-Based Voting in London', *Comparative Politics*, 5.9 (1977), pp. 219–29, and 'Class and the Vote Before the First World War', *British Journal of Political Science*, 5.8 (1978), pp. 441–57. See Professor Wald's much more extensive statements on this subject in *Crosses on the Ballot: Patterns of British Voter Alignment Since 1885* (Princeton: 1983).

[15] V. O. Key, Jr., 'A Theory of Critical Elections', *Journal of Politics*, 17 (1955), pp. 3–18; W. D. Burnham, *Critical Elections and the Mainsprings of American Politics* (New York: 1970); Joel H. Silbey, Allan G. Bogue, and William H. Flanigan (eds.), *The History of American Electoral Behavior* (Princeton: 1978); Jerome M. Clubb, William H. Flanigan, and Nancy H. Zingale, *Partisan Realignment: Voters, Parties, and Government in American History* (Beverly Hills: 1980); Blewett, *The Peers, the Parties, and the People*, chs. 1–2; Hugh Stephens, 'The Changing Context of British Politics in the 1880s: The Reform Acts and the Formation of the Liberal Unionist Party', *Social Science History*, 1.4 (Summer 1977), pp. 486–501, and 'Party Realignment in Britain, 1900–1925, A Preliminary Analysis', *Social Science History*, 6.1 (Winter 1982), pp. 35–66.

to a new partisan majority control over the Government. Continued electoral approval enables this partisan majority to hold office for a period sufficient to institutionalize its policy agenda. Time passes. Generational change among electors and their new policy demands lead to electoral and partisan decay: a decline of electoral support, the necessity of partisan coalitions, and the incapacity to govern. These circumstances produce a new critical election.[16] The elections of 1886 and 1906 have been understood by some students of British politics as realigning, or critical, elections.[17]

According to realignment theories of this kind, Irish policy formation and partisan change are expressions of changes in constituencies. Elections are political devices for tension management. Governing structures tend to be stable and static. Social and economic structures tend to be dynamic. Constituencies, since they are closest to these social processes, change first, and critical elections are those which bring governing élites into accord with social relationships. In so doing they reduce tensions between government and society by altering the composition of the governing élite.

How far, in the present state of our knowledge, this can be taken is difficult to say. Some of the most distinguished work by modern scholars had been done on this question. As one would suppose, a body of criticism has arisen, and scholarly debate rages among advocates of various positions. Some criticism is general, fixing attention on the problem of identifying the characteristics of realigning elections. Other criticisms focus on the difficulty of assessing the connection between electoral and policy change.[18] In fact, some work regards the actions of governing élites, in the aftermath of realignments, as more important than electoral change. Policy-making, in this view, completes and confirms realignments, and leaders rather than voters determine the shape and direction of the political system.[19] More important for the present study, objections have been raised to the view that the elections of 1886 and 1906 were realigning ones.[20] For most of the nineteenth century in Britain, in

[16] I owe this summary to Professor Ballard Campbell's review of Clubb, Flanigan, and Zingale, *Partisan Realignment: Voters, Parties, and Government in American History*, in *Social Science History*, 6.2 (Spring 1982), p. 260.

[17] Blewett, *The Peers, the Parties, and the People*, chs. 1–2; Stephens, 'The Changing Context of British Politics in the 1880s', *passim*.

[18] Ballard Campbell, review of Clubb, Flanigan, and Zingale, *Partisan Realignment*, p. 262.

[19] Richard L. McCormick, 'The Realignment Synthesis in American History', *Journal of Interdisciplinary History*, 13.1 (Summer 1982), pp. 85–105.

[20] Kenneth D. Wald, 'Realignment Theory and British Party Development: A Critique', *Political Studies*, 30 (1982), pp. 207–20.

contrast to the Continent, there was not much interest in elections. Until 1885 a large proportion of seats remained uncontested, and although the proportion of uncontested elections declined, nearly a quarter of the constituencies were uncontested in December 1910, and a tithe remained uncontested in the election of 1931.[21] Elections in the nineteenth century seem out of touch with the pulsating movements of the time, industrialization and urbanization. Moreover, Governments achieved policy changes contrary to the electoral surges which brought them to power. One thinks of the repeal of the Corn Laws. One might also think of Gladstone's Home Rule policy, and its relation to the general election of 1885, which might also be seen in the same way. Moreover, the great political reforms of the nineteenth century, in 1832, 1867, and 1884–5, had been preceded by no significant electoral transformations. British political institutions had a capacity for accommodation which enabled partisan élites to introduce changes in their policy agenda without prior changes in constituency demands. Pressures from without found their expression in agencies other than constituency characteristics and organizations.[22] Members paid great attention to the electors who had returned them, but there is little evidence that electors required obedience to electoral mandates.[23]

One would not dash willingly into the teeth of these controversies, and what follows does not propose to do so. Whatever reservations one has about the high politics school, theories of social conflict, and theories of electoral realignment, each has made a distinguished contribution to our understanding of modern politics. At the least, each offers points of purchase and preliminary hypotheses which can be tested further. At the most, each offers a view of politics the terms of which can be specified with greater precision by further examination. The present study begins with an analysis of the general election of 1885 to discuss the nature of the House of Commons which sat in 1886. It turns then to a discussion of voting patterns in the House of Commons as a means of describing the points of substantive cleavage in parliamentary politics. It proceeds then to a consideration of the ways in which partisan affiliation, social class,

---

[21] W. O. Aydelotte, 'A Data Archive for Modern British Political History', *Quantification in History*, (Reading, Mass., Menlo Park, Calif., London, and Don Mills, Ontario: 1971), p. 108.

[22] Patricia Hollis (ed.), *Pressure from Without in Early Victorian England* (London: 1974), ch. 1 and *passim*.

[23] W. O. Aydelotte, 'Constituency Influence on the British House of Commons, 1841–1847', in *The History of Parliamentary Behavior*, ed. W. O. Aydelotte (Princeton: 1977), p. 246. See also Chapter 5 below.

and constituency background shaped political action. It examines the break-up of the Liberal party over Home Rule, and shows the relationship between this disruption and previous disagreements within the Liberal party. The study ends with a discussion of the general election of 1886, to trace the consequences of the political crisis over Home Rule in the House of Commons.

This study is based upon two kinds of evidence: statistical data drawn from the division lists of the House of Commons, and detailed information concerning the partisan, social, and constituency backgrounds of Members of Parliament; and unpublished manuscript evidence drawn from the archives of late Victorian politicians. The evidence of parliamentary voting, subjected as it is to numerical methods, has been the subject of some debate. Counting noses, as Louis Halle once said, is not the same thing as exploring minds, and this is doubtless true. But, like most witticisms, it is true only so far as it goes. Quantification is merely a device for describing the incidence, frequency, and variation of a certain kind of observable behaviour. It allows us to gain some understanding of the beliefs and values of such men as William Wither Bramston Beach, an elegant landed gentleman sitting for the Andover division of Hampshire, who apparently exerted great influence upon his colleagues in private but rarely spoke.[24] (Beach entered the debates in 1886 but once. He asked whether 'a patent had been granted to one particular firm for supplying ensilage devices'.)[25] The evidence of parliamentary voting, moreover, has the cardinal advantage of being information derived from the putting of uniform propositions to an entire population of individuals. So far as it goes, the evidence of the division lists is unambiguous and complete. As John Buchan said, when speaking of Sir Walter Scott's study of the law, 'its complexity and exactness formed a valuable corrective to a riotous imagination'.[26]

Voting, of course, does not tell the whole story. Some issues did not come to votes. However, without knowing the positions of Members as recorded in the division lobbies we are left to helpless speculation, guided only by the statements of a few in the parliamentary debates or in their private papers. Additionally, not all Members vote on all occasions, and most legislatures have a high incidence of absenteeism. During the Long Parliament, little more than half

---

[24] Mrs Adrian Porter, *The Life and Letters of Sir John Henniker Heaton, Bt.* (London and New York: 1916), pp. 26–7.

[25] Hansard (1886), 306: 831.

[26] Quoted in Richard Usborne, *Clubland Heroes* (London: 1953), p. 85.

the House was present for the debate on Stafford's attainder.[27] Sir Richard Temple's voting record, by his own account, set to shame almost all his colleagues, yet even Temple was absent from the House from March 24 to April 14 for reason of illness.[28] Others were absent because of business or professional demands, or because of their rural pleasures. After describing various personal and professional motives for entering the House, Temple addressed himself to the question of attendance.

On critical occasions all Members without distinction will be present to vote. But on ordinary occasions it happens that, with these several motives overlying the fundamental motive, the attendance of Members in the House will be varied. In other words, some will attend more and others less. It does not follow that he who makes politics his pursuit, as a grand profession, will be very regular in attendance. If he be in office there will be public business to which he must apply himself, even though he be within beck and call of the House at a moment's notice. If he is not in office he may be engaged in important meetings outside the House; and for speeches to be delivered inside the House much preparation in his study at home will be needed. The man of business, being occupied all day, will not attend the House till late in the afternoon. The man of social status will have many public banquets claiming his assistance; indeed nearly all the engagements and avocations of metropolitan society affect Members of Parliament in a greater or lesser degree.[29]

It is impossible to explain all issues all the time, or to account for the actions of all individuals on all occasions using this evidence, or any other evidence for that matter. The most which can be hoped for is to discover some general patterns and trends which cover most of the issues most of the time.

Parliamentary voting, and the meaning of a parliamentary vote, is no simple matter. Clear breaks within parties rule out a narrow cause and effect relationship between partisan affiliation and voting. Parliamentary voting involves simultaneous considerations of both political strategy and ideological principle. To consider voting as simply one or the other is a false dichotomy which trivializes political experience. Parliamentary voting involves an appreciation of many things: the measure before the House and its relationship to other measures, the future of the Government, the reputations of individuals,

---

[27] Valerie Pearl, 'In Pursuit of the King', *The Times Literary Supplement*, 18 June 1982, p. 670.

[28] Sir Richard Temple, Bt., *The Story of My Life* (London, Paris, and Melbourne: 1896), vol. 2, p. 260; The Parliamentary Letters of Sir Richard Temple, Bt., BL Add. MS 38916, f. 59.

[29] Sir Richard Temple, Bt., *Life in Parliament, Being the Experience of a Member in the House of Commons from 1886 to 1892 Inclusive* (London: 1893), pp. 1–3.

the career aspirations of leaders and back-benchers, the size of one's electoral majority, the nearness of a general election, one's personal and social background, and the characteristics of one's constituency.

The evidence of the parliamentary division lists cannot tell us everything about parliamentary behaviour during the Irish Home Rule crisis, but they reveal some things which cannot be known in any other way: the general characteristics of political behaviour in 1886; the dimensional structure of voting in the House; the nature of parties, their voting patterns, and their ideological cohesion; the relationship between voting and partisan affiliation, social background, and constituency influence. To limit the study of the Home Rule crisis and the great separation in the Liberal party to what can be learned from the observations of parliamentary leaders obscures these more general considerations. And what is obscured as well is the nature of formative and institutionalizing processes in modern politics.

As this recitation may serve to indicate, this study, with its reliance on statistical methods rather than on the narrative, and with its interest in political behaviour rather than the recounting of a story, owes much to what has been called the new political history. But caution requires certain strictures to be admitted here. This research does not utilize statistics of a high power. Frequently it is satisfied with the calculation of a few percentages. The nature of the data does not do more than permit the rounding of them to the nearest percentile. It does not rely on extensive model-building, nor does it seek to build a model of politics itself. Frequently, it sacrifices conceptual clarity and elegance to the messy business which has always preoccupied historians: the getting of facts right, and the marshalling of them in the most effective manner possible.

In addition, more than most exercises in quantitative history or studies of legislative behaviour, this research makes extensive use of the considerable manuscript materials and unpublished papers of Members of the House of Commons. Gladstone himself understood the importance as well as the abundance of this evidence. As he put it shortly after the Home Rule crisis, 'the History of our time, and probably still more of coming times, seems menaced by the danger of being crushed beneath the weight and mass of its own materials'.[30] Daunted, but resolved to make the best possible use of manuscript materials, this research benefited by a reading of the unpublished letters of Members of the House of Commons. Five

---

[30] W. E. Gladstone, 'The History of 1852–1860 and Grenville's Latest Journals', *English Historical Review*, 2 (1887), p. 281.

political diaries have been of special value: those of Sir Richard
Temple, Bt., who was called the ugliest man in the House,[31] Reginald
Brett, W. S. Blunt, Lewis Harcourt, and Edward Hamilton.[32] These
men were not themselves, we are reminded, 'practitioners in the
central areas of British life'.[33] But 'as men in the antechambers of
power', their observations clarify and illuminate the politics of the
period in as intimate a manner as we are likely to find.

The use of political diaries and private correspondence in 1886
serves two purposes. First, they frequently supply ideas and hypotheses which quantitative evidence can verify. In turn, statistical tables
often point toward questions which can be followed up in archival
research. Second, the voting lists of the House of Commons raise
questions about the way partisan associations were achieved, how
back-bench opinion was formed, and whether back-bench opinion
influenced policy formation. The letters and diaries of politicians
shed light on their political behaviour and preferences and their
relationships with their colleagues. Legislative assemblies, after
all, are to no little extent worlds unto themselves, with their own
socializing experiences. The behaviour of Members, therefore,
cannot be explained solely in terms of their individual attributes;
account must also be taken of the interaction among them. This is
what Namier was getting at when, in discussing the Parliament of
1761, he drew upon Aeschylus' metaphor of crook-taloned birds
consorting together.

It is this consorting together of Members in the precincts of
Westminster, with their mutually dependent patterns of behaviour,
as revealed in their votes and individual attributes and correspondence, which is the subject of this study of the Home Rule crisis in
1886. It is organized around two general contentions. First, rather
more than is generally assumed, ideology, rather than social interest

[31] Diary of Alfred Pease, 21 May 1886, in Sir Alfred Pease, *Elections and
Recollections* (London: 1932), p. 133. T. P. O'Connor likened Temple's visage to
a 'curious Japanese grotesque mask'. Known as 'the Burmese idol', Temple could sleep,
apparently, at any time or place, including the House of Commons which, 'when
sitting had been late and heavy, resounded to his sonorous snore'. Hamilton Fyfe,
T. P. O'Connor (London: 1934), p. 117. His sleeping habits did not prevent Temple
from compiling a highly detailed record of life in the House of Commons.

[32] Esher, or Reginald Brett as he then was, sat for Plymouth from 1880 to 1885
and contested, but lost, the borough in 1885. Blunt contested, but lost, the Camberwell
division of London as a Tory in 1885, and contested, but lost, Kidderminster, standing
as a Gladstonian Liberal in 1886. Lewis Harcourt followed and assisted the career
of his father, Sir William Harcourt, with great zeal and interest. Hamilton was an
intimate of Gladstone's circle.

[33] Vincent, 'Introduction' to *Disraeli, Derby, and the Conservative Party*, p. xi.

and constituency pressure, counts for much in the explanation of parliamentary behaviour, even in the midst of constitutional crisis. Second, political parties, often overriding the influence of social background and constituency pressure, served as the agencies for mobilizing political support and for integrating the political community. Parliament, where leaders and back-benchers scrutinized policy formation, was the centre of political action. The House of Commons in 1886, composed of those disparate Members thrown up by the general election of 1885, framed a Unionist policy settlement for the Home Rule crisis which prepared the way for a period of Conservative dominance lasting the better part of twenty years. The general election of 1886 ratified this settlement. The Liberal party, cast from power and shorn of the Liberal Unionists, remained in the wilderness, but the parliamentary session of 1886 had prepared them, with vast numbers of new and more radical Members, for a return to power, briefly in the 1890s and then, more impressively, in 1906.

1

The General Election of 1885
and the New House of Commons

My election, owning to my agent having softening of the brain is very uncertain. I have only just found this out, & I think I can by a series of local meetings held nightly put things right. If I go to Balmoral this is impossible. Can I refuse, & if so should I do it through you, or off on my own bat. . . .

Stumping & a heavy department are bad enough, but to dance attendance on Royalty in the northern latitudes at the same time is heart breaking.

Lord George Hamilton to Salisbury, 27 October 1885[1]

In the next House, admirable or the reverse as it may be, the changes in the men are certain to be numerous beyond all precedent since the first Reform Act. . . . For a time the House will be like a flock of sheep just descended from a railway train, and despatched into unexplored pastures.

The Times, 21 November 1885[2]

I am very sorry you are not in the House. Though destined no doubt to have a short life, the Parliament is likely to have a merry one — and in the general imbroglio which I foresee your particular gifts would I think have found a great sphere. You must look out for some political bride: — mistress would perhaps be the most appropriate term considering the brevity, and the cost, of the connection indicated.

A. J. Balfour to Reginald Brett, 4 December 1885[3]

Introduction

Hicks Beach sat in the House of Commons in 1886, as did Lord Randolph Churchill and Aretas Akers-Douglas. Chamberlain sat there, as did Hartington, Goschen, and, of course, Gladstone. In addition to these great men in parliamentary life, however, there sat the lesser lights, the back-benchers, the parliamentary foot-soldiers: Joseph Arch, a Primitive Methodist preacher who had been the leader of the agricultural labourers' agitation; Ernest Baggallay, the barrister; Lawrence Baker, who had been to India and was a trustee of the London Stock Exchange; Joseph Gillis Biggar, the

---

[1] Hamilton to Salisbury, 27 Oct. 1885, Third Marquess of Salisbury MSS Class E. [2] *The Times*, 21 Nov. 1885, p. 9.
[3] Balfour to Brett, 4 Dec. 1885, Esher Papers 5/3/146–9.

Belfast provision merchant; Colonel Henry Blundell-Hollinshead-Blundell, who served in the Crimea and owned the Pemberton colliery; James Edward Hubert Gascoyne Cecil, Viscount Cranborne, the heir of the third Marquess of Salisbury; four sons of the first Duke of Abercorn; Leonard Lyell, the nephew of the geologist; and Sir George Sitwell, Bt., who, while at Eton, had devised a toothbrush which played 'Annie Laurie' and a revolver for shooting wasps. Later he invented a synthetic rectangular egg for sportsmen and travellers, and sired the literary family. Sitwell fought his election in 1885 on crutches.[4] They were brought to Westminster, these and 661 others, by the general election of 1885, an election cast in the structures of a newly reformed electoral system.

The General Election of 1885

Vastly imperfect, leaving large numbers of men off the electoral register,[5] the electoral system created by the reforms of 1884–5 had the cardinal advantage of an enfranchisement of agricultural labour and an electoral redistribution. These new features of electoral life raised new anxieties about the nature of the parliamentary and political world which would emerge from the contest. *The Times* estimated a large turnover in the House of Commons; the election would return a majority of Members 'untried in political life'. More to the point, this turnover would have a social basis: 'With today's dissolution passes away, for good or evil, the direct power of the middle classes in English politics, as the direct power of the aristocracy passed away in 1832.'[6] The great questions posed by the election were institutional and political; they had to do with the ways new men and new policies would be assimilated. Who would enter the House? How many of them would be inexperienced? How far would they resemble men who had sat there previously? What policies would emerge in the election contest, and what bearing would they have on parliamentary life in the new session? And what about the Irish? Even before the outcome of the election could be foretold, Reginald Brett wrote, '. . . in the new Parliament all political questions will be subordinated to one question, which is how to deal

---

[4] Sir George Sitwell, Bt., to Salisbury, 26 Dec. 1885, Third Marquess of Salisbury MSS Class E.

[5] For the limitations of the electoral system after 1885, see H. C. G. Matthew, R. I. McKibbin, and J. A. Kay, 'The Franchise Factor in the Rise of the Labour Party', *English Historical Review*, 91 (July 1976), pp. 725 ff., and Paul Thompson, *Socialists, Liberals, and Labour: The Struggle for London, 1885–1914* (London: 1967), p. 90. See also Chapter 5 below.

[6] *The Times*, 18 Nov. 1885, p. 9.

with the Irish party. The Government of the day will be forced to deal with the Irish party and their demand for Home Rule.'[7] But who would form the Government, and what would be their political resources? The Liberal and Conservative parties appeared to *The Times* to have approached equilibrium.[8] On the Liberal side, the force of Gladstone's personality threw a weight in favour of party unity. New voters added to the electoral rolls by franchise reform would weigh in favour of the Liberals as well. On the Conservative side, Salisbury's reputation for 'intellectual power', for 'prudence', and for 'moderation' would count. And the record of the previous Liberal Administration would count as well, whether for its history of foreign policy or for its 'tampering with unsound theories' and 'rejection of accepted principles'. The Tory–Parnellite electoral alliance, *The Times* noted, would produce, at one and the same time, 'a strong feeling of disgust' and Catholic votes against Liberals. The upshot was uncertain. New political forces were at work, and the House of Commons in 1886 would have to find the means for reconciling those elements with the traditions of parliamentary and cabinet government.

The scramble for seats, however, began long before the first nominations, even before the redistribution features of electoral reform were settled. Here is what John George Lambton wrote to Reginald Brett on 11 January 1885:

I don't like the political outlook here. The local manufacturing & coal owning plutocrats mean to divide [the county of Durham] amongst them . . . Jos. Pease is to have Barnard Castle, Henry Fell Pease, Bishop Auckland; D. Dale [?] Joicey—Gateshead; a nominee of the Peases (probably Havelock-Allan!)—North Tees; Palmer, Jarrow; Laing—Sunderland; and the miners' representative, Crawfurd [*sic*], [?]. Dale, Joicey, Laing & co are political non-entities. Havelock-Allan is mad—but the Peases & Palmer, & Crawfurd [*sic*] are proper candidates.[9]

By 18 December all polling was completed. It was a vibrant election: 81 per cent of the electorate polled its votes. This was the most substantial turn-out in British elections before the great Liberal revival in the first decade of the twentieth century. At the next election, in 1886, the turn-out fell to 74 per cent. It rose slightly to 77 per cent in 1892, and slightly again to 78 per cent in 1895. The turn-out declined marginally to 75 per cent in 1900, but then increased dramatically to 83 per cent in 1906, and even more strikingly to

[7] Letter to *The Times*, 2 Dec. 1885, p. 8.
[8] *The Times*, 24 Nov. 1885, p. 9.
[9] Durham to Brett, 11 Jan. 1885, Esher Papers 10/7.

87 per cent in the January election of 1910.[10] In 1885 the highest turn-out occurred in Wales and Scotland, where the percentage of electors polled was 82.2 per cent and 82 per cent respectively. But it was only marginally lower in England. The turn-out was lowest in Ireland, where 75 per cent of the electorate voted.

Despite the fact that the Government in office at the time of the dissolution was Conservative, Lord Salisbury having taken office in 1885 in a caretaker capacity, the Conservatives put what they judged to be the failures of Gladstone's second Administration before the electors: Egypt, Chinese Gordon's ill-fated mission to Khartoum, Kilminham, the Land War, the unpreparedness of the army and the navy.[11] As Robert Uniacke Penrose Fitzgerald put it to his electors, the Conservatives have 'both the will and ability to rescue England from many of the perils and dangers into which she had plunged, in South Africa, in Afghanistan, in Egypt and Soudan, by the wavering, uncertain, and evershifting policy of the late Liberal Government'.[12] There were additional issues of an economic nature which Conservatives laid, though with rather more difficulty, at Liberal feet. These issues, the depression in trade and agriculture, which Ellis Ashmead Bartlett wished to make dominant in the election,[13] gave Lord George Hamilton in the Ealing division of Middlesex, and other Tories elsewhere, the opportunity to call for protection.[14] Though Ashmead Bartlett believed this would have working-class appeal, the Liberals could counter-attack, and, as Sidney Herbert ruefully reported, 'hundreds of agricultural workers in the more distant villages firmly believe that the Conservatives wanted to abolish the "cheap loaf" and to grind down the labourers, and nothing would drive the idea out of their minds'.[15]

The Church question was the liveliest to be put before the electorate, and, indeed, for one student of this election, it outstripped all others in importance.[16] It was especially important in Scotland,

[10] F. W. S. Craig (ed.), *British Electoral Facts, 1885–1965* (London: 1968), pp. 1, 75.

[11] See Christopher N. Johnson to Lord George Hamilton, Third Marquess of Salisbury MSS Class D/27/184.

[12] Robert Uniacke Penrose Fitzgerald, *To the Elector of the Parliamentary Borough of Cambridge* (Cambridge: 1885).

[13] Ashmead Bartlett to Salisbury, 7 Nov. 1885, Third Marquess of Salisbury MSS Class E.

[14] *The Times*, 28 Nov. 1885, p. 6.

[15] Sidney Herbert to Salisbury, 2 Dec. 1885, Third Marquess of Salisbury MSS Class E.

[16] Alan Simon, 'Church Disestablishment as a Factor in the General Election of 1885', *The Historical Journal*, 18.4 (1975), p. 792.

where one observer believed 'this senseless attempt to cram Liberation down our throats' would damage the Liberal party seriously. In Wales, *The Times* reported, 'Toryism is synonymous with Churchmanship, and Liberalism is synonymous with Dissent'.[17] Herbert Gladstone, speaking for Pitt Lewis in the Barnstaple division of Devonshire, said that the Tories had loosed '20,000 gentlemen, educated men, trained in speech' against disestablishers as well as the whole of the Liberal party.[18] The Conservative party, Sir William Hartcourt charged, 'had fled to the church as to sanctuary and were hanging on the horns of the altar'.[19] The disestablishment issue was sufficiently troubling to have Lord Richard Grosvenor, Gladstone's chief whip, place cautious advice before his chief. 'You can only with safety sail along the line which you have already taken up, but the more you urge its postponement to the "dim and distant future" the better.'[20]

The Church question was but one of a series of related issues put forward by the radicals and Joseph Chamberlain in this election. These had the effect of dividing political opinion because of both their substance and their form. Originally articulated in the pages of the *Fortnightly Review* in 1883, the demands for housing for the poor, agrarian reform, the amendment of local government and taxation, free education, and religious freedom formed the essence of the *Radical Programme* which was published in July 1885.[21] Whether these proposals were counter-revolutionary efforts to preclude the more fundamental attacks on property offered by Henry George and H. M. Hyndman,[22] or whether they constituted an attempt on the part of experienced parliamentarians to move a constitutional working class eager to sustain middle-class values toward radicalism,[23] their substance had the effect of shaking the complacency of Conservatives and moderate Liberals alike. These issues were the more pointed because they took the form of radicals seeking to attack their own leader, effect a coup, and displace and purge their more moderate colleagues. Chamberlain, it was widely

---

[17] James Graham to Lord Richard Grosvenor, 4 Nov. 1885, BL Add. MS 44316, f. 90ᵛ; *The Times*, 11 Dec. 1885, p. 3.

[18] *The Times*, 28 Nov. 1885, p. 6.   [19] Ibid.

[20] Lord Richard Grosvenor to Gladstone, 7 Dec. 1885, BL Add. MS 44316, ff. 98–9.

[21] C. H. D. Howard, 'Joseph Chamberlain and the "Unauthorized Programme"', *English Historical Review*, 65 (1950) and Richard Jay, *Joseph Chamberlain: A Political Study*, (Oxford: 1981), pp. 75, 112–13.

[22] Peter Fraser, *Joseph Chamberlain* (London: 1966), p. 46.

[23] Jay, *Joseph Chamberlain*, p. 77.

suspected, had placed one of his henchmen, B. F. C. Costelloe, in the contest against Goschen in the Eastern division of Edinburgh in this election.[24] Chamberlain dealt pretty bluntly with Gladstone, and was not above putting rather sharp ultimata to the Liberal leader. As Chamberlain himself described the situation, 'I have told Mr G. that I will not join any Govt which does not give Dilke and self a free hand as to Local Government including the powers to acquire land compulsorily and which does not also leave us free to speak and vote on Free Education.'[25] Lord Richard Grosvenor, as whip, leaped into the breach and corresponded with Chamberlain in an effort to avoid an open division in the Liberal party. As Grosvenor warned, 'a split *now*, would I am sure, let the Tories in, & once in they would sacrifice every principle both to the Irish & others to keep in' for four or five years.[26] In consequence, anxieties rose on all sides. As R. U. P. Fitzgerald wrote in his election manifesto, 'the struggle of Mr Chamberlain and the "caucus" for supremacy in the Councils of the State will, should the Liberal Party regain power, paralyse all effective handling of foreign or domestic affairs.'[27] How far these divisions in the Liberal party would lead to an internal crisis would be answered only with the meeting of the new House of Commons and the Home Rule crisis in six months' time.

Irish Home Rule was the issue, as Gladstone's critics would later point out, which was not fully ventilated in the election. A few, such as John Morley, brought it forward, but on the whole references to Irish government were cautious and guised. Hugh Childers, at Pontefract, spoke in favour of local self-government for the Irish, but even here he protected himself. The formula Childers used— 'giving the Irish as much self-government as is consistent with the integrity and unity of the Empire'—was an incantation used by many as they sought ways to bridge the gap between the nationalist aspirations of the Irish and the requirements of imperial unity. Viscount Ebrington, who became a Liberal Unionist in 1886, analysed the Liberal election manifestos. Upwards of one third of these, he discovered, made no mention whatever of Ireland. Only twenty-one Liberal candidates had 'generally a sympathetic leaning toward the Irish cause'. And tabulation of successful Liberal candidates in the

---

[24] *The Times*, 26 Nov. 1885, p. 11; Michael Barker, *Gladstone and Radicalism: The Reconstruction of Liberal Policy in Britain, 1885–1894* (Hassocks, Sussex: 1975), p. 16; Jay, *Joseph Chamberlain*, p. 114.

[25] Chamberlain to Harcourt, 20 Sept. 1885, Chamberlain Papers JC5/38/147.

[26] Grosvenor to Chamberlain, 30 Oct. 1885, 3 and 5 Nov. 1885, Chamberlain Papers JC5/37/2, 3, 5.

[27] Fitzgerald, *To the Electors of the Parliamentary Borough of Cambridge*.

election who favoured Home Rule fully shows that only six of these
came to the House committed to an extensive Irish government
measure.[28] While the votes of Irish electors would make the question
of Irish government a large one in the new Parliament, the caution
with which candidates approached it in the election of 1885 reveals
their uncertainty and uneasiness in framing their views on this fraught
subject.

Violence and hooliganism had a deep tradition in British electoral
politics, and it is unsurprising that the issues advanced in 1885
should have provoked violence to an intense degree. Street fights
broke out in the Montgomery district of Wales when the victory
of Pryce Jones was announced. Windows were smashed, the banner
of the Salvation Army was shredded, and the coat of the rector was
thrown in the river. In Loughborough, Leicestershire, Mr Middleton,
a county magistrate, attacked Mrs Johnson-Ferguson, the wife
of the Liberal candidate, giving her a blow on the breast. A crowd
seized Middleton, footballed his hat, and rolled him in the mud.
At Northwich, in Cheshire, a disturbance broke out and windows
were smashed in the Central Conservative Office when a Conservative election official assaulted a drunken man carrying an
emblematic big loaf. At Colchester a 'venerable farmer', who was
a Liberal, had his horse and four-wheeled chaise painted blue. In
the Aylesbury division of Buckinghamshire, Ferdinand de Rothschild
several times 'had to save his life from the fury of the mob —
once in his own (Ferdy's) village of Waddesdon where he was
attacked and his carriage wrecked'.[29] W. S. Blunt's supporters
in the Camberwell division of London demonstrated for him by
pulling his carriage through the streets. 'In the course of it', Blunt
wrote, 'they ran over a woman but no great harm was done & after
parading Camberwell road they left me at the Catholic Club.'[30]
In Derby, Sir William Harcourt's agents sent his 'bruiser', whose
name was Yellow Jack, into a meeting before the candidate, and he
came back reporting that the room was filled with Irishmen who
had staves up their sleeves, and that they intended to break heads
as well as to break up the meeting. A local parson in Derby advised
the men and boys of his choir to attend Harcourt's meetings for
the purpose of disrupting them. 'I have always been in favour of

---

[28] Viscount Ebrington, 'Liberal Election Addresses', *Nineteenth Century*, Apr.
1886, pp. 607, 611. Devonshire Papers, 349, 1938, cited by Michael Hurst, *Joseph
Chamberlain and Liberal Reunion* p. 39 n. 1.
[29] Harcourt Journal, 5. Dec. 1885, Harcourt dep. 374, f. 17.
[30] Blunt Diary, 23 Nov. 1885, Blunt MS 333-1975, f. 209.

disestablishment in theory and I am now so in practice', Lewis Harcourt responded.[31]

Riots in the Camborne division of Cornwall; violence in Dudley; a drunken row at Oxford; a chair through the window of Henry Broadhurst's committee room in the Bordesley division of Birmingham; the calling out of the York and Lancaster Regiment in the East division of Nottingham and the Lancashire Regiment in Derry to suppress violence. In the Evesham division of Worcestershire, a band of Sir Richard Temple's followers invaded a meeting for his opponent, Arthur Chamberlain, Joseph Chamberlain's brother. What destruction they wrought cannot be known, but Chamberlain's supporters retaliated by breaking up one of Temple's meetings. Temple determined to hold a rally in a barn where Chamberlain expected to hold forth. 'So I went', Temple wrote, 'with a potent body-guard of the stalwart market gardeners for which Evesham was renowned.' His bully-boys preserved order inside, but a 'tumultuous' free-for-all prevailed without.[32] Violence was also present in the contest for the North-west division of Norfolk. The supporters of Lord Henry Cavendish-Bentinck, the brother of the Duke of Portland, held a meeting in a village known for its attachment to Joseph Arch. Arch's adherents threw stones through the windows and on to the roof of the schoolhouse in which the meeting was held. Still dissatisfied, they released fireworks inside the building. As Bentinck's brother observed, 'it is not easy to explain one's political views when at the same time one was bombarded by roman candles!' On leaving in a dog-cart, these Conservatives were set upon again with mud and stones. Colonel Loftus Tottenham (known for his size as 'Lofty Tot') refused to have his clothing brushed until he had hung his overcoat in the Carlton as an indication of the 'perils he had gone through, and the savages he had encountered in Norfolk'.[33]

Fought under new conditions and in new constituency arrangements, the election of 1885 was highly effervescent. Only forty-five of the seats held by these 680 Members, less than 7 per cent, had been uncontested. Twenty of these were in Ireland. This is the lowest portion of uncontested seats in elections during the period from 1832

[31] Harcourt Journal, 19 and 20 Nov. 1885, Harcourt dep. 373, ff. 61–2, 66.
[32] Temple, *The Story of My Life*, vol. 2, pp. 106–7.
[33] W. J. C. Bentinck, Duke of Portland, *Men, Women, and Things: Memoirs of the Duke of Portland* (London: 1937), pp. 372–3. See also Norman Gash, *Politics in the Age of Peel* (London: 1953), pp. 137–53; Asa Briggs, *Victorian People* (London: 1954), pp. 108, 111; Donald Richter, 'The Role of Mob Riot in Victorian Elections, 1865–1885', *Victorian Studies*, 15.1 (Sept. 1971), pp. 19, 20, 22, 26.

to 1924.[34] Though highly contested, the election of 1885 was less expensive than previous contests. Despite the additions to the electoral rolls of an expanded electorate which the reforms of 1884–5 had produced, the Corrupt Practices Act of 1883 had its effect. The total cost of electioneering declined from £1,736,781 in 1880 to £1,026,645 in 1885. Thereafter the cost for contested seats never attained the 1880 level, though it increased slightly to more than £2,000 in the elections of 1906 and January 1910.[35]

Excited by contests though it was, the general election of 1885 demonstrated the settledness of the nation's electoral habits and instincts, and the era of modern elections began with it. This election was characterized by high levels of partisanship, and most contests were fought between two major parties. The exception to this is found in the Celtic fringe, which became an arena of political experimentation. The fringe was, at one and the same time, more radical and less stable than other parts of the United Kingdom. In England and Wales the contesting pattern was a partisan one in which Liberals and Conservatives faced each other directly and with little internecine conflict. *The Times* had predicted a large number of duplicate Liberal candidates competing for the same seats, and a consequent weakening of the Liberal forces.[36] In Lord Richard Grosvenor's view this was an exaggeration. There were thirteen duplicate candidates in London, all under control, and fourteen in the rest of the country. Grosvenor rid himself of most of these with ease, and, in fact, he started a duplicate candidate of his own in an abortive effort to keep Sir George Campbell out of what proved to be one of the safest Liberal seats, Kirkcaldy Burghs. 'Killing duplicate candidates goes on much faster & better than killing stags', Grosvenor wrote.[37]

Some Liverpool constituencies, those with heavy concentrations of Irish electors, had their electoral passions stimulated by the active intervention of Parnell and the Irish Nationalists. Parnell, or so it was rumoured, planned to stand for the Exchange division, with

---

[34] For a summary of uncontested elections, see W. O. Aydelotte, *Quantification in History* (Reading, Mass.: 1971), p. 108.

[35] 'Return of Charges made to Candidates at the General Election in 1885, by Returning Officers', *Parliamentary Papers*, 1886, 52, p. 482. 'Return of Charges made to Candidates in the General Election of 1886, by Returning Officers', *Parliamentary Papers*, 1886, 52, p. 562. William B. Gwyn, *Democracy and the Cost of Politics in Britain* (London: 1962), pp. 51, 55. Neal Blewett, *The Peers, the Parties, and the People* p. 290.

[36] *The Times*, 18 Nov. 1885, p. 4.

[37] Lord Richard Grosvenor to Gladstone, 25 Sept. 1885, BL Add. MS 44316, ff. 40–1.

T. P. O'Connor standing for the Scotland division, J. Barry for the West Toxteth division, J. Redmond for the Bootle division of Lancashire, and another Nationalist in the Abercrombie division.[38] In the event, O'Connor fought the Scotland division, and won it, as he was to do until 1910 by vast majorities, making it 'the old, obdurate, impenetrable foxhole of Nationalism'.[39] Redmond fought, but lost, the Kirkdale division. Captain William Henry O'Shea entered the contest for the Exchange division, and the Liberals there, subsequently, adopted him. Gladstone, drawn into the situation by the entreaties of Mrs O'Shea, blessed the adoption by reason of O'Shea's general support of the Liberal policy and his assistance to the Government in 1882 during the Land War and the Kilmainham crisis.[40] All for nothing, because the Conservative candidate, L. R. Baily, defeated him by a narrow majority.

North of the Tweed, *The Times* reported bitter rivalries pitting Liberal against Liberal: 'The contests are almost as frequent between two Liberals as between a Conservative and a Liberal.'[41] Though this was an exaggeration, Liberals contested other Liberals in 13 per cent of the Scottish seats in contrast to 1 per cent of the English seats. Moderate against radical, east against west, Churchman against disestablisher, agrarian reformer against landlord; wherever one turned, Scottish Liberals were divided amongst themselves.[42] These internal challenges were sometimes close. A direct appeal to the Liberal electors in the St Rollox division of Glasgow settled the dispute between McCulloch and Cardwell, 2,475 of whom supported the former and 2,413 the latter.[43] The history of the Liberal party in Scotland made such divisions possible, and safe. After 1832, Whig and Radical support for the Scottish national interest converted the sympathies of the Scottish electorate into support for the political

---

[38] *The Times*, 23 Nov. 1885, p. 8.

[39] *The Liverpool Courier*, 6 Dec. 1910, cited in Blewett, *The Peers, the Parties, and the People*, p. 198.

[40] Gladstone to Lord Richard Grosvenor, 18 Nov. 1885, BL Add. MS 44316, f. 111ᵛ.

[41] *The Times*, 18 Nov. 1885, p. 4.

[42] Ibid. See also D. C. Savage, 'Scottish Politics, 1885-6', *Scottish Historical Review*, 40.130 (Oct. 1961): James G. Kellas, 'The Liberal Party and the Scottish Church Disestablishment Crisis', *English Historical Review*, 79 (Jan. 1964); 'The Liberal Party in Scotland, 1876-1895', *Scottish Historical Review*, 44.137 (Apr. 1965); James Hunter, 'The Politics of Highland Land Reform, 1873-1895', *Scottish Historical Review*, 53.155 (Apr. 1974); James Hunter, 'The Gaelic Connection: The Highlands, Ireland, and Nationalism, 1873-1922', *Scottish Historical Review*, 54.158 (Oct. 1975).

[43] *The Times*, 23 Nov. 1885, p. 8.

left, and there was little change in this pattern between the first and second reform bills. By 1868, the Liberals, as the party of national patriotism, could count on taking all but six or seven of the Scottish seats. Despite a slight Conservative revival in Scotland in 1874, there was an atmosphere of Liberal permanence at the end of the century.[44] In the election of 1885, *The Times* saw little hope for the Conservatives; its most generous estimate was twelve Tory seats.[45] With little threat from the other side, Scottish Liberals could afford the luxury of fighting out their internal disputes. Consequently, in Scotland the great ideological questions of the day were thrashed out amongst Liberals, rather than between Liberals and Conservatives.

The contest in Ireland did not set Liberals against Conservatives, but the Irish Nationalists against what *The Times* called 'the two old constitutional parties'.[46] Despite this — perhaps because of it — the level of partisanship, indicated by straight two-party fights was high. In Ulster there were twenty-five straight-party tests: sixteen in which Irish Nationalists and Conservatives opposed each other, eight in which Conservatives and Liberals opposed each other, and one between an Irish Nationalist and a Liberal candidate. In the south there were forty-nine straight-party tests: thirty-nine in which Nationalists and Conservatives opposed each other, and ten in which Nationalists and Liberals contested each other. In the whole of the island there were but two three-cornered tests. The effective opposition to the Nationalists, it is clear, was provided by the Conservatives. The Liberal effort was slight. The potential for nationalism is indicated by the high proportion of uncontested seats in Ireland, all of which were taken in the south by the Parnellites, who took as well the majority in the north.[47]

In contrast to the solidarity of the Parnellites, the loyalist Liberals and Conservatives, *The Times* observed, 'seem almost everywhere unprepared, and in the north especially are directed at enmity the one with the other, more so even than with the Nationalists'.[48] On 20 November, for example, Charles H. Rankin announced his intention to stand for the southern division of Kerry as a 'Conservative Home Ruler'. In the event, partisan reason prevailed and he withdrew,

---

[44] H. J. Hanham, *Elections and Party Management: Politics in the time of Disraeli and Gladstone* (London: 1959), pp. 155–69.

[45] *The Times*, 24 Nov. 1885, p. 9.

[46] Ibid., 10 Dec. 1885, p. 6.

[47] The exception to Nationalist solidarity in Ireland was the dispute in Louth over the candidacy of Phillip Callan. *The Times*, 30 Nov. 1885, p. 6.

[48] Ibid., 18 Nov. 1885, p. 4.

to be replaced by a Conservative with a more orthodox manifesto.[49] Co-operation between Irish Conservatives and Liberals in the formation of electoral compacts was possible in some places, especially in the western districts of Ulster. In the Northern division of Tyrone, for example, the Liberals withdrew their candidate to allow the election of Lord Ernest Hamilton, the youngest son of the Duke of Abercorn. In other places, such as Antrim and Down, 'the old battles of Whig and Tory are being fought again'.[50] The Nationalists, confident of their electoral strength throughout the island, identified fourteen contests—two in the south and twelve in the north—on which to focus their attention.[51] In the election they won ten of these.

Interesting as these electoral developments in Ireland were, the great question concerning the Irish vote in the election of 1885 was the effect it would have in English contests. In late November, a manifesto, approved by Parnell, and issued over the name of T. P. O'Connor, the President of the Irish National League of Great Britain, instructed Irish electors to vote for Conservative candidates if no Nationalist candidate was standing. It called for the Irish to vote against all members of 'the servile and cowardly and unprincipled herd that would break every pledge and violate every principle in obedience to the call of the Whip and the mandate of the caucus'.[52] From these requirements Parnell and his lieutenants exempted only five: R. Lloyd Jones, an independent Liberal standing for the Chester-le-Street division of Durham, T. C. Thompson, who stood for the borough of Durham, Joseph Cowen in Newcastle, Henry Labouchere in Northampton, Samuel Storey in Sunderland, and Captain O'Shea. In Ulster, Parnell imposed his manifesto against some Conservatives, who were opposed by Liberals, rather than Nationalists: for John Barbour against Macartney in South Antrim, for Dickson against O'Neill in Mid Antrim, for DeCobain 'the Orange Labour Candidate' against Sir J. P. Corry 'the Tory Capitalist' in the Eastern division of Belfast.[53]

---

[49] Ibid., 21 Nov. 1885, p. 7.

[50] Ibid., 19 Nov. 1885, p. 7; 23 Nov. 1885, p. 8.

[51] Ibid., 20 Nov. 1885, p. 7. These contests were: the Southern division of Dublin county; St Stephen's Green, Dublin; North and South Tyrone; North and South Fermanagh; East Donegal; South Down; South Londonderry; South and Mid Armagh; West Belfast; Londonderry City; Newry. The Conservatives won North Tyrone, Mid Armagh, West Belfast, and Londonderry City. The Southern division of Dublin county was considered the Alsace–Lorraine of Ireland because Unionists held it for much of the period between 1885 and 1910. In the elections of 1885 and 1886, however, Nationalists took the seat. Blewett, *The Peers, the Parties, and the People*, p. 389.

[52] *The Times*, 23 Nov. 1885, p. 11.

[53] Ibid., 24 Nov. 1885, pp. 6–7; 26 Nov. 1885, p. 8.

How effective the Nationalist flirtation with the Tories proved to be cannot be known with any exactitude. The Irish in England suffered the bias of the electoral rolls: they were a part of that section of society least likely to be found on the register. Moreover, large Catholic densities were likely to provoke a strong Protestant backlash, working for the Liberals in 1885, and swamping whatever intentions Irish electors might have.[54] The Irish Nationalists were divided about the desirability and the consequences of their compact with the Tories. William O'Brien believed the Irish vote could have delivered a Conservative majority by turning over dozens of the great manufacturing towns in the north of England and in the Clyde valley. Michael Davitt, however, with his 'fanatical devotion to British democracy', opposed the arrangement.[55] Shaw-Lefevre believed his defeat by the Tory banker Charles Townsend Murdoch at Reading could be attributed to the 'defection of seventy to eighty Irish Catholics who had promised to vote for me on previous occasions and the very undue influence of the Church party'.[56] Other Tories did not feel they had Murdoch's advantage. 'I have not won by the Irish vote at all', T. H. Sidebottom wrote to Salisbury from Stalybridge, 'as I made them no [promise?] and I believe only about thirty voted for us. . . . I won the election in your celebrated words "trade follows the flag," and the Church and Religious Education Question.'[57] At Oldham 'the Irish did not vote straight and their strength had been seriously exaggerated'.[58] In the Central division of Sheffield, according to Charles Vincent, 'the Irish by no means supported me in a body, & . . . not more than 260 votes in my majority of 1149 over Mr Plimsoll & of 1009 over both the Liberal & Radical candidates combined, were contributed by the local branch of the National League which the late Government allowed to arise on the ruins of the suppressed Land League.' The same state of affairs probably prevailed in other English constituencies.[59] And in York, Frank Lockwood, a Liberal Member, believed the Liberals had been carried by the Irish vote.[60] According to Herbert

[54] Michael Kinnear, *The British Voter: An Atlas and Survey Since 1885* (Ithaca, NY: 1968), pp. 13–14.

[55] William O'Brien, *Evening Memories*, (Dublin and London: 1920), pp. 91–2.

[56] Shaw-Lefevre to Chamberlain, 28 Nov. 1885, Chamberlain Papers JC5/52/7.

[57] T. H. Sidebottom to Salisbury, 25 Nov. 1885, Third Marquess of Salisbury MSS Class E.

[58] John Maclean to Salisbury, 6 Dec. 1885, Third Marquess of Salisbury MSS Class E.

[59] Vincent to Salisbury, 8 Dec. 1885, Third Marquess of Salisbury MSS Class E.

[60] *Harcourt Journal*, 3 Jan. 1886, Harcourt dep. 375, ff. 98 f.

Gladstone's estimate, twenty seats were lost to Conservatives as a result of the manifesto. Morley thought twenty to forty seats were affected.[61] Chamberlain thought twenty-five seats were at stake. Edward Hamilton put the estimate somewhat higher, at thirty to forty seats, though, in 1886, when the Liberals were to be the recipients of Irish benefactions, he suspected the Irish vote had been overrated. As might be expected, T. P. O'Connor thought the Irish vote could shape the returns in nineteen contests in London and forty-six seats in the country.[62] Modern analysis puts the figure at the more astringent, and probable, estimate of five to twelve seats.[63] It is difficult to see how the Irish could have a significant impact on English elections. Canon McGrath, in Camberwell, told W. S. Blunt 'that it will be very difficult to bring them to the poll. They care for nothing in this district—men from Kerry he said are a bad lot, not one out of ten even comes to Mass'.[64] Few in numbers, they were at the most 10 per cent of the electorate. Moreover, their political sympathies pulled them three different ways. Religion, the commitments of their priests, and the question of education might draw them toward the Conservatives. Home Rule pulled them toward the Liberals. With the growth of trade unionism amongst the unskilled, they would be attracted toward the Socialist clubs.[65] This is not the stuff of which an effective voting bloc is made.

In the election contest, Liberal candidates feared the worst but put the most positive face on the situation. Osborn Morgan, in Denbighshire, likened the new-found sympathy of the Nationalists for the Tories to Jonah's gourd or the beanstalk in the nursery story: 'it had grown up over night'. At Leicester, Sir Henry James, after attributing Liberal defeats in London and Lancashire to the Irish vote, said, 'The Tory party was now brought down to the humiliation of trying to retain their position by an alliance with those who a few months ago they were denouncing as rebels.'[66] In the event, the Parnellite flirtation with the Conservatives proved impermanent because it was a negative association. As Parnell's manifesto of November 1885 shows, the alliance rested on a rejection

---

[61] John Morley, *The Life of W. E. Gladstone* (London: 1903), vol. 3, p. 244.

[62] J. L. Garvin and Julian Amery, *The Life of Joseph Chamberlain* (London: 1935–1969), vol. 2, p. 189. Edward Hamilton Diary, 19 May 1886 and 7 July 1886, BL Add. MSS 48643, f. 132 and 48644, f. 57. *The Nation*, 19 Dec. 1885.

[63] Kinnear, *The British Voter*, p. 13.

[64] Blunt Diary, 22 Nov. 1885, Blunt MS 333-1975, f. 208.

[65] Lynn Hollen Lees, *Exiles of Erin: Irish Migrants in Victorian London* (Ithaca, NY: 1979), p. 237.

[66] *The Times*, 3 Dec. 1885, p. 6; 28 Nov. 1885, p. 6.

of Gladstone's second Administration, not on a positive identification with Tory policy. When the parties assembled in Westminster, it did not take long for the Irish Nationalists and the Conservatives to part their ways.

As polling approached, early predictions favoured the Liberals, but with an ever-diminishing majority. In September, Lord Richard Grosvenor believed the Liberal majority would be sufficiently large to deal with the Irish; that is, to avoid Home Rule. 'Grosvenor', Edward Hamilton wrote, 'is very sanguine about the result of a general election.'[67] Liberal organizers, Balfour reported to Salisbury in early October, expected a majority of fifty over the combined Conservatives and Nationalists.[68] The day before the old Parliament was dissolved, Grosvenor predicted an overall majority of forty-six.[69] In little more than a week's time he was less easy. With the borough vote and its disappointment behind, and with the uncertainty of the county poll ahead, Grosvenor could bring himself to estimate only a bare majority.[70] The borough returns marked a resurgence of Tory strength and Tory optimism. 'There had been a gt. improvement the last ten days', Sir William Hart Dyke, Bt., told Lord Carnarvon, '& . . . almost anything is possible.'[71] Akers Douglas called attention to 'some remarkable wins'.[72] On 3 December, *The Times* rendered the result at 320 Liberals, 270 Conservatives, and 80 Irish Nationalists. Gladstone, *The Times* concluded, could not challenge Lord Salisbury with such a balance of forces, and, therefore, the Conservatives were likely to continue in office.[73] On 7 December the Liberals had a majority of seventy-one over the Conservatives alone, and were in a minority of two if the Nationalists combined with the Tories.[74] The picture was confused. Grosvenor wrote to Gladstone:

. . . as you truly say, if the Govt is to be in the hands of the party who have the majority in the House of Commons, according to ancient custom,

---

[67] Hamilton Diary, 10 Sept. 1885, BL Add. MS 48641, f. 71.

[68] Arthur Balfour to Salisbury, 2 Oct. 1885, Third Marquess of Salisbury MSS Class E.

[69] Lord Richard Grosvenor to Lyttleton, 17 Nov. 1885, BL Add. MS 44316, ff. 107–9.

[70] Lord Richard Grosvenor to Gladstone, 29 Nov. 1885, BL Add. MS 44316, ff. 118–21.

[71] Carnarvon Diary, 21 Nov. 1885, BL Add. MS 60925, unbound and unfoliated.

[72] Akers Douglas to Salisbury, [?] Nov. 1885, Third Marquess of Salisbury MSS Class E.   [73] *The Times*, 3 Dec. 1885, p. 9.

[74] Lord Richard Grosvenor to Gladstone, 9 Dec. 1885, BL Add. MS 44316, 139–40.

the question is to ascertain which party is in the majority! Even if the Irish party put us in on an amendment to the Address they would promptly put us out on our *first* measure of proposed reform, viz. the Reform of Procedure.[75]

At the end of the day, the electors returned 249 Conservatives, 335 Liberals, and 82 Irish Nationalists. (In by-elections during 1886, six additional Conservatives, four Liberals, and four Irish Nationalists were added to these figures.) When adjustments are made for two Member constituencies, the Conservatives had polled 43.5% of the vote, the Liberals 49.6 per cent, and the Nationalists 6.9 per cent. Therefore, the Liberals enjoyed a majority of eight-six over the Conservatives alone, who could maintain themselves in office only with the support of the Irish. When the Conservatives rendered this improbable support impossible by their declaration of a coercionist policy for Ireland, they severed themselves from the Parnellites.

Table 1.1 reveals some of the salient features of the election results and shows a sectional character. England, though the Conservatives and Liberals found themselves evenly divided, remained the region in which, in addition to Ulster, the Conservatives did best. Moreover, reflecting a continuing pattern in the electoral history of the party, the Conservatives did well in the boroughs. In fact, they gained

TABLE 1.1 *The General Election of 1885**

	Irish Nationalists		Liberals		Conservatives		No.
	No.	%	No.	%	No.	%	
Members by their party and region:							
England	1	0.2	244	53	218	47	463
Wales	0	0	31	89	4	11	35
Scotland	0	0	63	89	8	11	71
Ulster	17	50	0	0	17	50	34
Southern Ireland	68	100	0	0	0	0	68
University	0	0	1	11	8	89	9
TOTAL	86	13	339	50	255	37	680
Members by their party and type of constituency:							
County seats	74	19	186	49	122	32	382
Borough seats	12	4	152	53	125	43	289
University seats	0	0	1	11	8	89	9

*These figures include all Members who sat in the House of Commons in 1886, those originally elected as well as those fourteen additional Members who came to the House in the by-elections fought in 1886.

[75] Ibid., ff. 141–2.

everywhere in borough constituencies except for the West Midlands where, as *The Times* put it, 'Liberalism was protected by the caucus'.[76] However, even there the Conservatives could take some considerable measure of satisfaction. Lord Randolph Churchill came within 800 votes of defeating John Bright in the Central division of Birmingham. Salisbury wrote to Churchill, 'You have given old Bright a shake— & anyone with less of a record than he has, you would have evidently beaten.' Sir John Gorst echoed this sentiment. 'Such a defeat is almost a victory and with Bright and Dilke winning by the skin of their teeth we are doing very well.'[77] Salisbury also expressed himself fulsomely to Rowland Winn, First Baron St Oswald:

We are in pretty good spirits down here, & of course the borough polls have encouraged our men. Exeter went quite mad, for the Liberals had made sure of winning & the instant the majority was announced they took for granted that it was on their side, lit their illumination, drank their first glass of champagne & were dancing round the table when the truth was made known. Poor [Edward] Johnson [the sitting Liberal] was terribly overcome and is said to have fainted. Our people made such a rush to get at our son that they pulled down the stair-bannister against which he was leaning & gave him a bad fall. He is getting on well but has to be kept very quiet.[78]

In an oft-quoted letter, Gladstone attributed the Conservative successes in the boroughs to 'Fair Trade + Parnell + Church + Chamberlain . . . in what I think their order of importance'.[79] Sir Henry James concurred in the notion that Chamberlain's radical campaign had in some cases worked against the Liberals.[80]

The Liberals, for their part, riding the wave of popularity rising from the enfranchisement of agricultural labour, did well in English counties. 'I had no idea', Sir Michael Hicks Beach wrote to Salisbury, 'this part of England [Gloucestershire] would go so strongly against us, though I did not anticipate that we should do really well in it.'[81] 'We committed political *felo de se* when we let Mr Gladstone pass the county franchise', Ashmead Bartlett believed, but this need not be permanent. Good Conservative candidates, who were 'active,

---

[76] *The Times*, 25 Nov. 1885, p. 11.

[77] Lord Salisbury to Churchill and Sir John Gorst to Churchill, 25 Nov. 1885, Lord Randolph Churchill Letters 1/11/1091, 1091a.

[78] Salisbury to Lord St Oswald, 27 Nov. 1885, Third Marquess of Salisbury MSS Class D/84/198.

[79] Gladstone to Grosvenor, 27 Nov. 1885, BL Add. MS 44316, f. 117.

[80] Sir Henry James to Lord Randolph Churchill, 7 Dec. 1885, Lord Randolph Churchill Letters 1/10/1147.

[81] Hicks Beach to Salisbury, 7 Dec. 1885, Third Marquess of Salisbury MSS Class E.

well-to-do, locally popular', who could 'speak more or less', and with a fair organization, the Conservatives could hold their own in the counties, except for the mining districts.[82] Though they had done poorly in the counties in 1885, Salisbury also held hope open for the future. 'In the past new voters have always begun with a Radical fling. It by no means follows that they will continue to be unmanageable hereafter.'[83] Conservative pessimism concerning their electoral prospects in Wales and Scotland[84] proved to be correct, and there was a solid Liberal triumph in these regions. 'There has come a turn in the tide & the Liberals are drawing ahead. We are equal in England & Wales (in spite of the Welsh Liberal majority) but Scotland with its dead weight over powers us', Carnarvon recorded.[85] Conservatives could only take satisfaction in the hope that Conservative electors had helped to return the most moderate Liberals in constituencies where no Conservative stood. 'In these cases the Conservatives naturally preferred a Moderate Liberal, who satisfied them on the Church question, to a pledged disestablisher.'[86]

In Ireland, nationalism and electoral reform had their effect, and the election of 1885 completed a revolution there. Southern Ireland became a one-party state forged by the power of national solidarity.[87] The highest proportion of uncontested elections in the United Kingdom were found in southern Ireland, all of which returned Nationalists. Lord Richard Grosvenor interpreted this high proportion of uncontested seats and the lower electoral turn-out as evidence against the Parnellite claim that they represented the Irish nation. (Grosvenor got his facts wrong: 25 per cent, not 33 per cent, of the Irish electorate failed to poll their votes.) Nevertheless, he advised Gladstone against 'coquetting with Parnell' because negotiations would damage the Liberals. Grosvenor advised Gladstone to refuse office since he had heard from Carnarvon that there would be trouble in Ireland and he wanted the Tories to deal with it by imposing a sharp law and order policy on the country.[88] Whatever conclusions Grosvenor drew of the Irish election results,

---

[82] Ellis Ashmead Bartlett to Salisbury, 6 Dec. 1885, Third Marquess of Salisbury MSS Class E.

[83] Salisbury to J. A. Thynne, Fourth Marquess of Bath, 3 Dec. 1885, Third Marquess of Salisbury MSS Class D/82/114.

[84] *The Times*, 24 Nov. 1885, p. 9.

[85] Carnarvon Diary, 30 Nov. 1885, BL Add. MS 60925, unbound and unfoliated.

[86] *The Times*, 12 Dec. 1885, p. 4.

[87] Hanham, *Elections and Party Management*, pp. 179–87; Blewett, *The Peers, the Parties, and the People*, pp. 225–6, 286–7.

[88] Grosvenor to Gladstone, 14 Dec. 1885, BL Add. MS 56446, unbound and unfoliated.

the Liberals were dismissed from the whole of the island and the
Tories were dished in the south. The only constituency which the
Conservatives hoped to take in the south, the St Stephen's Green
division of Dublin,[89] returned Edmund Dwyer Gray, the Nationalist
candidate over his Conservative rival, Sir Edward Guinness, with a
majority of 11 per cent of the total poll. In the south the Nationalists
routed Conservatives and Liberals alike. J. C. O'Flynn, in the
Northern division of Cork, received 4,982 votes to his Liberal
opponent's 102. In the Northern division of Kilkenny, Edward Marum
received 4,082 votes in contrast to the 174 votes cast for the Hon. C.
Bertram Bellew, the Conservative candidate. And so throughout the
south, driven by the forces of electoral reform and nationalism, it
went. When *The Times* reported the results of the contest in county
Carlow it called attention to the 'signal proof of the great change
which has been effected in the character of the representation. . . .
A comparison of the old and new constituencies generally will show
how great a revolution has been effected by the new law.'[90]

The Nationalists made strong inroads in Ulster as well. Indeed,
they took half of the province's seats. *The Times* ascribed this success
'to the divisions and feuds'[91] in Liberal and Conservative ranks.
Much as this might be the case, the division of Ulster between
Conservatives and Parnellites fell along lines of religious density.[92]
Where Protestants were in a distinct minority, in the south-west
portion of Ulster, Nationalists had overwhelming success, taking all
seats. Even in those portions of the province in which the Catholics
and Protestants were equally balanced, the Nationalists had great
success, winning five of the six seats. 'The one certain result of the
general elections', *The Times* reported, 'is the commanding position
secured by Mr Parnell.'[93] The Nationalists found themselves frustrated only in the north-east, in the part of Ulster having a decided
Protestant majority. Here Conservatives took fifteen of the nineteen
seats. Joined by a group of Irish MPs sitting for English constituencies
united by party, family, and Irish land in some cases, the Ulster
Conservatives constituted a more formidable political faction in the
House than their numbers would imply.[94]

---

[89] David Plunkett to Salisbury, 14 Aug. 1885, Third Marquess of Salisbury MSS
Class E.

[90] *The Times*, 5 Dec. 1885, p. 6.   [91] Ibid., 10 Dec. 1885, p. 6.

[92] I take these estimates of religious density from Patricia Jalland, *The Liberals and
Ireland: The Ulster Question in British Politics to 1914* (New York: 1980), pp. 50–1.

[93] *The Times*, 7 Dec. 1885, p. 9.

[94] For a discussion of this faction see D. C. Savage, 'The Origins of the Ulster
Unionist Party, 1885–6', *Irish Historical Studies*, 12.7 (Mar. 1961).

In addressing his Midlothian electors in December, once the results of the county polling had become known, Gladstone attributed the election results to the people, 'not to the Church, nor the nobles, nor the landlords, nor the rich'.[95] The election results did not reveal so clear a meaning to all. For some, the electors had shown the Liberal party to be a fractured political force. Liberal defeats in the boroughs may have set back Chamberlain and the radicals as they sought to seize control of the party, but the conflict between these factions was sending over to the Conservatives recruits from 'the heterogeneous party opposed to them'.[96] It was 'plainly . . . not one party, but at least two, divided on many points'.[97] W. H. Smith described the Liberals as 'a mixed, medley party, composed of those holding every variety of crotchets and fads'.[98] The election also suggested something of the nature of the Conservative party. By accepting the results of electoral reform, the Conservative party would not be the party of reaction: in future it would be progressive. With new strength in the boroughs, the 'Toryism of the past', *The Times* declared, 'is now extinct'. A conclusion followed from this. 'Modern Conservatism is hardly to be distinguished from moderate Liberalism.'[99] Some believed, whether on the basis of hope or of fact, that the election had been a victory for moderate elements. As Henry Howarth put it in a letter to Viscount Cranborne, 'the victory is really a Whig victory if anything'.[1] And a further conclusion followed. As the polling drew to a close and as observers assessed its results, some called for an alliance of moderate forces in the Liberal and Conservative parties to resist the extremism of Irish nationalism and English radicalism. Whether Liberal disunity would frustrate them, whether the Conservatives could be something other than a party of reaction, whether an alliance of moderate forces was possible, were questions which would be answered in the precincts of Westminster when the new House of Commons gathered there.

'The New Westminster Club'[2]

A total of 680 men were elected to the new House of Commons between the time of the general election of 1885 and the time of its

---

[95] *The Times*, 4 Dec. 1885, p. 7.   [96] Ibid., 25 Nov. 1885, p. 11.
[97] Ibid., 5 Dec. 1885, p. 9.   [98] Ibid., 26 Nov. 1885, p. 8.
[99] Ibid., 26 Nov., 1885, p. 11; 8 Dec. 1885, p. 9.
[1] Henry Howarth to Cranborne, 3 Dec. 1885, Fourth Marquess of Salisbury MSS Bundle 1.
[2] *The Tablet*, 19 Dec. 1885, p. 965. In drawing comparisons between the House of Commons in 1886 and other Houses, I have consulted the following works: Sir John Neale, *The Elizabethan House of Commons* (London: 1949); D. Brunton

dissolution in June. Of these, 666 men had been elected in the general election. Four Irish Nationalists had enjoyed double returns and had been elected to two seats each. Professor John McKane and Sir George Harrison died before Parliament assembled, and W. E. Forster and John Brooks died during the session. Henry Wyndham West, Jesse Collings, Harry Bullard, and David Duncan were unseated on petition for election violations. More happily, William Grantham resigned on his appointment as Judge of the Queen's Bench, and Lord Richard Grosvenor resigned to take a seat in the House of Lords as First Baron Stalbridge. It was the replacements[3] for these fourteen men which raised the total membership of this House of Commons to 680.

The Members of the new House of Commons were older, had less previous parliamentary experience than the Members of earlier

and D. H. Pennington, *Members of the Long Parliament* (London: 1954); Namier, *England in the Age of the American Revolution* (London: 1930); Ian Christie, *The End of North's Ministry, 1770–1782* (London: 1958); Gerrit P. Judd, *Members of Parliament, 1734–1832* (New Haven: 1955); W. O. Aydelotte, 'The House of Commons in the 1840's', *History*, 39 (Oct. 1954); W. L. Guttsman, *The British Political Elite* (New York: 1964); J. P. Cornford, 'The Parliamentary Foundations of the Hotel Cecil', *Ideas and Institutions of Victorian Britain*, ed. Robert Robson (London: 1967); Blewett, *The Peers, the Parties, and the People*; J. F. S. Ross, *Parliamentary Representation* (London: 1948); R. B. McCallum and Alison Readman, *The British Election of 1945* (London, New York, and Toronto: 1947); Michael Rush, 'The Members of Parliament', *The Commons in the Seventies*, ed. S. A. Walkland and Michael Ryle (London: 1977); J. A. Thomas, *The House of Commons, 1832–1901* (Cardiff: 1939), *The House of Commons, 1906–1910* (Cardiff: 1958); John Ramsden, *The Age of Balfour and Baldwin, 1902–1940* (London and New York: 1978).

[3] Replacements to the House of Commons of 1886:

Originally elected:	Replacement:
E. D. Gray (double return)	John Aloysius Blake
T. M. Healy (double return)	Patrick O'Brien
Arthur O'Connor (double return)	Stephen O'Mara
T. P. O'Connor (double return)	William O'Shea
Sir George Harrison (died)	Hugh Childers
W. E. Forster (died)	George Shaw-Lefevre
John Brooks (died)	Sir W. C. Brooks, Bt.
Professor John McKane (died)	Sir J. P. Corry
H. W. West (unseated on petition)	Lord Elcho
Jesse Collings (unseated on petition)	Charles Dalrymple
Harry Bullard (unseated on petition)	Samuel Hoare
David Duncan (unseated on petition)	W. S. Caine
William Grantham (resigned on appointment as Judge of the Queen's Bench)	Sidney Herbert
Lord Richard Grosvenor (elevated to the House of Lords)	Samuel Smith

Houses of Commons, and the House contained more businessmen and professional men. These differences are great, and indicate the adaptive capacities of legislative institutions. The differences were insufficient to prevent the assimilating and integrating features of parliamentary life from preserving the House as a club, rather than allowing it to be transformed into a cock-pit.

On average, as the ages of these MPs show, this was an older House of Commons than those of earlier centuries. Upwards of 40 per cent of the Members were forty years of age or younger in the eighteenth century. This is true of Members in the 1840s. In 1886 only 26 per cent of the Members were forty or less. Three hundred and twenty Members (48 per cent) were over fifty, and twenty-three (3 per cent) exceeded seventy-one years of age. Francis Bingham Mildmay, the newly elected Liberal Member for the Totnes division of Devon, who was the son of the banker, the great grandson of Earl Grey, and who had been to Eton and Trinity College, Cambridge, was at twenty-five the youngest Member of the House. The oldest Member was the eighty-four-year-old Charles Pelham Villiers, the Liberal Member for Wolverhampton South, who had become famous in the 1830s and 1840s for his repeated motions against the Corn Laws. Villiers, however, was not Father of the House, the Member with the longest continuous service. Villiers had sat continuously since 1835, but the eighty-three-year-old Christopher Rice Mansel Talbot had sat uninterruptedly for Glamorganshire since 1830.

Of the Members whose marital status can be ascertained, sixty-three were bachelors. Eighty-six Members had contracted second marriages, and five had married a third time. The proportion of these Members who had been to public school was 31 per cent, a figure which is lower than for both preceding and succeeding periods. In the eighteenth century the percentage of public school men in the House exceeded a third of the total membership and verged on 40 per cent. In the 1840s nearly half the House had been to public school. In 1918 the figure approached two-thirds of the House. Though the numbers decay for the House elected in 1945, when only 30 per cent of the Members had been to public school, they rose again in the 1950s. In the 1970s, 48 per cent of the Members had been to public school.[4] The schedule of Members of the House of Commons who had attended university holds to a flatter profile. The *Pall Mall Gazette* had anticipated that the House of Commons in 1886 would be like others in having a large number of university men.[5] This

---

[4] Rush, 'Members of Parliament'.
[5] *Pall Mall Gazette*, 10 Dec. 1885, p. 12.

proportion in 1886 was 47 per cent, a figure approximating the reckonings which have been made for the eighteenth century. In 1831 and for the period 1841–7, however, calculations of university men sitting in the House had been significantly higher, 59 and 62 per cent respectively. In the inter-war decades of the twentieth century, the figures declined to as low as 38 per cent. More recent figures, on the other hand, are higher, and significantly so. Sixty per cent of the Members sitting in the 1970s had been to university.[6] That Members of the House of Commons in 1886 had some measure of prestige and reputation in their local communities is shown by the fact that 40 per cent held, or were holding, county offices, and 23 per cent had borough offices.

It is not easy to get at the religious affiliations of these men. Arthur Balfour, for example, was an observer of the Presbyterian Church while in Scotland, and the Church of England when in England. Henry Joseph Wilson had been raised as a Congregationalist and had often attended Quaker meetings, but his intense dislike of all forms of religious authority kept him from an identification with any particular denomination. When once asked why he did not attend chapel more often, Wilson responded, because 'I so often want to move as amendment to the sermon!'[7] While the information on this subject is extremely limited, it is possible to say that no fewer than 154 Members were Nonconformists. Twenty-five were Methodists, twenty-two were Unitarians ('the Liberal party at prayer'), eleven were Quakers, and seven were Jews. One Member was an agnostic, and two were atheists. At least twenty-five Roman Catholics sat in this House of Commons: twenty-two were Irish Nationalists, twenty-one sitting for Irish seats and one (T. P. O'Connor) sitting for the Scotland division of Liverpool. Three (D. H. Macfarlane, Charles Russell, and H. B. Sheridan) were Liberals, one sitting for a Scottish seat and two holding English seats. But the information about the religious preference of Members is so incomplete—the religious affiliations of only 203 (30 per cent) Members of the House of Commons can be determined—that it would be folly to attempt any generalization based upon it.

The social composition of the House of Commons is quite another matter, however, and this is a subject to which it will be necessary to return when it comes time to ferret out from these figures their

---

[6] W. O. Aydelotte finds that 48% of the House in the 1840s had been to public school and 62% to university. Rush, 'Member of Parliament', p. 40.

[7] W. S. Fowler, *A Study in Radicalism and Dissent: The Life and Times of Henry Joseph Wilson, 1833–1914* (London: 1961), p. 24.

implications for political behaviour. The great work on this subject has been done for the sixteenth, seventeenth, eighteenth, and early nineteenth centuries, but the end of the nineteenth, and especially the period after the reforms of 1884–5, have remained prosopographical

TABLE 1.2 *The Social Composition of the House of Commons in 1886*

	No.	%
Relationship to the landed élite:		
Irish peers	1	0.1
Heirs of peers	27	4.0
Younger sons and grandsons of peers	43	6.3
Related to the peerage through the maternal line or marriage	16	2.4
Baronets	54	7.9
Sons or grandsons of baronets	24	3.5
Related to the baronetage through the maternal line or marriage	10	1.5
Landed gentry	78	11.5
Sons or grandsons of gentry	28	4.1
Related to landed gentry through the maternal line or marriage	26	3.9
Not related to the landed élite in any way	373	54.8
Summary:		
Peerage–baronetage–landed gentry (male line only)	255	37.5
Peerage–baronetage–landed gentry (through the female line or marriage)	52	7.6
Unrelated	373	54.8
Relationship to the professions:		
All professions	352	51.7
Lawyers (barristers and solicitors)	181	26.6
Army officers	70	10.3
Naval officers	10	1.5
Newspapermen	26	3.8
Academics	32	4.7
Diplomatic service	7	1.0
Civil service	19	2.8
Business interests:		
Active and substantial business interests	224	32.9
Bankers	38	5.6
Brewers or distillers	21	3.1
Colliery owners	22	3.2
Merchants	65	9.6
Textile manufacturers	31	4.6
Manufacturers of metal products	24	3.5
Shippers	21	3.1
Railway directors	75	11.0
Relationship to the working classes:		
Working men	14	2.0

terra incognita. Table 1.2, however, describes the major features of the evidence on this subject for the House of Commons in 1886. In the social world of this House, changed social structures accompanied changed tone and resonance, and for the first time landowners began serving a decorative rather than a substantial function. It was a world increasingly dependent on full-time professionals who worked under the increasingly abstract requirements of public opinion, rather than those of social intimacy.[8] Yet the social character of the House of Commons in 1886 indicates that forceful changes of this sort were more ironic and less symmetrical than the polemics of social reformers in the nineteenth century would imply.

The most important point to which Table 1.2 calls attention is the dramatic decline in the proportion of Members having connections with the peerage–baronetage–landed gentry. It depends, of course, on the manner in which such figures are tabulated. If one excludes MPs whose connections with the landed classes were attained through their mothers or wives alone, and there were fifty-two of these, only 37 per cent of the House was landed in its social background. This, however, is an underestimate. If one takes a less astringent definition of landed society and admits those Members who were connected to the peerage–baronetage–landed gentry through the maternal line or through marriage, a definition fully supported by the realities of such a social world, the proportion becomes 45 per cent of the House. What neither calculation disputes is that less than half the House of Commons was connected to landed society, and this for the first time.

According to Sir John Neale, 80 per cent of the House was landed in the late sixteenth century. The corresponding proportion for the seventeenth century was 77 per cent, and Namier found 93 per cent of the House to be landed in 1761.[9] The figures for landed gentlemen in the nineteenth century reveal a constant, though gradual, decline until the last fifteen years of the nineteenth century, and then the bottom dropped out. Different scholars, having different intellectual interests, have collected various numbers using various criteria, and the consequent picture, while not completely comparable, presents the general trend. J. A. Thomas, for example, calculating the number of economic interests in each Parliament, shows a decline

---

[8] David Spring, 'Some Reflections on Social History in the Nineteenth Century', *Victorian Studies*, 4 (Sept. 1960), p. 58; J. M. Lee, *Social Leaders and Public Persons: A Study of County Government in Cheshire since 1888* (Oxford: 1963), p. 5.

[9] Neale, The *Elizabethan House of Commons*, ch. 15; Namier, *England in the Age of the American Revolution*, pp. 215 ff. See also Judd, *Members of Parliament, 1734–1832*, pp. 54 ff.

in the number of landowners from 489 in 1832 to a number only one-third that after the general elections in December 1910. These figures, however, have to be regarded as an underestimate, because Thomas included only landowners in his calculations, not the heirs, younger sons, or grandsons of landed gentlemen, whose status entitled them to consideration amongst the landed classes.[10] Another study, one which deals with the period from 1865 to 1880, includes MPs who could be considered landed gentlemen both by economic interest and by social status and finds a declining proportion of landed gentlemen of about 21 per cent during the period of the second electoral system, an estimate which does not differ greatly from Thomas's for the same period.[11] Calculations for the 1840s and 1870s are rather more certain, and reveal the proportion of landed gentlemen in the House of Commons to have declined by 15 per cent during the intervening period, from 81 per cent to 66 per cent.[12] In 1886, Table 1.2 shows, the proportion of landed gentlemen had declined by an additional 21 per cent, to 45 per cent of the House. While comparable figures for the House of Commons in the twentieth century are harder to come by, Blewett's assessment of the social background of candidates for parliamentary seats in general elections of 1910 reveal a very much lower percentage of landed gentlemen.[13] Ramsden found a remnant of eighty-three landowners in the Liberal and Conservative parties (about 14 per cent of the House) on the eve of the Great War.[14]

This survey suggests two points. First, after remaining stable in its social composition for centuries with the landed classes dominating parliamentary life, for the first time in 1886 the non-landed element in the House of Commons became larger than the landed. This was a sudden event. The reforms of 1884–5 did what those of 1832 and 1867 did not do; they broke the numerical hold of the landed élite in the House of Commons. The decline in the number of landed gentlemen in the House of Commons coincided with other events which imply a crisis in the aristocracy. The numbers of armorial

---

[10] Thomas, *The House of Commons, 1832–1901*, pp. 4–7, 14–17; *The House of Commons, 1906–1911*, p. 14.

[11] William Henry Whiteley, *The Social Composition of the House of Commons, 1868–1885* (unpublished Ph.D. dissertation, Cornell University: 1960), pp. 577–8. Like Thomas, Whiteley gives no clue to the bases and criteria of his social classifications.

[12] Aydelotte, 'The House of Commons in the 1840's', pp. 254–5; James Cook Hamilton, *Parties and Voting Patterns in the Parliament of 1874–1880* (unpublished Ph.D. dissertation, University of Iowa: 1968).

[13] Blewett, *The Peers, the Parties, and the People*, pp. 229–30.

[14] Ramsden, *The Age of Balfour and Baldwin*, p. 98.

bearing on carriages and for quarterings on writing paper, family silver, and cutlery, after growing throughout the century, ceased their expansion or declined in the 1890s. Figures such as these imply a change in public values, and an end to what one scholar has called the Victorian 'rush to gentility'.[15] Second, another implication of the proportion of landed gentlemen in the House of Commons ought not to be forgotten. Forty-five per cent is no insubstantial figure, and testifies to the continuing influence of the landed interest in British politics. The Victorian landed classes' history is the story of survival.[16] While they were fewer in the House of Commons, the landed classes and the social symbols affixed to them could not be ignored or discounted. As Lord Percy of Newcastle has observed, landed gentlemen do 'not run to types, and [their] best fruits are apt to be out of season. A mild bent toward eccentricity and anachronism, is indeed [their] virtue and [their] salvation'.[17]

Businessmen alone, as Table 1.2 also makes clear, did not fill the social room which landed gentlemen had evacuated by 1886. The proportion of businessmen in the House had not exceeded 12 per cent in the period from the sixteenth to the eighteenth centuries.[18] Their proportion, of course, grew in the nineteenth century, but not as much as some have claimed. J. A. Thomas, for example, had sharply inflated estimates of the number of businessmen in the nineteenth century House of Commons because he counted economic 'interests' rather than individuals, and because he made no distinction between MPs having substantial business activities and those who were only tangentially concerned with trade, industry, or commerce.[19] In the House of Commons which sat between 1841 and 1847, only 17 per cent of the Members were active businessmen.[20] This

---

[15] F. M. L. Thompson, 'Britain', *European Landed Elites in the Nineteenth Century*, ed. David Spring (Baltimore and London: 1977), pp. 22–44.

[16] Walter L. Arnstein, 'The Survival of the Victorian Aristocracy', *The Rich, the Well Born and the Powerful: Elites and Upper Classes in History*, ed. Frederic Cople Jaher (Urbana, Chicago, and London: 1973), pp. 203–57.

[17] Eustace Percy, *Some Memories* (London: 1958), p. 9.

[18] Neale, *The Elizabethan House of Commons*, ch. 15; Namier, *England in the Age of the American Revolution*, pp. 220 ff.; Judd, *Members of Parliament, 1734–1832*.

[19] Thomas, *The House of Commons, 1832–1901*, pp. 14–17; *The House of Commons, 1906–1910*, pp. 14–17. As Thomas realized, MPs often had more than one interest. Therefore, if one divides the number of business interests by the number of MPs having business interests (Aydelotte, in 'The House of Commons in the 1840's', p. 255, shows that each MP having business interests had, on average, two business interests), a very much more plausible figure emerges.

[20] For a preliminary discussion of this point, see Aydelotte, 'The House of Commons in the 1840's', pp. 255–7.

proportion grew to 24 per cent of the House in the 1870s,[21] and, as Table 1.2 shows, increased to 33 per cent in 1886. The same general pattern can be seen in other legislatures. In the United States House of Representatives, for example, the percentage of businessmen increased slowly from 13 per cent in the first decade of the nation's history to a maximum of 24 per cent during the 1930s, whereafter it declined slightly.[22] What apparently happened was that the number of active businessmen in the House of Commons grew slowly in the nineteenth century to a level which remained fairly constant into the twentieth century. The proportion of businessmen standing in the general elections of 1910 was 25 per cent; the percentage holding Liberal or Conservative seats in 1919 was 26 per cent, and this figure increased to 32 per cent in the 1970s.[23] The increased average age of MPs in the late nineteenth century, which would have enabled businessmen to enjoy parliamentary careers after they had established themselves in their firms, apparently, did little to affect these proportions.

It was professional men who took the place of landed gentlemen in the late Victorian House of Commons. Their increase, in the first place, simply took the form of increased numbers. The combined increase of lawyers and MPs in the non-service professions in 1886, when compared to the social composition of the House of Commons in the 1840s, was 22 per cent. In the 1840s, 40 per cent of the MPs had professions of some kind. This proportion declined in the 1870s, but only slightly, to 37 per cent, but then grew to better than half of the House (52 per cent) in 1886. Secondly, the character of the professions in the House of Commons changed. In the 1840s the largest group of MPs with professions were those with army or navy commissions (50 per cent of the MPs with professions and 20 per cent of the House). In 1886 only eighty Members (23 per cent of the professional men and 12 per cent of the House) held military commissions. If J. A. Thomas's figures for the nineteenth-century Houses of Commons are used,[24] there was a slight increase in the

---

[21] Whiteley's figures on this point (*The Social Composition of the House of Commons, 1868–1885*) are confirmed by those of Hamilton (*Parties and Voting Patterns in the Parliament of 1874–1880*).

[22] Allan G. Bogue, Jerome M. Clubb, Carroll R. McKibbin, and Santa A. Traugott, 'Members of the House of Representatives and the Processes of Modernization, 1789–1960', *Journal of American History*, 63.2 (Sept. 1976), p. 284.

[23] Blewett, *The Peers, the Parties, and the People*, pp. 229–30; Ramsden, *The Age of Balfour and Baldwin*, p. 98; Rush, 'The Members of Parliament', p. 42.

[24] Thomas, *The House of Commons, 1832–1901*, pp. 4–7, 14–17; *The House of Commons, 1906–1910*, pp. 22–3.

proportion of MPs with service commissions in the 1850s and 1860s, perhaps corresponding with a period of Palmerstonian bellicosity (more likely, however, coinciding with the end of the Crimean War and the return to civilian life of men commissioned in the services), and then a long-term decline in those proportions for the remainder of the century. The same general trend can be observed in the proportions of commissioned officers sitting in the United States House of Representatives in the nineteenth century. The largest proportion of such men (47 per cent) sat in the Congresses of the first decade of the nation's history, after which the figures decline to 18 per cent in the decade immediately preceding the Civil War. They rose again to 37 per cent in the 1870s, but then sharply declined to 9 per cent during the decade of the Great War.[25] The decline of the military services in the social composition of the House of Commons in the nineteenth century is of some considerable interest because it occurred during a period of heated public interest in the Empire and foreign policy, during the Boer War, and the run-up to the Great War, during periods of both Gladstonian and Cecilian dominance. Britain, like the United States, and unlike the Continent, did not rely on a professional military élite, and whatever increased foreign policy or imperial bellicosity there was in the last two decades of the nineteenth century was not the result of a penetration into the political system of the military corps.

As the proportion of MPs with service commissions diminished, the proportions of lawyers and MPs in the newer professions grew. In the 1840s, 134 members were lawyers (40 per cent of all professional men and 16 per cent of the House). In 1886 these numbers increased to 181 lawyers (51 per cent of all professional men and 27 per cent of the House). For purposes of comparison, it is possible to see the same trend in the United States House of Representatives during the same period. There was a higher proportion of lawyers in the House of Representatives at the beginning of the period (45 per cent in 1800), which proportion grew to 67 per cent in 1850, and then diminished to 60 per cent in 1920.[26] Additionally, by 1886, members of the new professions had entered the House of Commons. Journalists and academics, engineers, and architects joined members of the diplomatic and civil service there. It is the proportion of these Members which shows some of the sharpest growth in the nineteenth century, from 5 per cent of the House in the 1840s to 15 per cent

[25] Bogue, Clubb, McKibbin, and Traugott, 'Members of the House of Representatives and the Processes of Modernization', pp. 286–7.

[26] Ibid., pp. 284–5.

in 1886. In consequence, by 1886 more men of the professions had entered parliamentary politics, and many of these displaced members of the military professions who had connections with the traditional élite. These additions and subtractions gave the social composition of the House of Commons a new character, distinguishing it from earlier Houses. With the emergence in political prominence of professional politicians and the rise of the Labour party, with the consequent increase in the number of working class MPs at Westminster, the proportion of professional men declined slightly in the twentieth century. Though the proportion of professional men standing for parliamentary seats in the general elections of 1910 was 37 per cent, the proportion of such Members sitting in the Liberal and Conservative parties in 1916 was 51 per cent, and the corresponding figure for MPs in the 1970s was 38 per cent.[27]

Table 1.2 identifies the small contingent of working-class Members in parliamentary politics in 1886. These included Henry Broadhurst, who had been associated with the parliamentary committee of the Trade Union Congress, and who was admitted to Gladstone's Ministry in 1886. Conscious of his appearance, Broadhurst refused to appear at Court until he had earned enough of his official salary to buy his Court dress.[28] Gladstone was also aware of his appearance, and 'praised Mr Broadhurst and told again the story, which story, which evidently delights him, how Mr Broadhurst made all his clothes'.[29] Thomas Burt rose to the House, and eventually to the Privy Council, from the coal pits. These Members also included Joseph Arch. Arch failed to make a favourable impression. W. S. Blunt described him as 'a heavy lump of a farmer, very thick witted I thought & dull, but they say he is a good speaker on his own subjects. . . . Arch dresses in coloured clothes & wears a billy cock hat—no pretence of being a gentleman or a clever man.'[30] According to Sir Richard Temple,

Arch however must needs speak and his speech confirmed the impression I already had that (apart from the impression of his influence *outside*) he will make *no* moral impression of this H. of Commons. He is much inferior to the other 'Labour Representatives' (MPs) as they are called—Burt & others. He may have similar ability to theirs (tho' I rather think not) but

[27] Blewett, *The Peers, the Parties, and the People*, pp. 229–30; Ramsden, *The Age of Balfour and Baldwin*, p. 98; Rush, 'Members of Parliament', p. 42.

[28] Salisbury to Lady John Manners, 4 Mar. 1886, Third Marquess of Salisbury MSS Class D/48/274.

[29] Lady Dorothy Stanley's Diary, 8 Mar. 1886, Chamberlain Papers JC8/2/2.

[30] Blunt Diary, 23 Feb. 1886, Blunt MS 334-1975, f. 58.

they have been in industrial centres, whereas he has been among Hodges & clod-hoppers all his life. He has got into a rhetorical groove,—a low & simple one—from which he cannot get out of. So he actually addresses *us* in the House just as if he were addressing a rural audience from a platform in a village barn.[31]

The powerful working of the kinds of social distinctions found in Blunt's and Temple's remarks reveal how difficult it was for working-class MPs to be accepted in the existing political structures, though Broadhurst's admission to Gladstone's Government was a more hopeful sign. Moreover, their loyalties were uncertain and divided. Arch, during the election contest, expressed some ambiguity himself concerning the relationship of working-class MPs to the political world they were entering when he described himself as standing in 'the Liberal and labouring class interest'.[32]

Arch believed these interests were compatible, and, as he admitted in his memoirs, he had the political 'patronage of several of the local gentry' who loaned him their carriages for getting electors to the polls.[33] On the one hand Arch identified himself with working-class political action and attempted to preserve the force of social independence. This is the way he described his first appearance in the House of Commons in 1886:

. . . I meant to wear my ordinary dress in the House, not to make myself conspicuous, but because I was determined to do like the Shumanitish woman of whom I read in the good old book, and who had great opportunities of enriching herself—I would live and die with my brethren.[34]

On the other hand, Arch was as confident of upward mobility as the best labour aristocrat, and preferred political to direct action. He encouraged the working classes to seek their objectives within existing economic arrangements, and he gave them good bourgeois advice as he did so. 'Let the lower classes of society rise and become thrifty, and provident, and happy with plenty to eat and plenty to do, with good wages, fairly earned, and then every other class of society will be raised, will be strong and happy in proportion.'[35] The same tensions, though in a more strictly political sense, can be seen in Burt's career. Arch considered Burt a straight-party politician, but as late as the 1890s Burt held to an independent line and would commit himself neither to the Liberal nor to the emerging Labour party. Valuing 'independence above every other possession', Burt

---

[31] Letters of Sir Richard Temple, 15 Apr. 1886, BL Add. MS 38916, ff. 62ᵛ–63.
[32] Joseph Arch, *Joseph Arch, The Story of His Life* (London: 1898), p. 355.
[33] Ibid., pp. 386–8.   [34] Ibid., pp. 358–9.   [35] Ibid., pp. 370–1.

claimed he 'had never been asked, and if . . . asked . . . would never have consented to give a political pledge to support any political party'.[36]

The cardinal features of modern British society are found in these figures. Highly elastic, highly landed, highly bourgeois, and even more highly professional, the House of Commons in 1886 consisted of social elements which required political integration and assimilation. Nowhere is this more true than with regard to another feature of the evidence describing the background of MPs: their previous parliamentary experience. Nearly half the Members of the new House of Commons (48 per cent) were returned to Westminster for the first time. The comparative figures for this shows that in the sixteenth and seventeenth centuries there had been similar high rates of turnover. The proportions for this earlier period exceed 50 per cent frequently and sometimes exceed two-thirds. For the most part, the eighteenth and nineteenth centuries were periods of low turnover in the House of Commons—less than a third, for example, in the 1840s. In the twentieth century the rate of turnover has been reduced, on the whole, from the level of 1886, save for those elections where one would expect increases. In 1906, for example, turnover rose to 42 per cent of the House, and in 1945 it rose to 53 per cent.[37] The high rate of turnover in 1886, therefore, was an anomaly in nineteenth-century Parliaments, the highest percentage of the century. Moreover, this turnover rate was reflected in all three parties sitting there, with relative equality. Forty-seven per cent of the Conservatives sitting in the House of Commons in 1886 had no previous parliamentary experience, and the corresponding figure for the Liberals was 48 per cent. For the Irish the percentage was higher, 56 per cent. But it would not always be so. With the establishment of the Nationalists in Irish constituencies, once returned an Irish Nationalist could consider a seat his for life, if he could avoid the squabbling of consitituency factions.[38] The necessity of political assimilation in 1886 was a prospect some observers regarded as an advantage. As *The Tablet* put it: 'the new Westminster Club has at least one element which is necessary to the

---

[36] Ibid., p. 355; Thomas Burt, *Thomas Burt, M.P., D.C.L., Pitman and Privy Councillor, An Autobiography* (London: 1924), pp. 261, 287, 289.

[37] Neale, *The Elizabethan House of Commons*, ch. 15; Brunton and Pennington, *Members of the Long Parliament*; Namier, *England in the Age of the American Revolution*, p. 217; Judd, *Members of Parliament, 1734–1832*, pp. 27–9; Aydelotte, 'The House of Commons in the 1840's', p. 253; Ross, *Parliamentary Representation*, pp. 36–7; McCallum and Readman, *The British Election of 1945*, p. 274.

[38] Blewett, *The Peers, the Parties, and the People*, pp. 225–6.

success of such an institution. There is sufficient variety in the character and composition of its members.'[39] Other observers were not so certain.

Misgivings about the increased number of Members without previous parliamentary experience raise the question of political socialization and integration, the question of how new Members were to be reconciled to the old, and how quickly inexperienced Members could be introduced into the folk ways of the House of Commons. Turnover is an indicator of institutionalization,[40] the degree to which an institution is distinct and insulated from its environment. A high degree of turnover, such as that found in the House of Commons in 1886, reveals an ease of entry into the House; it reveals that the electorate placed less value on seniority and previous political experience. Therefore, it is important to assess the degree to which, and in what characteristics, experienced MPs differed from their inexperienced colleagues. An index of similarity, by comparing these two groups according to personal, social, and constituency variables, can measure the amount of assimilation the circumstances in 1886 required.

Table 1.3 shows the percentages of experienced and inexperienced Members having each of these qualities, and provides a calculation of their similarity by comparing these proportions. The evidence of which this table is a summary suggests that on most variables there was little difference between these groups of Members. The average of these similarity scores for the whole House is very high, 95.5. Even if these scores are disaggregated and calculated for each party separately, they remain elevated: 93 for the Conservatives, 92 for the Liberals, and 90 for the Irish Nationalists. Figures such as these support the calming assessment made by *The Times* at the election's conclusion in 1885:

There are no signs of the cataclysm feared by many nervous observers. The voice of reason, commonsense, and experience has not been drowned in the clamour of unreasoning ignorance and prejudice. No great wave has threatened to engulf our institutions or undermine our social order. Some extreme men have found their way into the House of Commons, but so they have done under every electoral *regime*. Upon the whole, they are neither so numerous nor so influential as they were in the last Parliament.[41]

This is not, however, the whole story.

[39] *The Tablet*, 19 Dec. 1885, p. 965.
[40] Nelson Polsby, 'The Institutionalization of the U.S. House of Representatives', *American Political Science Review*, 62 (Mar. 1968) pp. 144 ff.
[41] *The Times*, 8 Dec. 1885, p. 9.

TABLE 1.3 *The Similarity of New Members and Experienced Members of the House of Commons in 1886**

	New Members (%)	Experienced Members (%)	Similarity score
Landed gentlemen	31	58	73
Professional men	51	52	99
Businessmen	43	42	99
Working class	4	.6	97
Public school men	28	35	93
University educated	41	52	99
Held county constituencies	60	52	92
Held borough constituencies	39	46	93
Held university seats	.3	2	98
Seats in southern England	35	31	96
Seats in northern England	34	37	97
Welsh seats	3	7	96
Scottish seats	10	11	99
Ulster seats	5	5	100
S. Irish seats	12	8	96
0–4,999 electors	6	9	97
5,000–7,599 electors	18	17	99
7,500–9,000 electors	24	20	96
9,000 + –12,500 electors	50	52	98
12,500 + electors	8	11	97

*S = 100 – (% of new Members with a particular attribute – % of experienced Members with that attribute). Perfect similarity = 100. The Mean of these indices is 95.5.

The figures so far cited are averages which, necessarily, obscure variations and extremes. When the detailed figures in Table 1.3 are examined, it is possible to identify those grounds on which inexperienced Members differ from those MPs who had sat in previous Houses of Commons. One of these is indicated by the variable describing the relationship of experienced and inexperienced MPs to the landed élite. A high percentage of experienced Members enjoyed connections to landed society. This was less true for parliamentary newcomers in 1886, and, as a consequence, the similarity score measuring this difference declines sharply to 73. And it is low for each of the parties taken individually: 71 for the Conservatives, 74 for the Liberals, and 84 for the Irish Nationalists. Another ground for difference is revealed in the figures for two closely related variables, those describing the relationship of experienced and inexperienced Members according to the types of constituencies for which they sat. This does not come out so clearly in the similarity scores in Table 1.3, but it is apparent in the percentages found there. While experienced MPs divided themselves almost equally between county and borough seats, a higher proportion of inexperienced Members sat for county seats.

The barriers separating the experienced from the inexperienced Members in the House of Commons in 1886, therefore, were two, social and constituency. In all parties new Members had a lesser connection to the landed classes than their experienced brethren. Among Conservatives, inexperienced Members, reflecting the increasing success of Tories in urban constituencies, sat for borough seats in higher proportions. Among Liberals, inexperienced Members, reflecting the electoral rewards for the extension of the franchise, sat for county seats in higher proportions. The House of Commons in 1886 was able to reconcile and assimilate these differences, and, for this, as Chapter 3 will show, partisanship was one of its agents. These differences failed to produce policy splits among the Conservatives, who could present a united and consolidated opposition to Gladstone's Government. These differences, and especially social differences, account for internal differentiation in the Liberal party, but they did not produce the great separation in the Liberal party. The Liberal party was able to preserve its unity despite these differences. When the party broke up, it did so under quite special circumstances. As the dimensional analysis of voting patterns in the House of Commons shows, forceful integrating agencies were at work assimilating the new to the old, providing at one and the same time ways for advancing and for resisting reform. This was the forging work of the parliamentary regime, and it is the story of the parliamentary session which lasted from January to June in 1886.

Conclusion

In one sense, any new House of Commons is an uncertain political world; but the House of Commons in 1886 opened a world which was less certain than most. A new franchise and a new electoral distribution had returned a three-party legislature in which it was impossible to know who could form a Government or how long any Government could survive. By their numbers the Irish Nationalists could turn out the Conservatives and put-in the Liberals, and by their numbers they could displace the Liberals in their turn. Parliamentary politics in 1886 confronted a crisis in which the dominance of the Liberal party, which had lasted the better part of two decades, ended and was replaced by a period of Conservative hegemony lasting, in its turn, twenty years. At the end of the parliamentary session *The Times* assessed its history: 'It wrecked more than one reputation, broke up political parties, and plunged the country into a whirlpool of excitement.'[42] This, however, was a political crisis, not a crisis in society. Politics was not caught in the pincers of class struggle or in a struggle between urban and rural regions. As a political crisis, it tested the nature of parliamentary institutions and structures. An assessment of the structures of parliamentary life requires a dimensional analysis of voting in the House of Commons, and it is to this subject that this study now turns.

[42] *The Times*, 26 June 1886, p. 11.

2

The Dimensions of Parliamentary Voting

I look upon this as a thoroughly working Parliament. . . . The Queen's Speech before the dissolution gives but a jejeune [*sic*] notion of the work actually done. This work has been really great in quantity for the *short* broken session of which nearly half was taken up with Ireland. Not only have public Acts been passed, but also a large number of private Acts relating to general improvements of all sorts. Many subjects were also investigated by special Committees. The independent workers, especially among the new Members, are numerous. Legislation was by no means left to the Government, but individuals were always trying to signalize themselves by promoting some new measure. The general temper of the House was earnest and industrious. Again, much time was given to several comprehensive measures, which, after all, had to be dropped when the Session was abruptly terminated — for instance the Railway and Canal Traffic Bill. Among the Acts passed, that relating to the Scotch Crofters was discussed in considerable detail.

Sir Richard Temple, Bt., 26 June 1886[1]

Introduction

Though the question of Irish government came to dominate the lifetime of this House of Commons, it is not possible to dismiss it as a single-issue legislature.[2] Assessed in terms of the questions taken to the division lobbies, this House faced both the ordinary matters of parliamentary life, the estimates and tests of confidence in Salisbury's and Gladstone's Administrations, and the major issues of the day. The House debated and voted upon questions of Church and State, land policy, political reform, foreign, imperial, and military policy, and social questions, such as shop hours, the Contagious Diseases Acts, and temperance. And then there was Irish Home Rule and other aspects of Irish policy.

Toward such diverse questions, naturally, there was a welter of attitudes and it is difficult to identify a common thread which might be used to interpret the period. The difficulty of finding a consistent theme in the content of legislation with which the House of Commons dealt was compounded, in fact, by the introduction of the Home

[1] Temple Letters, 28 June 1886. BL Add. MS 38916, f. 162ᵛ.
[2] D. W. Crowley, 'The Crofters' "Party", 1885–1892', *The Scottish Historical Review*, 35.2 (Oct. 1956), p. 119; Cooke and Vincent, *The Governing Passion*, p. 16.

Rule question into an already heady mix. It served to throw many observers and participants into a state of crisis and confusion. For Lady Sophia Palmer, orthodox values had been rendered obsolete. 'We all lost a great deal of time when we learned the 10 commandments—to rejoice in the Magna Charta [*sic*] and ached our heads over Adam Smith—Fawcett, and even J. S. Mill! It is all disproven—and we have to unlearn and learn anew.' For the Duke of Argyll 'there is no principle of Government which is not put into the furnace and crucible'. He wrote to Gladstone, 'we have no guidance in which any man can feel confidence.'[3] And these were not casual or inexperienced observers. Lady Sophia was the highly intelligent and deeply political daughter of the Earl of Selborne and the sister of Lord Wolmer, who sat in this House of Commons and who became a Liberal Unionist during the Home Rule crisis.

The present study centres its analysis on distinctly legislative evidence, the House of Commons division lists, to discover the central strands which exist in the vast materials which remain from the Home Rule crisis. The name of the various approaches to the study of such evidence is legion. What follows, however, uses dimensional analysis of the sort developed for the study of legislative politics in America, Britain, France, and Germany.[4] A detailed discussion of the procedures involved in the discovery of parliamentary voting dimensions must be put in its proper place (see Appendix II), but since it lies at the heart of this study a brief description is necessary here.

The idea of a dimension is simplicity itself. A group of legislative items (bills, resolutions, motions, votes of supply) may be said to belong to a common dimension if they satisfy two interrelated conditions. First, it must be possible to rank them in order of their degree of radicalness, or moderation. How is it known which items

[3] Lady Sophia Palmer to Sir Arthur Gordon, 6 Apr. 1886, published in *A Political Correspondence of the Gladstone Era: The Letters of Lady Sophia Palmer to Sir Arthur Gordon*, ed. J. K. Chapman (Philadelphia: 1971), p. 33; Argyll to Gladstone, 29 Jan. 1886, BL Add. MS 44106, ff. 92-3.

[4] Duncan MacRae, *Dimensions of Congressional Voting* (Berkeley, California: 1958); W. O. Aydelotte, 'Voting Patterns in the British House of Commons in the 1840s', *Comparative Studies in Society and History*, 5.2 (Jan. 1963), pp. 134-63; Donald J. Mattheisen, 'Liberal Constitutionalism in the Frankfurt Parliament of 1848: An Inquiry Based on Roll-Call Analysis', *Central European History*, 12.2 (June 1979), pp. 124-42; Woodruff Smith and Sharon A. Turner, 'Legislative Behavior in the German Reichstag, 1898-1906', *Central European History*, 14.1 (Mar. 1981), pp. 3-29; Aage Clausen, *How Congressmen Decide* (New York: 1973); Gerhardt Loewenberg, Samuel C. Patterson, and Malcom E. Jewell (eds.), *Handbook of Legislative Research* (Cambridge, Mass. and London: 1985).

are more radical and which are moderate? If they belong to the same dimension, the votes of Members tell us. Those items enjoying the least support (the fewest positive votes) are the most radical, the most extreme, because they were the hardest to vote for. More moderate measures have more support. Those items having the greatest support in the House are the most conservative measures. The secondary necessary condition if one is to claim the existence of a dimension of legislative items is consistent voting on these questions by Members. Some Members may support all items; some Members may oppose all items; some Members might support some items and oppose others. However, none may oppose a more moderate item, as judged by the proportion of the House voting for the measures, while supporting more extreme items. Irregular voting of this kind casts items out of a dimension. Using these two conditions, it is possible to establish ordinal scales which order legislative items according to their degree of radicalism or moderateness, and which rank Members on these scales according to their support, or opposition, to the measures which fit the dimensions. To facilitate the analysis, a searching statistic, Yule's Q, serves as a device to measure the degree of irregular voting and, in this manner, to determine which items fit a dimension and which do not. (See Appendix II.)

To discover dimensions in the votes of Members of the House of Commons, or any other legislative body, is a finding of great importance and interest because it shows political behaviour, in those settings, to be based upon ideology, rather than upon individual, social, or economic interest. By ideological behaviour here I do not mean that Members or parties were bound to narrow or abstract sets of doctrines or dogmas. Nor do I mean that Members were bound together by an overwhelming consensus and agreement, nor that they held to their positions with a particular emotional intensity. In the present analysis, ideological behaviour refers to the consistent and regular responses of Members to policy based upon their beliefs and political values.

Moreover, the existence of dimensions identifies the political centres of gravity, the major political agendas of the period, by discriminating between those questions which were central and those which were not. Those legislative questions on the periphery of the policy agendas defined by dimensions of legislative items are consigned there by the Members themselves. Their votes show a *shifted*, or different, basis of ideological support. That is to say, Members reveal a different posture on some questions because they voted for more extreme measures as judged by the proportion of the House voting in favour of them, while opposing more moderate measures. A dimension visualizes legislative action—the support and opposition to detailed questions of policy—on a continuum. It identifies those points on a political continuum which ordinary discourse labels as 'left' and 'right'. In this way, by outlining the ideological character of a political system's policy agendas, it is possible to characterize the reactions of politicians to them. Dimensions reveal the limits and range of choice and conflict in the House of Commons. They do not describe the external realities of the political universe, or the objective meaning of political issues, if there is such a thing. Rather, dimensions summarize, in a highly parsimonious manner dozens of votes of Members and, in so summarizing, reveal the subjective responses of Members toward their political world. They are descriptions of values and attitudes, descriptions of the shape and meaning of politics as Members understood it.

The greater the number and variety of legislative questions which can be fitted into dimensions of this sort, the more coherent the political system may be said to be. And by this test the world of parliamentary politics in 1886 was highly coherent and integrated. In the first place, dimensions of a high statistical quality can be discovered along lines of common policy. For example, one dimension consists of votes on ecclesiastical questions, and there are others of land policy, and social and political reform. There is one on Ireland and Irish policy, and another on imperial, military, and foreign policy votes. In the second place, many of the items which fit these various content dimensions also fit a large cross-content dimension which, as a consequence, contains all of the major questions of the time. Findings of this sort are too regular and consistent to have been produced by chance, and they run contrary to conceptions of politics which view political behaviour as *sui generis*, or view political motivation as resting solely on personal interest and ambition.

The Substantive Lines of Cleavage

Kitson Clark, in describing politics a half-century earlier, spoke of the 'smell of religion in the air'. The aura and odour of religion filled no less the politics of the 1880s. It is not surprising, therefore, to find a dimension of religious and ecclesiastical questions in the parliamentary divisions of 1886. The question of disestablishment excited the general election of 1885 with grave emotional force.[5] This was less the result of encouragement by the Liberation

---

[5] Alan Simon, 'Church Disestablishment as a Factor in the General Election of 1885', pp. 791–820.

Society[6] and more greatly the work of Scottish disestablishers, Joseph Chamberlain campaigning on behalf of the unauthorized programme, and Tories seeking to rouse Anglican support. The 'Church in danger' was one of the most important political cries. As Lord Balfour of Burleigh put it, 'among the many questions of domestic policy which will be submitted to the new electorate for decision, that of the relation between Church and State will be one perhaps of the earliest in point of time, as it will certainly not be the least in the point of difficulty and importance.'[7] This matter was, or so Gladstone and William Rathbone believed it to be, an attempt on the part of the Tories to split the Liberals.[8]

The Church question emerged in the House of Commons of 1886 in several forms. On 9 March, Lewis Llewelyn Dillwyn raised the question of the Church of England in Wales in a resolution which attacked it as 'an anomaly and an injustice which ought no longer to exist'. This resolution initiated a stream of parliamentary events which included Albert Grey's amendment for the reform, but not for the disestablishment of the Welsh Church, and three parliamentary divisions.[9] On 17 March, John Finlay's Church of Scotland Bill advanced to its second reading. Since it ought to restore the Scottish Free Church to the Scottish Church, it contained the principle of ecclesiastical establishment. Critics of this principle, such as Dr Charles Cameron, opposed it because the measure 'would strengthen the National Church at the expense of the Dissenting Presbyterian communities'.[10] On 30 March, Cameron introduced his own resolution calling for the disestablishment and disendowment of the Church of Scotland.

Late in the parliamentary session, the Tithe Rent-Charge (extra-ordinary) Redemption Bill raised the Church question in a different manner. This was a private Bill, with extensive parliamentary support, introduced by T. H. Bolton, James Thorold Rogers, William Copeland Borlase, and Sir John Lubbock, to eliminate the tithe on hops in Sussex and Kent and to make the rent-charge on hops, in future, payable by the landowners rather than the tenants. This Bill, in fact, was one of three which was discussed by a Select

---

[6] D. A. Hamer, *The Politics of Electoral Pressure: A Study in the History of Victorian Reform Agitation* (Hassocks, Sussex: 1977), pp. 139–64, and especially p. 157.

[7] Lord Balfour of Burleigh, 'Church and State in Scotland', *Fortnightly Review*, new series, 44 (1885), p. 277.

[8] Gladstone to the Earl of Southesk, 27 Oct. 1885, Rathbone to Gladstone, 6 Nov. 1885, BL Add. MSS 44548, ff. 47–8, 44493, f. 47.

[9] Hansard, 303: 305 ff. and 322 ff.   [10] Ibid., 303: 1086.

Committee, and this one had been produced by agreement among Liberals and Conservatives on the Committee.[11] Though concerned with local interests, the debate on the Bill had implications for the Church and the social order. Its proponents viewed the Bill as a means for the integration of institutions in rural society through the reduction of tensions between clergy and parishioners, between landlords and tenants.[12] Those opposed to it viewed the Bill as they viewed disestablishment, as a measure of spoliation. As Stanley Leighton put it, 'I am perfectly astounded when I find Radicals—Radicals of Radicals—and Irish Members proposing to take property from one set of individuals who represent Church property, and not private property, and to put it in the hands of landowners.' Members such as Leighton were aided in their conception of this legislation by statements of some of its adherents. Alfred Illingworth, in the second reading debate, addressed the question of disestablishment itself. One of Lord Cranborne's correspondents, on this legislation, appealed to Cranborne 'and the Conservative interest and Party to again befriend the Church'.[13]

The Church question, when it came before the House, shocked the sensibilities of ecclesiastical defenders such as Sir Richard Temple, who found horrifying the spirit and tone of Dillwyn, Richard, and other disestablishers.[14] It left neither Gladstone nor his Government sanguine. Aware of the sentiments of Chamberlain, Morley, and Trevelyan within the Cabinet, aware that he also needed their support for other and, to his mind, more important questions, Gladstone could not press them. To Trevelyan, indeed, he allowed a free hand in the division on Finlay's Bill. Yet Gladstone on the other hand sought to marshal opposition within the Cabinet to Welsh disestablishment, and on another still attempted to mollify disestablishment and antidisestablishers in Scotland with the view that this was a Scottish question to be settled there by the electors. In England it was to be resisted altogether. The principle at work here, as Gladstone put it in a letter to Dr Rainey, was one of severance. 'On this principle of severance I have acted during the present autumn, and shall continue so to act.' Severance was a political conception Gladstone had used before, with regard to land policy, and with regard to the Church question in Ireland, and which

[11] Ibid., 306: 1434.

[12] See the speeches of two Conservative Members, Robert Norton and George Burrow Gregory: Hansard, 306: 1769, 1758.

[13] Hansard, 306: 1768, 1778; 303: 1736–8; J. K. Aston to Cranborne, 16 June 1886, Fourth Marquess of Salisbury MSS Bundle 1.

[14] Temple Letters, 11 Mar. 1886, BL Add. MS 38916, f. 38.

he was to use again in connection with Irish Home Rule. It was a means of limiting the imperial implications of a reformist policy by the application of regional, rather than English, solutions to the questions his Government faced. For Gladstone disestablishment was a question whose time had not yet come, though, as we shall see, the parliamentary Liberal party did not wholly accept this view. Though 'real beyond Tweed, and . . . rising in Wales, in England it is, and may long continue, little more than what is termed academic'. These matters, to Gladstone's involved mind, were secondary to the 'great controversy of belief which seems to me to be the one really absorbing subject'.[15]

Church questions induced, therefore great excitement, and the parliamentary reaction can be assessed by a consideration of the division lists in 1886. As the display of voting evidence in Table 2.1 shows, all divisions save one (about which more in a moment) were conceived by Members as belonging to a common scheme of things, as related questions. Whatever their differing positions on them, whether they supported or opposed them, Members treated Church questions in 1886 according to a common basis of ideological support. Why one of the divisions on Welsh disestablishment fails to fit this dimension illustrates the point, and can be puzzled out from the twisted history of voting on Dillwyn's Motion. After Albert Grey introduced his Amendment to reform, but not to disestablish, the Church in Wales, the House divided, first on whether or not it wished to put the vote on the Resolution as amended or as unamended. It decided to vote on the Resolution as amended. The House took a second division, shortly afterwards, as to whether Grey's words should be inserted in the Resolution. The House decided it should be. Here the proceedings become murky,[16] for the amended Resolution was sharply defeated (Division 26). Some Members who had supported the Resolution in previous divisions now voted against it. In so doing, they voted contrary to the logic of an ideological dimension because, having previously and strongly voted in support when the question was put in more extreme forms, it would be only consistent to support it now in a more moderate form. By showing their disdain for a measure which had been amended into a form unacceptable

[15] Gladstone to Childers, 9 Mar. 1886, Gladstone to Trevelyan, 12 Mar. 1886, BL Add. MS 44548, ff. 59–60; Gladstone to the Rev. Dr Hutton, 28 July 1885, Gladstone to Dr Rainey, 3 Nov. 1885, Gladstone to the Rev. Sir G. Prevost, Bt., 24 Apr. 1886, Gladstone to Sir W. Farquhar, Bt., 27 Sept. 1886, printed in *Correspondence on Church and Religion*, ed. D. C. Lathbury (New York: 1910), vol. 1, pp. 182, 183, 186, 187.
[16] *Annual Register* (1886), pp. 66–7.

TABLE 2.1 *Ecclesiastical Policy*

	24	25	26	36	53	126	127
24. Church of England in Wales, Dillwyn's Motion, 9 March	—	.99	.15	1.0	1.0	1.0	.76
25. Church of England in Wales, Grey's Motion, 9 March		—	− .39	1.0	.99	1.0	1.0
26. Church of England in Wales, Bill as Amended, 9 March*			—	.42	− .07	.30	1.0
36. Church of Scotland Bill, 17 March				—	1.0	1.0	1.0
53. Disestablishment of the Scottish Church, 30 March					—	1.0	1.0
126. Tithe Rent-Charge Redemption Bill, 10 June						—	.92
127. Tithe Rent-Charge Redemption Bill, 17 June							—

*No. 26 fails to fit a scale with the other items, but, with this excluded, the remaining items scale together with Q values exceeding .76.

to them, these Members cast this division out of a dimensional relationship with the other items with which it had an obvious substantial association. This division fails to fit the dimension of ecclesiastical questions because the ideological basis of support for it shifted. With this division excluded from the analysis, the remaining items form a dimension of a very high quality. Six divisions fit together when the minimum threshold is set at .75, and, of these, five fit together when the threshold is raised to .90. Elevated values of this sort, since they are reckoned according to the degree of irregular voting on these questions, shows the way in which Members treated various items as part of a highly consistent and coherent pattern, a treatment only possible if they regarded them as related.

If the underlying theme in the dimension on ecclesiastical questions was *l'église en danger*, the debate over land reform in the House of Commons in 1886 raised the theme of property in peril. The most important land legislation to come before the House was the Crofters Bill. An extension to Scotland of the principles of Irish land legislation (fair rent, fixity of tenure, compensation for improvements, but not free sale), this Bill was a Government measure which had been preceded by rural protest and violence and the report of a Royal

Commission.[17] Members on both sides threw up amendments to advance or to limit the application of the Bill. If radicals, aided by the Irish, took every opportunity to expand the range and meaning of it, the Bill's opponents, such as the Duke of Argyll and A. J. Balfour, while believing defeat of the Bill impossible, took every chance open to them on the other side. Consequently, Amendments to include the cottars and fishermen in its provisions, and Amendments on the use of seaweed and deer forests stood cheek-by-jowl with Amendments offered by Balfour which would weaken it by allowing landlords to dispose of their lands when 'the State steps in and takes from [them] the management of [their] land'.[18] Indeed, opponents of the Bill had no little success in fighting a rearguard action. On the third reading some of the strongest supporters of the measure voted against it. Their efforts, they charged, had been dashed by a coalition of the front benches on a measure which had been insufficient in the first place. They became subject to further frustrations. When the Crofters Bill re-emerged into the Commons with the Lords' Amendments attached, it was even further restricted, and the Bill became the object of further sharp debate and further divisions. As W. A. Hunter put it in a parliamentary eulogy on the Bill: 'we proposed many Amendments in the House, all to no purpose. The Government narrowed the scope of the bill to such an extent that, in the opinion of the Crofter Members, it was completely valueless. The Lords have now narrowed it further.'[19]

Henry Chaplin dismissed the Crofters measure as a 'horrible' bill,[20] but he, a squire's squire and a Tory's Tory, with other Conservatives,[21] introduced the Cottagers' Allotment Gardens Bill, which illustrates the interest the land question had on both sides of the House. Intended to provide labourers with the opportunity to acquire half-acre allotments, this measure, Chaplin sought to reassure

---

[17] H. J. Hanham, 'The Problem of Highland Discontent, 1880–1885', *Transactions of the Royal Historical Society*, series 5, 19 (1969), pp. 21–65.

[18] 'The Crofter Bill is a question of tactics. The Whole Bill shd as such legislation must be. — But *can* [it] be opposed wholly? What earthly chance have we?' Argyll to Arthur Balfour, 5 Mar. 1886, BL Add. MS 48900, ff. 7–7ᵛ; Hansard, 304; 148–52, 168. For Balfour's Amendment, see Hansard, 304: 942. The Government rejected Balfour's Amendment, believing it would render the legislation 'absolutely nugatory'. The Lord Advocate condemned Balfour's speech on this occasion as a second reading speech against the Bill. Hansard, 304: 946–7.

[19] Hansard, 305: 678–9; 306: 960.

[20] Chaplin to Salisbury, 20 Apr. 1886, Third Marquess of Salisbury MSS Class E.

[21] Sir William Hart Dyke, Edward Harcourt, Viscount Curzon, and Charles Hall.

Salisbury, was strewn with abundant safeguards.[22] And in a later letter Chaplin sought to be even more reassuring.

I agree with you entirely that allotments are and ought to be advantageous to the landlords, as well as the tenants—and I fully expect that the effect of any measure of this kind would be simply to accelerate the process which is going on already—and to make the system practically universal, without the powers of compulsion being used at all.

And Chaplin went on to explain how the Bill would gain the confidence of the labourers whose votes were going to be important 'in the greater questions which are now before us—but which at present they neither care for, nor understand'.[23] Arch, the spokesman for agricultural labourers in the House, rejected the Bill as 'derisory, as flimsy, worthless', and as 'an insult and mockery to us'.[24] While an indication of a Conservative approach to the land question, Chaplin's sedulous interest, as his letters to Salisbury serve to indicate, was not greeted with unalloyed enthusiasm by all Conservatives. As Lord Randolph Churchill put it to Salisbury, who was then taking his rest in the south of France, 'I hear Chaplin at Monte Carlo has been as stupid with the tables as he was with his allotments.'[25]

The House of Commons in 1886 also divided on other aspects of the land question: the Compulsory Purchase of Land Compensation Bill, the Copyhold Enfranchisement Bill, the Conveyancing (Scotland) Act (1874) Amendment Bill, James Barclay's and Donald Horne Macfarlane's Amendments to the Address on the Queen's Speech,[26] and, of course Jesse Collings's 'Three Acres and a Cow' Amendment which brought down the Conservative Government.

The Collings Amendment was an issue important both as a stroke of partisan politics and as a point of policy. Labouchere believed Parnell would vote against the Amendment to keep the Conservatives in until such time as they 'could be turned out with profit'.[27] Profit's

---

[22] Chaplin to Salisbury, 20 Apr. 1886, Third Marquess of Salisbury MSS Class E.

[23] Chaplin to Salisbury, 4 May 1886, Third Marquess of Salisbury MSS Class E.

[24] Hansard, 305: 1786.

[25] Churchill to Salisbury, 9 Mar. 1886, Third Marquess of Salisbury MSS Class E.

[26] Charles B. B. McLaren, W. H. Houldsworth, Joseph Bolton, and Jesse Collings introduced the Compulsory Purchase of Land Compensation Bill. Barclay's Amendment expressed 'the pressing necessity for securing without delay to the cultivators of the soil such conditions of tenure as will aid and encourage them to meet the new and trying circumstances in which the Agriculture of the Country is placed' (Hansard, 302: 348). Macfarlane's Amendment addressed itself to the condition of the people of the highlands and islands of Scotland (Hansard, 302: 642).

[27] Herbert Gladstone to Labouchere, 23 Jan. 1886, BL Add. MS 46015, f. 165.

time came directly, for the Conservative Government declared itself for legislation to proscribe the National League, and on this division the Liberals and the Irish Nationalists turned out the Tories. Edward Hamilton regarded one measure as good as any other for bringing the Conservatives down, though 'it would have been more dignified to come to grief over some more serious obstacle than J. Collings has put up'.[28] Some observers saw the Amendment as a device for internal Liberal unity. It, according to *The Times*, 'casts the net widely to catch votes', and Lady Courtney believed Gladstone's acceptance of it was a means to buy radical support for an emergent Irish policy.[29] Whatever these twists and turns of partisan fortune, 'the Three Acres and a Cow' Amendment had policy entwined in it. The 'cow' had been widely debated in the election of 1885, particularly by Chamberlain, and Collings's triumph represented 'the adoption by the Liberal leader of more than one point of the "unauthorized programme" advanced by Mr. Chamberlain and his followers'. And this point has been seized on by modern scholars who emphasize Gladstone's conversion to radical policies late in his career.[30] This was not lost on the Duke of Argyll: 'the parliamentary prominence you give to a mere nostrum of the Radicals, distinctly outside your own programme, marks a decided patronage on your part of the Radical sections as against the reasonable Liberals.'[31] Even more was at work here. *The Times* saw the Collings Amendment as the first fruit of the influence to be exercised in the House by the extension of the household franchise to the counties. It is a futile exercise to seek to separate policy from expediency in such a tangled web. Even contemporaries could not do it. Of the eighteen Liberals who voted with the Conservatives against the Amendment, *The Times* found it 'impossible to say whether they were chiefly influenced by their opinions on the ostensible issue placed before the House', or whether they were motivated, in a premonition of alarm, by their fears about what Gladstone's Home Rule policies might turn out to be.[32]

When the votes of Members of the House of Commons on these various questions are inspected, a highly satisfactory dimension can be discovered in the division lists. As Table 2.2 shows, voting on items in this dimension was the most regular of any discovered for

[28] Edward Hamilton Diary, 26 Jan. 1886, BL Add. MS 48642, f. 104.
[29] *The Times*, 25 Jan. 1886, p. 9; Lady Courtney's Journal, 25 Jan. 1886, quoted in G. P. Gooch, *Life of Lord Courtney* (London: 1920), p. 248.
[30] *The Times*, 27 Jan. 1886, p. 9; Barker, *Gladstone and Radicalism*, p. 44.
[31] Argyll to Gladstone, 29 Jan. 1886, BL Add. MS 44016, f. 91.
[32] *The Times*, 28 Jan. 1886, p. 9.

TABLE 2.2 *Land Policy**

	3	47	54	61	65	71	90	96	98	103	117
3. 'Three Acres and a Cow' 26 January	—	.97	1.0	1.0	.99	1.0	.95	.99	1.0	.99	.99
47. Crofters Bill, McLaren's Motion, 29 March		—	.97	.97	.92	1.0	.96	.92	.96	.98	.97
54. Crofters Bill, Macfarlane's Amendment, 1 April			—	.99	1.0	1.0	.99	1.0	1.0	.97	.96
61. Crofters Bill, Stafford's Amendment, 5 April				—	.98	.98	.98	.98	.96	.97	.98
65. Crofters Bill, Balfour's Amendment, 6 April					—	1.0	1.0	.98	.95	.97	1.0
71. Copyhold Enfranchisement Bill, 13 April						—	.96	1.0	1.0	1.0	1.0
90. Crofters Bill, Opposition to the Third Reading, 10 May							—	.91	.95	.97	.98
96. Compulsory Purchase of Land Compensation, Second Reading, 12 May								—	.93	.96	1.0
98. Conveyancing (Scotland) Acts (1874) Amendment Bill, 18 May									—	.99	.98
103. Cottagers' Allotments Gardens Bill, Opposition to the Second Reading, 21 May										—	.98
117. Crofters Bill, Opposition to the Lords' Amendment, 3 June											—

*This Q Matrix contains only some of the items fitting the land policy dimension. For a more complete discussion, see Appendix II.

this House. Forty items, indeed, fit a dimension with a threshold of .65, and not an item is lost when the threshold is raised to .70. Thirty-seven items fit at .80, 32 at .90, and even 16 items at .95. Elevated values such as these suggest extremely regular voting on land policy questions, and encourage the view that the land question was among the more highly crystallized and clarified matters in the parliamentary mind. Because the 'Three Acres and a Cow' Amendment to the Address on the Queen's Speech fits this dimension, it is possible to suggest that Members regarded it in ideological terms, as much for its policy as for its expediential value. If it had been a question solely of the latter, irregular voting would have prohibited it from the dimension.

Throughout the Home Rule crisis, the land question remained at the centre of parliamentary politics. Indeed, just as Lord Salisbury resumed office in July of 1886, William Tyssen-Amherst reminded him of the pressing importance of the allotments question for Conservative policy.[33] However, as Chaplin's letters reveal, the Tory approach to this question differed rather sharply from Liberal policy. The parliamentary disputes over land centred themselves on the role of government, Westminster and local, and on this consideration Members parted ways. As Lord Salisbury put the issue, 'the point to which personally speaking, I am *not* prepared to go, is to give the local authority power of taking any man's land compulsorily. Parliament has never allowed the compulsory taking of land except where it has itself designated the particular land to be taken, and no case, has to my mind, been made out for departing from this wise rule.'[34] To such sentiments a Liberal, such as Leonard Courtney, could give a hearty assent.[35] On the other side, moved by the spirit of Henry George and guided by the public positions of Joseph Chamberlain,[36] vigorous land reformers raised sharp criticism of landlords and landlordism. The Conservative cry of confiscation, Sir William Harcourt protested, was merely a reiteration of the traditional Tory credo announced whenever an effort was made to redress injustices. Harry Lawson Webster Lawson, in supporting the Compulsory Purchase of Land Compensation Bill, said it 'was most unjust that the public should be

---

[33] William Tyssen-Amherst to Salisbury, 28 and 30 July 1886, Third Marquess of Salisbury MSS Class E.

[34] Salisbury to the Third Duke of Buckingham and Chandos, 3 [Jan.?] 1886, Grenville Correspondence, Third Duke of Buckingham and Chandos Papers STG, Box 118/34.

[35] Courtney to a constituent, 27 Jan. 1886, printed in Gooch, *Life of Lord Courtney*, p. 249.

[36] J. A. Spender, *Life, Journalism, and Politics* (London: 1927), vol. 1, p. 34.

robbed at every turn simply to give a bribe and a sop to the landed interest'.[37]

More than the issue of government, or the baneful influence of landlords, the debate over land reform in 1886 became a battle over competing economic theories.[38] On one side the Duke of Argyll, Sir Richard Temple, and men of their kidney defended an orthodox view stressing the principle of economic equilibrium and the importance of uniform laws structured naturally in the very stuff of the economy. In this spirit Argyll called Collings's Amendment 'the nostrum of allotments', and prided himself on more traditional views. 'I began as a Peelite and remain of that complexion', he wrote. And in this spirit he wrote to Balfour about the Crofters Bill insisting upon uniform principles of land valuation and for the protection of contracts. Temple believed the Crofters Bill lay on the very extremity of economic orthodoxy.[39] By way of contrast, the land policy of Gladstone's Government, as expressed in the Crofters Bill, rested on a realization fully consistent with the position taken by Gladstone's former Administration with regard to the question of Irish land.[40] Differential customary development had bred differential conditions. This was a situation which did not admit of the application of uniform treatment based upon uniform and natural laws. If the questions of Irish Church and Irish land, and eventually the question of Irish government, required Irish rather than English solutions, the question of Scottish land required a Scottish solution. This *The Times* realized when it described the Crofters Bill as an effort 'to restore the Crofter to the position he formerly occupied after the creation of large sheep farms and then their conversion into deer forests'.[41] John Stuart Blackie, the Professor of Greek in the University of Edinburgh and a leader of the Celtic revival, argued sharply for land reform in Scotland based upon the country's unique economic and cultural character. He condemned

. . . the process by which the glens of my beloved Highlands have been denuded of their natural population, and the very pitch and marrow of the

---

[37] Hansard, 305: 861, 863.

[38] Clive Dewey, 'Celtic Agrarian Legislation and the Celtic Revival: Historicist Implications of Gladstone's Irish and Scottish Land Acts, 1870–1886', *Past and Present*, 64 (Aug. 1974), pp. 30–70.

[39] Argyll to Gladstone, 29 Jan. 1886 and 2 Oct. 1885, BL Add. MSS 44106, ff. 91, 92; Argyll to Balfour, 6 and 26 Mar. 1886, BL Add. MS 49800, ff. 9–12, 13–15.

[40] E. D. Steele, *Irish Land and British Politics: Tenant Right and Nationality, 1865–1870* (Cambridge: 1974).

[41] *The Times*, 26 Feb. 1886, p. 9.

rural life in the Highlands sacrificed to economic theories alike inhuman and impolitic, and to aristocratic pleasure hunting which sowed the seeds of disaffection and stirred up class against class throughout the land.[42]

Nostalgic, even romantic these views, and they drew together a reforming impulse and a vision of social harmonies incompatible with economic theories based on natural lawfulness.

If ecclesiastical and land policy raised the questions of the Church in danger and property in peril, foreign and imperial matters coming before the House of Commons in 1886 posed fears of the empire and the nation in danger. When William Alexander Hunter brought before the House his Motion against charging the military expenses for the annexation of Burma to the Indian budget, Hartington and Gladstone attempted to contain its policy implications and tried to treat the issue in technical terms, as an issue dealing with the manner in which military action would be paid for.[43] This did not hold. Hartington had warned Gladstone that Hunter 'will probably contend that the preliminary consent of Parliament ought to have been obtained', and, in fact, Hunter did so, raising the while themes of national honour and colonial exploitation.[44] Henry Richard, who followed Hunter in the debate, construed the question in large terms indeed, and regretted the narrow scope of the Motion. Richard wanted an examination of Britain's imperial policy. 'For my part', he said, 'the summary annexation of that kingdom was an act of high-handed violence for which there is no adequate justification.'[45]

Other divisions on the supply estimates drew out similar criticisms of imperial policy. T. M. Healy, in his Motion to reduce the estimate for the salaries of colonial governors, protested against the suppression of a rebellion in Canada. The debate on this Motion contained expressions of discontent with the expense of empire (see Peter Rylands' speech[46]) and produced invective and abuse between Parnellite and Ulster Conservatives about the treatment of colonial peoples, Irish nationalism, and British patriotism.[47] Bradlaugh's Motion, on 1 March, to reduce the supply estimates for embassies and missions, criticized Sir Henry Drummond Wolff's mission to Constantinople and Egypt, and Members used it as a vehicle for

---

[42] John Stuart Blackie, *The Scottish Highlands and the Landlaws; An Historico-Economical Enquiry* (London: 1885), pp. viii–ix.

[43] Hansard, 302: 964.

[44] Hartington to Gladstone, 25 Jan. 1886, BL Add. MS 44148, ff. 208–9; Hansard, 302: 945.   [45] Hansard, 302: 948.

[46] Ibid., 302: 1248.   [47] Ibid., 302: 1254, 1249, 1247.

even broader objections to Egyptian policy.[48] On the same day Labouchere's Motion to reduce the supplementary sum asked for African expenses was an occasion for a debate on South African policy.[49] Then, on 19 March, the House divided twice on Henry Richard's Motion on national engagements, which Motion advanced the concept that 'it is not just or expedient to embark in wars, contract engagements involving grave responsibilities to the Nation, and add territories to the Empire without the knowledge and consent of parliament'.[50]

In addition to these divisions, taken on matters explicitly imperial, a series of divisions were taken on military estimates which raised imperial considerations less directly. On 25 March, Charles Cameron, a prominent radical, proposed a Motion to reduce the naval estimates as a protest against waste in military expenditures.[51] On the same day, Sir George Campbell proposed to reduce the army estimate and called for the withdrawal of troops from Egypt in his criticism of Egyptian policy.[52] Shaw-Lefevre, as another gesture toward government economies, on 10 June sought to reduce the naval estimate by eliminating the part of it proposed for the construction of iron-clads.[53] In contrast to these efforts to reduce the military estimates there were those, Lord Charles Beresford on 15 March and Howard Vincent on 22 March, who tried to achieve their increase, the former for the navy and the latter for the army auxiliary force.[54] Finally, any consideration of imperial questions must include the great question of 1886, Irish Home Rule. In this sense Gladstone proposed it, and in this sense the House of Commons debated it. Gladstone regarded his Bill as a measure which would strengthen the empire. Goschen believed it would show 'every subject race . . . India . . . [and] Europe that we were no longer able to cope with resistance, if resistance were offered'.[55] Sir Richard Temple denounced Gladstone's Bill thus: 'The Act of Union [Gladstone] vilified in the strongest terms, — what on earth was the use of raking up those old old stories, except to make mischief in the present? *No real Englishman* would have made that speech.'[56]

[48] Ibid., 302: 1550 ff.

[49] Ibid., 302: 1614 ff.

[50] Ibid., 303: 1386.

[51] Ibid., 302: 1286.

[52] Ibid., 303: 1892, 1894.

[53] Ibid., 306: 1286 ff.

[54] Ibid., 303: 827 ff, 1506 ff.

[55] See Gladstone's speech on the introduction of the Government of Ireland Bill, 8 Apr. 1886, Hansard, 304: 1036–85. See Goschen's speech on 13 Apr. 1886, Hansard, 304: 1477.

[56] Temple Letters, 17 Apr. 1886, BL Add. MS 38916, f. 68ᵛ. The speech to which Temple referred was Gladstone's speech on the Irish Land Bill, which both Temple and Gladstone understood as a necessary aspect of the Government's Irish policy.

TABLE 2.3 Imperial, Military, and Foreign Policy*

	9	10	11	12	13	31	38	39	40	44	124	125
9. Military Operations in Burma, 22 February	—	.86	.86	.96	.89	-.85	.90	.91	-.90	.93	.89	.91
10. Salaries of Colonial Governors, 25 February		—	.92	.95	.95	-.88	.97	.97	-.92	.93	.90	.98
11. Naval Estimates, 25 February			—	.93	.94	-.90	.96	.96	-.71	.85	.78	.96
12. Expenses for Embassies, 1 March				—	.97	-.96	.97	.97	-.86	.96	.94	1.0
13. African Expenses, 1 March					—	-.92	.98	.98	-.79	.90	.98	.97
31. Beresford's Motion on the Navy, 15 March						—	-.93	-.94	.99	-.90	-1.0	-1.0
38. Foreign Involvements, 19 March							—	1.0	-.92	1.0	.89	.95
39. Foreign Involvements, 19 March								—	-.93	.93	.89	.96
40. Vincent's Motion on the Army, 22 March									—	-.86	-.97	-.97
44. Army Estimates, 25 March										—	.93	.94
124. Home Rule, 8 June											—	1.0
125. Navy Estimates, 10 June												—

*When items 31 and 40 are excluded from the table, the remaining items fit together in a scale with Q values exceeding .78.

When the voting patterns on these several imperial–military questions are examined, the voting relations among them may be expressed as in Table 2.3. The votes of Members show, with two exceptions, a close association among these items. Beresford's motion to increase the naval estimate and Vincent's motion to increase the army auxiliary force estimate fail to fit this dimension because they had a different basis of ideological support. They were proposed by Conservatives, and the opposition to them came from the left. The other items, those fitting the dimension, had been advanced and supported by the radicals and the Irish Nationalists in the House. With these divisions excluded, however, a dimension appears which is of a very high statistical order. It contains nine divisions which are related to each other not only at a threshold of .65. but also at .80, an indication of great voting regularity on imperial and military questions.

Since this dimension contains together items on the empire and items on military readiness, its meaning is not a simple one. The debate on these questions pitted against each other two rather different conceptions of the imperial and international policy. On the one side was a view which, if not wholly jingoist, at least placed great importance on the national interest. Empire and war, far from being unholy concepts, in the period before 1914 were the accepted quiddities of a confident age. For many, perhaps for most, the empire, the greatest force for good since the fall of Rome, had brought the advantages of peace and prosperity and civilization to vast areas. What had been so successful deserved respect and expansion and defence, by war if necessary.[57]

The only hope for our Party lies in a straightforward, national policy, which will draw to us all moderate men, disgusted and alarmed as they are at Gladstone–Chamberlainism, and we must look to gain confidence *in the country*, & not to intrigue in the House of Commons for our success.

So said Edward Hardcastle.[58]

On the other side resided a conception of the international world which brought together morality and political economy. While not isolationist, it placed great importance upon a policy of settling international quarrels by satisfying grievances through negotiation

---

[57] Michael Howard, 'Empire, Race, and War in Pre-1914 Britain', *History and Imagination: Essays in Honour of H. R. Trevor-Roper*, ed. Hugh Lloyd-Jones, Valerie Pearl, and Blair Worden (London: 1981), pp. 340 ff.

[58] Edward Hardcastle to Salisbury, 27 July 1885, Third Marquess of Salisbury MSS Class E.

and compromise. Peace was at the same time moral and cheap.[59] The Marquess of Ripon expressed such a view to John Bright in the fall of 1885 on the occasion of the Tory Government's annexation of Burma.

Of the danger [of annexation] I have no doubt. It will add to our burden and responsibilities; it will lead to fresh demands for an increase of the army and for other military expenditure; and by making our frontiers conterminous with those of China and very soon with those of France it will multiply the chances of disagreement with those countries. . . . Powerful agencies are being brought to bear in support of annexation. . . . There is a strong party in India in favour of it; & the English Jingoes are sure to back it up.[60]

Dr Gavin Clark seized on these themes when the House debated the annexation of Burma. 'It was a kind of freebooting Expedition undertaken against Burma—one of the wars entered into at the instance of these modern freebooters, the commercial Jingoes, who believe they are entitled to do anything in the name of British trade.[61] Others approached imperial questions in rather more measured tones, considering these issues as matters of political means rather than ultimate ends. In a speech praised by Wilfred Scawen Blunt, Colonel Duncan, a Conservative as well as an army man, said, 'many of us are perfectly at one in our anxiety to get out of Egypt; but we differ very much as to the means'.[62] Throughout, political economy assisted morality. The House, according to Handel Cossham, ought to halt the 'excessive military expenditure and extension of territory, which had created that gigantic National Debt now weighing so heavily on the industry and commerce of the country'.[63]

The political economy and morality of imperialism had constitutional implications, as the debate on Richard's motion against national commitments without parliamentary consent showed. This measure sought to redefine the relative roles of the legislative and the executive in the conduct of policy. For those advancing this

---

[59] See Paul Kennedy, *The Realities Behind Diplomacy: Background Influences on British External Policy, 1865–1980* (London: 1981), chs. 1 and 2; 'The Tradition of Appeasement in British Foreign Policy, 1865–1939', *British Journal of International Studies*, 2.3 (Oct. 1976), pp. 195–214; 'The Theory and Practice of Imperialism', *Historical Journal*, 20.3 (1977), pp. 761–9.

[60] Ripon to Bright, 24 Oct. 1885, BL Add. MS 43635, ff. 166–9.

[61] Hansard, 302: 994.

[62] Blunt Diary, 1 Mar. 1886, Blunt MSS 334-1975, f. 63; Hansard, 303: 1896–7. How sincere Duncan was in this 'means rather than ends' speech may be mooted. Later, in the same speech, he said: 'Let them resolve upon leaving Egypt when Egypt was ready to be left; not upon a certain day or in a particular month.'

[63] Hansard, 303: 1415.

proposal, and other items fitting this dimension, it was an effort to recover the initiative in these matters by the House of Commons. Members of the Liberal Government were caught in a cleft stick. They could sympathize with such policies, but they needed their estimates. James Bryce, the Under-secretary of State for Foreign Affairs, pointed to practical difficulties in a process of a continuing parliamentary consultation, and assured Members that any Government proceeding without the support of the House in these matters was a doomed thing.[64] Gladstone also adopted this line. 'I, for my part,' he said, 'would be delighted if it were practicable to associate the Executive more with the Legislative in these great and responsible proceedings, but I do not see how it can be done.'[65] Others were deeply shocked by Richard's proposal. The debate and the division on it, according to *The Times*, decreased the respect in the country for the constitutional principle separating the legislative from the executive. The size of the parliamentary support for it 'shows that the fundamental principles on which the Constitution rests are virtually at the mercy of an unexpected, and almost accidental, vote of the House of Commons'.[66] The fact that the great division on the Government of Ireland Bill also fits this dimension of imperial and military policy questions is of great importance, for it reveals Home Rule to be not an isolated or local or eccentric question, but one which Conservatives, Irish Nationalists, and some Liberals considered a part of the policy agenda of the age.

Gladstone's first Home Rule Bill was the Irish measure outstripping all others in importance in 1886, yet other Irish issues consumed parliamentary attention, and it is important to know the extent to which Irish policy in the House of Commons formed a single voting dimension. On 4 March Hugh Holmes brought in his Resolution on the maintenance of the social order in Ireland. Prepared by Hicks Beach and Lord Randolph Churchill, this Resolution attempted to flush out Gladstone, to force him to declare his Irish policy at a moment for which he was unprepared.[67] An Arms Bill, restricting the sale and possession of firearms, came to four divisions late in the session. Additionally, several measures sought political and social reform in Ireland. One of these last, a bill to amend the Irish Labourers Acts, was in aid of sanitary housing. Measures of Irish political reform attempted to reduce election expenses by restricting bogus candidates whose presence in the contest, even when there

---

[64] Ibid., 302: 1320. [65] Ibid., 303: 1405–6.
[66] *The Times*, 20 Mar. 1886, p. 11.
[67] Hicks Beach to Salisbury, 1 Mar. 1886, Churchill to Salisbury, 9 Mar. 1886, Third Marquess of Salisbury MSS Class E.

was little chance of success, drove up the cost of standing. Another, introduced by T. M. Healy and P. A. Chance, initially limited the security of candidates, but Labouchere amended the Bill by throwing the returning officers' charges on to the rates.[68] A third contrived to facilitate inexpensive registration, and included a provision for separating voting from ratepaying.[69] Sexton's Amendment to the Belfast Main Drainage Bill would have reformed elections in Belfast by assimilating the Belfast Corporation franchise to the parliamentary franchise. The Municipal Franchise (Ireland) Bill would harmonize the franchises of England and Ireland. Though it was not introduced as a specifically Irish measure, the Police Forces Enfranchisement Bill became one because of the prominence given in the debates to the Royal Irish Constabulary. The Poor Law Guardians (Ireland) Bill also had political content, since it sought the reform of Poor Law guardians' elections through the introduction of the secret ballot, by the elimination of proxy voting, and by the reduction of the number of *ex officio* guardians. Finally, two Irish measures concerned themselves with the economic development of the country: the Ulster Canal and Tyrone Navigation Bill and the Tramways Order in Council (Ireland) Bill.

Though their content was various, the Irish measures fit a common voting dimension of no little coherence and statistical integrity. As the display of evidence in Table 2.4 shows, only three items fail to fit this dimension. These fail to fit because their ideological basis of support differed from that for items in this dimension. Macartney's Amendment to the Irish Labourers Acts Bill was a liberalizing Amendment; it would have enlarged the scope of the Bill. Macartney, an Ulster Conservative, was joined in this by the Parnellites. Their support is consistent with the voting logic of this dimension; one would expect their support throughout. However, the votes of Tories in this Amendment's favour (30 per cent of the Conservatives voting in this division supported the amendment) is not expected because they had opposed more moderate items in the dimension. It is these votes which prevent the division on this Amendment from fitting the dimension. The second division on the Police Forces Enfranchisement Bill fails to fit this dimension, but fits a different one, one enjoying the patronage of Conservatives, and these circumstances will find their discussion in due season. The Ulster Canal and Tyrone Navigation Bill fails to fit this dimension because it reflected local rather

[68] Hansard, 306: 1436–7, 1604–6.
[69] See Dillon's speech on the Registration of Voters (Ireland) Bill, Hansard, 306: 784–5.

TABLE 2.4 *Irish Policy**

	16	30	34	70	86	95	99	101	115	124	127	140
16. Irish Social Order, 4 March	—	.98	.19	1.0	-1.0	.99	.99	1.0	1.0	1.0	1.0	.99
30. Labourers' Acts Amendment, 15 March		—	.67	1.0	-.96	.99	.99	1.0	.99	.95	1.0	1.0
34. Labourers' Acts Amendment, Macartney's Amendment			—	1.0	-1.0	-.06	.23	.94	.43	.44	.63	.60
70. Police Forces Enfranchisement, 13 April				—	-1.0	1.0	1.0	1.0	1.0	1.0	1.0	1.0
86. Police Forces Enfranchisement, Parnell's Motion					—	-1.0	-1.0	-1.0	1.0	-.95	-1.0	-.92
95. Parliamentary Elections Bill, 12 May						—	.99	1.0	.99	.99	1.0	.97
99. Poor Law Guardians Bill 19 May							—	1.0	1.0	1.0	.99	.99
101. Opposition to the Arms Bill, 20 May								—	1.0	1.0	1.0	1.0
115. Registration of Voters Bill 2 June									—	1.0	.99	1.0
124. Government of Ireland Bill Second Reading										—	1.0	1.0
127. Parliamentary Elections, 10 June											—	1.0
140. Belfast Main Drainage, 21 June												—

*For a discussion of voting on all items fitting an Irish policy dimension, see Appendix II.

than national or imperial interests and, therefore, had a different basis of ideological support. By way of contrast, the Tramways Order in Council (Ireland) Bill, no less a matter of local improvement, fits this Irish policy dimension. The Ulster Canal Bill had been caught in intense rivalries between Irish Nationalists and Ulster Conservatives. The Tramways Bill was introduced into the Commons after passing the Lords; the Liberal Government was much interested in having it passed without amendment.[70] The former Bill found itself caught in local squabbles; the latter was advanced as a public bill.

These few cases of voting irregularity ought not obscure the principle finding in Table 2.4: Members took Irish legislation in 1886, though it was highly varied, as parts of a whole, and their votes reveal a common ideological base. There was greater ideological coherence in this than some contemporaries understood. Salisbury, for example, believed there was no connection between Holmes's Resolution on the maintenance of Irish social order and the Home Rule or Irish land questions.[71] Yet, of the twenty-three items which fit this voting dimension when the minimum threshold is set for .65, 96 per cent also fit when the threshold is raised to .70, and 91 per cent fit at .80. Irregular voting affects the dimension in a major way only when the Q threshold is elevated to .90, and even here 57 per cent of these items fit a common dimension. Statistical values of this sort, testifying to stable and highly regular voting patterns, reveal the existence of shared conceptions concerning Irish policy, even if they disagreed about the responses appropriate to it. When Joseph Chamberlain compared the Irish question to his gout,[72] he was declaring himself unwilling to treat on the Home Rule question, but he none the less understood the Irish government question as an aspect of Irish policy.

The conflict over Irish policy—and the Government of Ireland Bill is an illustration of this—dealt with the place of Ireland in British imperial institutions, and how far it was possible to accommodate

---

[70] See H. H. Fowler's speech on 24 June 1886, Hansard, 307: 227. Both of these divisions had extreme marginal frequencies: only seven MPs voted against one and only five against the other. Yule's Q cuts with great force on such frequencies, and a single vote can powerfully affect the statistical values. One might be included in a dimension and another excluded by the freak vote of a very few Members. Therefore, it is probably not worth the labour to seek in the debates, or in the measures themselves, explanations for these results.

[71] Salisbury to Goschen, 4 Mar. 1886, Third Marquess of Salisbury MSS Class D/26/31.

[72] O'Brien, *Evening Memories*, p. 5. O'Brien reported Chamberlain to have said, 'they are both equally detestable and both absolutely incurable.'

those institutions to Ireland's requirements. Towards accommodation the Irish Nationalists pressed. Conservatives and some Liberals poised themselves in opposition.[73] The Arms Bill for Ireland is a useful demonstration of the way the various parliamentary forces ranged themselves against each other. It was introduced to renew the Peace Preservation Act (1882) which, in John Morley's opinion, had done much to reduce agrarian outrages. The Parnellites and radicals opposed this policy, and, therefore, opposition to the measure represents a more liberal position on it. It was a violation of the right to bear arms, Parnell protested, using a profoundly English argument to fit a curious Irish case. Moreover, it constituted an act of harrassment against Nationalists.[74] Charles Lewis, the Member for Londonderry, approved of this measure but criticized the Government for inconsistency and for being 'backward in coming forward with the Act'.[75] Cutting through it all, Members discussed special Irish conditions and discussed ways of meeting those peculiarities. As Patrick Chance put it in the debate on the second reading of the Police Forces Enfranchisement Bill, 'he would, under all circumstances, and *having regard to the peculiar constitution and mode of administration of the force in Ireland*, give his most strenuous opposition to this Bill as far as its extension to Ireland was concerned.'[76]

As to the other aspects of Irish policy, some sought to reform the franchise, others attempted to liberalize Irish political structures. All constituted attacks on privilege. 'They were now living in democratic times', James Tuite said. 'Parliament was in large measure democratic in its character, and the cost of entering the House should be made democratic and popularized.'[77] And on the Poor Law Guardians Bill, Captain Edmund Verney observed, 'the principles of the Bill were more trust in the people and the lowering of the property qualification, [and I] should wish to see that qualification abolished altogether.'[78] Labouchere believed his Amendment to throw the returning officers' charges on to the rates would work to the advantage of the Conservatives because the Tories would do, with their greater

---

[73] Broderick's motion to report progress on the effort to amend the Irish Labourers Bill was one of the few divisions in which Ulster Tories were able to form a voting alliance with the Nationalists. William Johnson (and one cannot imagine a more resolute Ulsterman) rose on the occasion to say: 'On a former occasion I supported the Motion to Report Progress made by my hon. friend (Mr. Broderick); but in the interest of the labourers of Ireland I do not think it is well the progress of the measure should be any longer delayed.' Hansard, 303: 917–18.

[74] Ibid., 305: 1537.   [75] Ibid., 305: 1552.

[76] Ibid., 304: 365 (emphasis mine).

[77] Ibid., 305: 830.   [78] Ibid., 305: 1426.

partisan discipline, what the Liberals could not: prevent bogus candidates. 'Why did I propose this essentially Conservative reform?' Labouchere asked Churchill. 'Simply because it is really too great an absurdity that candidates should pay such expenses, and I don't like absurdities.'[79]

On the other side, the Ulster Conservatives joined this debate by opposing the use of private bills, and what they called limited measures, to advance major reforms. Charles Lewis rejected the Registration of Voters Bill because it was 'really a new Reform Bill under the guise of a Registration Bill'.[80] Colonel Waring believed the essence of the measure could be summarized in a single phrase: 'a Bill to establish Manhood Suffrage in Ireland'.[81] Edward King-Harman believed efforts to prevent the standing of bogus candidates, thereby reducing the cost of elections, deprived minorities 'of the right of expressing their opinion at [the] polling booths'.[82] Sir Richard Temple agreed. 'The object was to prevent *Loyalist* candidates from coming foward in *Nationalist* counties where they had no chance of success. . . . It is nothing but an attempt to *extinguish minorities*.'[83] Others, in their aggressive resistance to reform proposals for Ireland, defended *ex officio* Poor Law guardians and the Royal Irish Constabulary. On the Bill to amend the Irish Labourers Act, Members such as Saunderson charged the Parnellites with a politicalization of the Act's operation. Membership in the National League, they protested, was a requirement before anyone could benefit from it.[84]

As the several measures for political reform in the Irish policy dimension show, some issues had escaped the reform bills of 1884–5. To these proposals for the registration of voters and returning officers' expenses in Ireland the House of Commons added others concerned with electoral policy in England, Scotland, and Wales. These included a Bill to extend the parliamentary franchise to women, a police forces establishment Bill, and a Scottish returning officers Bill. Still there were others whose substance was freighted with the content and spirit of political reform: Labouchere's proposals to reduce the estimates for royal parks and royal palaces, his motion against the House of Lords, Thorold Rogers's motion on the incidence of local taxation, and, of course, the Irish Government Bill. On these

---

[79] Labouchere to Churchill, 17 June 1886, Lord Randolph Churchill Letters 1/13/1536.
[80] Hansard, 306: 788.   [81] Ibid., 306: 791.   [82] Ibid., 305: 831.
[83] Temple Letters, 12 May 1886, BL Add. MS 38916, f. 88.
[84] Hansard, 302: 1822.

questions the House contested the further limits of political reform, and debated the degree to which they should be extended.

Table 2.5 examines the voting patterns on these legislative questions and considers the degree to which they fit a common dimension of political reform policy. Three divisions on political reform questions fail to fit this dimension. The second division on the Police Forces Enfranchisement Bill (Division 86), taken on Parnell's motion, does not belong here. It enjoyed a different basis of ideological support since it was initiated by Conservatives and voting on it will be discussed at a later point. J. H. Puleston regretted that the previous Salisbury Government had not had a chance to pass these measures, and Ashmead Bartlett regarded them as being well within the scope of the Conservative party.[85] He thought it would be better if the Liberals proposed the women's franchise Bill, but in the event the sponsors came from both sides of the House. Three were Liberals (Illingworth, Stansfeld, and Woodall) and three were Tories (Sir Robert Fowler, Bt., Houldsworth, and Yorke). Treated as an open question by the Liberal leadership,[86] the women's franchise Bill came to two divisions.[87] Consistent with the radical position, the Irish Nationalists unanimously supported the women's franchise. The other parties divided, but narrowly. In the first of these divisions the Liberals and the Conservatives, by thin majorities, opposed the Bill, and in the second division, while remaining divided, a majority of both parties supported it. In the second division the support of the Conservatives was rather greater: sixty Conservative MPs supported it and thirty-five opposed it. And this is the nub of the matter. Throughout the history of the women's suffrage movement the Conservatives provided the hardcore of the opposition, but not in 1886. Sir Richard Temple was a member of the Central Executive Committee of the Women's Suffrage Association. Even Lewis Harcourt identified the Tories with this question. 'It really will be too disgusting', Harcourt remarked, 'if this becomes law and I fear in this instance we cannot even depend on the House of Lords to

---

[85] J. H. Puleston to Salisbury, 18 July 1885, and Ellis Ashmead Bartlett to Salisbury, 6 Dec. 1885, Third Marquess of Salisbury MSS Class E.

[86] William Woodall to Gladstone, 11 Feb. 1886, BL Add. MS 44494, ff. 229–30.

[87] The official division lists of the House of Commons show only a single division on this Bill. Actually, however, there were two. As the debates show, Division 5 (which is listed as a division on the shop hours Bill) was taken on the franchise measure. James Beresford-Hope rose to move the adjournment because of the 'lateness of the hour'. But Leonard Courtney rose to say: 'The action of the right Hon. Gentleman is too transparent. . . . The next Bill upon the paper [the women's franchise bill] is one of which the right Hon. Gentleman does not entertain a high opinion.' Hansard, 302: 688–9.

TABLE 2.5 Political Reform*

	6	18	28	41	70	86	115	124	131	132	141	142
6. Women's Franchise, 28 February	—	.53	.41	.10	.80	-.71	.12	.16	-.12	.01	.46	-.38
18. Representative Government, 5 March		—	.95	.98	1.0	-.97	1.0	.95	1.0	1.0	.97	1.0
28. Supply: Royal Parks, 11 March			—	.88	1.0	-.98	.98	.95	.93	.95	.91	.88
41. Incidence of Local Taxation, 23 March				—	1.0	-1.0	1.0	.99	.98	.99	.98	1.0
70. Police Forces Enfranchisement, 13 April					—	-1.0	1.0	1.0	1.0	1.0	1.0	1.0
86. Police Forces Enfranchisement, Parnell's Motion						—	-1.0	-.95	-1.0	-1.0	-.98	-1.0
115. Registration of Voters, 2 June							—	1.0	1.0	1.0	1.0	1.0
124. Government of Ireland Bill, 8 June								—	.98	.99	.98	.99
131. Returning Officers (Scotland) Bill, 16 June									—	1.0	1.0	1.0
132. Parliamentary Elections (Returning Officers) Act Amendment Bill, 16 June										—	1.0	1.0
141. Municipal Franchise (Ireland Bill), 21 June											—	1.0
142. Belfast Main Drainage Bill, 24 June												—

*For a discussion of voting on all items fitting this dimension, see Appendix II.

throw the Bill out as it would be so essentially a Conservative measure.'[88] Support by Conservatives for a moderate measure, judged by the proportion of the House voting for it, prevented it from fitting this dimension. The women's franchise Bill would have fit the political reform agenda in this House of Commons only if Conservatives had supported questions which had even greater support in the House (divisions on the reduction of estimates for the royal parks, or on Sexton's Amendment to the Belfast Main Drainage Bill, for example). This they did not do, and their inconsistent voting on the women's franchise Bill threw it out of the political reform dimension.

With the division on the franchises for the police force and women excluded from this analysis, however, the remaining items fit a dimension of common political experience in a highly satisfactory manner. Eighteen are related with minimum statistical values of .65, but, even more impressively, the same sustain their relationship when the statistical threshold is elevated to .80. At this point. voting irregularity begins to take its toll, yet twelve items fit a dimension at .90. On one end of this dimension were men who wished to remove from the electoral system anomalies untouched or partially touched by the reform settlement of 1884–5. At the other end were those Members who believed reform had gone far enough, or who wished more time to pass before the electoral question was attacked further. In between were men who supported some measures, but opposed others. All, though they might support or oppose these questions, saw the same meaning in them.

As Table 2.5 indicates, the House of Lords question came before the House of Commons in 1886 as a political reform question rather than as a matter of social class. Lord Salisbury did not share Bagehot's view, or the view of the Liberal party, on the political function of the Lords. He had used the upper chamber with great effectiveness, even while the Liberals had a majority, during the reform crisis of 1884–5.[89] It should, in his view, be the Conservative party's creature, and, taking its lead from the nation rather than the Commons, should be used to cripple Liberal legislation when the national interest required it. Salisbury was aware of the difficulty

---

[88] Brian Harrison, *Separate Spheres: The Opposition to Women's Suffrage in Britain* (London: 1978), p. 27; Temple to Salisbury, 19 Mar. 1885, Third Marquess of Salisbury MSS Class E; Harcourt Journal, 19 Feb 1886, Harcourt dep. 377, f. 162.

[89] Peter Marsh, *The Discipline of Popular Government: Lord Salisbury's Domestic Statecraft, 1881–1892* (Hassocks, Sussex: 1978), pp. 35–47; Corrine C. Weston, 'Salisbury and the House of Lords, 1868–1895', *Historical Journal*, 25.1 (1982), pp. 103–29.

of managing the Lords. 'We have no kind of hold over them: and unless we can persuade them the interests of the party are involved, they will not interfere with the Government in matters that are ordinarily left to it.'[90] However, Salisbury remained confident of the Lords' powers to control radical energies. To this Gladstone, the Liberals, and the Irish Nationalists objected. Gladstone, while defending the hereditary principle, believed the Liberal party could not be satisfied with 'the present working composition of a great chamber which more than any other single force resists, postpones and cripples measures which, in eleven Parliaments out of thirteen, the constituencies had returned it to promote'.[91] Labouchere's Motion on Representative Government attacked the peerage in its political capacity. He called the House of Lords an English Land League legislating in the interests of the landlords; it was nothing more than a political instrument of the Conservative party. 'There was no more partizan assembly in the country. The air of the House of Lords was too foul and stagnant for Radicals to live in it. There was no Radical there; even Liberalism drooped in that House. The Upper House was an Assembly of Conservative partizans.'[92] Despite Gladstone's affection for the aristocracy, and though he opposed the abolition of the hereditary principle, he did not defend the 'legislative action of the House of Lords', and he recognized 'sufficient and ample reason . . . for large and important change'.[93]

   Though not inspired by republicanism, Labouchere's Motions to reduce the estimates for the royal parks and palaces used a radical political economy in the service of democratic principles. These were attacks on privilege. Alfred Illingworth, in his intervention in the debate on royal parks, said: 'We have now in this House a real and genuine popular representation, both in regard to town and country, and I think we ought to undertake genuine economy in the administration of the affairs of the country.'[94] To the Government's embarrassment, Labouchere's Motion succeeded on 11 March, and the estimate required re-commitment for the funds to be restored. When it was, on 18 March, Labouchere was ready with a second Motion, one to cut from the estimate funds for the Bailiff of Royal Parks and the Ranger of Windsor Forest. In his speech on the Motion to reduce the estimate for royal palaces, Labouchere kept himself

---

[90] Salisbury to Churchill, 19 May 1886, Third Marquess of Salisbury MSS Class D/15/192.
[91] Gladstone to the Queen. 6 Mar. 1886, in Philip Guedalla, *The Queen and Mr. Gladstone, 1880–1898* (London: 1933), vol. 2, pp. 395–6.
[92] Hansard, 303: 26–8.   [93] Ibid., 303:48.   [94] Ibid., 303: 498.

at some distance from an attack on the monarchy. 'It was only reasonable', he said, 'with a Monarchy we should have a palace in London, and another in the country. But why keep up a number of Palaces which are not in the occupation of Her Majesty, or even of Her Majesty's family.'[95] He even offered the irreverent suggestion that vacant properties might be sold. But Labouchere came close to the Royal Family again in his speech concerning the fees for the Ranger of Windsor Forest, which Ranger was the Duke of Cambridge, the Queen's first cousin. 'These Parks are the people's Parks', Labouchere urged; they are 'not for eminent Noblemen to turn into game preserves for themselves'.[96]

James Thorold Rogers's Motion on the Incidence of Local Taxation was a matter both of land policy and political reform. As a matter of fact, both divisions on this Motion could be included in the land policy dimension. Moreover, one of its considerations was a protest against the inequitable rating of country houses. But this is the point. The thrust of the motion directed itself against political privilege in the form of an unequal incidence of local rating. This incidence, Rogers argued, struck most sharply on the occupier of land, and he proposed to have the owners pay at least a 'moiety' of these taxes.[97] At issue was the relative political power of social groups. 'The Democracy of the country', William Rathbone warned, 'if the majority of the wealthy classes continue to dissociate themselves from the work of the country, might soon ask for the *raison d'être* of such a class.'[98] Justification by political works rather than by the inherent grace of social value, this. As Llewellyn Atherley Jones (appropriately, the son of the Chartist) put it, the motion did not intend to impose taxes on landed property, nor to remove them from small property owners. It was a 'recognition of the principle that capital value should be the subject of taxation rather than earnings or income'.[99] The politics of land and its privileges carried the burden of the matter. 'The division of rates between owner and occupier would remove a sense of injustice', Robert Lacey Everett argued. Handel Cossham 'hoped the new House, in close touch with the people as it was, would do what it could to redress the wrong inflicted in the past by putting the weight of the burden on trade and commerce rather than on the landed interest represented on the other side of the House.'[1] Arthur Balfour took speeches such as these as expressions of 'a disease which is now extremely common

[95] Ibid., 303: 482.
[96] Ibid., 303: 1310–11.
[97] Ibid., 303: 1643.
[98] Ibid., 303: 1661.
[99] Ibid., 303: 1664.
[1] Ibid., 303: 1670, 1680–1.

in this Parliament. I mean "Landlordphobia" '.[2] The political reform dimension in 1886, therefore, describes the parliamentary conflict over the political weight and influence of social groups. Though these proposals might be favoured by some as a reasonable extension of reform and opposed by others as inappropriate attacks on certain social groups, Members were in agreement upon the meaning and significance of these questions. They were not talking past each other.

It is neither unimportant nor accidental to find questions of political reform for Ireland, which also fit the Irish policy dimension, fitting this dimension of political reform issues for England and Scotland. Parliament integrated Irish policy into the more general political agenda of the period. The debates on these questions give some clues about the manner in which this integration was effected. To some considerable extent in 1886 various groups and factions quarrelled over the character of public policy. For some, those favouring a uniform policy, 'English' solutions should be imposed on Ireland. For others, those coming to sympathize with the special qualities of special regions, an 'Irish' policy could be used in England. Irish nationalism had not been easily accepted by British radicals,[3] but by 1886 some British radicals treated Irish questions as testing grounds for reform policies. That Irish Nationalist Members proposed many of these questions shows a growing relationship between the Parnellites and English radicals, not on the basis of tactics or political calculation, but on the basis of policy and ideology.

Ireland became a laboratory for political experimentation. As Captain Edmund Verney, in his nautical manner, put it, 'Irish Gentlemen are always getting to the windward of English Members.'[4] Handel Cossham called for the application of the returning officers' charges Bill to England and Scotland.[5] Charles Crompton applauded the Irish for pressing their voters' registration Bill. It was evidence of the responsible action he anticipated of them once they had got Home Rule. 'And there could equally be no doubt that they [the Irish Nationalist MPs] were in advance of English Members in all these social matters which they had studied so carefully.'[6] T. H. Bolton concurred, and believed the Bill should be extended to England with the helping hand of the Government to enlarge its scope.[7] Thomas Coote and Joseph Arch wanted the Irish Poor Law

---

[2] Ibid., 303: 1697.
[3] T. W. Heyck, *The Dimensions of British Radicalism: The Case of Ireland, 1874–95* (Urbana, Chicago, and London: 1974), *passim*.
[4] Hansard, 305: 1425.
[5] Ibid., 305: 834.
[6] Ibid., 306: 797.
[7] Ibid., 306: 800.

guardians Bill to be applied to England. As Coote said, it was 'monstrous to prevent the labourers from having the right of representation on Boards of Guardians merely because they did not pay the rates directly'.[8] The debates and private communications of Members amplify what voting on the political reform dimension implies. Members of the House of Commons generalized from Irish political problems to general questions which affected the whole of the empire. Members did not isolate their thinking about Irish issues and consider them in terms and categories other than those used for the analysis and treatment of English, Welsh, and Scottish questions. If this reveals the capacity of English and Scottish radicals to support Irish reforms, it also indicates the capacity of Irish Nationalists to stimulate and support advanced policies for England.

The highly regular and disciplined voting patterns found in the ecclesiastical policy, land policy, military–imperial policy, and political reform dimensions in 1886 stands in contrast to voting on social policy questions. These include Barclay's Amendment to the Address to the Queen's Speech on behalf of agricultural labourers and Chaplin's Cottagers' Allotments Bill, which also fit the land policy dimension, and the Irish Labourers Acts Amendment Bill, which fits the Irish policy dimension. This is not the extent of it, however. Sir John Lubbock introduced a Bill to regulate the hours of young persons apprenticed to shopkeepers. Sir Joseph Pease, Bt. introduced a Motion for the abolition of the death penalty. Sir John Kennaway, Bt. proposed an Amendment to Stansfeld's Motion for the repeal of the Contagious Diseases Acts which would continue hospital care for prostitutes. Sir Lyon Playfair's Medical Acts Amendment Bill sought reform of the medical profession by requiring compulsory examinations, supervised by a medical council, to insure proper qualifications for practitioners. Sir Richard Assheton Cross, the Home Secretary in previous Conservative Governments, proposed a Bill for regulating conditions of safety in coal-mines. Additionally, three temperance questions came before the House: Sir Joseph Pease's Bill on the sale of intoxicating liquors on Sunday, Theodore Fry's Bill to apply the principle of local option to the sale of intoxicants on Sunday in Durham, and Charles Augustus Vansittart Conybeare's Bill to prevent the sale of liquor to children.

The rather more extensive degree of irregular voting on social policy questions, as compared to voting on the other policy agendas of the period, is shown in Table 2.6. Here the low statistical values in voting on the Shop Hours Bill (Division 137) and the highly

---

[8] Ibid., 305: 1428, 1439.

TABLE 2.6 Social Policy*

	1	30	32	43	93	103	119	121	135	136	137
1. Agricultural Depression, 25 January	—	.99	-1.0	.98	.92	.99	.99	.98	.96	.97	.39
30. Irish Labourers Acts Amendment, 12 March		—	-.98	.98	1.0	1.0	1.0	.93	.97	.99	.22
32. Coal Mines Bill, 15 March			—	-.97	-1.0	-1.0	-1.0	-1.0	-.98	-.97	-.28
43. Sale of Intoxicating Liquors, 24 March				—	.82	.92	.97	.84	.97	.96	.49
93. Resolution to Abolish the Death Penalty, 11 May					—	.96	.94	.91	1.0	1.0	.48
103. Cottagers' Allotment Gardens Bill, 21 May						—	1.0	.98	.93	1.0	.68
119. Terms of Removal (Scotland) Bill, 3 June							—	.94	.98	.99	.14
121. Public Health Acts Bill, 3 June								—	.79	.81	.46
135. Shop Hours Regulation Bill, 17 June									—	.98	.08
136. Shop Hours Regulation Bill, (in Committee), 17 June										—	.44
137. Shop Hours Regulation Bill (cl. 9) 17 June											—

*For a summary of voting on all items fitting a social policy dimension, see Appendix II.

negative values in voting on the Coal Mines Bill (Division 32) reveal differing patterns of attitudes on social questions. Members did not see the same meaning in these items, and consequently voted differently on them. And this is not all. The Medical Acts Amendment Bill, Kennaway's Amendment to the Motion to repeal the Contagious Diseases Acts, a division on the Irish Labourers Acts Amendment Bill, and the divisions on the temperance question also fail to fit a social policy dimension.

The division on Westlake's Motion to reject the clause exempting members of shopkeepers' families from the Shop Hours Bill[9] illustrates the kind of irregular voting which prevented some questions, with a clear social content, from fitting a social policy dimension. Westlake found support for his more liberal Amendment among a rump of Liberals and Conservatives, but a majority of the Conservatives, all of the Irish Nationalists, and a high proportion of Liberals voted for the clause and against the Amendment. It is the votes of Liberals and Nationalists, who normally supported more liberal positions, against this Amendment which prevent it from fitting the social policy dimension. An unusual alliance of parliamentary forces, drawn from different ideological bases, produced the voting irregularity revealed in this comparison.

Voting inconsistency on the Medical Acts Amendment Bill reveals a different conjunction of ideological forces. The divisions on this Bill occurred on Amendments which were not directly related to the Bill's central purposes: the establishment of qualifications for the medical profession. Rather, Sir Henry Roscoe and Dr Robert Farquharson proposed Amendments to provide places on the Medical Council for representatives from Victoria University and the University of Aberdeen. Dr Balthazar Foster saw through this. The point of the Bill, he indicated, was to increase the professional character of medical practice by having medical men themselves judge their colleagues; corporations of the sort found in the Amendments were in fact over-represented.[10] The local character of these amendments, their representation of local interests, makes them different from questions fitting the social policy dimension, and partially accounts for different parliamentary responses to them. Moreover, these were fairly moderate questions; they had the support of a large proportion of the House. Yet Members who had supported questions of a more radical character opposed them. This was sufficient to keep them from the social policy dimension.

---

[9] Ibid., 306: 1866-7.
[10] Ibid., 306: 601, 606-7.

Since the founding of the United Kingdom Alliance, the temperance question hovered over party politics.[11] That divisions on temperance questions should fail to fit a dimension with other social reform questions is a surprise because of the importance of temperance in moral reform programmes both in Britain and the United States. In the general election of 1885, temperance was relegated to a subordinate position,[12] but in some cases it served as a political test. A Conservative deputation asked Wilfred Scawen Blunt, then proposing to stand as a Tory, if he would support Sir Wilfred Lawson's local option Bill. Blunt told them that he 'had no intention of voting for it. . . . After all England is a Xian country and must have its beer.'[13] One wonders how he would have responded to the same test the next year when he was standing as a Liberal. Though he had come out in favour of the principle of local option at Newport in October 1885,[14] Salisbury and the Conservatives, for the most part, tried to be the party of the publicans. According to Lord Willoughby de Broke, measures of the sort being proposed would rob the poor man of his beer. 'The public house would be closed on Sunday while the rich Liberals could drink champagne in the Reform Club.'[15] Tories such as Temple regarded these measures as virtually unpatriotic. 'This is one of the first inroads, if not the very first inroad, by the Temperance Party into the *English* system, whereby there is not any closing except during the time of divine services.'[16] Thomas Milvain recapitulated the usual arguments against reforms of this sort. They violated vested interests and citizens' liberties; they constituted special legislation for particular regions; they would fail in their moral objectives.[17] However, as Temple realized, not all Conservatives shared these views. In the second reading on Pease's Bill 'it became apparent that our Conservatives were not united in opposition'.[18] Consequently, when the Durham Sunday closing Bill passed its second reading in the Lords, Temple wrote to Salisbury asking him to renew the opposition, even into the committee stage and the third reading.[19]

---

[11] A. E. Dingle, *The Campaign for Prohibition in Victorian England: The United Kingdom Alliance, 1872–1895* (London: 1980), pp. 101 ff.

[12] Hamer, *The Politics of Electoral Pressure*, p. 237.

[13] Blunt Diary, 16 July 1885, Blunt MS 333-1975, f. 72.

[14] Dingle, *The Campaign for Prohibition in Victorian England*, pp. 106–7.

[15] Lord Willoughby de Broke, *Passing Years* (London, Bombay, and Sydney: 1924), p. 174.   [16] Temple Letters, 24 Mar. 1886, BL Add. MS 38916, f. 58.

[17] Hansard, 303: 1756.

[18] Temple Letters, 12 Mar. 1886, BL Add. MS 38916, ff. 39^v–40.

[19] Temple to Salisbury, 12 May 1886, Third Marquess of Salisbury MSS Class E.

The kind of counter-pressure Salisbury felt from other sections of his back benches is revealed in a letter from C. J. Valentine, an ironmaster sitting for the Cockermouth division of Cumberland. 'It is a fact which is well within the cognizance of social reformers whose political convictions cause them to support the Conservative party, that their party loses the adhesion of thousands of the best of our young men yearly, because of the attitude of hostility against the Temperance legislation which our leaders take up.'[20] These disagreements within the Conservative party came to express themselves in acceptable levels of voting irregularity in most divisions on temperance questions. The proportion diverging from the party position ranged from 4 to 7 per cent. However, in the division of the Sale of Intoxicating Liquors on Sunday Bill on 2 April the proportion of internal disagreement within the Conservative party rose to 14 per cent.

However, it was the positions struck by the Irish Nationalists on temperance questions which played the largest role in preventing them from fitting the social policy dimension. While some Parnellites, including Parnell himself, favoured temperance measures as instruments of social reform, others viewed them as anti-nationalistic and, indeed, anti-Irish. Others found other grounds for opposition. John O'Connor, for example, criticized Conybeare's Bill restricting the sale of liquor to children because he regarded it as 'inhuman and unjust', and a measure which would prevent the ill and disabled from sending children to fetch refreshment for them.[21] Because of deep divisions in their party, O'Connor and Parnell wished Ireland to be excluded from the provisions of Conybeare's Bill, to which request Conybeare agreed.[22] For Parnell, the control of the liquor trade in Ireland was a question which the Irish Parliament should settle. 'I believe, more firmly,' he said, that this House will never satisfactorily deal with the liquor trade in Ireland.'[23] Internal disagreements amongst the Irish Nationalists, and the proportion of Parnellites deviating from the party position in these divisions, served to throw votes on temperance questions out of a dimensional relationship with other social reform questions. With a minimum Q value established at .70, divisions on temperance questions came into conflict in more than a fifth of the comparisons with voting on other social reform

---

[20] C. J. Valentine to Salisbury, 20 May 1886, Third Marquess of Salisbury MSS Class E.

[21] Hansard, 304: 678.   [22] Ibid., 304: 678, 693.

[23] Ibid., 304: 694. Elizabeth Malcolm, 'Temperance and Irish Nationalism', *Ireland Under the Union: Varieties of Tension*, ed. F. S. L. Lyons and R. A. J. Hawkins (Oxford: 1980), pp. 91–5, and *passim*.

questions. These were divisions on the Irish Labourers Acts Amendment Bill, the Resolution on the death penalty, and the Public Health Acts Bill.

Incidentally, it is incorrect to regard Liberal disagreements on local option or other efforts to control the liquor trade as in some way connected to the Home Rule split.[24] Those who became Liberal Unionists were not in any noticeable way more opposed to these measures than other members of the Liberal party. No future Liberal Unionist opposed the Sale of Intoxicating Liquors Bill on 24 March (Division 43) or the Sale of Intoxicating Liquors on Sunday Bill on 2 April (Division 59); only four are found in the Opposition division lobby for the Intoxicating Liquors (Sale to Children) Bill on 2 April (Division 60); and only four again for the Sale of Intoxicating Liquors on Sunday Bill on 4 June (Division 123).

Even when the temperance measures, the shop hours Bill, the coal-mines Bill, the medical acts Amendment Bill, and the Amendment to the Motion to repeal the Contagious Diseases Act are removed from the analysis, the remaining social policy dimension is not, from a statistical point of view, very satisfying. Fifteen items fit the dimension with minimum statistical values of .65 and thirteen at .70, but only five fit the dimension at .80 and only four at .90. And this in contrast to the dimensions on Church policy, land reform, imperial and military policy, and political reform. A high degree of voting irregularity on social policy questions leads to the inevitable conclusion that they were untypical of policy formation in the House of Commons in 1886. But this is not the whole of it, and a larger implication lurks in these reckonings. For half a century the House of Commons had had legislative experience with social reform and Government interventionist measures. In the 1840s, these questions were not accepted as part of a coherent political programme. As a consequence, parliamentary voting on the ten hours Bill and the Poor Law did not fit the major ideological dimensions of the period.[25] They had not become integrated into the general thrust of parliamentary politics, into the major political agenda of the age of Peel. As Table 2.6 shows, social reform had become more fully integrated into the political agenda of the age of Gladstone, but integration remained incomplete. The place of such questions in the

---

[24] Dingle, *The Campaign for Prohibition in Victorian England*, p. 103.

[25] Aydelotte, 'Voting Patterns in the British House of Commons in the 1840s', pp. 155 ff. I myself have had something to say about Government intervention on social questions in *The Politics of Government Growth: Early Victorian Attitudes Toward State Intervention, 1833–1848* (Newton Abbot and Hamden, Conn.: 1971).

politics of the 1880s was unclear, even to Members themselves. Some they could associate with the general understandings they had of their politics; others they could not. Only later, perhaps as late as the decade before the Great War, would the ideological bases underlying social reform resemble, and become associated with, other policy dimensions.

The Progress and Limits of Reform in 1886 — the Great Parliamentary Voting Dimension

These voting patterns which identify these policy agenda also identify the political centres of gravity around which politics turned. In their different ways, each posed the great question of the age: how is the maldistribution of power, privilege, and wealth to be reconciled with what many took to be an age of reform? Some demanded continuing reform, consolidation, and extension. Others, championing the same principles (none, for example, wished to revert to the pre-1884 period), based their actions on reservations and restrictions which, to them, established the limits of policy and safe political action. These dimensions describe areas of public policy about which Members had common understandings and about which they spoke a common language, and about which the essential disagreements concerned matters of degree, not matters of kind. For some, the time to halt was not yet. For others, the time to halt had occurred. William Tyssen-Amherst wrote to Salisbury: 'all true Conservatives and I believe constitutional Liberals have discarded the possibility of concessions of principle in even so small a degree in the hope of staving off a revolution.'[26] And Sir Henry Tyler: 'If Mr. Gladstone now succeeds in forming an Administration, it cannot, I apprehend, last long. And then another opportunity will arise for a combination of loyalists and anti-socialists under your leadership, which is the only hope, as far as present appearances go, of saving the Country from serious disaster.'[27] Tyssen-Amherst and Tyler represent one extreme on this continuum. Labouchere represents another. In the midst of the Home Rule crisis, in the midst of his efforts to salvage Chamberlain for the Liberal party, Labouchere wrote, 'there never was such an opportunity to establish a Radical party and to carry all before it. Is it worth while wrecking this beautiful future, for the sake of some minor details about Irish

[26] William Tyssen-Amherst to Salisbury, 12 Oct. 1885, Third Marquess of Salisbury MSS Class E.

[27] Sir Henry Tyler to Salisbury, 30 Jan. 1886, Third Marquess of Salisbury MSS Class E.

Govt?'[28] Both positions, and those in between, were—to use Tyssen-Amherst's word—constitutional. That is, political behaviour on these policy agenda were points on continuums. Behaviour on questions which fit these dimensions did not wander off into actions or beliefs which could not be squared with the accepted constitutional standards of the period.

Nor is this all. A larger construction should be put on this. As the tables above and Table 2.7 make clear, many of the divisions fitting specific voting dimensions on specific types of policy questions fit, as well, a larger voting dimension which transcends these specific points of policy. Of the 143 divisions in which Members of this House of Commons voted, ninety-five (66 per cent) fit a common dimension at a statistical threshold of .65. That this is a dimension of high statistical quality, with little irregular voting, can be shown by elevating the statistical threshold. Of these ninety-five divisions, ninety-two (97 per cent) fit a dimension of .70, and eighty-one (85 per cent) fit at .80. Since questions of Church policy and land, political reform and the empire, Irish policy and social reform fit this dimension, it is not possible to label it in such a manner as to describe its contents. It is a description of ideological behaviour.

The existence of such a voting dimension shows two things about the nature of parliamentary life in the 1880s. First, it reveals underlying and uniform patterns of behaviour which were unaffected by the episodic excitements of which the Home Rule Bill in 1886 was most important. Political responses to particular policy questions were part of a larger ideological framework which went beyond personal ambition, interest, and parliamentary tactics. Had such latter factors bulked larger in the motivations of Members, there would not be one large dimension but many of them, and each would be smaller. Secondly, it shows the way in which episodic excitements were integrated by the forces of parliamentary life, the ways in which various voting interests were domesticated, and the extent to which all voting groups, whether social or political, were drawn together in the kind of commitment which is necessary for all stable systems.[29]

These are findings of the greatest importance and interest. Studies of American legislative behaviour have not produced comparable results. Votes in the Confederate Provisional Congress, for example, could be fitted into but two small dimensions, and these, together,

[28] Labouchere to Chamberlain, 31 Mar. 1886, Chamberlain Papers JC5/50/69.
[29] Gabriel A. Almond and Bingham Powell, Jr., *Comparative Politics: System, Process, and Policy*, 2nd edn. (Boston: 1966) pp. 98–127.

TABLE 2.7 Some Items Fitting the Major Voting Dimension*

	9	13	24	38	44	47	101	103	115	124
9. Military Operations in Burma, 22 February	—	.89	.96	.92	.93	.80	.89	.91	.96	.89
13. Colonial Expenses in Africa, 1 March		—	.98	.98	.90	.96	.98	1.0	1.0	.93
24. Welsh Disestablishment, 9 March			—	.98	1.0	.99	1.0	.99	1.0	.98
38. Foreign and Imperial Involvements, 19 March				—	.92	.97	1.0	.90	1.0	.89
44. Army Estimate, 25 March					—	.89	.94	.91	1.0	.93
47. Crofters Bill, 29 March						—	.98	.98	1.0	.91
101. Arms Bill, 20 May							—	.98	1.0	.98
103. Cottagers' Allotment Gardens Bill, 21 May								—	.98	.95
115. Registration of Voters, 2 June									—	1.0
124. Home Rule, 8 June										—

*For a discussion of voting on all items fitting the major voting dimension, see Appendix II.

consisted of only fifteen roll-calls (26 per cent).[30] It is rather a different story for the British House of Commons throughout the nineteenth century. In the 1840s, of the 188 divisions selected for analysis, 120 (64 per cent) fit together in a single dimension. In the House of Commons which sat between 1852 and 1857, a period which historians have regarded as important because of its political incoherence, seventy-four of the 145 divisions tabulated and analysed (51 per cent) belonged to the same dimension. Similarly, in the House of Commons of 1861, another time in which political structures and values seem to have been fluid and confused, the voting of Members fitted powerfully ordered dimensions.[31] And not for British politics only. Legislative studies of German Parliaments which sat in Frankfurt and Berlin between 1848 and 1849, and the Reichstags of 1898–1903 and 1903–6 show remarkably coherent voting patterns in which roll-calls fit dimensions of considerable size.[32] What all of these cases of European legislative politics illustrate is the capacity and tendency of Parliaments to integrate and organize political agendas, not by eliminating conflict, but by shaping it and directing it into constitutionally legitimate paths.

There are two chief illustrations of this in the political agenda of the House of Commons in 1886: imperial affairs and Irish Home Rule. Contrary to American legislative politics in which foreign and domestic policy fit two distinct voting dimensions, as Table 2.7 indicates, imperial questions and domestic questions in the House of Commons fit one dimension. There is a very high statistical relation between the divisions on military operations in Burma or colonial expenses in Africa and Welsh disestablishment or the Crofters Bill. And two implications follow from this. First, Members considered questions of internal and external affairs in the same political terms.[33] They

---

[30] Thomas B. Alexander and Richard E. Beringer, *The Anatomy of the Confederate Congress: A Study of the Influence of Members Characteristics on Legislative Voting Behavior, 1861–1865* (Nashville, Tenn.: 1972), p. 266.

[31] W. O. Aydelotte, *The British House of Commons, 1841–1847* (Regional Social Science Data Archive, Iowa City, Iowa: 1970), p. 20; J. R. Bylsma, 'Party Structure in the 1852–1857 House of Commons', *Journal of Interdisciplinary History*, 7.4 (Spring 1977), p. 618; Valerie Cromwell, 'Mapping the Political World of 1861: A Multidimensional Analysis of House of Commons' Divisions Lists', *Legislative Studies Quarterly*, 7.2 (May 1982), pp. 281–97.

[32] Mattheisen, 'Liberal Constitutionalism in the Frankfurt Parliament of 1848', pp. 124–42; 'German Parliamentarism in 1848: Roll-Call Voting in the Frankfurt Assembly', *Social Science History*, 5.4 (Fall 1981), pp. 469–82; Smith and Turner, 'Legislative Behavior in the German Reichstag, 1898–1906', pp. 3–29.

[33] A. J. Mayer, 'Domestic Causes of the First World War', *The Responsibility of Power*, ed. L. Krieger and F. Stern (London: 1968), pp. 261 ff.; Kennedy, *The Realities Behind Diplomacy, passim.*

did not have one grammar and rhetoric for one set of political issues and another system for other issues. A Member who favoured a radical domestic programme also favoured a radical imperial and foreign policy. Secondly, imperial policy had the same basis of support, both in the House and in the country, as domestic questions had. Members did not represent different policy constituencies on these different questions. External and internal policy were related.

Irish Home Rule, Table 2.7 also shows, also fits the major dimension of parliamentary voting. This is a finding of the highest importance. Clearly related to other aspects of Irish policy, Home Rule was one of the thirteen items which fitted the Irish policy dimension with statistical values exceeding .90. A similarly close relation is found here between the Irish government question and other items in this dimension. Much has been made of Ireland as an alien culture about which politicians knew little and cared less. Whatever they may have lacked in sympathy and patience, these figures reveal that Members of the House associated Home Rule ideologically with the other questions they faced. This is surprising on a volatile question of this sort. It was not so in other places and other political cultures, where nationalism was too difficult a creature to tame. In the Frankfurt Parliament of 1848, German nationalism did not fit the major policy agenda of the period. Rather than dividing themselves into ideological left- and right-wing groups as they did on liberal reform questions, deputies divided into *Kleindeutsch* and *grossdeutsch* groups according to the their preferences for a Prussian or an Austrian solution to the unification question.[34] This different basis of ideological support prevented roll-calls on nationalism from fitting a common dimension with liberal reform questions. Irish nationalism, as in the case of other nationalisms, was an example of extreme, even violent, populist romanticism, an emotion as much as it was a policy. Spirits such as this are notoriously unsusceptible to political solutions of the parliamentary sort. They do not often obey the political rules of debate, discussion and compromise. Therefore, to find the Home Rule question in a dimension with other questions on the major policy dimension of the period reveals it to be an issue which the integrating forces of Parliament contained and tamed, at least for the short term. This taming and containing was accomplished at the expense of the ninety-four Liberals who defected to the Conservative party.

[34] Mattheisen, 'German Parliamentarism in 1848', pp. 471–2.

Other Voting Dimensions

As the preceding discussion shows, not all questions coming before the House of Commons in 1886 fitted the major dimensions of parliamentary voting. These, because of the ideological bases of support they enjoyed, found places only on the fringe of parliamentary life. But they are worth passing examination because of their intrinsic interest, and because they reveal the extent to which behaviour in this House of Commons was multi-dimensional, requiring more than one voting dimension to describe it. These items fit two very small dimensions. The first consists of a miscellaneous lot, the primary characteristic of which seems to be its Conservative basis of support. The second dimension consists of a small group of divisions on railway questions.[35]

As one who examines the tables found earlier in this chapter will see, some divisions fail to fit the various dimensions in a dramatic manner. It is not just that they fail to attain the necessary statistical values for inclusion in the dimensions, but they have negative values approaching or attaining -1.0. These are, in fact, inversely related to divisions fitting the dimensions. For example, in Table 2.3, Beresford's motion concerning the readiness of the navy and Vincent's motion on behalf of the army auxiliary force are strongly and inversely related to every other military–imperial question. On the other hand, as Table 2.8 shows, Beresford's and Vincent's motions (Divisions 31 and 40), when compared with each other, reveal a strong positive relationship ($+.99$). Similarly, Tables 2.4 and 2.5 show an elevated inverse relationship between the division taken on Parnell's Amendment to the Police Forces Enfranchisement Bill and items fitting the Irish policy and political reform dimensions. Comparisons of voting on social policy show a strong inverse relationship between divisions on Cross's Coal Mines Bill and Kennaway's Amendment to the Motion for Repeal of the Contagious Diseases Acts. While these items hold a negative relationship to divisions in dimensions in which one would expect them to find a place, they fit a common dimension by themselves. To these, as Table 2.8 shows, others can be added. The House took three divisions on questions in which a Tory social consciousness may be detected. One was on Sir John Kennaway's amendment to Stansfeld's Motion for Repeal of the Contagious Diseases Acts. These Acts had created a system of regulated prostitution between 1864 and 1886 to protect members of the services from the consequences of venereal disease.

---

[35] W. C. Lubenow, 'Ireland, the Great Depression, and the Railway Rates'. *Opinion in the House of Commons in 1886.*

TABLE 2.8 *The Conservative Initiative*

	31	32	35	40	75	76	86	89	94	130
31. Royal Navy, 15 March	—	.99	.98	.99	1.0	1.0	1.0	.95	.98	.98
32. Coal Mines Bill, 15 March		—	.99	1.0	1.0	1.0	1.0	.96	.98	1.0
35. Contagious Diseases Acts, 16 March			—	.97	1.0	.75	1.0	.85	.97	.87
40. Army Auxiliary Force, 22 March				—	.83	.89	.93	.92	.98	.98
75. Highway Acts Amendment, 16 April					—	.99	1.0	1.0	1.0	.75
76. Highway Acts Amendment, 16 April						—	.98	1.0	.78	.91
86. Police Forces Enfranchisement Bill, 19 April							—	.91	.85	.92
89. Charterhouse Bill, 7 May								—	.85	.93
94. Income Tax Inquiry, 11 May									—	.96
130. Coal Mines Bill, 11 June										—

They embodied provisions for identifying prostitutes, for examining them, and, if infected, for detaining them in hospital for specified periods. Several assumptions lay behind this legislation. Men of the services were regarded as a special creation, set off from society, and requiring special discipline and special social protections. Women, not men, were regarded as responsible for the spread of venereal disease. While degrading to men, inspection was not regarded as degrading to women because they were already degraded, having satisfied men's beastly urges. Defenders of the Acts, bolstered by the medical profession, regarded them as examples of progressive enlightenment. Critics, such as Josephine Butler outside parliament, and James Stansfeld and H. J. Wilson within, attacked the Contagious Diseases Acts as immoral, as abuses of the constitution, and as an extension of the excessive powers of the state.[36] Strictly speaking, Kennaway did not offer his Amendment in opposition to the Motion for Repeal. Extended in the spirit of humanitarianism, it provided for a continuation of hospital treatment, though under voluntary conditions, for prostitutes in Portsmouth.[37] As Kennaway observed, 'the Acts were passed to meet terrible evils that could not be allowed to exist in a civilized country without a legislative attempt at remedy.'[38] Sir Richard Temple echoed this, but went further in his private letters than Kennaway could have gone in a public speech. 'Now there's to be total repeal and the streets will be quite as bad as ever! A horrid physical evil will be perpetuated for the sake of maudlin sentiment. Alas, what *asses* some of the well meaning folks are'.[39] Stansfeld, in his speech on repeal, took the straight liberal reformist line. He sought to avoid the grounds of sentiment and offered the House a choice, *tout simple*, between freedom and coercion: between these principles 'there was no half-way house'.[40] Gladstone and Campbell-Bannerman, speaking for the Government on this occasion, opposed Kennaway's search for such a house on administrative and governmental grounds. In their view, the Amendment would limit the 'freedom of the House' on a matter which was the responsibility of the local authority.[41] Voting on Kennaway's Amendment fits this dimension, and not the major parliamentary voting dimensions, because the ideological forces here arrayed were diametrically the reverse of those on other occasions. Support for this Amendment

---

[36] Paul McHugh, *Prostitution and Victorian Social Reform* (London: 1980); Keith Thomas, 'The Double Standard', *Journal of the History of Ideas*, 20 (1959), p. 199.

[37] Hansard, 303: 989.   [38] Ibid., 303: 989.

[39] Temple Letters, 18 Mar. 1886, BL Add. MS 38916, ff. 47ᵛ–48.

[40] Hansard, 303: 983.   [41] Ibid., 303: 996, 997.

came from those who opposed questions found in the social policy dimension; opposition came from those who supported other measures of social reform.

Cross's coalmines Bill can also be construed as a measure reflecting a concern for the social condition of England, and fits this voting dimension for the same reason Kennaway's Amendment does. Those who had opposed other measures of social reform supported this; Members who had supported other social reform questions opposed Cross. Sir Richard Assheton Cross took the line of an old social reformer in his speeches, as indeed he was. More than Disraeli, Cross had been responsible for the social reforms of the Government which had held office between 1874 and 1880.[42] His Bill, caught in a labyrinth of parliamentary manoeuvring, competed with measures introduced to the same end by the Government and Arthur O'Connor. Cross faced arguments and criticisms of mixed nature. Sir Joseph Pease spoke of the difficulties the House faced when they had 'a confusion of Bills' before them.'[43] Broadhurst and Burt, as working-class Members, had a difficult position on this question, and Broadhurst's was enhanced by his membership in the Government. Speaking for the Government, he tried to delay action on Cross's Bill out of regard for the other mining measures, and the Members supporting them, before the House.[44] Thomas Burt complimented Cross on the Bill, but rejected it as a partial measure, and objected to dealing with the subject in a 'piecemeal and fragmentary manner'.[45] How far electoral considerations lurked, with an election in sight, can only be conjectured at, but Members were not insensitive to the political consequences of their actions. Once Cross's Bill had gone to the House of Lords, Cranborne telegraphed his father and requested, on Cross's behalf, that the Bill receive immediate treatment in the other place. Cranborne, on the same day, followed this with a letter. 'It is of great importance to the mining vote. Cross says he hopes you will force it through somehow.'[46]

Efforts to advance the military also found a favoured place in this Conservative initiative. On 15 March, Lord Charles Beresford took to a division his Resolution for the improvement of the Royal Navy's efficiency. 'This splendid Empire,' he told the House, 'which was built by their forefathers, and which extended to every point of the

---

[42] Paul Smith, *Disraelian Conservatism and Social Reform* (London and Toronto: 1967).   [43] Hansard, 303: 908.
[44] Ibid., 303: 910–11.   [45] Ibid., 303: 912.
[46] Cranborne to Salisbury, 16 June 1886, Third Marquess of Salisbury MSS Class E.

compass, depended entirely on our supremacy at sea.'[47] Sir William Harcourt, for the Government, offered another view to 'the noble Lord and his gallant Colleagues'. 'Besides ships and torpedoes there is a great resource in war — namely, the sinews of war, in the credit of a nation whose finance is sound.'[48] Alfred Illingworth sounded the call for economies from the back benches and for back-bench reasons. Anxious about the great depression, he regarded taxes as already burdensome and asked for 'a little breathing time' for taxpayers.[49]

The next week, on 22 March, the House debated similar themes when it considered Howard Vincent's Motion to increase the grant for the Army auxiliary forces.[50] Gladstone leaped into this debate, and, in Edward Hamilton's words, 'fairly and perhaps unnecessarily jumped down the throats of those who supported the motion'.[51] Increasing the military estimates, Gladstone argued, had not reduced the 'appetite for further augmentation'. Furthermore, in his judgement, the House of Commons sat at Westminster to diminish, not to increase, Government expenditure. 'That is the function of the House of Commons in our Constitution, and it is a function which I, for one, mean to adhere, and I do not mean to be party to a transgression on the part of any House of Commons beyond the lines that the Constitution prescribe to it.'[52] This particular battle between those seeking an increase in the military estimate and those resisting it was settled only very narrowly in the Government's favour, and this only with the support of 'Mr. Parnell's vigilant and well-disciplined band'.[53] Sir Richard Temple left a vivid description of the occasion:

We went to a division — and very nearly defeated the Government as they had only a majority of 20 with the help of the Irish. Apart from the Irish — as regards *British* Members, we had a large majority. It is the old story — our men were not in their places. *Had they been* Gladstone would have been beaten — on a small issue indeed, but one which in a pompous and verbose manner he had declared to be virtually vital.[54]

That the political right should support expenditures for the military forces is unsurprising, and this is confirmed in the election manifestos

---

[47] Hansard, 303: 837.   [48] Ibid., 303: 892.
[49] Ibid., 303: 901–2.   [50] Ibid., 303: 1506.
[51] Hamilton Diary, 23 Mar. 1886, BL Add. MS 48643, ff. 50–1.
[52] Hansard, 303: 1520–1.   [53] *The Times*, 23 Mar. 1886, p. 9.
[54] Temple Letters, 22 Mar. 1886, BL Add. MS 38916, ff. 54–54ᵛ. As these statements show, if the voting polarities on these questions were reversed (see Appendix II on this point), these items would fit the imperial–military affairs dimension as well as the major dimension of parliamentary voting.

for the period. As Baron De Worms declared, the naval and military forces 'should be kept in the highest state of efficiency'. 'I hold those to be mistaken economists who begrudge the supplies to the services.'[55]

The forces of the political right also championed the Police Forces Enfranchisement Bill. As early as 18 July 1885, J. H. Puleston wanted the Tory Government to advance such a Bill. According to C. H. Vincent's estimate, seven-tenths of the unenfranchised were 'staunch Conservatives', and Ellis Ashmead Bartlett viewed it with naked partisan interest as well.[56] Voting on the Bill in 1886 was a highly complex matter. The principle of the Bill turned upon franchise extension, and a division on clause 1 of the measure fits the political reform agenda and the major dimension of parliamentary voting. Having extracted from the Bill's promoters the promise to exclude Ireland from its provisions, the Irish Nationalists supported it.[57] Directly, however, the twisting fortunes of Nationalist–Ulster Conservative conflict plunged the tale into very much deeper waters. No sooner had the first division been taken when Parnell realized that he had no firm agreement on the exclusion of Ireland. As Parnell said of Selwin-Ibbetson, a sponsor of the Bill, 'he now tells me that he cannot meet us in the direction of the promise made during the discussion.'[58] Thereupon the debate centred on what Members regarded as a violation of parliamentary trust and confidence. 'Although I should be willing to grant the Constabulary the franchise', John Clancy said, 'I cannot continue to support this Bill, because I believe that a gross breach of faith has been committed.'[59] The general terms of a Bill for the British Isles were not before the House.

Now it was a question of the Royal Irish Constabulary. In the event, Parnell moved to postpone the measure and the Nationalists voted against the Bill, against a position they had formerly supported. This is an illustration of political fragmentation in the House of Commons in 1886. It was a fragmentation produced by the collapse in a belief in reciprocity upon which dimensional voting depends. The Irish Nationalists could take no confidence that the same parliamentary rules were being applied to issues in which they had an interest. Moreover, the Nationalist suspicion of the Royal Irish Constabulary led the Conservatives to feel that reciprocal treatment

[55] A copy of De Worms's election manifesto, dated Sept. 1885, can be found in the Third Marquess of Salisbury MSS Class E.

[56] J. H. Puleston to Salisbury, 18 July 1885, C. H. Vincent to Salisbury, 28 Sept. 1885, and Ashmead Bartlett to Salisbury, 6 Dec. 1885, Third Marquess of Salisbury MSS Class E.   [57] Hansard, 304: 374–5.

[58] Ibid., 304: 1559–60.   [59] Ibid., 304: 1562.

could not be expected from the Irish. Major Saunderson 'was not surprised that hon. Members from Ireland should feel a little sore on the subject of the Irish constabulary. They had had a large experience of that force at various times, and probably they would have again.'[60]

In 1886 the Governors of Charterhouse put a plan for alterations before the House of Commons, and the division on this plan fits this dimension of Conservative initiatives. The Governors appealed to Gladstone for his support,[61] and Sir Richard Webster, himself a Carthusian, advanced the proposal in the House of Commons. In brief the scheme proposed to alter Washhouse Court to permit the construction of a street through two walls.[62] It will surprise only those who do not know Gladstone to learn that the Liberals, joined by the Irish Nationalists, opposed this measure. Walter James regarded it as 'an act of Philistinism and of Vandalism, which the House is asked to sanction, under the patronage of these great names of the Governors of the Charterhouse, by sweeping away a monument of this character'.[63] James Bryce, similarly, deplored the destruction of 'Memorials of our medieval life'.[64] The Tories supported it, and Sir Richard Temple found this constellation of ideological opinion surprising. 'Oddly enough the Tory arguments, about not disturbing ancient historical and venerable buildings came from the *Liberal* side. The rank and file of the Conservatives sympathized with the Liberal view, and by a Division we compelled the promoters to withdraw the Bill.'[65] Actually, Temple vastly exaggerated Tory back-bench opposition to the measure. Ninety per cent of the Conservative leadership supported the Bill, and 65 per cent of the rank and file followed them.

On May 11 George Christopher Trout Bartley brought before the House, and took to a division, his Motion for a Select Committee to inquire into the income tax. His concerns were two: the rate of taxation, which taxed gross incomes rather than profits; and the manner of taxation, a system of tax-farming in which collectors were paid a percentage of what they collected.[66] That this issue was initiated from a conservative impulse to protect property from increasing taxation is clear in Sir John Whittaker Ellis's speech on this occasion. The income tax, he feared, was coming to be regarded

[60] Ibid., 304: 372–3.
[61] Harry Lee to Gladstone, 16 Jan. 1886, BL Add. MS 44494, ff. 39–40.
[62] Hansard, 305: 499.   [63] Ibid., 305: 503.   [64] Ibid., 305: 520.
[65] Temple Letters, 7 May 1886, BL Add. MS 38916, ff. 80–80ᵛ.
[66] Hansard, 305: 801–3.

as a permanent tax capable of continuous enlargement. This motion 'raised a question of the deepest interest to the community, in as much as a tendency had been indicated to throw a larger burden on all forms of property'.[67] Henry Fowler expressed the Government's position on the matter in sharp terms. Committees had twice examined the assessment of the income tax; twice they had failed to propose changes; there was not, therefore, much advantage to press ahead with yet another committee.[68]

A Select Committee on the income tax, the Charterhouse Bill, a Police Forces Enfranchisement Bill, increases in the military estimates, a Coal Mines Bill, an amendment to the notion for the repeal of the Contagious Diseases Acts: there is something here. Wilfred Scawen Blunt described Conservative policy in 1886 as a Bismarckian counter-revolution,[69] but that goes too far. There is insufficient substance to this dimension. Yet it reveals the Conservative position in 1886 to be not wholly one of resistance. Though there is no common theme cutting through the issues which fit this dimension of Conservative initiatives, and though it is an extremely small voting dimension, it was highly consistent and identifies a positive, if anti-liberal, programme.

Conclusion

Voting patterns in the House of Commons of 1886 show a process of political integration. Issues were related to each other in extensive voting dimensions which were bound together ideologically. In patterns too coherent and extensive to be the result of chance, domestic, imperial, and Irish questions found their places in the political repertoires of Members of the House. While it goes to the bounds of what one can reasonably say to observe that 'legislation is the way in which gossip transforms the suggested into the customary',[70] it is a thought which points up the workings of the legislative process in this House of Commons.

The binding together of legislative items into ideological dimensions is a political matter, but in the institutional sense rather than in the cynical, wire-pulling sense of the expression. Political integration in 1886 involved Members' responses to several influences and audiences, all of which provided various kinds of political support.[71] Whatever

---

[67] Ibid., 305: 805.   [68] Ibid., 305: 803.

[69] Blunt Diary, 2 Mar. 1886, Blunt MS 334-1975, f. 64.

[70] Quoted in John C. Wahlke and Heinze Eulau (eds.), *Legislative Behavior: A Reader in Theory and Research* (Glencoe, Ill.: 1958), p. 5.

[71] On this point see Joel H. Silbey, *The Shrine of Party: Congressional Voting Behavior, 1841–1852* (Pittsburgh: 1967), p. 240; and MacRae, *Dimensions of Congressional Voting*, p .278.

their dispositions on the hustings, their arrival at Westminster imposed new demands on Members, demands which shaped their behaviour as surely as their nursery experiences did. Wishing to be returned again, Members were sensitive to their electors' opinions. Wishing to support or oppose the Government, they respected the views of their party leaders and whips. Wishing to obtain office or place, or to retain office or place, they understood the requirements of loyalty. Wishing to cut a figure in London society, they abided by the conventions of society. And these motivations are not inconsistent with loyalty to principle. They merely indicate the ways in which political principles, values, and ideas are formed, modified, and brought to bear on questions coming to the House.

Political crises of the sort which sent *frissons* through life in Parliament in 1886 do not occur in isolation, and Members do not live isolated political lives. The House of Commons, like other legislatures, was a social system with its own processes for socialization and for the structuring of political behaviour.[72] Politics may be about people governing institutions, but it is just as surely the story of institutions governing people.[73] In the House of Commons of 1886 partisanship, the social background of Members and constituency influence were the factors which might be taken to be the forces most likely to forge the strong patterns of dimensional voting found there. Each has its problems.

The growth of party discipline, to which A. Lawrence Lowell called attention at the beginning of this century,[74] is the influence most frequently pointed to in discussions of politics in the late Victorian period. Political parties by 1886, it might be argued, summarized in their respective positions the major attitudes toward questions coming to divisions in the House of Commons. Party voting, or near-party voting, might explain the highly disciplined voting patterns revealed by the policy agendas and the major dimension of parliamentary voting. Some students of these matters, notably the high politics scholars, may wish to push this point further. The power of party discipline (the whips in the House and the caucuses in the constituencies) dragooned Members into the division lobbies, coercing from them the patterns of regularity the dimensions describe.

---

[72] Duncan MacRae, Jr., 'The Sociology of Legislatures', *Il Politico*, 32 (Sept. 1967), p. 578.

[73] Clive James's review of the Crossman diaries, 'Dissatisfaction of Power', *New York Review of Books* (31 Mar. 1977), p. 22.

[74] A. Lawrence Lowell, 'The Influence of Party Upon Legislation in England and America', *Annual Report of the American Historical Association* (Washington, DC: 1902), vol. 1, pp. 319–542.

And for this, and as the next chapter will show, there was a strong relationship between partisanship and voting in 1886. However, this is a complex question which requires separate treatment because straight-party votes occurred on only one-fifth of the items which fit the major voting dimension. The voting regularity which the dimension describes, therefore, was obtained through means other than blind, unthinking, coerced discipline. Moreover, even if the level of party voting were higher, it might not yet be sufficient to regard it as an adequate explanation of ideological voting. A dimension may reflect partisanship, but, just as easily, partisanship and the choice of party affiliation may be the consequence of the ideological pattern outlined by a dimension.

Social class and the social background of Members is also given as the source of political divisions in the period following 1885. For Sir Robert Ensor and W. H. G. Armytage, the political conflicts of the 1880s pitted Gladstone and his followers against those hosts representing the regnant social and economic powers and authorities. Land legislation and Irish government together constituted an assault on an order which resisted these reforms for the sake of class interest.[75] And one can find in the parliamentary debates many interesting examples of such an interpretation. Whatever social conflict these examples describe, it was not conflict between rich and poor, but conflict between several kinds of wealth. Fourteen Members of this House of Commons had their origins in the working classes, and, to be sure, most of these held the more radical positions in the House. But not all. Henry Broadhurst, after a long association with the Trades Union Congress and now a junior member in Gladstone's Government, voted moderately. The role of social class and background in parliamentary voting, like that of partisanship, is a complex question which wants careful treatment and qualification.

The debates and the divisions here examined also turn up instances in which Members felt bound by their constituencies, and the influence of electors may be one of the forces forging voting regularity in this House of Commons. Certainly, in the division on the Manchester Ship Canal Bill the pattern of votes has a character which allows one to stress the importance of constituency awareness. Similarly, in the division on Macartney's Amendment to the Irish Labourers Acts Bill, Ulster Conservatives and Irish Nationalists

---

[75] Ensor, 'Some Political and Economic Interactions', and W. H. G. Armytage, 'The Railway Rates Question and the Fall of the Third Gladstone Ministry', *English Historical Review*, 65 (Jan. 1950), pp. 18–52.

joined in an alliance which seems bonded by constituency interests. It remains for an examination of the relationship of constituency attributes to parliamentary voting to determine which characteristics of the constituencies served to shape parliamentary behaviour. First, however, the roles of partisanship and the social background of Members require an examination, and to these subjects this study now turns.

3

The Partisan Basis of Political Behaviour in the House of Commons

If I were like you—a party man—I should be in very low spirits just now, but being a mere looker-on I suffer but slightly. Still the look-out for all concerned is as black as black can be, and I can see no blue beyond.

Sir Henry James to Lord Randolph Churchill, 25 December 1885[1]

Our actual party names have become useless and even ridiculous. It is absurd to speak of a Liberal when no man can tell whether it means Mr. Gladstone, or Sir Henry James whom no offers however dazzling, and no ties however sacred can induce to accept Mr. Gladstone's policy. It is absurd to speak of a Radical when the word may denote either a man like Mr. Chamberlain, who has repeatedly affirmed his unqualified hostility to any proposal directly or indirectly involving the disruption of the Empire, or a man like Mr. John Morley, who avowedly makes the disruption of the Empire his chief aim. Notwithstanding the hard words which the politicians fling at one another in their moments of excitement, it is ridiculous to maintain a distinction between moderate Liberals and moderate Conservatives, which no man can define or grasp, and which breaks down under every test that can be applied by the practical politics of the day.

The Times, 4 March 1886

Introduction

By 1886, after five decades of partisan combat,[2] the age of the independent Member had long been over. Despite what Sir Henry James wrote to Churchill, all Members were party men, though within parties men might differ according to the degree and intensity of their engagement. The period, and the period which followed, are full of testimony to the compelling power of party loyalty. Lord Stockton told a story about the Duke of Devonshire, the nephew of Hartington and Stockton's father-in-law, and the Marquess of Lansdowne, who left the Liberal party in 1873 and who went on to assume high offices in Unionist administrations. Upon leaving the House of Lords one day, being drenched with rain, the Duke

---

[1] Sir Henry James to Lord Randolph Churchill, 25 Dec. 1885, Lord Randolph Churchill Letters 1/10/1209.

[2] D. E. D. Beales, 'Parliamentary Parties and the "Independent" Member, 1810–1860', in *Ideas and Institutions of Victorian Britain*, ed. Robert Robson (London: 1967), pp. 1–19.

suggested shelter in the Carlton Club. The Marquess, casting a horrified look as if the Duke had said something scandalous or had committed an unspeakable act, said, 'What do you mean Victor, go in there? Not at all.' Whereupon he insisted they walk on through the rain to a Liberal club.[3] Such was the force of partisanship, and the latent manner in which it affected even apostates, and some little time after significant changes had occurred in their political relationships. Yet, as the quotes above show, James and *The Times* witnessed what they regarded as a party system in disarray and in the process of realignment. The story of partisanship in the 1840s has been well told, and the modern history of British political parties has found its historians for the 1850s and 1860s. Indeed, much has been said about the whole of the nineteenth century on this point.[4] Not everything, however, has yet been said about the relationship between party and voting, and especially for 1886, about which scholars have made much. Therefore, this chapter considers the role of partisanship in the House of Commons during the Home Rule crisis.

The nature of party systems, and the importance of policy in partisan behaviour, has been a controversial subject for nearly a century. Is a party an agent of theoretical positions which represent distinct and coherent approaches to public policy, or is it a loose coalition of opinion and support which allows little unity behind policy positions? Is it the function of parties to exclude Members by the application of strict tests of loyalty to particular policy choices, or is it their function to include Members by allowing generalized understandings of policy objectives? Two general answers have been offered to these questions.

The first is to view parties as mere coalitions of opinion. Rather than being distinguished by distinct programmes, they have been held

---

[3] Harold Macmillan, *The Past Masters: Politics and Politicians, 1906–1939* (New York, Hagerstown, San Francisco, and London: 1975), p. 194.

[4] Frank O'Gorman, *The Emergence of the British Two-Party System, 1760–1832* (London: 1982); Gash, *Politics in the Age of Peel*; *Reaction and Reconstruction in English Politics, 1832–1852* (Oxford: 1965); W. O. Aydelotte, 'Isssues and Parties in Early Victorian England', *Journal of British Studies*, 5.2 (1966); John R. Bylsma, 'Party Structure in the 1852–1857 House of Commons: A Scalogram Analysis'; J. B. Conacher, 'Party Politics in the Age of Palmerston', *1859: Entering an Age of Crisis*, ed. Philip Appleman, William A. Madden, and Michael Wolff, (Bloomington, Indiana: 1961), pp. 163–80; Hanham, *Elections and Party Management*; A. L. Lowell, 'The Influence of Party Upon Legislation in England and America'; Cromwell, 'Mapping the Political World of 1861', pp. 281–97; Hugh Berrington, 'Partisanship and Dissidence in the Nineteenth Century House of Commons', *Parliamentary Affairs*, 21 (1968), pp. 338–74.

to consist in alliances of individuals competing for power. At the most, according to this view, parties differ as to legislative means, rather than policy ends. Ideas, ideologies, even issues, therefore, mean little. These are important for a parliamentary party only in an instrumental sense; they are devices for rallying majorities and criticizing opponents. Sir Lewis Namier's prestigious work in the 1920s and 1930s contributed to this conception of partisan behaviour through his minute analysis of eighteenth-century politics, as well as in his insightful observations on twentieth-century public affairs. Namier taught a whole generation of historians to disregard ideology and to study the relationship between personal interest and political motivation. This view of partisan behaviour was also expressed by Robert de Jouvenal in his witty observation that 'there is more in common between two deputies, one of whom is a revolutionary, than between revolutionaries, one of whom is a deputy'.[5] As R. T. McKenzie has argued, there are greater policy differences between the front benches and back benches of the same party than between the policy positions of different parties.[6] Robert Blake also describes partisan politics in non-doctrinaire terms. A party in office, especially, has little reason to frame its positions in inflexible terms. 'Why should it as long as things are going well? Problems come up one after another and are solved—or not solved—by empirical criteria.'[7] This point of view pushes research on partisan behaviour away from the speeches and statements of Members, away from the programmes of parties, and turns attention toward questions of organization, within and without the House of Commons. This view turns analysis away from the objectives of political action, since parties are not believed to differ according to their policy objectives, and toward high politics research, the study of tactics and manoeuvre.

In the several discussions of party politics in the 1880s there was a tradition of discussing partisan politics in non-policy terms. On the Conservative side, both Henry Cecil Raikes and A. J. Balfour commented on methods of manoeuvre which would take advantage of loose ideological distinctions during the period from 1880 to 1885, when their party was out of power and perhaps not likely soon to return to it. Raikes, who had been Chairman of Ways and Means and Deputy Speaker from 1874 to 1880, believed every party had a section which is closer to the 'Opposition than the rest of the party

---

[5] Quoted in Aydelotte, 'Issues and Parties in Early Victorian England', p. 100.
[6] R. T. McKenzie, *British Political Parties* (New York: 1964).
[7] Robert Blake, *The Conservative Party from Peel to Churchill* (London: 1970), pp. 257–8.

to which it belongs'.[8] Because parties were not neatly separated, potential alliances across party lines existed, and in such a situation much of political behaviour could be accounted for by the quest for power. Balfour, reflecting on his experience with the fourth party during Gladstone's second administration, also emphasized the importance of individual action, and, like Raikes, he tended to disregard partisan policy differences. Ascribing considerable latitude to members of an Opposition party, untroubled by the constitutional obligation to maintain a ministry, and enjoying looser party discipline, these Members had great opportunities for personal initiative since 'the art of attack offers to the ingenious Parliamentarian a greater scope and variety of method than the counter-art of defence'.[9] Edward Hamilton, before the general election of 1885, in commenting on the respective policy positions of the Liberal and Conservative parties, believed 'the policy of the present [Conservative] Govt is practically a continuance of the policy of the late [Liberal] Govt'.[10] *The Times* on 1 January took a view which fully squared itself with those of Raikes and Balfour and Hamilton when it pointed out that Gladstone's 'authorized programme' during the general election recently completed was 'substantially the programme of the Conservative Government'.[11] As events worked themselves toward the Home Rule crisis, Reginald Brett saw little to distinguish the Liberals from the Conservatives. As he put it privately, 'if as a party we have no policy which can be distinguished from that of the Tories, there seems to be no adequate reason for putting us in office.'[12] Brett made the same point in the *Fortnightly Review*:

It is true that Salisbury's policy so closely resembles the policy of the Liberal manifesto, that he might save himself trouble, and rely on the Liberal party to give effect to it. . . . So that, putting aside the question as to whether Tweedledum or Tweedledee was guilty of plagiarism, or to what degree the Conservatives have been 'hypnotised' by Mr Gladstone, a disinterested politician—if there is one—might well look with indifference upon the results of Mr Parnell's decision as to which party was to enjoy the privilege of introducing so much excellent reform.[13]

---

[8] Henry Cecil Raikes, 'The Function of an Opposition', *Nineteenth Century*, 13 (Jan. 1883), p. 156.

[9] Arthur James Balfour, *Retrospect: An Unfinished Autobiography, 1848–1886* (Boston and New York: 1930), p. 137.

[10] Hamilton Diary, 15 Aug. 1885, BL Add. MS 48461, f. 53.

[11] *The Times*, 1 Jan. 1886, p. 7.

[12] Brett to Joseph Chamberlain, 9 Dec. 1885, Esher Papers 2/7.

[13] Reginald Brett, 'Liberal Reverses and the Cause, Procrastination or Policy?', *Fortnightly Review*, new series, 39 (1 Jan. 1886), p. 5.

Labouchere's cynical assessment of the party system, after the Home Rule crisis had passed, was not terribly different. He wrote to Harcourt: 'Parties just now do not hang together by principle. They are gangs greedy of office.'[14] One remembers James Bryce's aphorism about American political parties—two bottles, each having a label denoting the kind of liquor it contains, but each of them empty. Statements of this kind testify to the degree to which practitioners of late Victorian parliamentary politics rejected notions of party membership as requiring allegiance to sets of ideas or political programmes. For these, the primary qualities of partisanship consisted of organization and loyalty to parliamentary leaders. Parties consisted of unities of men, not ideas or policies.

Parties, on the other hand, especially for Continental politics, have been regarded as instruments for the implementation of decidedly stated positions. Some have applied this notion to American and British politics. Ivor Bulwer-Thomas, for example, characterized British political parties as associations of persons 'for the purpose of promoting a set of principles' by winning elections and by gaining control of the machinery of government.[15] The classic statement of this position is, of course, Burke's, for whom parties consisted of men acting for the general interest 'upon some particular principle on which they are all agreed'. Disraeli came close to this sentiment when, in reference to ecclesiastical factions, he referred to parties as 'organized opinion'.[16] A. L. Lowell, the pioneer of legislative studies, viewed partisanship as the wave of the future, as a phenomenon rendered inevitable, virtually, by the development and the advance of democratic reforms.[17] More recently Samuel Beer, in his analysis of British politics in the twentieth century, has come to hold the view that, despite the acceptance of collectivism by both parties, Conservatives and Labourites remain divided by profound ideological principles: those involving the meaning of the party system, the nature of the constitution, and the character of modern democracy.[18] As Ivor Jennings summarizes the case, British parties 'are not mere

---

[14] Labouchere to Sir William Harcourt, n.d., but written at the time of Lord Randolph Churchill's resignation from Lord Salisbury's second administration, in Percey Colson (ed.), *Lord Goschen and His Friends (The Goschen Letters)* (London, New York, Melbourne, Sydney, and Cape Town: n.d.), p. 85.

[15] Ivor Bulwer-Thomas, *The Growth of the British Party System* (London: 1967), vol. 1 p. 3.   [16] *The Times*, 26 Nov. 1864, p. 6.

[17] Lowell, 'The Influence of Party Upon Legislation in England and America', pp. 332, 222, and *passim*.

[18] Samuel H. Beer, *British Politics in the Collectivist Age* (Random House, New York: 1969).

electioneering organizations. . . . In preferring one party to another, then, the electorate not only prefers one Government to another but prefers one line of policy to another.'[19]

Again, one can find support for this vision of politics in the political memoirs of the 1880s, where it was another convention of political discourse and practice. For example, certain Liberal politicians practised the politics of partisan exclusion. Joseph Chamberlain was one of these, and he predicated his efforts in the general election of 1885 on the development of a coherent radicalism with which he wished to reconstruct the Liberal party.[20] For Gladstone there was greater ambiguity in the relationship between issues and party unity. He was, as his activities on the occasions of the Bulgarian atrocities and Irish Home Rule demonstrated, committed to questions of great moral principle. Yet this could be squared in his complex mind with an appreciation for the unity and effectiveness of the party with which his career had become identified. He expressed this at Midlothian on 11 November 1885:

Far be it from me to say that the unity of any political party is an object that at all times is to be preferred to every other. If we come to a point at which our convictions go radically apart, and if matters at issue are of vital importance, then I, who am now teaching and preaching unity to the best of my ability, would hope that the Liberal party will sever and split rather than sacrifice conscience and conviction. There are questions which do not admit of compromise.[21]

But how are questions which will admit of compromise to be separated from those which will not? This is the essential question for both leaders and rank and file, and, in the passage quoted here, knowing he needed a united party with the Whigs and the radicals and with Hartington and Chamberlain to do whatever dealing he could do with the Irish question, Gladstone engaged in those deft efforts, for which he was famous, to sustain the unity of his party. For Gladstone, the Liberal party was the party of action and movement, always restrained by conservative motives, whose organizational features consisted in diversity and spontaneity.

---

[19] Ivor Jennings, *The British Constitution*, 4th edn. (Cambridge: 1961), p. 188.
[20] Joseph Chamberlain, *A Political Memoir, 1880–1892*, ed. C. H. D. Howard (London: 1953), p. 109; C. H. D. Howard, 'Joseph Chamberlain and the "Unauthorized Programme" ', *English Historical Review*, 60 (Oct. 1950), pp. 479, 483–6; Donald Southgate, *The Passing of the Whigs, 1832–1886* (London: 1965), pp. 364–5; Barker, *Gladstone and Radicalism*, pp. 18 ff.
[21] W. E. Gladstone, *Political Speeches in Scotland, November 1885* (Edinburgh: 1886), p. 71.

Therefore, for purposes of party management, Gladstone attempted to use and maintain this spirit of vitality while preventing organizational and ideological chaos. Much of this came to rest on the force of his own personality. While he was prepared to 'leave behind those who can't keep up with' him,[22] the Grand Old Man was unwilling, and here he was unlike Chamberlain as he was in many respects, to deal with questions of Liberal policy in terms of exclusion. Consequently, Gladstone tolerated, in secondary and tertiary positions, a variety of political questions which were important to the various sections of his party. The result was a pluralism of policy, in which members could assert their objectives through internal pressure and manoeuvre, which was not inconsistent with the unity of the party.

As these views illustrate, two concepts of partisanship have been treasured in Western democracies, and it is difficult to reconcile them. On the one hand, the notion of parties unified around opposing policies has been admired as a condition for producing appropriate policy decisions through a consideration of alternatives; they avoid policy stagnation by always presenting different ideas and approaches. Policy agreement amongst parties, however, has also been admired because it is a condition for political stability; parties sharing common values and assumptions and policies resolve their differences through normal electoral and parliamentary processes.

Parties, it is clear, must share certain values sufficiently for them to be prepared to suffer electoral and parliamentary defeats without indulging themselves in behaviour, calculated or uncalculated, which will destroy the system. On the other hand, parties must have sufficient policy distinctness so that they can govern with the force of a majority upon assuming office, or so that they can challenge the policies of a majority party if they are in Opposition. The sharpest partisan differences may reveal themselves on the hustings. As Lord Randolph Churchill put it to Sir Henry James, 'you must clear your mind of the ordinary polemics which are good enough for elections, but do not form part of statemanship.'[23] Churchill was aware, as this shows, of a distinction which has been made between electoral and parliamentary parties.[24] Lord Blake has put the matter

[22] Quoted in Paul Smith's review of Dudley W. R. Bahlman (ed.), *The Diary of Sir Edward Walter Hamilton, 1880–1885* (Oxford: 1972), *English Historical Review*, 89 (Oct. 1974), p. 919.

[23] Churchill to James, 30 Nov. 1885, in George Ranken Askwith [Lord Askwith], *Lord James of Hereford* (London: 1930), p. 146.

[24] Richard Rose, 'Parties, Factions, and Tendencies in Britain', *Studies in British Politics: A Reader in Political Sociology*, 1st edn. (London: 1966), pp. 314–16.

succinctly: 'A party has two main problems: how to obtain power, and what to do with it once obtained.'[25] How distinct from each other these conceptions are is unclear, and both require an emphasis on partisan differences and a toleration of internal dissent.

As a practical matter, internal agreement and disagreement, and the distinctness of parties on grounds of policy, are twin conditions of party systems. Therefore, the task is to explore the limits of each condition. Put this way, the problem is more complex than asking whether parties were united or divided. Instead, what has to be shown is the *extent* to which parties were cohesive, *how far* they divided internally (and the sorts of question on which these disagreements occurred), and the *degree* to which parties resembled each other in terms of the public policy positions they held. For this, the statements of party leaders have limited value. This is not to take the cynical view and assume that leaders will say anything to obtain power. Party chieftains, however systematically they may express themselves, rarely shed light on the ways in which legislative choices, the detailed decisions of back-benchers, are taken. For this it is more useful to adopt what *The Times*, in the statement quoted at the outset, called a 'test that can be applied by the practical politics of the day'. This requires an assessment of the relationship between partisanship and issues. This, in turn, requires an examination of the aggregate decisions of members of political parties as reflected in their votes in parliamentary divisions. Using the division lists, three detailed tests are possible: a calculation of the internal cohesion for each political party, an enumeration of the number of straight-party votes, and an assessment of the dispersion of partisan voting patterns along the various voting dimensions in the House of Commons in 1886.

Partisan Cohesion

Table 3.1 displays a summary of cohesion values,[26] in the form of averages for each party on the major parliamentary voting dimension and on the various legislative content dimensions developed for this study. This evidence, and especially the average cohesion scores for parties on the major parliamentary voting dimension, shows the high degree of unity enjoyed by the Conservatives and Irish Nationalists in contrast to the Liberals in 1886. The Liberals, indeed, attained but half the cohesion of the other parties on this voting dimension.

---

[25] Blake, *The Conservative Party from Peel to Churchill*, p. 243.
[26] The Rice Index of Cohesion is given by the formula: $C = Ayes - Nays$ (or $Nays - Ayes$)/party members voting.

This can be put another way. The threshold for partisan unity used as a convention in legislative research is 90 per cent of the party voting on the same side of the question. This is a score of 8.0 when measured by the Rice Index of Cohesion.[27] Evaluated according to this standard, the Conservatives and the Irish Nationalists attained almost absolute party unity on the questions summarized in the major parliamentary voting dimension. From this standard the Liberals fell far short. Indeed, of the eighty-one legislative questions in this dimension, the Irish Nationalists were unified on eighty occasions, the Tories on seventy-nine, and the Liberals on only twenty-three.

The average party cohesion scores for the major parliamentary voting dimension, however, gives little indication about the ways in which unity might be related to issues because it is a pattern of voting calculated across lines of legislative content. If cohesion values are reckoned for legislative items fitting the same dimension but having common content as well, interesting variations emerge because party unity was not uniform on all issues. The Irish Nationalists and the Conservatives were almost fully united on almost all questions. Their unity levels become deflated only on social and ecclesiastical policy.

Stalwart unity of the sort displayed by the Conservatives in 1886 is at odds with the interpretations of the high politics scholars for whom policy diversity is a necessary condition if politicians are to respond to all opportunities to seize power. It also fails to square with what Tories themselves were saying in 1886. The councils of Conservative leaders, where strategy and policy became one, were not undivided, and Salisbury was deeply sensitive to the problem of unity. As he said to Churchill regarding overtures to the Irish Nationalists, to make such gestures 'would be quite fatal for the cohesion of our party'.[28] Churchill was more adventurous, and policy as well as power had directed his attacks against Northcote and the Tory leadership between 1880 and 1885 (the 'mandarins' as he had referred to them).[29] He had concerned himself, beyond questions of organization, with a popular, though not necessarily a

---

[27] Lowell, 'The Influence of Party Upon Legislation', *passim*; Berrington, 'Partisanship and Dissidence in the Nineteenth Century House of Commons', p. 340. If 117 members of a party (91%) voted in the affirmative in a division, and 11 voted in the negative, then $C = 117 - 11/128 = 8.3$.

[28] Salisbury to Churchill, 9 Dec. 1885, Lord Randolph Churchill Letters 1/10/1157a.

[29] The Earl of Midleton, *Records and Recollections, 1856–1939* (London: 1939), p. 114.

TABLE 3.1 *Average Cohesion Scores for Parties in the Voting Dimensions for 1886* *

	Conservatives	Liberals	Irish Nationalists
Major parliamentary voting dimension	9.6	5.0	9.9
Ecclesiastical policy	7.8	8.1	9.8
Land policy	9.7	6.0	9.8
Foreign policy	9.9	4.1	8.4
Irish policy	9.5	8.0	9.7
Political reform	9.7	6.9	9.9
Social reform	8.3	6.9	9.3

*For this table the cohesion values for each party in each division in each dimension were averaged together. 10.0 = perfect cohesion; 0.0 = perfect disunity.

radical Tory programme.[30] 'Our task', he wrote, 'should be to keep the boroughs as well as to win the counties; this can only be done by an active progressive—I risk the word, a democratic—policy, a casting-off and burning of those old, worn-out, aristocratic and class garments from which the Derby–Dizzy lot, with their following of county families, could never, or never cared to extricate themselves.'[31] Balfour, on the other hand, opposed an approach based upon partisan programmes because this imposed on party leaders the task of devising policies which 'shall be at once harmless and imposing. This necessity is getting more and more difficult to satisfy.'[32]

And from the back benches came an interest in reformist programmes. Ellis Ashmead Bartlett advanced one which would have included imperial federation, Church reform, and land and educational reform.[33] Conservative unity in the division lobbies was not something Tory observers could take for granted. This was true on temperance, a question on which the Conservatives might have been presumed to have great agreement. Sir Richard Temple described the debates on Pease's Sunday closing Bill:

As the afternoon wore on, it became apparent that our Conservatives were not united in their opposition. So we judged that the best plan would be to talk the matter out. You see by the rules of the House the Speaker must

[30] Roland Quinault, 'The Fourth Party and the Conservative Opposition to Bradlaugh, 1880–1888', *English Historical Review*, 91.2 (Apr. 1976), pp. 315–40; 'Lord Randolph Churchill and Tory Democracy, 1880–1885', *Historical Journal*, 22.1 (1979), pp. 141–65.

[31] Churchill to Salisbury, 9 Dec. 1885, Lord Randolph Churchill Letters 1/10/1157b.

[32] Balfour's Memorandum, 10 Dec. 1885, BL Add. MS 49838, f. 219.

[33] Ashmead Bartlett to Salisbury, 6 Dec. 1885, Third Marquess of Salisbury MSS Class E.

close the Debate as the clock strikes a quarter to six. Therefore any Debate which is protracted up to that time must cease without any decision being arrived at. So this is what we decided on without challenging a decision, we let the Debate die a natural death and put off Pease & his motion to the Greek islands.[34]

Neither was Temple sanguine about Conservative unity in the division on Vincent's motion to increase the army auxiliary force estimate, which he believed a majority of the House favoured.[35]

How far the Tories were capable of playing a 'green card' in 1886 by supporting some species of Irish nationalism has been widely debated.[36] The Conservative leadership had contacts, though uneasy ones, with the Irish Nationalist leaders. In the winter of 1885, Rowland Winn met with Parnell over the terms of the Irish franchise in the redistribution reforms. There is also a memorandum in the Winn letters of the Salisbury correspondence describing a conversation with Richard Power, the Nationalist whip, about candidates for the Irish administration. Hart Dyke's name is on the list, but Henry Chaplin's is stricken off as too unpopular—he had too many friends in Ireland and his speeches would be quoted against him. The conversation also dealt with an elections Bill to reduce sheriff's expenses, a labourers Bill, and the number of elections in England the Irish vote could affect. But these contacts were so fraught with embarrassment that secrecy was essential. The memorandum concluded: 'No arrangement, compact, or agreement was come to between us, nor was anything of that nature either asked for or alluded to by either of us.' It was accompanied by a letter in which Winn said that he was keeping no copy himself 'so that there will be no other than the one I send you'.[37] The much more famous contact between Lord Carnarvon and Parnell is well known. Carnarvon was the most sympathetic of the Conservative leaders, and favoured a solution to the Irish question which would include 'some extension of local self-government'. But Carnarvon was no Home Ruler along Gladstonian lines, and on his return from Portofino, Carnarvon met privately with Salisbury and denounced

---

[34] Temple Letters, 12 Mar. 1886, BL Add. MS 38916, ff. 39–40.

[35] Ibid., 22 Mar. 1886, BL Add. MS 38916, ff. 54–54ᵛ.

[36] Cooke and Vincent, *The Governing Passion*; Foster, *Lord Randolph Churchill*; 'To the Northern Counties Station: Lord Randolph Churchill and the Prelude to the Orange Card', *Ireland Under the Union: Varieties of Tension*, ed. F. L. S. Lyons and R. A. J. Hawkins (Oxford: 1980), pp. 237–88; Roland Quinault, 'Lord Randolph Churchill and Home Rule', pp. 377–403.

[37] Rowland Winn (Lord St Oswald) to Salisbury, 28 Feb., 2 Mar., and 20 June 1885, Third Marquess of Salisbury MSS Class E.

Gladstone's Home Rule plan as unsafe and impractical. Salisbury, therefore, knew of Carnarvon's views, and his approach to Parnell, but as Carnarvon admitted, 'you [Salisbury] have been quite consistent in yr objections to Home Rule or whatever may be included under that elastic word'.[38]

The Conservative leadership warned its rank and file against flirtations with a Home Rule scheme. Churchill, who W. S. Blunt came to realize was being educated by Lord Salisbury rather than the reverse, advised Blunt against alluding in his election manifesto to 'an alliance with the Irish leaders' and 'was doubtful abt. my saying anything regarding an Irish Parliament'.[39] Churchill advised Blunt against a Conservative Home Rule policy in December, 1885. 'It is out of the question. If you want Home Rule you must go to Mr. Gladstone. We cannot touch it.'[40] So Blunt did, and concluded that Salisbury had never entertained a serious notion of Irish Home Rule. 'What is more likely is that he allowed Churchill & Ld. Carnarvon to pretend that he did in order to secure the Irish vote at the elections.'[41] Salisbury, with a keen eye on the past, was wholly unprepared to lead his party into a policy adventure on Ireland. As he wrote to the Marquess of Bath, 'I never admired the political transformation scenes of 1829, 1846, 1867: and I certainly do not wish to be the chief agent in adding a fourth to the history of the Tory party.'[42] If the Conservative leadership became united against Home Rule, they were divided on the question of coercion in Ireland. They had great difficulties in achieving agreement in January 1886 about what should be expressed in the Queen's Speech. In a cypher telegram to the Queen on 16 or 17 January, Salisbury summarized the situation in the Cabinet, 'Humble duty. Great differences in the Cabinet today. Sir M. Beach, Lord R. Churchill, Lord G. Hamilton, and Viceroy (Carnarvon) were against measure for suppressing National League; the other twelve were in favour.'[43]

[38] Carnarvon Diary, 6 and 7 May 1886, Carnarvon to Salisbury, 23 June 1886, BL Add. MSS 60926, ff. 66ᵛ–67, 60927, f. 14ᵛ.

[39] Blunt Diary, 14 Jan. 1886, 23 July 1885, Blunt MS 334-1975, f. 18, 333-1975, ff. 81–2.

[40] Ibid., 27 Dec. 1885, Blunt MS 333-1975, f. 224.

[41] Ibid., 21 June 1886, Blunt MS 335-1975, ff. 117–18.

[42] Salisbury to the Marquess of Bath, 27 Dec. 1885, Third Marquess of Salisbury MSS Class D/82/115.

[43] Salisbury to the Queen, 16 or 17 Jan. 1886, Third Marquess of Salisbury MSS Class D/87/318. See other correspondence between Salisbury and the Queen: 14 Dec. 1885, 15, 21, and 24 Jan. 1886, Third Marquess of Salisbury MSS Class D/87/295, 307, 321, 287. See also, on this point, Eric Alexander, Third Viscount Chilston, *Chief Whip: The Political Life and Times of Aretas Akers-Douglas, first*

On the back benches there were signs of support for a moderate Irish government policy. After the general election of 1885 and after the fall of Gladstone's Government the following June, John Henniker Heaton wrote to Salisbury requesting the appointment of a 'Commission fairly representative of all sections of the House of Commons to inquire how far we might safely go in the direction of domestic Government for Ireland without infringing on the powers and privileges of the Imperial Parliament'. This, though not Home Rule in Gladstone's or Parnell's sense, was closer to Carnarvon's position, and was somewhat in advance of the Tory leadership. It was a moderate policy to protect Conservative interests. Henniker Heaton feared a Liberal government plan for Ireland. 'It is especially the interest, therefore, of the Ulster members and their constituents—if the arrangement is inevitable—that it should be made by their friends who will guard their interests.'[44] W. S. Blunt hoped for a policy favourable to the Irish. He himself stood as a Home Rule Tory in the general election of 1885, and was defeated. His hope for a Conservative policy favouring Irish nationalism faded, and he resigned from the Carlton Club in June 1886, and stood as a Gladstonian candidate in the general election of 1886.[45] During the parliamentary session in 1886, however, Blunt, who always had a sharp ear for parliamentary gossip, believed there was Tory back-bench support for a Home rule policy. John Evelyn, the Member for Deptford, was 'well disposed abt. Ireland'. 'He wd like to support the [Home Rule] Bill, but does not do it alone among the Tories, so is going to vote against it. Poor good man, he had not the fibre of a fighter'.[46] Blunt and T. P. O'Connor 'talked over the possibility of getting together some Conservative M.P.s favourable to Home Rule'. O'Connor and Blunt 'thought Jennings of Stockport, Henniker Heaton of Canterbury, & McLean of Oldham might do so, as they were all entirely at the mercy of the Irish vote at the next election'. How far deluded he was by his own nationalist sympathies cannot be known, but Blunt believed even such stalwarts as Henry Chaplin and Howard Vincent could go over

---

Viscount Chilston (London: 1961), p. 60; *W. H. Smith* (London and Toronto: 1965), pp. 200–4; Cooke and Vincent, *The Governing Passion*, p. 300.

[44] Henniker Heaton to Salisbury, 9 Dec. 1885 and 6 Aug. 1886, Third Marquess of Salisbury MSS Class E.

[45] For Blunt's progress toward Home Rule see, Blunt Diary, 16 July 1885, 6 Aug. 1885, 7 Sept. 1885, 24 Oct. 1885, 12 Nov. 1885, 12 Dec. 1885, 10 Jan. 1886, 12 June 1886, Blunt MS 333-1975, ff. 72, 112, 140–1, 143, 183, 198, 219; 334-1975, f. 12; 335-1975, f. 100.

[46] Ibid., 16 Feb. 1886, 14 May 1886, Blunt MS 334-1975, ff. 38–40, 54, 189.

to Home Rule.[47] The cohesion scores of legislation fitting the Irish policy dimension reveal such estimates and hopes to be wholly without foundation. The Conservatives in 1886, from the front benches to the back benches, on policy from Home Rule to all other features of reform, were virtually unqualified in their resistance.

The deflated levels of Conservative cohesion on the ecclesiastical policy dimension in Table 3.1 is something of a surprise, considering their strong and unanimous opposition to disestablishment. But this surprise disappears when it is remembered that this policy dimension includes two divisions on the Tithe Rent-Charge Redemption Bill, on which the Tories suffered deep internal divisions. It is these votes which mask the unity of the Conservative party on Church questions.

As to social policy, the erosion of Tory unity, revealing some support for social questions, assists those interpretations of the Conservatives in the late Victorian period which attributes to them some malleability on such matters. It gives life to theories of Tory social reform, but not enough to press very far. In the 1840s Conservatives took no consistent position on the question of factory legislation, and they sharply resisted other Government intervention measures of the period.[48] In 1886 they strongly supported Kennaway's Amendment to the Motion to repeal the Contagious Diseases Acts, an Amendment which would have provided a measure of humanitarian hospital care, and the Coal Mines Bill; but these matters were exceptional, and fail to fit the social reform dimension as well as the major parliamentary voting dimension for the session. No Conservative majority supported any of the questions which fit the social reform agenda in the House of Commons in 1886, and minorities exceeding 21 per cent of the Tories voting supported only four of them. A commitment to the Church, to property, and a vision of partisanship which sought to assist the party in resisting the forces of political and social disintegration, hindered a social ethic in the Conservative party.[49] Such an approach could not go very far in offering legislative remedies to the social problems of the period.

---

[47] Blunt Diary, 4 Feb. 1886, 10 Feb. 1886, 12 June 1886, Blunt MS 334-1975, ff. 43, 47; 335-1975, f. 100.

[48] W. O. Aydelotte, 'The Conservative and Radical Interpretations of Early Victorian Social Legislation', *Victorian Studies*, 11.2 (Dec. 1967), pp. 231–6; Lubenow, *The Politics of Government Growth*, pp. 40–1, 82–3, 116–17, 147, 195, 203, 210, 214.

[49] Peter Marsh, 'The Conservative Conscience', in *The Conscience of the Victorian State*, ed. Peter Marsh (Syracuse University Press, Syracuse, New York: 1979), pp. 216, 232 ff.

The picture of disunity amongst the Liberals, which the cohesion values in Table 3.1 reveal, documents the reputation Gladstone's party had for a haphazard and diffuse political programme. This deserves a general comment because it is a finding which bears on the continuing debate about the motivations lying behind partisan conflict in the late Victorian and Edwardian periods. If these disputes were solely concerned with the quest of leaders for power, policy disagreements should not appear in descriptions of the political behaviour of the rank and file. Since cohesion scores are constructed from the votes of all members, they show Liberal disunity was not limited to the manoeuvres of the ministerial élite but rather cut deeply into the parliamentary groups they led. Moreover, policy disagreements in the Liberal party were nothing new in 1886, and studies of parliamentary voting for the 1840s and the 1870s reveal deep internal cleavages amongst Liberals during those periods.[50] The high level of Liberal dissent shows that Liberals frequently felt their constitutional obligation to keep a Government in office was not inconsistent with their responsibility to press for reform.

The general election of 1885 had returned large numbers of radicals to the ranks of the parliamentary Liberal party in 1886. These members took parliamentary service as their opportunity to advance measures of reform. These policies could not help but divide moderate from radical in the Liberal party. This was a traditional condition on the parliamentary left. But to it, however, must be added certain structural features of Liberal politics in the 1880s. In contrast to partisan discipline developed by Lord Salisbury for the Conservatives, the Liberal leadership encouraged a pattern of policy-making which stimulated rather than discouraged inter-party disputes between moderates and radicals. This is what has been described as a collective leadership in descriptions of Liberal ministerialists.[51] But it also extended itself down into the Liberal back benches. Gladstone's handling of the Home Rule question, sometimes misguided, prevented the hardening of internal policy disputes. In fact, it allowed a situation of fluidity which discouraged the settlement and resolution of internal cleavages.[52] Moreover, Gladstone's devotion to Home Rule, and his

---

[50] The Liberals were united in seventy-six of 186 (40%) divisions during the period 1841-7, and twenty-two of fifty (44%) divisions during the period from 1874-80. W. O. Aydelotte, 'The Disintegration of the Conservative Party in the 1840s: A Study of Political Attitudes', *The Dimensions of Quantitative Research in History*, ed. W. O. Aydelotte, Allan G. Bogue, and Robert William Fogel (Princeton: 1974), p. 324; Hamilton, *Parties and Voting Patterns in the Parliament of 1874-1880*, ch. 3.

[51] Cooke and Vincent, *The Governing Passion*, pp. 62, 78-9, 83.

[52] Ibid., p. 388.

absences from the House while framing his Irish policy, gave freer play to Labouchere and other radicals, who used the session of 1886 as the occasion to develop a variety of policy initiatives and to press these to divisions.[53] Gladstone himself, in relinquishing office in the summer of 1886, believed Liberal unity could be achieved more easily with the Tories in power. 'It is in opposition,' he wrote in a secret memorandum, '& not in Govt, that the Liberal party tends to draw together.'[54]

It is inadequate to treat internal disputes as matters of organization and manoeuvre alone. The average cohesion scores given for the Liberals in Table 3.1 show that Liberal disunity was related to issues. To put the matter in slightly different language, Liberal unity and disunity was not uniform across all policy dimensions, but varied according to issues. There are some surprises in these figures. The comparatively low levels of cohesion is what one might expect, but the Liberals attained an average party unity threshold $(C = .80)$ on two dimensions: ecclesiastical policy and Irish policy. The average cohesion scores for matters of Church policy is higher than might be expected. As the *Pall Mall Gazette* reported before the general election of 1885, of the 579 Liberal candidates in England, Scotland, and Wales, 403 (70 per cent) committed themselves to disestablishment.[55] Since 90 per cent of the parliamentary party came to support disestablishment Motions in the session which followed, either the proportion of disestablishers elected to the House was greater than the proportion who stood for election, or some of those uncommitted to disestablishment in 1885 changed their views once returned.

The other surprise here is the high level of Liberal unity on Irish policy in 1886. Of course, Irish policy as expressed in this voting dimension includes more than the Home Rule vote. But this is quite the point. Whatever their disagreements concerning a Dublin Parliament and the exclusion of Irish Members from Westminster, these disagreements failed to communicate themselves to all aspects of Irish policy. On questions of social and electoral reform, and especially on the question of coercion, Liberals shared a united Irish policy. Even the Liberal Unionists, those who separated themselves from the Gladstonians on the Home Rule matter, Gladstone believed had 'an important point in common with us, they refused

---

[53] Barker, *Gladstone and Radicalism*, pp. 165–6.
[54] Gladstone's Memorandum (marked secret), 12 July 1886, BL Add. MS 56445, unbound and unfoliated.
[55] *Pall Mall Gazette*, 11 Sept. 1885, p. 1.

to contemplate coercion as the proper means to be adopted in governing Ireland'.[56]

For the rest, the cohesion values of the Liberals in 1886 show them to be deeply divided on land and political reform and, especially, on foreign policy. On social reform, if the cohesion scores reveal the Conservatives to be unable to mount a consistent programme of social policy, the scores for Liberals reveal the party of the left to be as incapable of developing a consistent partisan position on such an agenda. There is, however, a larger point to these figures. If one were to attempt to predict the break-up of the Liberal party in 1886 from these cohesion scores, and went by these alone, one would not look to Irish policy as the centre of internal Liberal rivalry; one would look to foreign policy, or social or political reform. And this leads to two conclusions. First, Home Rule was a special case of Liberal policy disagreement, and the party's unity on other aspects of Irish policy masked the problems which emerged over the question of Irish government. Second, the break-up of the Liberal party over Home Rule seems unrelated to other questions on the Liberal policy agenda. It was not rooted deep in the traditional policy disputes of the party, but emerged in 1886. These are leads which will be examined at a later point.

Straight-Party Voting

A further indicator of the importance of partisanship, and the relationship between partisanship and issues, emerges when the number of straight-party votes for this session is estimated. Policy disagreement between the parties was not haphazard because for each voting dimension a similar pattern can be found. When the legislative items are ranked according to the proportion of Members voting in the negative, and are then cross-tabulated against the Members' political affiliation, the questions uniting Conservatives but dividing Liberals are all found at one end of the dimension, the questions uniting Liberals but on which the Conservatives were divided are found at the other end, and the straight-party votes, those questions on which the Liberals and Conservatives opposed each other, are found in between. Table 3.2 shows the proportion of items in each dimension in which the two major parties squared off against each other unanimously, or nearly so, in straight-party votes.

In the major parliamentary voting dimension, slightly better than a quarter of the questions divided the House of Commons along

[56] Gladstone's Memorandum (marked secret), 12 July 1886, BL Add. MS 56445, unbound and unfoliated.

TABLE 3.2 *Percentage of Straight-party Votes** *in each Parliamentary Voting Dimension*

	%	No.
Major voting dimension	26	21
Ecclesiastical policy	17	1
Land policy	18	7
Foreign policy	0	0
Irish policy	57	13
Political reform	50	9
Social policy	22	4

*A straight-party vote, for this table, as well as for this study, is defined as those occasions on which 90%, or better, of the Conservative party opposed 90%, or better, of the Liberal party. This follows the conventions established by Aydelotte in 'Parties and Issues in Early Victorian England', and Berrington in 'Partisanship and Dissidence in the Nineteenth Century House of Commons'.

partisan lines. Members of all parties felt the pull of partisan loyalty strongly. As Edward Harcourt put it, rather late in the session, 'had it not been for my respect for party discipline I really should have been much tempted to say a few words in the House of Commons, in correction of the very garbled history which has passed current [*sic*] there during the past week on Irish affairs.'[57] Henry Chaplin was careful to reassure Lord Salisbury that he was not presenting his work on behalf of the Cottagers' Allotment Gardens Bill as the party's policy on land reform. 'I readily adopt your suggestion that it [the Cottagers' Allotment Bill] should be announced, not as a Party measure, but as the sole responsibility of its authors. Indeed I spoke in the House of Commons very much to that effect upon the occasion of the 2nd reading of Jesse Collings' Bill, which I opposed.'[58]

The Collings Amendment, since it was one of the three votes during the session which served as tests of confidence in Tory or Liberal Governments, raised the question of partisan loyalty directly. The occasional Tory, such as the Hon. Arthur H. J. Walsh, Lord Ormathwaite's heir, wished to support it. 'I asked Walsh . . . what he was going to do about Jesse Collings' agricultural motion and he admitted that he was in a great difficulty and said he would like to vote for it', wrote Lewis Harcourt.[59] Some Liberals opposed the

[57] E. W. Harcourt to Salisbury, 6 June 1886, Third Marquess of Salisbury MSS Class E.
[58] Chaplin to Salisbury, 4 May 1886, Third Marquess of Salisbury MSS Class E.
[59] Harcourt Journal,, 22 Jan. 1886, Harcourt dep. 376, f. 116.

Collings Amendment, a scene which Sir Richard Temple described vividly.

Goschen rose and declared against Gladstone in a masterly speech. Again, a strange sight. Goschen sitting on the same bench with Gladstone & the Liberal leaders, denouncing their conduct amidst *silence* from them but jeers and interruptions from the Radicals and the Irish.[60]

Walsh and Goschen were the parliamentary sports on this occasion; party voting was typical. The second test of confidence in a Government occurred in the division on Hugh Holmes's Motion on the Social Order in Ireland. It was a frail effort. Lewis Harcourt wrote that Holmes 'spoke for an hour and a half and was very forcibly feeble. Gladstone replied in a short incisive and for him humorous speech.'[61] Some Tories were dissatisfied with the Holmes motion. John Evelyn told W. S. Blunt that the debate on it 'was disgraceful business for the Tories. He would have voted agst Holmes if he had thought any other Conservative wd. As it was Sir Robert Peel voted agst him, & Evelyn did not vote.'[62] Party loyalty held on both sides, and this to the great satisfaction of the Liberals. As Lewis Harcourt put it, 'the Govt majority last night against Holmes' motion was 160. What fools the Tories are to register such a large majority in our favour on a question of this kind.'[63] The spectre of Liberal unity on this occasion troubled the Conservatives, who had taken heart from prospects of partisan disintegration on the Liberal side. Sir Richard Temple wrote:

. . . the Liberals seemed to have been deserting Gladstone and almost leaving him in the lurch. But they all seem united again last night. The magic of his influence seemed revived. Today it is currently reported that he will propose Home Rule & will carry it. Alas! I hope not but I begin to fear.[64]

A lower proportion of straight-party votes, therefore, occurred during this session, but it is difficult to attribute this to the Home Rule crisis. While comparative information is difficult to find, and what is available provides only mere impressions, the levels of straight-party voting seem lower during periods of Liberal Government than during periods of Conservative Government. During the life-time of the Parliament over which Disraeli's great Administration presided, 50 per cent of the divisions were straight-party votes. Lowell and

[60] Temple Letters, 30 Jan. 1886, BL Add. MS 38916, f. 13.
[61] Harcourt Journal,, 4 Mar. 1886, Harcourt dep. 377, f. 188.
[62] Blunt Diary, 11 Mar. 1886, Blunt MS 334-1975, f. 69.
[63] Harcourt Journal,, 5 Mar. 1886, Harcourt dep. 377, f. 189.
[64] Temple Letters, 5 Mar. 1886, BL Add. MS 38916, ff. 32-3.

Berrington provide samples for the analysis of straight-party voting in later Parliaments. In 1883, when the Liberals were in office, the proportion was 35 per cent, and in 1890, when the Tories held the Treasury Bench, the proportion was 65 per cent.[65]

Despite the lower level of straight-party voting in the major ideological dimension in 1886 when compared with other periods, the existence, on a certain number of issues, of persistent and disciplined partisan behaviour of this sort is a finding of great interest. On these issues at least there was a clear cleavage between the major parties on grounds of policy. It is a finding which is consistent with theories concerning the ideological integrity of political parties, and identifies an ideological basis for the nature of the party system. Furthermore, it is an indicator of the difficulty facing those, such as Lord Randolph Churchill, who believed time was ripe for a coalition between various moderate Liberals and the Conservative party. Moreover, the existence of a pattern of straight-party votes of this kind is inconsistent with the anxiety sometimes expressed in Liberal circles that an opportunistic pragmatism, reflected in the careers of Disraeli and Lord Randolph Churchill, had taken over political ground customarily held by the Liberal party.[66]

St John Brodrick, who succeeded his father as Earl of Midleton, and other contemporary observers, may have believed the 'Liberals and the Tories were divided *toto caelo* on foreign affairs and domestic politics' during this period,[67] but the figures in Table 3.2 reveal another picture. These assessments of the relative weight of straight-party voting in the several voting dimensions show how straight-party voting varied according to the issues. There was no uniform separation between the Liberals and the Conservatives on all questions of public policy. The two major parties diverged from each other most frequently on questions having to do with Ireland and political reform, and less frequently on questions having to do with land, the Church, and social policy. They diverged least frequently on foreign and military policy. Foreign policy, and this is a point to which a return will be warranted shortly, was not a partisan matter. The main ground of cleavage between Liberals and Conservatives in 1886, the points of policy on which these parties were the most distinct from each other, had to do with Ireland and political reform. The high

---

[65] Hamilton, *Parties and Voting Patterns in the Parliament of 1874–1880*, ch. 3; Berrington, 'Partisanship and Dissidence in the Nineteenth Century House of Commons'.

[66] Hamer, *Liberal Politics in the Age of Gladstone and Rosebery*, pp. 219–20.

[67] Midleton, *Records and Recollections*, p. 54.

proportion of straight-party votes on Irish questions indicates that possibilities existed for the addressing of the Irish government problem through the normal processes of partisan conflict, through electoral and parliamentary methods, without the disruption of the regime. The high proportion of straight-party votes on questions of political reform reveal continuity extending through the nineteenth century. In 1886, as in the period from 1832 to 1880, the cleft in the party system hinged on constitutional and political disputes, not on economic or social conflicts.[68]

That the policy cleavage denoted by this pattern of straight-party votes was central to the politics of 1886 is a point which a further examination of the division lists makes even more sharply. When all twenty-nine divisions on which straight-party votes occurred are compared using dimensionsal analysis, there is a strong and inter-related pattern of association. Two dimensions can be discovered in these materials, one of twenty-four divisions and the other of five. And when these dimensions are compared with each other, all the divisions in the larger dimension hold a strong inverse relationship with the divisons in the smaller dimension. Positive votes in divisions in the larger dimension, therefore, predict negative votes in the smaller dimension, and vice versa. Members, therefore, associated all the questions which divided the House of Commons along straight-party lines as aspects of a single, if complex, ideological pattern.

The primacy of these party questions becomes even clearer when they are compared, using the same dimensional analysis, with the great issue of the session, the division on the second reading of Gladstone's Government of Ireland Bill. All the divisions in the larger dimension were directly related, and all the divisions in the smaller scale were inversely related, to the Home Rule question. An examination of parliamentary voting during the previous decade found that Home Rule did not even fit the major voting dimension. Members of the House of Commons in the 1870s did not conceive of Home Rule as part of the general ideological scheme which subsumed the major questions of that period.[69] In 1886, on the other hand, Home Rule not only fitted the major parliamentary voting dimension, but it did so in such a manner as to put it at the focal point of partisan cleavage.

---

[68] Blake, *The Conservative Party from Peel to Churchill*, p. 34; Gash, *Reaction and Reconstruction in England*, chs. 5–6; Walter Arnstein, 'The Religious Issue in Mid-Victorian Politics: A Note on a Neglected Source', *Albion*, 6.2 (Summer 1974), pp. 134–43.

[69] Hamilton, *Parties and Voting Patterns in the Parliament of 1874–1880*, ch. 3.

It is one thing to discover a pattern of partisan behaviour, of course, but is quite another to account for it. Some have tried by calling attention to the power of the whips to coerce obedience; others to 'the proverbial effect which office has upon spirits which when out of it have less reason for restraint';[70] and even others to the less formal, but important, cosseting of back-benchers by the leadership (Evelyn 'thinks he has not been noticed by the "Party" ',[71] George Cubitt wrote to Salisbury). The evidence of straight-party voting in 1886 can be brought to bear on this question. In the first place, a majority of the twenty-nine straight-party votes which fit a common dimensional pattern, either positively or negatively, occurred on questions which originated neither from the Government nor from the leaders of the Opposition. Rather, they were frequently thrown up from the back benches. Nineteen of these twenty-nine divisions (66 per cent), to be exact, were on issues privately sponsored. Straight-party voting in the main, therefore, occurred on questions which interested the back-benchers more than they interested their leaders. The back-bench origins of many of these questions is itself a stimulating suggestion that partisan unity along ideological lines arose from the back benches, and was not imposed by the leaderships of the various parties.

Secondly, as Table 3.3 shows, the use of whips as tellers in straight-party votes was highly irregular. Now this may be a point without significance; the use of whips as tellers may have been a matter of convenience, rather than a form of discipline. But the whips were required to know much about their colleagues: their names, their constituencies, their policy preferences. George Leveson-Gower, who became a junior whip for the first time in 1886, described his duties.

One had, in the first place, to get to know by sight not only all the MPs of one's own flock, but also those of other parties. . . . One had also to remember, if possible, the constituency for which the Member sat, and if you could recollect the approximate amount of his majority, so much the better. By degrees one got to know something of the particular views of the various Members, which I fear we sometimes thought of as 'fads' or 'hobbies'.[72]

Discipline might be imposed in various ways, but on Leveson-Gower's own account, the knowledge required of whips was one means of asserting influence over the voting behaviour of party members.

---

[70] William Burdett-Coutts to Salisbury, 10 June 1885, Third Marquess of Salisbury MSS Class E.

[71] Cubitt to Salisbury, 3 July 1886, Third Marquess of Salisbury MSS Class E.

[72] Leveson-Gower, *Years of Content*, p. 236.

TABLE 3.3 *Whips serving as Tellers in Straight-party Divisions**

	Liberal whips only		Conservative whips only		Both Liberal and Conservative whips		Neither Liberal nor Conservative whips	
	No.	%	No.	%	No.	%	No.	%
Number of divisions	10	35	3	10	5	17	11	38

	Divisions in which Liberal whips served as tellers		Divisions in which Conservative whips served as tellers	
Number of divisions	15	52%	8	28%

*These divisions fit a common pattern, either positively or negatively, at Q = .65.

However, when the divisions in which the whips served as tellers are examined, the evidence is largely negative. On better than a third of the straight-party votes neither Liberal nor Conservative whips served as tellers, and both sets of whips served simultaneously as tellers in less than a fifth of these instances. As the figures in Table 3.3 may be taken to suggest, the emergence of partisan unity appears rather more spontaneous in the Conservative party, but then they were out of power during this parliamentary session. And even in the Liberal party, the whips served as tellers in only half of the straight-party votes. An air of general informality infused these cases, even for the Liberals. As Lord Ripon remarked to Lord Wenlock the preceding autumn, 'it must be borne in mind that all that the party is bound to is the measures sketched out in Mr. Gladstone's manifesto as those immediately dealt with beyond which everyone is free.'[73] While Ripon was describing the behaviour Liberals should follow on the hustings, his position makes clear that discipline was not a precondition for party unity. There was latitude for ideological agreement to develop as less formal pressures for conformity brought Members to a point of common understanding, and 'fads' and 'hobbies' were formed into a partisan programme.[74]

A final point about straight-party voting in 1886 is that the Home Rule issue seemed to have little effect on the incidence of partisan behaviour. If Home Rule had worked to dislocate the party system,

[73] Ripon to Wenlock, 25 Oct. 1885, BL Add. MS 43635, f. 173.
[74] For a discussion of the same problem, but in a different legislature, see Smith and Turner, 'Legislative Behavior in the German Reichstag, 1898–1906', pp. 17–18.

most of the straight-party votes would have occurred early in the session. Indeed, early in the session one would have expected the most intense partisan behaviour because the budget estimates moved through the division lobbies during those weeks. This was not the case. When the divisions on which straight-party voting occurred are arranged according to the order in which they occurred, the fewest straight-party votes took place during the earlier part of the sessions. The House divided along straight-party lines only twice before 15 March, and only nine times before 24 March, the day on which Gladstone notified the Queen that Chamberlain would leave the Cabinet. With the development of the Home Rule crisis the incidence of straight-party voting increased. Indeed, half the straight-party votes occurred after the introduction of the Home Rule Bill. This evidence, therefore, is consistent with the interpretation that the Home Rule crisis galvanized partisan action, rather than reduced it. It is also consistent with the view that the session itself served an educative function for Members, that it produced institutional integration.

Ideological Voting and the Various Patterns of Partisanship in 1886

The voting dimensions developed for this study go far to show the degree to which parties held positions distinct from each other's policy matters. Table 3.4 describes the distribution of Members, according to their partisan affiliation on the great parliamentary voting dimension. (See Appendix II for a discussion of these classifications.) The general ideological configuration of the House of Commons is clear from the totals at the bottom of the table. Reginald Brett had anticipated a House which would be slightly conservative in mood and policy. 'It is commonly reported', he wrote, 'to be a parliament

TABLE 3.4 *Partisan Affiliation and Voting on the Major Voting Dimensions in 1886* *

	Scale positions (%)			No.
	7–5	4	3–1	
Conservatives	0	0	100	192
Liberals	47	32	21	268
Irish Nationalists	100	0	0	79
	No.	%	No.	%	No.	%	
TOTALS	205	38	86	16	248	46	539

*The median scale position in this table is position 4.

conservative in sentiment, and bearing distinct marks, on the Liberal side, of the undoubted conservative feeling in the country, called Reaction.'[75] Brett was correct on two points. As the voting figures reveal, and especially the totals at the bottom of Table 3.4, the general ideological disposition of the House was toward the right. Sixty-two per cent of the Members are located in dimensional positions at the centre or on the right. Moreover, while the Irish Nationalists clustered themselves into positions on the extreme left, and the Conservatives located themselves in consistent positions on the extreme right, the Liberals dispersed themselves along the entire range of political opinion described by the dimension.

Indeed, the most striking feature of this evidence bears on the relationship of the Liberal party to the Irish Nationalists and Conservative parties in terms of the policy positions they took. The Liberals and the Irish Nationalists shared much common ideological ground, since 47 per cent of the Liberals and 100 per cent of the Irish Nationalists occupied the most radical dimensional positions. But this display of the evidence shows that some Liberals shared positions with Conservatives as well. This, however, merely reflects the summaries in the table. If the detailed figures are examined, they show that only three Conservatives held dimensional positions to the left of the most extreme position on the right, and only two Liberals occupied the rightwardmost dimensional position. Therefore, 99 per cent of the Conservatives fit the dimension at a point to the right of 99 per cent of the Liberal party. No more dramatic description of the ideological distinctness of the Liberal and Conservative parties is likely to be found. While there was a great diffusion of Liberal voting in 1886, much greater than for the other two parties, the direction of diffusion was clearly toward the left. And this in contrast to the Conservatives who stolidly dominated ideological positions on the right. This much points to a correlation of partisan affiliation and ideology. The Liberal and Conservative parties in 1886 were not mere ideological images of each other.

This is the general picture. By turning to the distribution of partisan voting on particular policy agenda, on the other hand, it is possible to identify some variations from that picture. Voting on the land policy dimension, as well as voting on most of the other substantive dimensions in 1886, resembles the pattern of votes found when partisan affiliation is compared with voting on the great parliamentary voting dimension. Conservatives clustered themselves at the extreme right, Irish Nationalists at the extreme left, the Liberals occupied

[75] Memorandum, 21 Jan. 1886, Esher Papers 2/7.

TABLE 3.5 *The Classification of MPs on the Land Policy and Foreign Policy Dimensions**

	Scale positions (%)			No.
	5–3	2	1	
Land policy:				
Conservatives	0	10	90	202
Liberals	61	38	0	270
Irish Nationalists	99	1	0	79
	No. %	No. %	No. %	
TOTALS	244 44	124 23	183 33	551[†]
Foreign–military–imperial policy:				
Conservatives	0	70	30	118
Liberals	26	56	18	176
Irish Nationalists	100	0	0	28
	No. %	No. %	No. %	
TOTALS	68 21	182 57	72 22	322[‡]

* The median scale position in this table is position 2.
† 81% of the House.
‡ 47% of the House.

all ideological positions. Some Liberals, as Table 3.5 shows, opposed the radicalization of land policy. However, the chief difference between the distribution of votes on the great parliamentary voting dimension and the land policy dimension lies in the higher proportion of Liberals who fit ideological positions on the left. Sixty-one per cent of the Liberals fit such positions on land policy, as opposed to 47 per cent in the leftwardmost positions on the dimension describing the general voting pattern for this House of Commons. Land policy drew out the more radical sentiments on the Liberal back-benchers, and a substantial portion of the party was prepared to go further than the Liberal leadership. This is further evidence for the contention that ideological unity developed amongst the rank and file, and was not imposed on them by party discipline.

Land represented an important stress-point in the party system. Chaplin was not the only Tory to favour land measures of a modest sort. William John Evelyn had similar sympathies. As he put it in a letter to Wilfred Scawen Blunt, 'as a counterpoise to the visionary cow and three acres, should we not offer to the agricultural labourer some sort of security in his actual holding, his cottage and garden, security from capricious eviction and from raising of his rent? Had the Conservatives offered this or something like this they would have gained many seats.'[76] Such a position, however, was exceptional, and Balfour, who made the defence of land and property the preserve of the Tory party, represented the main lines of thinking in the Tory party. 'Everything which facilitates the transfer, and makes clear the title of Landed Property, is as much or more the business of the Conservative party as it is of the Liberal party', Balfour wrote. He disapproved of schemes to allow the purchase of land, even by local authorities. Not merely a threat to landed interests, this was a wedge's thin edge. 'If the community is to lend money to small farmers to buy farms, I am utterly unable to see why it should not also lend money to small shopkeepers, to buy shops.'[77]

The general opposition of the Conservative party to the land reform in 1886 took clearest shape on the Crofters Bill. The Duke of Argyll put the problem to the Tories in Tory language. It was, Argyll said to Sir Richard Assheton Cross, a grand policy masquerading as a local one. 'But the *whole* "Land Question"', he wrote, 'is really involved, as Chamberlain's inflammatory speech at Inverness plainly showed.'[78] Balfour, in consequence, defined the crofter problem as one of distress, which could be addressed by humanitarian methods, rather than one of land tenure, which would require legislation. He distrusted the proposals advanced by parliamentary investigations as 'the extremely retrograde ones of revivifying and rendering permanent the moribund system of village communities'. Balfour did not understand Scottish agrarian discontent in cultural or historical terms, and consequently failed to accord to the Celtic fringe, both Scotland as well as Ireland, a special ethnic and cultural character. Iron economic law should be free to function everywhere. Therefore, while he opposed the further division of property, Balfour approved of the creation of freeholds which would achieve a French solution, an alliance of the peasantry with conservative social and political forces. Above all, Balfour's conception of the crofter question rested on his view of landlord rights. 'It is not fair', he wrote, while depriving the landlords of 'all the privileges of property, to leave them all the responsibilities; to prevent them from getting any enjoyment out of the land while throwing upon them the onerous and invidious task

---

[76] Evelyn to Blunt, 8 June 1886, in Blunt's memoir of Evelyn, found in Helen Evelyn, *History of the Evelyn Family* (London: 1915), p. 267.

[77] Memorandum dated 10 Dec. 1885, corrected in Balfour's hand, BL Add. MS 49838, ff. 216–17.

[78] Argyll to Cross, 16 Dec. 1885, BL Add. MS 51274, ff. 195–195ᵛ.

of seeing that the tenants do not abuse the privileges which the state has given them.'[79]

If the Conservative and Liberal parties diverged pretty sharply on land policy, they converged on foreign and imperial policy, a point which Table 3.5 also makes. A preliminary matter first, however. The vast majority of the House which participated in these divisions held ideological positions at the centre, or to the right of centre, on this dimension. Only a fifth of the House took positions to the left. This is a way of seeing in the aggregate what can also be seen in voting on questions of foreign or imperial policy separately. The high proportion of the House opposing these questions, in contrast to the lower proportions opposing such questions as land reform, sustained foreign and imperial policy questions in the great parliamentary voting dimension with other items. This is significant because students of other legislatures have found it necesssary to assemble roll-calls on foreign policy questions in dimensions separate from those containing domestic policy issues.[80] In British politics during the 1880s, as the Earl of Warwick and Brooke observed, the 'Empire was the chief concern of all legislators'.[81] The Irish Nationalists, as Table 3.5 shows, departed from this the most because all Irish Nationalists fit ideological positions on the extreme left of the dimension.

The most revealing aspect of this evidence, consequently, is that it is virtually impossible to distinguish the bulk of the Liberal party from the Conservatives in terms of their votes on foreign and imperial policy: 74 per cent of the Liberals occupied the same ideological positions held by the Tories. These were bipartisan issues in 1886; here, excluding the Irish, was parliamentary consensus. Sir Richard Temple, in describing the debate on the annexation of Burma, recognized as much. Sir Ughtred Kay-Shuttleworth, Bt., the Under Secretary for India, made, according to Temple, 'really a very good speech', as did Gladstone who spoke in a 'loyal and patriotic manner'. Gladstone found himself cheered by the Conservatives on this occasion.

Certainly the new Government is behaving *well* about this. They have specifically supported the Conservative action, the annexation is settled and the Natives will see that the two great English parties are united. . . . When

---

[79] Memorandum entitled Crofter Bill, initialled by Balfour, 12 Mar. 1886, Add. MS 49838, ff. 227–34.

[80] MacRae, *The Dimensions of Congressional Voting.*

[81] The Earl of Warwick and Brooke, *Memories of Sixty Years* (London, New York, Toronto, and Melbourne: 1917), p. 69. Warwick sat for East Somerset from 1879 to 1885, and for Colchester from 1888 to 1892.

we divided about Burma all the Leading *L*s and *C*s were in the same Lobby, a respectable and even a distinguished set. In the other Lobby, was a small & [scratch?] lot of about Eighty consisting of pestilent English Members, Scotch Rads, and a few treasonous Irish. Such a set.[82]

The Liberal occupation of a Tory ideological position is a finding of some interest. There may be in this something of the growth of Liberal imperialist sentiment, a body of opinion which would become associated with Lord Rosebery and would find its place in Liberal party politics in the next decade.[83] Some of this may be accounted for by the constitutional necessity of maintaining a Government. The Liberals in 1886, after all, were stuck with the Tory annexation of Burma. But they were not stuck with all foreign or imperial policies, and on these the Liberal instinct for economy and retrenchment came to bear. With whatever motives, policy consensus, on the whole, amongst Liberals and Conservatives was manifest chiefly on foreign and imperial questions. On some other occasions, as Chapter 6 will show, the Liberal front bench found itself sharing the division lobbies with the Tories, but foreign policy almost alone threw together leaderships and back benches of both parties, a condition found during other periods of British politics.[84] For the most part, as the classification of Members of the major dimension of parliamentary voting and on the land policy dimension indicate, Liberals and Conservatives took sharply different positions on policy. Despite the fissile state of the Liberal party, this shows the existence of partisan strength to a considerable degree.

The Liberals may have been divided over policy questions in 1886, but their divisions, despite what has frequently been written about them,[85] were not haphazard. As the figures in Tables 3.4 and 3.5 illustrate, the clear direction of Liberal dispersion was toward the left. Their voting positions on the great parliamentary voting dimension reveal a considerable measure of centrist opinion in the parliamentary party. A third of the Liberals fitted the median dimensional position. A small group of Liberals radiated toward the right (21 per cent), and a very much larger group radiated toward the left (47 per cent). Participants in these events often had a different view of the ideological complexion of the Liberal Party. Lord Richard

---

[82] Temple Letters, 23 Feb. 1886, BL Add. MS 38916, ff. 20-1.

[83] H. C. G. Matthew, *The Liberal Imperialists: The Ideas and Politics of a Post-Gladstonian Elite* (Oxford: 1973).

[84] See Cromwell, 'Mapping the Political World in 1861', pp. 291-5.

[85] H. V. Emy, *Liberals, Radicals and Social Politics, 1892-1914* (Cambridge, 1973), ch. 2.

Grosvenor, who would, by virtue of his position as whip, have been in the best position to know, believed the radicals constituted only a third of the Liberal party.[86] Even at the time of the gathering of parliament, Grosvenor held to this assessment.[87] Churchill believed that only sixty-five Liberals would follow the lead of Chamberlain, Dilke, Morley, and Labouchere.[88] Even Lewis Harcourt was 'afraid that this House is a very Whig one and that we shall not get much useful legislation from it'.[89] Parliamentary voting told quite another story. A modern scholar, using the subscription to one or more of Chamberlain's measures as a test of radicalism, puts the number of radicals in the Liberal party higher, at 180 MPs.[90] According to another scholar, using somewhat more ambitious statistical methods, 165 Liberals were radicals.[91] The figures in Table 3.4 record the proportion of the Liberals who can be assigned to positions on the major parliamentary voting dimension and who might, by virtue of their votes, be considered radicals. If one takes a limited definition of radicalism, for example ideological classifications in the two positions on the extreme left, or, or indeed, the most extreme position on the left, the proportionate strength of radicalism in the parliamentary party was, respectively, 29 per cent and 15 per cent. The former approximates Grosvenor's estimate. If, however, one allows a more generous definition of the radical position, an ideological location at any point to the left of the median, 47 per cent of the Liberal party in 1886 were radicals. This is very close to what other quantitative scholarship finds on this problem. If the definition of radicalism cannot be settled, at the very least figures such as these provide an estimate of the size of the most advanced section of the Liberal party. And, as this evidence suggests, the presence of a strong body of radicals in the Liberal party was antecedent to, rather than resulting from, the great separation in the Liberal party over Home Rule. Radical strength in the parliamentary party, therefore, cannot be regarded as a consequence of internal conflict. Rather, it was a precondition for such conflict.

The letters and unpublished papers of Conservatives in this parliament show them to be divided on grounds of both personality and policy. As one back-bencher remarked in 1885, 'the papers

---

[86] Grosvenor to Gladstone, 12 Dec. 1885, BL Add. MS 44316, f. 148.

[87] Labouchere to Chamberlain, 22 Jan. 1886, Chamberlain Papers JC5/50/67.

[88] Churchill's memorandum, n.d. but late in November 1885, Lord Randolph Churchill Letters 1/10/1126.

[89] Harcourt Journal, 12 Jan. 1886, Harcourt dep. 376, f. 56.

[90] Barker, Gladstone and Radicalism, p. 24.

[91] Heyck, The Dimensions of British Radicalism, pp. 247–52.

name Edward Clarke as a possible [?] member of a Conservative Administration. I therefore tell you that E*d* Clarke is *no* Conservative' because he advocated marriages between men and sisters of deceased wives. At about the same time another complained of Iddesleigh's elevation to the Lords and his loss to the House of Commons: 'We do miss your lead in Commons *terribly*. [Last?] night was simply disgusting. It must do a deal of harm to have such speeches as Gorst's coming from the Treasury Bench. I never expected to have been led by the 4th party.' And, in 1886, a third stated simply: 'I cannot accept Lord Randolph Churchill as my political leader.'[92] Quite another view of the Tories presented itself to the Liberals. Henry Labouchere remarked simply, 'the Conservatives are an army, the Liberals and Radicals a mob.' Edward Hamilton also found great Conservative unity. 'But curiously enough there is always plenty of independence among Liberals, and the Conservative always manages to find his own views in harmony with those of his party. One never finds a Tory taking a line of his own.'[93]

Indeed, the cardinal feature of Conservative voting behaviour in 1886 was a continuing cohesion. The cohesion scores, reported in Table 3.1, show them to be firmly established, with virtually no deviation, on the parliamentary right.[94] Conservative unity of this sort was a nineteenth-century phenomenon, not a response to the rise of Labour, as some have argued,[95] in the twentieth century. During the life-time of the House of Commons which sat from 1841 to 1847, the Conservatives were unified in 62 per cent of the divisions under analysis. Similar evidence has been found for Conservative unity in the 1850s and 1860s. During the period from 1874 to 1880, the Conservatives in the House of Commons were united in 88 per cent of the divisions which were

[92] John Hubbard to Salisbury, 10 June 1885, Third Marquess of Salisbury MSS Class E; E. W. Harcourt to Iddesleigh, 20 July 1885, BL Add. MSS 50042, ff. 135–135ᵛ; Lord Francis Hervey to Salisbury, 24 Sept. 1886, Third Marquess of Salisbury MSS Class E.

[93] Labouchere to Churchill, 17 June 1886, Lord Randolph Churchill Letters, 1/13/1536; Edward Hamilton Diary, 16 Apr. 1886, BL Add. MS 48643, f. 86ᵛ.

[94] The classifications of some Tories in the dimensional positions adjacent to the rightwardmost position in Table 3.5 are in some cases products of the rounding process, for which, see Appendix II. In no cases were Conservatives located to the left of the median on land or foreign policy. On the great parliamentary voting dimension (Table 3.4), all Tories held positions at the extreme right or in the dimensional position immediately adjacent.

[95] Robert J. Jackson, *Rebels and Whips, and Analysis of Dissension, Discipline, and Cohesion in the British Political Parties* (London, Melbourne, Toronto, and New York: 1968), p. 23.

studied.[96] A marshalling of Conservative unity, therefore, prepared the way for Tory dominance in parliamentary politics in the last fifteen years of the nineteenth century, and this was quite contrary to Salisbury's fear that he and his party would spend much of their time out of power in an age of advancing democracy.

In 1886 the Conservatives were divided on only nineteen of the 143 questions on which the House took divisions. Moreover, these incidents of Tory dissidence were ideologically unconnected and discontinuous. In contrast to the Liberals, whose cases of disunity can be assembled into ideological dimensions of various sizes, cases of Tory disunity can be assembled into dimensions of no size. Of these last, only two questions fit a cross-content dimension with a Yule's Q criterion of .80, and only four issues fit together when it is lowered to .65. Issues dividing Conservatives in 1886, therefore, were random, fragmented, and unrelated; they were not aspects of a consistent and extensive pattern of political behaviour. Tory unity was at the centre of parliamentary life and political action, but the issues dividing them, on the whole, were less consequential, and Conservative disunity was kept to the periphery of parliamentary politics in 1886.

To demonstrate the existence of Conservative unity in 1886 is easier than to account for it. Tory unity, however achieved, reveals a party fundamentally different in disposition, temperament, and policy from the Liberal party. The Liberals may have been rather like a club at the apex, but their roots were in the caucus where rival crusaders championed rival programmes and policies. There was a different relationship between policy and partisanship in the Conservative party. The Tories had some natural advantages. The party of the right, especially out of office, with its concern for consolidation and conservation, has fewer problems which might disturb internal unity.[97] Moreover, the identification of the Conservatives with national and imperial questions doubtless quickened centripetal forces.[98] But there was more to it than this. The Tories were able to transcend and conciliate internal differences. They evaded divisive

[96] W. O. Aydelotte, 'The Disintegration of the Conservative Party in the 1840s', p. 324; Bylsma, 'Party Structure in the 1852–1857 House of Commons'; Cromwell, 'Mapping the Political World of 1861', pp. 288–92; Hamilton, *Parties and Voting Patterns in the Parliament of 1874–1880*, ch. 3.

[97] E. J. Feuchtwanger, *Disraeli, Democracy and the Tory Party: Conservative Leadership and Organization after the Second Reform Bill* (Oxford: 1968), p. 53 and *passim*.

[98] Blake, *The Conservative Party from Peel to Churchill*, p. 130. For Salisbury's continuation of this policy, see Cooke and Vincent, *The Governing Passion*, p. 63.

issues by avoiding complex and comprehensive programmes. They were able to practise the politics of support rather than the politics of power.

Since the Tories were indisposed toward an extensive legislative programme, they were able to evade some questions of the day, which questions could be nothing but divisive. Though they were not wholly negative in their approach to policy, and while they undertook some social questions in the late 1880s which might have gained working-class support,[99] the Conservative posture was defensive rather than active. Preoccupied with the question of the Union, on which they would not legislate, and with foreign policy, which required little legislation, the policy achievement of the Salisbury administrations was not great. Salisbury, W. H. Smith, and Balfour were suspicious and resistant when, as part of his legislative recommendations at the end of 1885, Churchill set forward provisions to accelerate the legislative process by the use of *clôture*. 'I am not particularly anxious to expedite legislation just now, when the powers of evil are so strong', Salisbury wrote. Smith warned: 'have you fully weighed the possible results in Radical legislation upon *clôture* when they have an undisputed majority?'[1] Even Churchill's programme, and he was the most ambitious of all of them, seems slight, and even he was not sensible to any of the issues which would dominate the debates and parliamentary divisions in 1886, save, perhaps, for land reform.[2] Even this programme, of course, was lost after the Tories left government in January.

In 1886, while in Opposition, the Conservatives could practise the politics of support rather than the politics of power.[3] That is to say, with the policy obligations of power removed from them, the Conservatives could minimize internal differences, since they were under no requirement to make policy or to concur in those of their opponents. Opposition gave them the opportunity, which power does only rarely, for political purity, and the Conservatives had the luxury in these circumstances of contrasting themselves sharply as the party of the nation and the empire with the empire-breaking proposals of the Liberals. Moreover, Opposition provided respite, for which some

[99] Paul Smith, introduction to *Lord Salisbury on Politics: A Selection from his Articles in the Quarterly Review, 1860–1883* (Cambridge: 1972), p. 94.

[1] Salisbury to Churchill, 16 Dec. 1885, and W. H. Smith to Churchill, 3 Jan. 1886, Lord Randolph Churchill Letters 1/10/1177b, 1/11/1242.

[2] Churchill's memorandum to Salisbury, late Nov. 1885, Lord Randolph Churchill Letters 1/10/1145.

[3] The phrase is Andrew Gamble's in *The Conservative Nation* (London and Boston: 1974), p. 10.

Conservatives eagerly yearned in 1886. As Hicks Beach put it: 'perhaps it would be a pleasanter time for both of us if we had certain prospects of the pleasure of Opposition.'[4] Salisbury, as a matter of fact, anticipated in the early 1880s that his party was destined for an extensive period in the nation's service on the Opposition benches, where their function would be to inhibit radical legislation rather than to turn out Liberal Governments.[5] When he met the new Parliament as Prime Minister in 1886, Salisbury's object was to force Gladstone's hand on Ireland, not to form policy of his own.[6]

The Irish Nationalists, like the Conservatives, conform best to the notion of an ideological monolithic party. The unity of the Irish Nationalists is usually ascribed to their solidarity on the Home Rule question. The division lists in 1886 show them, however, to be radical on more questions than Irish policy, and reveal a general commitment to advanced policies located on the leftwardmost parts of the ideological voting dimensions. This is an important point because much opinion in 1886, and scholarly opinion since,[7] was divided over the relationship of the Irish Nationalist party to the British party system. Scholars have debated the degree of integration the Parnellites enjoyed *vis-à-vis* the other parties. Politicians in 1886 debated the same question, but called it the question of political and constitutional loyalty. John Bright summarized these anxieties in a letter to Sir Henry James. 'We are dealing with rebel party', he wrote. 'If they were friendly and loyal we might easily arrange something, but how can we give or offer anything which a rebel party can accept?'[8] These anxieties prevented Bright and others from understanding the similarities of the Nationalists and the other parliamentary parties. A party with agrarian interests and an agrarian base, the Parnellites, with their essential unity and cohesion, and through a persistent association with political questions beyond those of their region, found a home, one in which they were not always welcome perhaps, but a home none the less, in Westminster.

If internal unity is a characteristic of a modern political party, the Nationalists in 1886 were modern to an impressive degree. They were

---

[4] Hicks Beach to Churchill, 25 Dec. 1885, Lord Randolph Churchill Letters 1/10/1210.

[5] Smith, introduction to *Lord Salisbury on Politics*, p. 95.

[6] Salisbury to Churchill, 9 Dec. 1885, Lord Randolph Churchill Letters 1/10/1157a.

[7] Compare the following studies: Conor Cruise O'Brien, *Parnell and His Party, 1880–1890* (Oxford: 1957); Alan O'Day, *The English Face of Irish Nationalism: Parnellite Involvement in British Politics, 1880–1886* (Dublin: 1977).

[8] Bright to James, 18 Feb. 1886, [Askwith], *Lord James of Hereford*, p. 181.

internally divided on only sixteen of the issues taken to divisions in this House of Commons. What may be even more important, only one of these questions fits the major parliamentary voting dimension. The implication of this cannot be missed. Nationalist disunity was far removed from the centre of political action. It was quite incidental to the main thrust of political behaviour. Moreover, and in this the Irish Nationalists more nearly resembled the Tories than they did the Liberals, the questions which divided them in 1886 cannot be assembled into voting dimensions of any size or character. There was no pattern to Nationalist disunity, therefore; it was random, uncontained by statistical regularities.

The narrowing of recruitment patterns in the party assisted the development of Nationalist unity, and had consequences for nationalism as well. Since 1880 there had been a decline in the numbers of landed gentlemen and other members of the upper classes in the party. This did not result so much from a decline of upper-class elements as it did from an increase in the numbers of men with other social experiences who came into the party as a result of the electoral reforms of 1884-5. Political distinctions were more important than social differences in the Irish Nationalist party in 1886. The most important cleavage was between the old party, those Members elected in 1880 or before, and the new Members. The new men were less connected with the higher sections of society and were less well educated, but they had greater personal experience of Ireland. Twenty of those elected in 1880 or after had residences in their own constituencies, twenty-one had residences in Ireland, and only six had residences in England.[9]

If their political strength did not arise from the skills and qualities of deliberation—articulateness, formal knowledge, and parliamentary experience—other qualities, equally powerful in the shaping of unity and discipline, informed the political intelligence of the new men. The Irish Nationalist party increasingly consisted of those who had lived lives of action and commitment, rather than lives of reflection and deliberation. These were men raised to political consciousness by the Land War. Several had served prison sentences and some (J. F. X. O'Brien, McDonell Sullivan, Matthew Harris— 'the outrage Monger of the West in 1881-1',[10] James Gilhooly) had histories of direct action going back to Fenian times. Kevin Izod O'Doherty, indeed, had participated in the rising of 1848. Rather than being tested at Westminster, these men had their formative

---

[9] O'Brien, *Parnell and His Party*, p. 154.
[10] Harcourt Journal, 21 Jan. 1886, Harcourt dep. 376, f. 110^v.

experience in the work of protest. Such men did not require whips and mechanical discipline to guide their behaviour or to produce unified partisanship in the House of Commons. The commitment to nationalism was sufficient.[11]

Parnell opened the general election campaign in 1885 with the declaration that his party would have only one plank in its platform: legislative independence.[12] This was a self-conscious calculation on his part, a dramatization which has obscured the degree to which the Irish Nationalists were more than a single-issue party whose political interests went beyond Ireland and things Irish. It is a measure of their integration into the British political system that they associated themselves with the left wing of the Liberal party and its political interests. The Parnellite alliance with the Tories in the general election of 1885 had been an aberration. While the Irish might have found the Conservatives approachable on questions of land purchase or education,[13] there it ended. Labouchere, no disinterested observer, believed the rapprochement between the Tories and the Irish was becoming unstuck even before the general election in 1885 went to the poll.[14] In the preliminary fencing between parties over Home Rule before the parliamentary session got under way, Labouchere had attributed a conservative predisposition to the Irish:

The only trace of Radicalism is in their views on land, & this is a sort of Conservatism. The Irish have a [?] desire to manage their own local affairs, and . . . the mass of them—including their leaders, are far more afraid of the Fenians than we are, and would therefore gravitate into conservative—in the real not the party sense—ways.[15]

These remarks, however, were an apology for the Irish. They were addressed to the faint-hearted in the Liberal party in an effort to quell anticipations of Irish disloyalty and to make Home Rule more palatable. Others were aware of the close sympathy which existed between Irish issues and radical questions. The Duke of Argyll, for example, touched on the relationship between the Irish and Scottish land questions. The Irish Land Act, he said, 'had debauched the public mind in these matters . . . and a great deal of agitation brought

---

[11] O'Brien, *Parnell and His Party*, pp. 155–6.

[12] See T. P. O'Connor, *The Parnell Movement, with a Sketch of Irish Parties from 1843* (London: 1886), p. 542.

[13] F. S. L. Lyons, *Charles Stewart Parnell* (London: 1977), pp. 617–18.

[14] Labouchere to Chamberlain, 18 Oct. 1885, Chamberlain Papers JC5/50/28.

[15] Labouchere to Herbert Gladstone, 25 and 18 Dec. 1885, BL Add. MS 46015, ff. 114, 125ᵛ

on in the Highlands had simply been the echo of the Irish Land Act'.[16] Labouchere, when he was not soothing fearful spirits, pointed out the ideological relationship between the Parnellites and the Liberal party. He described a conversation he had with T. P. O'Connor on the way to the railway station:

I said that I supposed it would end in some sort of alliance with the Liberals as the Conservatives could give nothing. He agreed, and said that he himself was a Radical, & that he would do anything in reason.[17]

The Times described the working together of Irish Nationalists and radicals: 'How far English Radicals and Scotch Anti-Establishment Presbyterians are contented to work with such allies and for such objects it is for them to settle with their conscience and their constituents.'[18]

The evidence from the divisions in 1886 confirms these impressions about a Parnellite–radical political alliance. In the first place, counterpoised as they were at different ends of the various ideological dimensions developed from these votes, the Irish Nationalists shared no policy ground with the Conservatives. A majority of the Irish voting in the divisions in 1886 allied themselves with the Tories on only two occasions (in the votes on the international penny post and in the Motion for the Derby Day Adjournment), both of which were trivial in the parliamentary sense because neither fitted the major parliamentary voting dimension in 1886. Second, Irish engagement in voting coalitions with the Liberals is a vastly larger and more complex story. As I have shown elsewhere,[19] and, as I shall show in Chapter 6 at some length, there were two kinds of ideological cleavage in the Liberal party in 1886: left-wing revolts and right-wing revolts. In the former of these, the most numerous, the Irish joined the Liberal extremists against the leaderships and back-bench supporters of both parties. The Irish Nationalists, as a consequence, associated themselves with the policy positions of the left in attacks on foreign policy and the empire, and in efforts to extend the scope of the Crofters Bill. W. S. Blunt, always one to take a deep interest in colonial matters, even though he did not sit in the House, described the combination of radicals and Irish in the debate and division on Egyptian policy. 'I had written to McCarthy & Parnell to get their help & they voted, forty-five of them, [besides?] forty Radicals—not

[16] Hansard, 305: 1485.

[17] Labouchere to Herbert Gladstone, 12 Dec. 1885, BL Add. MS 46015, f. 85.

[18] *The Times*, 10 and 23 Mar. 1886.

[19] W. C. Lubenow, 'Irish Home Rule and the Great Separation in the Liberal Party in 1886: The Dimensions of Parliamentary Liberalism', *Victorian Studies*, 26.2 (1983), pp. 161–80.

a bad division for all things considered.'[20] Gladstone, on the occasion of the division in the House of Commons on Labouchere's motion against the House of Lords, also called attention to the relationship between the Irish Nationalists and radicalism:

Radicalism also derives very great strength from the presence of the Irish members in the House of Commons; so long as they sit there, it is morally certain that they will form a large part of the Radical wing, because of the total oppposition of the Tories to their views. Had the Irish Nationalists been absent from the division on Friday, the minority against the House of Lords would have been small, instead of being large and formidable.[21]

In right-wing revolts, on the other hand, in which Liberal dissidents deserted Gladstone and acted together with Conservatives, the Nationalists supported the Liberal Government and, in so doing, helped sustain Gladstone on questions where the position of his Government in the House might be at risk. Voting of this sort, it needs pointing out, was also of the more radical kind because the left wing of the Liberal party also supported Gladstone in these.

Though W. S. Blunt believed that 'the alliance between the Catholic Irish & the atheistical English Radicals is not a natural one & may be broken at any moment',[22] the voting lists show it to have been pervasive and durable. The proportion of the Irish Nationalist party participating in these voting coalitions was uniformly high and in most cases they voted unanimously. Moreover, as Table 3.6 indicates, the participation of Irish Nationalists was most telling in Liberal left-wing revolts. The Irish MPs constituted a majority of these coalitions in 40 per cent of these occasions. (By way of contrast, the Irish were in a majority in a voting coalition with the Liberal leadership against Liberal right-wing revolts only once, in a small division on a municipal franchise bill for Ireland.) The presence of Irish Nationalists as a majority of the coalition in left-wing revolts occurred principally on Irish questions. In the larger number of left-wing revolts, on the other hand, the Irish made up a minority of the coalition, the majority consisting of English and Scottish radicals. Therefore, the influence of the Irish Nationalists in the House of Commons in 1886 was larger than the Home Rule issue alone. While not dependent upon them, the radicals in the Liberal party and in the House of Commons drew support from the Parnellites. Sometimes this support was decisive.

[20] Blunt Diary, 1 Mar. 1886, Blunt MS 334-1975, f. 63.
[21] Gladstone to the Queen, 8 Mar. 1886; Guedalla, *The Queen and Mr. Gladstone*, vol. 2, pp. 397–8.
[22] Blunt Diary, 10 May 1886, Blunt MS 334-1975, f. 181.

TABLE 3.6 *The Proportion of Irish Nationalists in Coalitions with Liberals**

% of coalition Irish	Coalitions in which Irish Nationalists were allied with Liberal dissidents against the leadership of both Liberal and Conservative parties.		Coalitions in which Irish Nationalists were allied with the Liberals against Conservatives and Liberal dissidents.	
	Divisions		Divisions	
	No.	%	No.	%
91–100	1	1.6		
81–90	2	3.3		
71–80	3	5.0	1	2.8
61–70	9	15.0		
51–60	9	15.0		
41–50	15	25.0	3	8.5
31–40	18	30.0	10	28.5
21–30	2	3.3	11	31.4
11–20	1	1.6	9	25.7
1–10			1	2.8
	60		35	

*To get the largest view of the matter, this table includes all items fitting the major parliamentary voting dimension when the Q threshold is set at .65.

Conclusion

It is useful to consider, by way of summing up, the general question which was posed at the beginning of the chapter: the degree to which parties in the House of Commons in 1886 were ideologically distinct, the extent to which they diverged on policy. Because there was a relationship between parties and issues, clear patterns of partisan behaviour emerged in 1886, and this despite the Home Rule crisis. For this there are three pieces of evidence in the voting lists: high cohesion scores for the Tories and the Irish Nationalists; the existence of straight-party voting on the major parliamentary voting dimensions, and on the policy dimensions concerning political reform and Irish questions; and, especially, the different positions occupied by Liberals and Conservatives on the major parliamentary voting dimension and on the land policy dimension. The correspondence of party affiliation with the positions occupied by Members on these broad policy fronts is especially convincing evidence for the ideological distinctness of parties in 1886. To this there are two exceptions: a pattern of bipartisan voting among Liberals and Conservatives on foreign and imperial policy; and the great separation in the Liberal party over

Irish Home Rule, a question so important that it deserves the separate treatment it will receive below.

This strong pattern of partisanship makes it possible to identify, from the votes of Members, the nature of the political programmes which separated parties. The Tories were more than the party of the Union, though they were that. They were also the party of resistance to the threat they observed in land reform and in further modifications in the electoral system. To their political minds the threats of Home Rule, land reform, and further electoral reform would together undermine and weaken the organic unity of the State and contribute to its disintegration. The Liberals were the party of disestablishment, land and political reform, and they became the party of Home Rule. These were policies calculated to accommodate and incorporate into the political community groups who had been excluded. It was an effort to consolidate the regime by reconciling divergent interests and claims. There is much traditional, even conservative (as Gladstone recognized) in this because it was based upon values of retrenchment and governmental efficiency which had long been present amongst Liberals. Their programme was itself traditional in so far as it made no gestures in the direction of social democracy; the Liberals no more than the Conservatives adopted, or were agreed about, a programme of social reform.

It has not been fully appreciated that the House of Commons in 1886 was a three-party legislature, at least in policy terms. The tactical and strategic significance of a Liberal–Irish Nationalist alliance, for purposes of Home Rule, have always been recognized. The Irish could not gain legislative independence without the suppport or co-operation of one of the major parties. The Irish Nationalist agenda, as their votes show, was larger than nationalism. They also supported the radical programme: disestablishment, land reform, further political reform. With some qualifications which are noted above, they supported criticisms of the empire and an extensive foreign policy. Moreover, they supported social legislation more regularly than either of the major parties. Support for policies of this sort leavened the loaf of radicalism, advanced it, and gave it strength.

These patterns of partisanship differed in character. The Conservative and Irish Nationalist parties were consensus parties whose internal unity emerged from different impulses. For the Tories, unity developed around considerations of government and empire. They wished to restrain popular passion, and they wished to prevent dismemberment. Indeed, Salisbury's party found its *raison d'être* in a union of strategy and policy in which power for the Conservative party became coincident with the unity of the empire. Parnell's party, of course, never had government as its concern, and its consensus, therefore, developed from the force of nationalism and the policies of radicalism with which nationalism readily associated itself.

The Liberals, despite the considerations of government, were a coalition party. Without the deference at work in the Conservative party, the Liberals were allied, albeit with considerable fragility, around several policies and ideological positions. This, however, was no random matter. As the positions of Liberals on the various parliamentary voting dimensions in 1886 show, they held various ideological positions, but those positions tended, with the exception of foreign and imperial policy, consistently toward the left. This was ideological unity of a special sort. It was not unity on a single policy, or on a single ideological position. The holding of various policy positions and the internal disagreement this reflects often appears to be a species of political pathology, or so the twentieth-century pattern makes it appear. But this is not necessarily the case, and it was not the case in the Liberal party in 1886. Neither crisis nor the constitutional obligation to protect a parliamentary majority produced cohesion in the Liberal party. Nor need it have done, because not all policy differences in the Liberal party posed a threat to its essential unity. Once Gladstone realized that there was no hope for a Nationalist–Tory alliance of convenience, he could form a Government in the certain hope that when the Irish failed to take his position, the position they would take would be consistently on his left, where they could be trusted. In fact, it could be argued that without the Irish a Liberal Government would have enjoyed the support of a Liberal party with fewer policy differences because it would have been a minimum winning coalition in which the support for the Government would have rested upon a smaller majority. The alliance of the Irish and the Liberals in 1886 makes it possible to speak of a consistent anti-Conservative coalition in 1886. It failed to keep a Liberal Government in power only because it lost the support of those Liberals for whom the basis of the Liberal–Irish Nationalist alliance, Home Rule, was intolerable.

The force for partisanship in the 1886 House of Commons often emerged from the back benches. The absence of whips serving as tellers in straight-party votes and the extensive degree to which straight-party votes occurred on issues arising from the back-benchers rather than from the leaders are good reasons for believing that an informal and spontaneous basis formed partisan ideology in 1886. In fact, it can be argued that the direction of partisan unity was upward, from the rank and file, while the direction for dissent and fission was downward, from the high political and parliamentary élites. This was the case when the Irish Nationalists split over the O'Shea divorce case in 1890–1. A personal crisis led to squabbling among the Nationalist leadership which they thrust down to the electors. This was also the case concerning Home Rule in the Liberal party, a point which Gladstone recognized. 'While we have this big Irish business on hand', he wrote, 'no other important issue of disturbing character should be raised. Many tactical lessons are to be learned from Peel's conduct, and I recollect that in 1846, with the repeal of the Corn Law in view, he went to very great lengths indeed, perhaps even too great, in order to avoid side issues.'[23] As a later chapter will show, side issues, other issues of a 'disturbing character', those driving and motivating the back benches, did not disrupt the Liberal party. The party was split by the issue Gladstone himself introduced, the Government of Ireland Bill. In the relationship between partisanship and issues, parties served as institutions mediating between independent political behaviour and previous experience. Partisanship shaped action and political behaviour at the Palace of Westminster.

[23] Gladstone to Lord Rosebery, 28 Apr. 1886, in Paul Knaplund, *Gladstone's Foreign Policy* (New York: 1935; London: 1970), p. 249.

4

The Social Basis of Politics in the House of Commons

We have some half dozen more than formerly of what are called 'labour candidates'. We have fewer squires on the other hand. Still we have a goodly proportion of the titled classes. Science, learning, and professional experience are well represented.

Sir Richard Temple, Bt.[1]

When I first entered the House of Commons it was rather a different place from what it was when I left it. In the former epoch, 1884, a very large proportion of the House still consisted of country gentlemen and the larger manufacturers and merchants. There were only two working men, Burt and Broadhurst. Another two were, however, soon added in the shape of Arch and Crawford—the latter a miners' representative. There were not many journalists, if indeed any. The country gentlemen and the large manufacturers and merchants have now greatly decreased in number. During the last Parliament in which I sat, 1906-1910, there were a large number of journalists and of working men, and I should think, from observation, a very much larger proportion of members of the House on both sides had their election expenses paid for them by party or other funds than was the case when I first entered the House.

James Stuart[2]

Introduction

Temple and Stuart were not the only observers of the social composition of Parliament, nor were they the only observers of larger patterns of social change. For Lady Dorothy Nevill, 'society'—'a somewhat exclusive body of people, all of them distinguished either for their rank, their intellect, or their wit'—was something forever gone.[3] Lady Battersea, the wife of Cyril Flower, who served as a Liberal whip in the House of Commons in 1886, and the daughter of Sir Anthony de Rothschild, Bt., described the 'new and difficult phase' into which the Home Rule crisis plunged London society.[4] These observers, of society at large as well as parliamentary society,

[1] Temple Letters, 28 June 1886, BL Add. MS 38916, f. 165-165^v. Temple here described the composition of the House of Commons which had just risen.
[2] Stuart, *Reminiscences*, pp. 238-9.
[3] Ralph Nevill (ed.), *The Reminiscences of Lady Dorothy Nevill* (London: 1906), p. 99.
[4] Lady Battersea, *Reminiscences* (London: 1923), pp. 193-4.

163

were interested in more than observation. They were interested in understanding this society, and they regarded social change and changes in recruitment to the House of Commons as clues to changes in public policy.

'Dukes do not emigrate' and 'old sergeants do not mutiny' are only two common aphorisms indicating a relationship between social position and political behaviour. Yet efforts to examine connections of this sort have not always proved gratifying. Detailed research has frequently failed to square with what scholars anticipated; and the regularities of public life often defy commonly accepted assumptions. Studies of the social basis of political behaviour in the American Confederate Congress, in the French Chamber of Deputies, in the Corn Laws Parliament, amongst British radicals and French peasants, and in American anarchist–feminist circles at the end of the nineteenth century have produced negative or inconclusive results. A comparative study of British, French, and German legislatures in the 1840s has shown little relationship between the social background of legislators and their political behaviour. A study of British electoral behaviour in the 1880s and 1890s reveals little of interpretative value in social class or social conflict theories.[5] However, the problem of the social basis of parliamentary politics deserves another examination, because theories concerning the social origins of political behaviour enjoy continued vitality, and because many of the great events of modern British politics, especially the Home Rule crisis, are cast in class terms.

It is easy to understand why this should be because, according to some of the most consoling beliefs in the study of Western politics, political groups are expressions of social stratification. Lipset described partisan conflict as a 'democratic translation of the class struggle'.[6] Key regarded changes in the party system as the result of 'changes in the relative size, number, and relations of the underlying

[5] Alexander and Beringer, *The Confederate Congress*, ch. 4; Patrick L.-R. Higonnet and Trevor B. Higonnet, 'Class, Corruption, and Politics in the French Chamber of Deputies, 1846–1848', *French Historical Studies*, 5.2 (Fall 1967), pp. 212 ff; W. O. Aydelotte, 'The Country Gentlemen and the Repeal of the Corn Laws', *English Historical Review*, 82 (Jan. 1967), pp. 47–60; E. Le Roy Ladurie, *Montaillou: The Promised Land of Error*, tr. Barbara Bray (New York: 1978); M. S. Marsh, *Anarchist Women, 1870–1920* (Philadelphia: 1981); Heinrich Best, 'Biography and Political Behavior: Determinants of Parliamentary Decision-making in Germany, France, and Great Britain in the Nineteenth Century' (Social Science History Convention, 1983), pp. 11–13, 22–4; Wald, *Crosses on the Ballot*, ch. 1, 2, 5, 6.

[6] Seymour Martin Lipset, *Political Man* (New York: 1963), p. 230, and *Revolution and Counterrevolution: Change and Persistence in Social Structures*, revised and updated edn. (Garden City, New York: 1974), ch. 5.

social interests'.[7] For Pulzer, 'class is the basis of British party politics; all else is embellishment and detail.'[8] Authorities such as these step high, wide, and handsome; but, of course they can afford to. Experienced and thoughtful, their research has made an enormous contribution to our understanding of modern politics. They have given great ideas with which to work.

Social conflict interpretations of politics got a good deal of play in the late nineteenth century, and such ideas arose with some force during the debates in the House of Commons in 1886. Alfred Illingworth supported Richard's Motion requiring parliamentary consultation in foreign and imperial affairs using such an argument. 'The Democracy was not in favour of a war system', Illingworth said. 'War had been the pastime of the governing classes, but the masses of people have been the sufferers.'[9] William Rathbone challenged the power of the landed classes in the debates on Thorold Rogers's motion on the incidence of local taxation.[10] And Arthur O'Connor, in addressing the House on the Scottish Returning Officers Charges Bill, criticized the Tory benches because they represented the 'old history of the House of Commons, when it was a preserve of the monied and privileged classes'.[11] Other examples could be added, and the manuscript evidence for the period contains continuing and ever-present references to the ways in which highly intelligent men allowed their anxieties about society to stimulate their political thinking. W. S. Blunt reduced the Irish Home Rule question to a mechanical social and economic interpretation. 'There is nothing real at the back of it except the Landlord interests of a few aristocratic Whigs & Tories & speculators who have money in Ireland on mortgages.' 'Met Lady Egmont at Mr Evelyn's, a strong "Loyalist"; her husband having property in Ireland.'[12]

Neither Conservative nor Liberal had a monopoly on social conflict interpretations of politics in the 1880s. Before this parliamentary session got under way, when Churchill proposed procedural reforms for the House of Commons, Salisbury wrote to him, 'someday clôture no doubt may be harmless, but it will not be till the present class-struggle has been fought out.'[13] After the Home Rule crisis, on the

---

[7] V. O. Key, *Politics, Parties, and Pressure Groups*, 5th edn. (New York: 1964), p. 167.

[8] P. G. J. Pulzer, *Political Representation and Elections: Parties and Voting in Great Britain* (New York: 1975), p. 102.　　　[9] Hansard, 303: 1418.

[10] Ibid., 303: 1661.　　　　　　　　　　　　　[11] Ibid., 306: 1647–8.

[12] Blunt Diary, 25 Jan. and 20 Feb. 1886, Blunt MS 334-1975, ff. 31, 56.

[13] Salisbury to Churchill, 4 Jan. 1886, Lord Randolph Churchill Letters 1/12/1241b.

occasion in which Lord Randolph Churchill was preparing the ground for his own demise from ministerial politics, Salisbury wrote a famous letter in which he said: 'I think the "classes and dependants of class" are the strongest ingredients in our composition.'[14] W. T. Ashton, describing class conflict, wrote to Lord Cranborne, 'I regret to say that I have noticed for some time back a growing hatred of landowners as a class, irrespective of their personal merits, and a sort of indefinite idea that if they support Mr Gladstone he will in some way give them something for nothing.'[15]

On the Liberal side of the situation, Gladstone himself had drawn the Home Rule struggle along class lines, using phrases Salisbury would quote. In 1886, in May, Gladstone wrote to his Midlothian electors:

On the side adverse to the Government are found as I sorrowfully admit, in profuse abundance station, title, wealth, social influence, the professions, or a majority of them—in a word, the spirit and power of Class. These are the main body of the opposing host. Nor is this all. As knights of old had squires, so in the great army of Class each enrolled soldier has, as a rule, dependants. The adverse host then, consists of Class and the dependants of Class.[16]

Sir Thomas Dyke Acland, Bt. used class arguments in his complaints about Collings's 'three acres and a cow' Amendment and the appointments of Chamberlain and Collings to the Local Government Board in the early months of 1886. He called this 'the heaviest blow dealt to our country gentlemen and others who honestly do their local duties'. In July he wrote again, this time attributing the Liberal defeat in the general election to 'fear (and also jealousy) of you among the property and culture classes'.[17] The Earl of Southesk[18] had long suspected Gladstone's policies, and viewed Liberal legislation as a horror and as a threat to all forms of property.[19] Southesk did not bolt from the Liberal party during the Home Rule crisis, but he did so shortly thereafter. The Duke of Argyll's objections to Gladstone's policies amounted to more than

---

[14] Salisbury to Churchill, 9 Nov. 1886, Lord Randolph Churchill Letters 1/14/1991.

[15] Ashton to Cranborne, 28 June 1886, Fourth Marquess of Salisbury MSS Bundle 1.

[16] W. E. Gladstone, *Speeches on the Irish Question in 1886* (Edinburgh: 1886), p. 176.

[17] Acland to Gladstone, 10 Feb. and 15 July 1886, *Memoirs and Letters of the Right Honourable Sir Thomas Dyke Acland, Bart.*, pp. 358, 360.

[18] C.G.E. ed., *Complete Peerage*, (London: 1910–59), vol. 12, p. 147.

[19] Southesk to Gladstone, 24 and 30 Oct. 1885, BL Add. MS 44492, ff. 230–1.

class interest,[20] but the Marquess of Lorne, Argyll's eldest son, warned the Liberal leader of the Duke's inclination to support the Conservatives 'as is natural when he sees such numbers voting for confiscatory land Reformers in the "illiterate" Counties in the Highlands'.[21]

And so it goes. Many other examples of this sort can be put forward to demonstrate a social conflict theory of politics. The problem, of course, is that examples can be found to support the other side of the argument. Members of the same family, presumably having similar social experiences, should, according to a social interpretation of politics, be delivered of similar views. However, when one examines families participating in the events of 1886 there is reason to stop and pause. Of the Gladstone brothers, Thomas remained a Conservative, while William moved to an increasingly radical position, all the time retaining a confidence in aristocratic values. Their brother Robertson, the president of the Financial Reform Association, held the landed interest to be hostile to the economy.[22] The Harcourt brothers, Sir William and Edward, sat in this House of Commons, one as a Liberal and the other as a Conservative. Sir Michael Bass and his brother Hamar, of the brewing family, sat as Liberals, but Sir Michael supported Gladstone's Home Rule policies and Hamar, who abstained on the Home Rule vote, stood as a Liberal Unionist in the general election of 1886. John Bright became a Liberal Unionist while his son, William Leatham Bright, remained loyal to Gladstone. The Howard brothers— Edward of Thornbury and Henry of Greystoke Castle—found themselves also divided by the Home Rule question. Edward Hamilton observed the sons of peers voting with Labouchere, contrary to their apparent social interest, in his Resolution against the House of Lords.[23]

This recitation of quotation and counter-quotation only serves to illustrate that an argument for each side of the case can be mustered by telling examples. Not much would be gained by such an exercise, however, and, following such a line, this chapter could be ended here. The discussion of the vexing relationship between social background and political behaviour, however, might be advanced

---

[20] Argyll to Gladstone, 2, 16, 24 Oct., 6 and 9 Nov., 9 Dec. [1885?]; 29 Jan. and 19 Apr. 1886, BL Add. MS 44106, ff. 11–16, 17–21, 22–9, 30–1, 38–44, 64–74, 79–84, 85–8, 89–93.

[21] Lorne to Gladstone, 9 Dec. 1885, BL Add. MS 44493, ff. 194–5.

[22] S. E. Checkland, *The Gladstones: A Family Biography, 1764–1851* (Cambridge: 1971), pp. 376–7.

[23] Edward Hamilton Diary, 7 Mar. 1886, BL Add. MS 48643, f. 34.

by comparing the detailed politics of the squires, the men of business, and the professions in the House of Commons with the evidence which can be assembled about their social background. Addressed in this manner, the problem has a number of interesting features. One of these is the matter of social mobility and political recruitment, changes in the social composition of the House of Commons and in the parties holding their seats there. Another has to do with the interrelationships among social groups, the degree to which it is possible to describe lines of clear social cleavage for the late nineteenth century. A third concerns the social composition of the parties, whether or not social background had anything at all to do with the partisan preferences of Members. Finally, it is important to consider whether or not the voting of Members was affected by their social background, whether or not political differences within parties had a relationship to social differences within parties. The most important of these last, of course, is the great separation in the Liberal party during the Irish Home Rule crisis.

A number of things may be said about these perplexing and stimulating matters. In the first place, social differences continued to be important, and one can discover in the social background of the Members of this House of Commons that ancient distinction between gentlemen and non-gentlemen. Second, there was a slight relationship between political preference and social background, but parties and factions in 1886 were not socially homogeneous. A relationship can be discerned between social background and the votes of Members, as described by their positions on voting dimensions, for the whole House and for the Liberal party. This gives more plausibility to the old notion that politics was polarized on social lines, especially after the Home Rule disruption in the Liberal party. However, social differences within the parties rarely communicated themselves to differences in particular divisions, and this is especially true of the Home Rule split. When one examines the Home Rule division closely, and most of the other divisions in this session as well, there is little relationship between the votes of Members and their social positions. The only exceptions to this are those occasions when the party system broke down: that is to say, when it failed to produce the policy preferences of parliamentary rank and file. In these cases political action produced class conflict; class conflict did not produce political action.

The Social Composition of the House of Commons

Table 4.1 shows the history of changes of the social composition of the House of Commons in the nineteenth century. The general

TABLE 4.1 *The Social Composition of the House of Commons in Three Nineteenth-Century Parliaments**

	1841–7		1874–80		1886	
	No.	%	No.	%	No.	%
The landed classes:						
Irish peers, sons, and grandsons of peers	205	25	134	17	71	10
Baronets, their sons or grandsons	137	17	108	14	78	11
Landed gentry, their sons or grandsons	248	30	204	26	106	16
Land connected[†]	—	—	80	10	—	—
Related to the PBG[‡] through the maternal line or marriage	68	8	—	—	52	8
Total PBG	658	81	526	66	307	45
Non-PBG	157	19	270	34	373	55
Professional men:						
All professional men			295	37	352	52
Law	145	18	124	16	181	27
Army officers	126	15	111	14	70	10
Naval officers	37	5	18	2	10	1
Business men:						
All business men	—	—	—	—	.289	43
Active and substantial business men only	139	17	188	24	224	33
Bankers	70	9	24	3	38	6
Manufacturers	49	6	50	6	91	13
Merchants	63	8	76	10	65	10
Railway Directors	144	18	7	1	75	11
Brewers	8	1	14	2	21	3
Working class	—	—	—	—	14	2

*The percentages in this table are calculated on the basis of the total number of Members in each House, which was 815 for the period 1841–7, 796 for the period 1847–80, and 680 for 1886.
†This is a residual category for the period 1874–80, consisting of Members whose wives and mothers were connected to the peerage–baronetage–landed gentry, or who are listed in Bateman's *Great Landowners*.
‡Peerage–baronetage–landed gentry.

features of this are clear. The House of Commons changed, with fewer landed gentlemen, more professional men, more businessmen, and a few working-class Members where before there had been none. All groups of landed gentlemen—peerage, baronetage, landed gentry—declined in their absolute numbers, and for the first time less than half the House consisted of landed gentlemen. The number of Members with professions increased, but this enlargement occurred with respect to the numbers of lawyers and men of the new professions, such as journalists. The number of army and navy officers — those of the more traditional professions — declined. The number of active and substantial business men increased as well, but not as sharply as one might have expected, and James Bryce called attention to the fact that 'men of commerce have not been able to sit in the House'.[24] In some business sectors the numbers of MPs in fact declined — for example, banking, railway directors. In some there was little change — merchants. In others were found the increases — manufacturers, brewers. Perhaps what is more striking about these data is the suddenness of the changes they express. After remaining stable for a very long period of time, the social composition of the House of Commons was altered in the 1880s.

These groups, of course, were not mutually exclusive. Indeed, this is one of the most interesting features of the evidence, and sheds light on a cardinal aspect of Victorian society. Social groups had interpenetrated each other and became highly interdependent. Evidence of this sort makes it extremely difficult to generalize about modern British politics as a conflict between different social élites. In fact, social penetration moved in a number of different directions simultaneously. Because they had connections with the business and professional worlds, landed gentlemen in the House of Commons cannot be regarded as backwoodsmen. For their part, professional men and business men introduced themselves into a world of landed society. Though their numbers have sometimes been exaggerated, some were welcomed.[25] In the 1840s approximately 10 per cent of the landed gentlemen in the House of Commons had business connections of a significant sort, and a total of 24 per cent were either business men or lawyers.[26] By way of comparison, 20 per cent of the landed gentlemen in the House of Commons of 1886 had active and substantial business interests, and 55 per cent held professions. The worlds of land, business, and the professions were not mutually

[24] Bryce to Gladstone, 12 Mar. 1886, BL Add. MS 56447, unbound and unfoliated.

[25] The family histories of the Peels, the Gladstones, the Whitbreads, and others testify to this well-known point. See Ralph Pumphrey, 'The Introduction of Industrialists into the British Peerage: A Study in Adaptation of a Social Institution', *American Historical Review*, 65.1 (Oct. 1959). For a sharply differing view, however, see Lawrence Stone and Jeanne C. Fawtier Stone, *An Open Elite? England 1540–1880* (Oxford: 1984).

[26] W. O. Aydelotte, 'The Business Interests of the Gentry in the Parliament of 1841–1847', appendix to George Kitson Clark, *The Making of Victorian England* (London: 1962), pp. 300, 302.

TABLE 4.2 *The Interpenetration of Land, Business, and the Professions in the House of Commons in 1886*

	Active and substantial business men (224)		Professional men (352)	
	No.	%	No.	%
Peerage (71)	1	1	45	63
Baronetage (78)	19	24	36	47
Landed gentry (106)	26	25	52	49
PBG through the maternal line and marriage (52)	16	31	35	67
Total PBG (307)	62	20	168	55
Not PBG (373)	162	43	184	49

exclusive. In consulting the Third Duke of Buckingham and Chandos about a chairman for the Aylesbury and Buckingham Railway, Sir Harry Verney, Bt. observed: 'the shareholders were quite contented as long as you occupied that position. They knew their property was as safe, and *as improving*, as circumstances permitted.'[27] Here were landed gentlemen who were as much committed to the values of an industrializing society as they were to those of land. Social values, like social groups, were not mutually exclusive; so much for sharp distinctions between traditional and modernizing élites.

The complexities of social interpenetration can be readily illustrated. Aretas Akers-Douglas, the Conservative whip, was deeply entrenched in landed society. He owned nearly 16,000 acres. He had been educated at Eton and University College, Oxford, and held a commission in the county yeomanry. He also held the patronage of a Church living. The family, as Burke's *Landed Gentry* indicates, originated in Lancashire and established themselves in the West Indies.[28] Akers-Douglas himself was a barrister, and held the directorship of four companies. Cyril Flower was connected to the landed classes through marriage to the Rothschilds. A merchant and barrister, he had additional associations with landed society by virtue of his education at Harrow and at Trinity College, Cambridge, and in his capacity as a lieutenant in the Bucks. yeomanry. Charles Edward Howard Vincent was the younger son of a baronet whose title dated from 1620. Vincent had the education, at Westminster, and the

[27] Sir Harry Verney, Bt., to the Third Duke of Buckingham and Chandos, 1 Dec. 1874, Huntington Library and Art Gallery, Stowe Collection, Grenville Correspondence Box 412 (57).

[28] Sir Bernard Burke, *A Genealogical and Heraldic History of the Landed Gentry of Great Britain and Ireland*, 7th edn. (London: 1886), vol. 1, p. 12.

associations, as a captain in the Royal Berkshire militia, of a landed gentleman. He was also a barrister; he had a distinguished military career; he reorganized the Criminal Investigation Division of Scotland Yard. Complex sets of social experiences, such as these, illustrate the nightmares of social taxonomy and the realities of social life in the House of Commons.

If some landed gentlemen in the House of Commons were bourgeois, so also some professional and business men were landed. In fact, of these Members, 28 per cent of the business men and 48 per cent of those holding professions were landed gentlemen by the definitions used here. Beyond this, some bourgeois Members, to a surprising degree, had social experiences associated with the life of land: public school educations, mothers belonging to the peerage–baronetage–landed gentry, wives with those relationships, or the possession of extensive landed territories. Better than one-third of the professional men in this House of Commons had public school educations. Nearly half of the business men sitting here held county offices. Better than a quarter of the professional men married women with connections to landed society, and themselves belonged to families possessing lands in excess of 3,000 acres.

The numerical decline of landed gentlemen in the House of Commons of 1886, the slight increase of business men, the larger increase of professional men there, and the interpenetration of landed, business, and professional worlds might lead to the tempting conclusion that social distinctions meant little, or at least less than before, at Westminster in the 1880s; that an age of egalitarianism had entered parliamentary politics; that there was little relationship between social and political behaviour in nineteenth-century politics because social class failed to mean anything. Taxonomic and conceptual nettles trouble the analysis of social distinctions, and these have long been known. When Trollope's Duke of Omnium explained the concept to his daughter, he said that the word 'gentleman' was 'too vague to carry with it any meaning as to what ought to be serviceable to you in thinking of such a matter'.[29] Bertrand Russell, who succeeded to the Russell earldom, regarded the concept of landed gentility as an aristocratic contrivance to keep the middle classes in line.[30] Despite the problems these statements suggest, the values of landed society, with the distinctions they implied, as Lord Annan has indicated, remained one of the age's convictions.[31]

[29] Anthony Trollope, *The Duke's Children* (Oxford: 1973), p. 67.
[30] Alan Brien, *The Sunday Times*, 1 Aug. 1977.
[31] Noel Annan, 'Victorian Swish', *New York Review of Books*, 19 July 1979, p. 16.

The sudden decline of the landed classes in the House of Commons, the elevated percentages of business men and professional men there, and the interpenetration of genteel and vulgar worlds might be advanced as evidence to explain the reduction of social conflict and the growth of homogeneity in the ruling élite: a demonstration of the theory of an open élite. Social transformation of these sorts may have facilitated peaceful change, but that change produced no easy social uniformity. It created, in fact, a system much more divided and complex than had existed before. In such an environment gentility became more, not less, important. Increased upward mobility produced growing social arguments about status, and it broadened notions of gentility. The landed élite, and its values was resurgent in the 1880s, and one scholar has talked about the 'counterrevolution' of gentry values.[32] The concept of the gentleman, after all, is peculiarly English (Taine said that the French did not have the word because they did not have the thing). The Baron Henry de Worms, the Conservative Member for the East Toxteth division of Liverpool, is not included in the company of landed gentlemen in this study, and for good reason: he had a foreign name as well as a foreign title. Arthur Forwood wanted him to change his name, and he wanted Lord Salisbury to elevate de Worms to the Privy Council to make him more English, and, in consequence, to make him more useful to the Conservative party.[33] W. S. Blunt described a dinner at Brooks's Club which was attended by Henry Brand, Lord Richard Grosvenor, Courtney Boyle, and George Christopher Trout Bartley, the newly elected Member for the Northern division of Islington and the only Conservative in the company. But Bartley's problems included his status as well as his politics. As Blunt put it, 'he is a vulgar fellow & seemed not quite at ease in the company of gentlemen.'[34]

The power of gentry values can be illustrated in another way, by the manner in which newcomers were taken into the political élite. Of these, none was more prominent than Joseph Chamberlain. During the general election of 1885, Chamberlain sought to force Hartington's hand and gain acceptance of his programme by threatening to form a separate Radical party in the House of Commons. Gladstone, in a letter to Lord Richard Grosvenor, criticized Chamberlain's tactics on a number of points: it 'was putting a pistol to the head of the

---

[32] Martin Wiener, *English Culture and the Decline of the Industrial Spirit, 1850–1980* (Cambridge: 1981), pp. 27–41.
[33] Forwood to Salisbury, 9 Sept. 1885, Third Marquess of Salisbury MSS Class E.
[34] Blunt Diary, 30 Dec. 1885, Blunt MS 333-1975, ff. 227–8.

man with whom he is in negotiation'; it was 'not a usual nor a convenient form of negotiating'. Fundamentally, Gladstone came down on Chamberlain's incapacity to act like a gentleman. Chamberlain's tactics would take 'all credit and dignity from any arrangement made', and, Gladstone concluded, 'it is only a question of manner'.[35] Chamberlain's colleagues in the Cabinet bitterly faulted his 'cleverness', his 'stirring up of the mob', and, above all, his failure to 'observe the traditions of the House'. He was not a patriot and he was not a gentleman.[36] Arthur Balfour objected to Chamberlain's 'voice and manner', and for Alfred Austin, later to become the poet laureate, Chamberlain lacked tact, wide culture, fine breeding, breadth of view, and the sympathy with all classes which was important in great public leaders. For Edward Hamilton, Chamberlain 'was not born, bred, or educated in the ways which *alone secure* the tact and behaviour of a real gentleman'.[37] Reginald Brett was equally damning: 'Chamberlain's faults all come from his upbringing. Clever as he is, he has never learnt the self-restraint which everyone learns at a great public school or at a university. I mean everyone with his immense capacity.'[38] In these attitudes toward Chamberlain there is revealed a complex pattern of assumptions associating ideals of status with notions of public service.

The persistence of landed values in the late nineteenth century may be seen in the strong arguments for status and position found in various criticisms offered against popular genealogy and the growing Burke enterprises.[39] Landed gentlemen such as Walter Long, who sat in this House as the Conservative Member for the Devizes division of Wiltshire, held Burke in contempt for slights committed against their families. 'Burke', Long wrote scornfully, 'the great autocrat in questions of genealogy and the authority and kindly framer of our pedigrees, declines to admit my descent from the original Longs of Wiltshire. But I am content to rely upon an abundance of local

---

[35] Gladstone to Grosvenor, 3 Nov. 1885, Chamberlain Papers JC5/37/4.

[36] Diary of Lady Dorothy Stanley, 14 Dec. 1885, Chamberlain Papers JC8/2/2.

[37] Lady Frances Balfour, *Ne Obliviscaris, Dinna Forget* (London: 1930), vol. 2, p. 332; Edward Hamilton Diary, 3 Dec. 1899, Sir Edward Hamilton Papers, BL Add. MSS 46875, quoted in Robert V. Kubicek, *The Administration of Imperialism: Joseph Chamberlain at the Colonial Office* (Durham, NC: 1969), p. 4; Alfred Austin, *'Skeletons at the Feast,' or the Radical Program* (London: 1885), p. 4.

[38] Esher to Maurice V. Brett, 21 Nov. 1901, *Journals and Letters of Reginald Brett*, vol. 1, p. 319.

[39] George Burnett, *Popular Genealogists, or The Art of Pedigree Making* (Edinburgh: 1865); Edward A. Freeman, 'Pedigree and Pedigree-makers', *Contemporary Review*, 30 (June 1877), pp. 11–44; J. Horace Round, *Peerage and Pedigree: Studies in Peerage Law and Family History* (Westminster: 1901).

evidence which is forthcoming.'[40] Other landed families sought to bolster their genealogical position through direct negotiations with the heraldic authorities. George Manners Morgan, the representative of a gentry family with seats in Carmarthenshire and Buckinghamshire, appealed first for a baronetage and then attempted to establish a more extensive pedigree when his son, the husband of the daughter of the Third Duke of Buckingham and Chandos, sought a licence to assume the surname and the arms of the Grenvilles.[41]

That gentry values continued to intrude themselves on politics can be shown by the importance politicians attached to matters of status in electioneering, and by the continued attachment of signs of dignity and status to the conferring of honours for political service. His political agents wanted Lord Salisbury to become a vice-president of a working-class borough Conservative Registration Association because 'gentlemen of position and title' had an effect upon political loyalties.[42] Lord Randolph Churchill arranged to have Viscounts Lewisham and Folkstone (respectively the heirs of the Earls of Dartmouth and Radnor) appear at a Camberwell meeting in support of W. S. Blunt. 'Which is satisfactory', Blunt wrote, 'as the working men insist upon having a Lord. "No M.P.s for us", they say, and two Lords ought to carry all before them.'[43] And status remained important even after MPs went to Westminster. As one observer remarked, 'with Liberals only less exclusively than with the Conservative party, it has, from time immemorial, been the custom to appoint as Chief Whip a scion of the peerage, or a commoner sanctified by connection with an old county family.'[44]

The association of gentry values with political service, public and electoral, which had been characteristic of nominations for honours in the mid-nineteenth century[45] continued in the 1880s. And this

[40] Walter Long, *Memories of the Right Honourable Viscount Long of Wraxall* (London: 1923), p. 1.

[41] George Manners Morgan to the Third Duke of Buckingham and Chandos, 28 Jan. 1868; Sir John Bernard Burke to Manners Morgan, 18 Mar. 1887; Sir Henry Farnham Burke to Manners Morgan, 5 Dec. 1890, 10 Jan. and 21 Jan., 14 Apr., and 17 June 1891, 21 Jan., 19 Feb., and 6 May 1892; Huntington Library and Art Gallery, Stowe Collection, Grenville Correspondence Box 125 (64), Manners Morgan Correspondence Box 209 (44), (33), (38), (35), (40), (41), (43), (37).

[42] The Battersea Conservative Registration Association to Salisbury, 29 July 1885, Third Marquess of Salisbury MSS Class E.

[43] Blunt Diary, 4 Aug. 1885, Blunt MS 333-1975, f. 104.

[44] Henry W. Lucy, *Later Peeps at Parliament from Behind the Speaker's Chair* (London: 1905), p. 275.

[45] H. J. Hanham, 'The Sale of Honours in Late Victorian England', *Victorian Studies*, 3 (1959-60), pp. 277-88. Professor Barry McGill, more recently, set himself

was true for both Liberal as well as Conservative Governments. When Lord Dalhousie, in 1886, recommended John Glencairn Carter Hamilton, the Member for the Southern division of Lanarkshire, for a peerage, he summarized these various qualities:

Mr. John Hamilton of Dalzell seems to me to be a fit subject for a peerage. It would be hard to find a more deserving case, I think. He has been 22 years in the House of Commons out of the last 27 years. He has fought four contested elections at his own expense entirely, and they were all of them expensive contests. . . . At the last election he lost his seat by 18 votes. He has always voted straight. He is a man of high and honourable character, wealthy, and of a very old family. He has always been very public spirited and unselfish in his political conduct, and ever ready and glad to sacrifice his own interests for the good of the party — a most loyal and chivalrous fellow. He has, besides, dignity and good manners.[46]

Political service to party and country were by themselves insufficient. To these were added wealth, old family, honour, character, dignity, and manners. This happy combination of public, social, and personal virtues is reflected in other correspondence concerning honours for Liberals in 1886.

On the Conservative side, Lord Salisbury was no more, or less, concerned with the application of appropriate social values in the granting of honours. As Lord Carnarvon remarked, 'Salisbury is so extremely chary of giving away honours that I know it is vain to ask for any.' Carnarvon regarded this as 'a very odd mental phenomenon in a man who I should have thought would not have cared a pin's head about such matters'.[47] This annoyed some Tories who wished to use the granting of honours as a more aggressive method for developing support for the party. As a correspondent in Wales put it to Captain Richard Middleton, Pennant and Pryce Jones are 'the life & soul of the Conservative cause' and 'it would

---

to this story and concludes that political service, which was by itself a kind of partisan contribution involving expenditures more than outright cash payment, was involved in awards of honours. See 'Glittering Prizes and Party Funds in Perspective, 1882–1931', *The Bulletin of the Institute for Historical Research*, 50.131 (May 1982), pp. 88–93. Such a position is not inconsistent with the examples cited here as well as with the correspondence on a peerage for Sir Michael Bass, Bt., and baronetages for Frederick Thorpe Mappin, Leonard Lyell (the nephew of the great geologist), and the baronetage claim made by Charles Hunter. For these last examples, see Harcourt to Gladstone, Dalhousie to Gladstone, 19 July 1886, and Hunter to Gladstone, 27 Feb. 1886, BL Add. MSS 44200, ff. 141–6, 44498, ff. 233–6, 44495, ff. 71–4.

[46] Dalhousie to Gladstone, 21 July 1886, BL Add. MS 44498, ff. 249–50.
[47] Carnarvon to Lord Harrowby, 7 Nov. 1885, BL Add. MS 60863, unbound and unfoliated.

cheer us all very much in our work' if they were honoured.[48] Ellis
Ashmead Bartlett appealed to Salisbury to grant a baronetcy to a
journalist who had published criticisms of the radical programme.
Salisbury refused. 'An innovation of this kind is sure to be watched
with the utmost jealousy, & I think on the whole it would have
created more discontent than would be the result of an opposite
course of conduct.'[49] On the other hand, Sir John Kennaway, Bt.
approached Salisbury in another spirit on behalf of Mark Stewart,
the Member for Kirkcudbrightshire who had invested great effort
in helping Sir Herbert Maxwell win Wigtownshire. Scottish seats
were important to the Tories. 'I would also ask you to remember
the great services Mark Stewart has rendered', Kennaway wrote. 'He
is a rich man and heir to large estates in Wigtownshire and would
be a worthy addition to the order of the baronets.'[50]

In November, 1885 William Beckett Denison wrote to Lord
Salisbury on behalf of his brother Sir Edmund Beckett, Bt. to
advance a peerage claim which Disraeli had denied because of
'certain pecularities of his which were quite well known in higher
quarters'. Denison, none the less, put forward the petition citing
his family's extensive political and electoral service, its extensive
estates, and the family's association with its county. When the
peerage was conferred, special acclaim was given to Beckett's work
in the restoration of St Alban's Cathedral, but Denison's application
had been based as much on family interest as on his brother's personal
merit.[51] As the life of Salisbury's caretaker Government was coming
to its close, Lord Carnarvon wrote to Hatfield recommending a
peerage for Arthur MacMurrough Kavanagh, the Irish politician
distinguished for the fact that he had been born legless and yet
had given powerful service to his party in Ireland and in the House
of Commons. Kavanagh, Carnarvon wrote, 'whom you probably
know— [is] a strange being physically, but by intelligence, influence,
[?] of character, [and] birth, [is] eminently acceptable to all the
gentry'.[52]

[48] Mr Nicholas to Captain Richard Middleton, 20 Aug. 1886, Third Marquess
of Salisbury MSS Class E.
[49] Ashmead Bartlett to Salisbury, 6 Dec. 1885 and 2 Feb. 1886; Salisbury to
Ashmead Bartlett, 1 Feb. 1886; Third Marquess of Salisbury MSS Class E, Class
C/6/251.
[50] Kennaway to Salisbury, 1 Jan. 1886, Third Marquess of Salisbury MSS
Class E.
[51] William Beckett Denison to Salisbury, 8 and 17 Nov. 1885, 11 Dec. 1885,
1 and 3 Feb. 1886, Third Marquess of Salisbury MSS Class E.
[52] Carnarvon to Salisbury, 9 Aug. 1885, Third Marquess of Salisbury MSS
Class E. Salisbury, as was not at all unusual, had his own ideas on these

These impressions, at once so vivid and persistent and illuminating, give bright hope to the thought that the distinction between gentle and non-gentle status might be verified in the evidence about the social background of Members of the House of Commons in 1886. And such proves to be the case. Dimensions of status can be discerned in these materials because certain social characteristics of Members indicated and predicted prestige and station.[53] Table 4.3 describes these status dimensions. As it shows, two sets of overlapping indicators defined the relationship between the status of Members in a world of community values on one hand and in a world of family values on the other.

Two social indicators form part of both of these status dimensions. Land in excess of 3,000 acres, whether owned personally or held by the family, and public school educations were attributes which were central to gentry values in the late Victorian period. Land was more than the basis of wealth, though it was that, of course; it was the sign and signal of social position and accomplishment. Landed status, since it could be separated from wealth, and especially from the new wealth of the industrial revolution, could be preserved from contamination. A few facts make this clear. Of the peerages conferred between 1833 and 1885, 75 per cent had been to politicians for service in governments or service in the House of Commons. Only twenty-five (20 per cent) owned land in amounts less than 2,000 acres. In 1911, one-sixth of all peers were first-generation noblemen with non-landed backgrounds, but less than 11 per cent of the House of Lords came from the business world.[54] Of the millionaires who died in the two decades after 1880, 37 per cent owned estates in excess of 2,000 acres, and 13 per cent owned estates in excess of 10,000 acres. These figures declined in the period from 1900 to 1914. Only 12 per cent of the millionaires who died during this period owned land in excess of 2,000 acres, and only 3 per cent held land in excess of 10,000 acres. These proportions

occasions. 'I have been very much pressed to recommend Bateson for a peerage. Would he not suit your purpose as well as the legless one? He would please the Orange men a great deal more; and though his service during the late crisis may have been less conspicuous, his services to the party are infinitely greater. He was a whip when I came into the House of Commons in 1854 — and has been working hard ever since. And he has *two* arms and *two* legs.' Salisbury to Carnarvon, 17 Aug. 1885, Third Marquess of Salisbury MSS Class D/13/130.

[53] See Appendix III for a description of the procedures used to construct these status dimensions.

[54] F. M. L. Thompson, *English Landed Society in the Nineteenth Century* (London: 1963), pp. 60, 297.

TABLE 4.3 Q Matrix* of Social Indicators of Members of the House of Commons in 1886 Showing the Social Threshold Separating Gentlemen and Non-gentlemen

	Community characteristics					Landed classes	Professional classes	Business classes
	1	4	5	9	10			
1. Public school	—	.75	.65	.64	.77	.80	.21	− .56
4. Church livings		—	.63	.90	.77	.85	− .38	− .22
5. Yeomanry/ militia			—	.69	.72	.73	− .07	− .40
9. Personal land in excess of 3,000 acres				—	.95	.91	− .27	− .35
10. Family land in excess of 3,000 acres					—	.98	.02	− .69

	Family characteristics							
	1	6	7	8	10			
1. Public school	—	.72	.77	.77	.77	.80	.21	− .56
6. Mother PBG		—	.70	.80	.84	.86	.007	− .66
7. Wife 1 PBG			—	.68	.84	.84	.003	− .53
8. Wife 2 PBG				—	.64	.72	.08	− .68
10. Family land in excess of 3,000 acres					—	.98	.02	− .69

*The values reported in this table are Yule's Q coefficient, a searching statistic and a measure of association. It measures for all Members of this House of Commons the degree to which they possessed, or failed to possess, each of these indicators in a manner designed to estimate whether or not the possession of one of these would predict the possession of all of them. Q advances toward 1.0 when Members possessed both or neither indicator. In so far as Members possessed some but not others, the Q value declines. See Appendix III for a fuller explanation of this procedure.

do not increase if only half-millionaires are considered. In the last two decades of the nineteenth century, 19 per cent of these held estates in excess of 2,000 acres, and 7 per cent held land in excess of 10,000 acres. In the fourteen years before the Great War, the proportions for half-millionaires owning in excess of 2,000 and 10,000 acres respectively are 11 per cent and 2 per cent.[55] While the business world had penetrated landed society, it had not done so sufficiently to dilute the values associated with the ownership of large estates.

[55] W. D. Rubinstein, 'The New Men of Wealth and the Purchase of Land in Nineteenth Century Britain', *Past and Present*, 92 (Apr. 1981), p. 130.

If the ownership of landed estates, or the membership in families owning landed estates, was the most obvious indicator of gentry values, attendance at one of the ancient public schools was no less important. The public schools became more important, rather than less, in the nineteenth century because they served as instruments for social and political integration. Unlike Winston Churchill, most old boys liked their schools and looked back on them with fond regard. Walter Long, Lord Willoughby de Broke, T. E. Kebbel, and many others testified to the significance of the school in shaping social and political behaviour.[56] M. R. James, who would be successively Provost at King's College, Cambridge and at Eton, wrote dreamily about the power of associations developed at such institutions:

How many have there been, how many are there now, who look back upon Eton and King's, with a love which no other spot on earth can inspire, and who say with the Eton poet, My brothers and my home are there? About these places have been woven cords of affection which bind together the most diverse natures and stretch over the whole world: cords which run through a man's whole life and do not part at the supreme moment of death.[57]

To be deprived of such associations and experiences, even for such a distinguished gentleman as Hartington, was to lessen the very character of individuals. As Reginald Brett wrote about Hartington during the Home Rule crisis: 'his weakness springs mainly from the circumstances that he was robbed of the advantage of a public school, and consequently has been forced to go through life with certain chambers of his heart and mind hermetically sealed.'[58] Constructed in an intense hierarchy of narrow yet sharply defined gradations, the public school experience never initiated, it always imitated. In so doing, it brought young boys into a world of trivial but essential rules in which they would live in colleges, in clubs, in the services, in country houses, and at Westminster. Tom Brown and the others learned competitiveness, discipline, and the life of leadership. Even in environment the school resembled the country

[56] Long, *Memories of the Right Honourable Viscount Long of Wraxall*, p. 27; Verney, *Passing Years*, p. 35; T. E. Kebbel, *The Old and the New English Country Life* (Edinburgh and London: 1891), pp. 44 ff. I have other evidence suggesting the importance of the public schools in the recruitment of local élites: W. C. Lubenow, 'Social Recruitment and Social Attitudes: The Buckinghamshire Magistracy, 1868–1888', *The Huntington Library Quarterly*, 40.3 (May 1977), pp. 265–6.

[57] Quoted in Michael Cox, *M. R. James, An Informal Portrait* (Oxford and New York: 1983), p. xix.

[58] Brett to W. T. Stead, 22 Apr. 1886, *The Journals and Letters of Reginald Brett*, vol. 1, p. 126.

house, built as it was frequently in the magical surroundings of parks and fields.[59]

Of the social dignities which make up the two dimensions of status which divided gentlemen from everyone else in the House of Commons of 1886, commissions in local militias and yeomanries might be regarded as having limited value in identifying thresholds of the social economy. Certainly the *Pall Mall Gazette* so regarded it.[60] These figures comparing the social backgrounds of MPs in 1886, however, give the lie to such an impression because they show a favourable correspondence between these commissions and other symbols of status, particularly public school education, the patronage of Church livings, and personal or family lands in excess of 3,000 acres. Moreover, the recruitment practices of at least one Lord Lieutenant in one county accorded great importance to these offices.[61]

To possess the indicators of status which made up these dimensions was to possess the badges of social respect and prestige. These dimensions identify that permeable barrier which was the filter of social mobility and the test of social advancement. As the comparison of these indicators with attachments to the active business community and the professions in Table 4.3 shows, they were strongly associated with membership of the landed classes. They show no relationship to the professions, and the relationship they reveal with men with active business interests is negative, and often strongly so. Whereas the holding of these indicators predicts membership of the landed classes, the failure to hold them tends to predict membership in the world of active business. Gentility stood for something; it was a lively social quality distinguishing élites in the late Victorian House of Commons.

The landed classes preserved their concern for the purity of their positions and estates, as the passion for genealogy and arms in the nineteenth century shows. Even Lord Salisbury, in 1886, declined a

---

[59] Jonathan Gathorne-Hardy, *The Old-School Tie: The Phenomenon of the English Public School* (New York: 1977), p. 120; and, of the vast literature on this subject, giving special attention to the boys at Harrow and Merchant Taylors', see Edward A. Allen, 'Public School Elites in Early Victorian England: The Boys at Harrow and Merchant Taylors' School from 1825 to 1850', *Journal of British Studies*, 21.2 (Spring 1982), pp. 87–107.

[60] *Pall Mall Gazette* 3 Dec. 1885, p. 4.

[61] Owen Peel Wethered (Commander of the Bucks Rifle Volunteers) to the Third Duke of Buckingham and Chandos, 5 June 1875, 11 Aug. 1882, 12 Nov. 1883, Huntington Library and Art Gallery, Stowe Collection, Grenville Correspondence Box 106, (48), (56), (60).

dukedom, believing 'his fortune would not be equal to such a dignity'.[62] When Sir Ughtred Kay-Shuttleworth accepted office under Lord Spencer in 1886, he lapsed into feudal language and spoke of his chief's statesmanship and chivalry.[63] Members who did not belong to this charmed circle held different values, and sustained them without apology. When John Brunner and his partner Ludwig Mond sought a site for their alkali works, they proposed to pay £200,000 for a ninety-nine-year lease on the property surrounding Winnington Hall, Cheshire. Winnington Hall, which was owned by Lord Stanley of Alderley, had a chequered history. It had been leased as a girls' finishing school; Sir Charles Hallé had given concerts there; John Ruskin visited to lecture and admired its architectural qualities. Yet the fee Brunner and Mond proposed to pay was not intended to include the stately home; they had no use for it and saw, therefore, little value in it.[64] Lord Blake, in his revealing biography of Bonar Law, shows how members of the business classes, who could frequently afford the symbols of landed society, often eschewed them out of disapprobation and even contempt.[65] Prosperous middle-class families, of the sort from which G. E. Moore sprang, driven by their nonconformist consciences and their residual hostility toward the aristocracy, distrusted the ancient public schools because they regarded them as too worldly and as the preserves of the upper class.[66] Joseph Leicester, the glass-blower MP, revealed working-class contempt at a radical meeting in Southwark when he observed that 'ignorance was better than knowledge in politics, that the educated class always went wrong & masses always right'.[67] Social cleavages, therefore, were important in the House of Commons in the 1880s, and it remains to be seen how far they had political consequences, how far they translated themselves into political conflict, how far they account for the political differences between Conservatives and Liberals, and between Liberals and Liberal Unionists.

The Social Basis of Partisanship in the House of Commons

The conventional wisdom about the relationship between social background and partisanship is that legislatures are stratified according

[62] Lord Salisbury to the Queen, 31 Jan. 1886, *Letters of Queen Victoria*, ed. G. E. Buckle (London: 1930), 3rd series, vol. 1, p. 34.

[63] Kay-Shuttleworth to Gladstone, 12 Apr. 1886, BL Add. MS 44496, f. 241.

[64] Koss, *Sir John Brunner, Radical Plutocrat*, p. 28.

[65] Robert Blake, *The Unknown Prime Minister: The Life and Times of Andrew Bonar Law, 1858–1923* (London: 1955), p. 25.

[66] Paul Levy, *G. E. Moore and the Cambridge Apostles* (New York: 1979), p. 36.

[67] Blunt Diary, 13 May 1886, Blunt MS 334-1975, f. 188.

to social class, and that parties express different class interests. There is only limited evidence to support this contention. Though British political parties had not been social or economic entities in the early nineteenth century,[68] the infusion of business and professional men might have structured the party system along class lines in the 1880s. Or so one might suppose. But despite the vague correlation between the social background and political preferences of Members, as Table 4.4 shows, this was not the case.

To take the landed gentlemen first, no matter whether reckoned according to the more astringent or the more generous definitions, few were Irish Nationalists. Less than half the landed gentlemen were Liberals and slightly more than half were Conservatives. A slightly higher percentage of the sons of peers (60 per cent) were Conservatives, but the proportions for the baronetage and landed gentlemen were closer: 52 per cent and 56 per cent were, respectively, Conservatives. Therefore, while a substantial proportion of landed

TABLE 4.4 *The Partisan Affiliation of Social Groups in the House of Commons in 1886*

	Irish Nationalists (86)		Liberals (339)		Conservatives (255)	
	No.	%	No.	%	No.	%
Landed gentlemen (255)*	4	2	110	43	141	55
Landed gentlemen (307)†	8	3	132	43	167	54
All professional men (352)	44	12	164	47	144	41
Army officers (70)	4	6	14	20	52	74
Navy officers (10)	0		6	60	4	40
Lawyers (181)	16	9	97	54	68	37
All business men (289)	28	10	173	60	88	30
Active and substantial business men only (224)	13	6	142	63	69	31
Bankers (38)	1	3	19	50	18	47
Brewers (21)	1	5	10	47	10	47
Merchants (65)	6	9	42	65	17	26
Textile manufacturers (31)	0		23	74	8	26
Railway directors (75)	2	3	55	73	18	24
Working classes (14)	2	14	12	86	0	

*The landed classes reckoned according to this definition include all Members connected to the peerage–baronetage–landed gentry through the male line, but exclude those Members so connected through their mothers or through marriage.

†The landed classes reckoned according to this definition include all Members connected to the peerage–baronetage–landed gentry through the male line and through their mothers and through marriage.

[68] Gash, *Reaction and Reconstruction in English Politics, 1832–52*, chs. 5–6.

gentlemen were Conservative in 1886, and substantial though declining proportions remained Conservative from 1886 to 1910,[69] the view that the Conservatives were the party of land—a traditional élite—as opposed to the Liberals—a non-landed modernizing élite—will not stand, and cannot be supported by the evidence from the House of Commons in 1886. Professor Vincent's calculations for the Liberal party from 1859 to 1874 show it to consist of large landowners to the extent of 39 per cent, and Professor Heyck has figures for the radical faction in the party, the least likely to include landed gentlemen, which show it to have nothing less than 5 per cent of its numbers drawn from the landed classes in the period from 1874 to 1892.[70] The figures for landed gentlemen in the parliamentary party in 1886 reveal a surprisingly high proportion to have been Liberals (43 per cent), which testifies to the political heterogeneity of social groups in late Victorian parliamentary politics.

The slight association between the landed classes and the Conservative party in 1886 shows up again, but reversed, in the distribution of business men and professional men among the parties in the House of Commons. On this ground Salisbury had critics within his own party which opposed and disapproved of social exclusiveness. As William Burdett-Coutts, the Conservative Member for Westminster, put it when writing to Salisbury to find a place for his brother—Ellis Ashmead Bartlett,[71] who sat for the Eccleshall

[69] Cornford, 'Parliamentary Foundations of the Hotel Cecil', p. 310. These figures are not fully compatible with mine because Cornford's percentages are proportions of the Tory party and mine are proportions of the landed classes in the House of Commons. They are close enough, however, to give a crude idea of the subject.

[70] John Vincent, *The Formation of the Liberal Party* (London: 1966), p. 3; Heyck, *The Dimensions of British Radicalism*, pp. 237–65. Again, these figures are not comparable to mine because they are proportions of the Liberal party and the radical faction in the Liberal party respectively, not proportions of landed gentlemen belonging to the various parties and factions. Moreover, Vincent's calculations, since he includes only Members or their sons listed in Bateman's *Great Landowners of Great Britain* having a gross rental of £2,000, may be underestimates.

[71] Ellis Ashmead Bartlett and his brother William Burdett-Coutts were political adventurers. They were the grandsons, on both paternal and maternal sides, of British subjects, but were born in Brooklyn, New York to Ellis Bartlett, of Plymouth, Massachusetts, and Sophia, the daughter of John King Ashmead, of Philadelphia. On their father's side they were descended from two of the Pilgrim Fathers. Ashmead Bartlett was educated at Torquay and Christ Church, Oxford, where he had been President of the Oxford Debating Society. Called to the Bar at the Inner Temple, Ashmead Bartlett was an examiner in the Education Department. He sat as the Conservative Member for Eye from 1880 to 1885. In 1885 he was appointed to Lord Salisbury's Government as a Civil Lord of the Admiralty. William Burdett-Coutts was educated at Torquay and at the Cholmeley School, Highgate. He won a

division of Sheffield: 'there is an impression abroad, most damaging to the party, that new blood is repressed, & that men — particularly young men — who make their own way, are less considered at head-quarters than men who belong to great families.'[72] When Salisbury was forming his first Administration in 1885, A. B. Forwood, who styled himself a Tory Democrat, wrote to him and asked for the recognition of 'Progressive Toryism' in ministerial arrangements. 'If we can only pull the party from under the wheel of mere County & Landed influence, & give to urban constituencies a just share, we shall infuse a new & strong life into our body politic.'[73] Forwood, dissatisfied and unappeased, wrote to Churchill during the formation of the second Salisbury Ministry in 1886 about the 'overpowering weight [which] is being given to landed property and status, to the exclusion of Bankers, Manufacturers, and Traders, the backbone of the country' in the composition of the ministry.[74] C. T. Ritchie regarded the commercial, the trading, and the working classes in the towns as the chief strengths of the Tory party, and wanted them represented in the distribution of offices.[75] Whatever their influence in the Conservative party, the number of business men was not unimportant. Depending upon the definition one uses, as Table 4.4 indicates, slightly fewer than a third of all business men were Tories and slightly less than two-thirds were Liberals. Various groups of business men divided themselves into different proportions amongst the parties. Bankers divided themselves very nearly equally between Liberals and Conservatives. And also the brewers. Despite Salisbury's view that 'we have to consider the Publicans' feelings more than James and Hartington are accustomed to do',[76] the Conservatives were not the party of beer in the House of Commons. For other groups, however, the balance of business men was not so narrowly split. Merchants, textile manufacturers, and railway directors tended to

scholarship to Keble College, Oxford and took an M.A. in 1876. In 1877 he volunteered to serve in Turkey as Special Commissioner for the Turkish Compassionate Fund, which Baroness Burdett-Coutts had originated. In 1881 he married this much older woman and assumed her name by Royal Licence. He sat in the House of Commons for the first time in 1886.

[72] Burdett-Coutts to Salisbury, 15 June 1885, Third Marquess of Salisbury MSS Class E.

[73] Forwood to Salisbury, 9 June 1885, Third Marquess of Salisbury MSS Class E.

[74] A. B. Forwood to Lord Randolph Churchill, 31 July 1886, Lord Randolph Churchill Letters 1/13/1606.

[75] C. T. Ritchie to Lord Randolph Churchill, 1 Aug. 1886, Lord Randolph Churchill Letters 1/14/1616.

[76] Salisbury to Lord Ashbourne, 25 May 1886, Third Marquess of Salisbury MSS Class D/24/28.

be much more one-sidedly Liberal. None the less, it would not do to argue that the Liberal party was the party of business. They had no monopoly on enterprise, just as the Conservatives had no monopoly on land. The Conservatives had strong connections with the business world; they were thoroughly bourgeois. The Churchills were connected to both aristocratic and plutocratic worlds. Winston Churchill's aunt, Lady Wimbourne, married into that great clan of iron magnates, the Guests. And she gave much financial support to her nephew, who spent much of his time in the Guests' circle.[77]

The presence of business men in these proportions (42 per cent of the Liberal party) is worth another word. Business men, the conventional wisdom on this question argues, deserted the Liberal party as its policies became increasingly radicalized. One scholar produced figures to show that the share of business men's seats in the party declined from 44 per cent in 1892 to 34 per cent in 1910.[78] These calculations, however, have been contested, and, if independent Labour MPs are removed from the reckonings for 1905, 1906, and 1910, the proportion of business men in the parliamentary party remained relatively constant during this period.[79] Whatever fluctuation there was in the proportions of business men in the Liberal party was linked to whether or not the Liberals had a majority in the House of Commons, and to the existence of political crisis. In 1885 and 1892, when the Liberals returned with majorities, the proportion of business men in their ranks was enhanced slightly because more Liberal candidates had been elected. In 1895 and 1900, when the Conservatives captured the House, the proportion of Liberal business men shrank slightly. There was another expansion of the proportion of business men in 1910, during the House of Lords crisis. Electoral results and crisis politics had as much to do with the waxing and waning of Liberal business men as economic or social interests. This can be shown further by the examination of non-landed millionaires and half-millionaires in the House of Commons between 1880 and 1939. These men divided themselves nearly equally between the Liberal and Conservative parties. There was no flight of wealthy men from the party of Gladstone to the party of Salisbury as a

[77] Julian Amery, 'If Churchill Were in Charge', *The Spectator*, 22 May 1976, p. 21.

[78] Emy, *Liberals, Radicals and Social Politics*, p. 103.

[79] G. R. Searle, 'The Edwardian Liberal Party and Business', *English Historical Review*, 98.386 (Jan. 1983), p. 32.

result of the new liberalism.[80] Business men continued to hold a third of all Liberal seats until 1930.[81]

In general, the distribution of professional men among the parties resembled the distribution of business men, save for the fact that the former were more heavily represented in the Irish Nationalist party than were business men, and more equally divided between Liberals and Conservatives. Within the professions, however, various groups distributed themselves variously and less equally. Army officers, for example, were strongly Conservative. As Sir Wilfred Lawson put it during the general election of 1886 in the Cockermouth division of Cumberland, 'I think it is almost as difficult for a soldier to be a Liberal as it is for a rich man to enter the Kingdom of Heaven.'[82] Naval officers, by narrow numbers, on the other hand, tended to sit on the Liberal side of the House. More than half the lawyers sitting there were Liberals, and if the Parnellites and Liberals are taken together, they placed themselves sharply to the left. The point to be made here is that if the professional and business classes had class interests, they were represented no more than were the landed classes by a single party. The system of parties in the House of Commons did not follow class lines; partisan cleavage in 1886 cannot be explained very far by the data or the theories of class struggle.

Though parties in the House of Commons did not stratify themselves along lines of social cleavage in 1886, one searches for social differences between the parties which might account for their different political behaviour. One can find an intimation of this in the degree of social deviation, the degree of social differentiation, within the Liberal and Conservative parties. This can be examined by constructing simple indices of representativeness for the front bench and the back benches of each party according to the attributes of status which were significant in this House of Commons (see Table 4.5).

While both Liberal and Conservative parties recruited all sections of society into their memberships, there was less difference between the social character of the Conservative front bench and back benches than between the Liberal leadership and their followers. The social distance between Conservative leaders and led was greatest with

---

[80] W. D. Rubinstein, *Men of Property: The Very Wealthy in Britain Since the Industrial Revolution* (London: 1981), pp. 165–6, tables 5.4–5.5.

[81] Searle, 'The Edwardian Liberal Party and Business', p. 34.

[82] G. W. E. Russell (ed.), *Sir Wilfred Lawson, A Memoir* (London: 1909), p. 186.

TABLE 4.5 *The Social Gap Between the Leaderships and Rank and File in the Conservative and Liberal Parties in the House of Commons in 1886* (Representativeness indices* for the front and back benches in the parties, and the difference between each index for each party)

	Conservatives			Liberals		
	Leaders	Followers	Difference	Leaders	Followers	Difference
Landed gentlemen†	1.18	.96	.22	1.56	.90	.66
Public school	1.26	.95	.31	1.75	.86	.89
Church livings	1.34	.93	.41	1.48	.91	.57
Officer militia yeomanry	.91	1.01	.10	1.11	.98	.13
Mother PBG	1.55	.89	.66	2.02	.81	1.21
Wife PBG	1.59	.89	.70	1.64	.88	.76
Personal land‡	.89	1.01	.12	1.28	.94	.34
Family land‡	1.43	.92	.51	1.72	.87	.85

* An index of representativeness is attained by dividing the proportion of leaders (or back-benchers) having an attribute by the proportion of the party as a whole with that quality. If the leadership (or back bench) is representative, the score will be 1.0. A score less than 1.0 indicates that on that attribute the leadership (or back bench) was under-represented; if the score is greater it indicates they were over-represented.
† Landed gentlemen in this reckoning include members of the landed classes through the male, female, and marriage lines.
‡ Personal or family land holdings in excess of 3,000 acres.

regard to MPs' maternal backgrounds, the social status of their marriages, and whether or not their families held extensive territorial possessions. For the Liberals, on the other hand, the only points of social proximity between front and back benches were the holding of commissions in local yeomanries and militias and the possession of lands in excess of 3,000 acres. For the rest, there was some considerable social separation between Liberal leaders and those they led. When these differences for each party are aggregated and the mean calculated, the social separation in each party becomes even clearer: for the Liberals the average difference was .68; for the Conservatives it was .38. This can be put another way if the average figures for Conservatives and Liberals, and their respective front and back benches, are calculated for the degree of deviation from representativeness. The detailed figures are: Conservative front bench, +.26 from representativeness; the Conservative back bench, −.06; the Liberal front bench, +.57; the Liberal back benches, −.11. The front benches of both parties were over-represented on this status dimension, and the back benches of each party were under-represented. But the degree of over-representation and under-representation for the Conservatives was half that of the Liberals. It was the function of parties to reconcile and transcend social divisions in their memberships for policy purposes. For the Conservatives in 1886 there was less reconciling and transcending to do. This implies a different distribution of social status attributes in the two major parties.

This lead can be pursued by employing the same test for each party separately as the one used to detect status thresholds in the House of Commons as a whole. In this manner it is possible to develop an empirical estimate of status variations between the Liberal and the Conservative parties. This test, as before, uses a comparison of indicators of social status, but this time holding partisan affiliation constant. This pattern of generally lower values for the Conservatives, relative to the Liberals, confirms the different distribution of these attributes in each party. For the Conservatives, the possession of one or more of these dignities does not predict the possession of others; for the Liberals, the distribution of these indicators shows a segregation of Members who held them from Members who did not. Among Conservatives, symbols of status were dispersed with a kind of random evenness among Members; among Liberals they were found clustered among certain Members only. In other words, the Liberal party in the House of Commons, but not the Conservatives, had a social structure in which Members possessing symbols of social status were located at one end of a status dimension, and

TABLE 4.6 Q Matrix of Social Indicators of Members of the Conservative and Liberal Parties Showing the Threshold Separating Gentlemen from Non-gentlemen

	1	2	3	4	5	6	7	8	Landed (141)	Professional (144)	Business (88)
Conservatives only:											
1. Public school (121)	—	.52	.48	.54	.52	.40	.61	.34	.65	.14	−.48
2. Church livings (38)			.33	.30	.22	.64	.87	.61	.73	−.49	−.14
3. Yeomanry/militia (63)				.27	.39	.18	.56	.62	.58	−.15	−.37
4. Mother PBG (86)					.59	.76	.35	.77	.74	.15	−.72
5. Wife 1 PBG (72)						.47	.54	.81	.79	−.01	−.47
6. Wife 2 PBG (8)							.32	.60	.35	−.17	−1.0
7. Personal land in excess of 3,000 acres (107)								.92	.85	−.39	−.40
8. Family land in excess of 3,000 acres (107)									.97	−.04	−.71
									(110)	(164)	(173)
Liberals only:											
1. Public school (91)	—	.81	.64	.77	.89	.92	.72	.79	.82	.23	−.52
2. Church livings (27)			.76	.60	.82	.58	.88	.81	.87	−.32	−.06
3. Yeomanry/militia (42)				.37	.67	.01	.67	.66	.71	−.07	−.13
4. Mother PBG (59)					.77	.81	.62	.87	.91	−.11	−.43
5. Wife 1 PBG (61)						.76	.78	.83	.85	−.02	−.29
6. Wife 2 PBG (12)							.12	.64	.83	.19	−.48
7. Personal land in excess of 3,000 acres (52)								.95	.91	−.18	−.15
8. Family land in excess of 3,000 acres (81)									.98	.05	−.50

*The landed classes by this reckoning excludes Members connected to the peerage–baronetage–landed gentry through the maternal line or through marriage to prevent the analysis from becoming circular.

those without indicators were located at the other. As Table 4.6 also shows (a point which has already been made for the House of Commons as a whole—see Table 4.3), Liberals with these indicators of status were rather more closely associated with the landed classes than were other Liberals or Conservatives. While both parties contained various groups in their social composition, these social differences carried greater weight and had rather different consequences for the Liberals than they had for Conservatives. The extent to which these differences played a role in parliamentary behaviour is the subject to which this study next turns.

The Social Background of Political Behaviour in the House of Commons

The pattern of interrelationships between political behaviour and social class upon which the analysis has so far depended is based upon a comparison of the partisan affiliation of Members and certain characteristics of their social backgrounds. These results, while not wholly negative, have not been impressive. Therefore, to get a more exact indication of political and social relationships it seems worth while to attempt a test which rests on a more precise indication of political position, the scores of Members according to their location on the great parliamentary voting dimension for this House of Commons. Partisan affiliation represents a tendency on the part of Members to support a particular party, its policy programme, and its leaders; it masks many differences. Scale position represents a tendency of a different sort: since it is a parsimonious summary of the specific decisions Members took on a large number of specific questions, it can express the deviations within partisan groups, deviations which may be accounted for by internal social differences.

When the political stances of Members of the House of Commons, as described by their positions on the major parliamentary voting scale, are compared with certain features of their social backgrounds, as in Table 4.7, a positive relationship sometimes emerges. The test for active business men and professional men and scale position reveals nothing. The distribution of percentages for these social groups among the political positions represented by the scale is in both cases flat, with slightly enlarged percentages to the right. Something more, though for limited numbers, is shown in the relationship of Members of the working classes and their political postures. Eighty-four per cent of them held positions to the extreme left, as compared to the 63 per cent of those Members who were not workers and who are found at the median or to the right of the median. Because of their greater numbers, it is with greater

TABLE 4.7 *Social Class and Ideological Positions on the Major Dimension of Parliamentary Voting*

	Scale positions			No.
	7-5 (%)	4* (%)	3-1 (%)	
Landed classes[†]	13	16	71	227
Non-landed classes	56	16	28	312
Active and substantial business classes	40	19	41	176
Non-business classes	37	14	48	363
Professional classes	37	16	47	284
Non-professional classes	39	16	45	255
Working classes	84	8	8	12
Non-working classes	37	16	47	527
Listed in Walford[‡]	17	19	64	306
Not listed	65	12	23	233

*Indicates median dimensional position.
†This reckoning of the landed classes included all MPs who were connected to landed society through male and female lines and through marriage.
‡Edward Walford, *The County Families of the United Kingdom* (London: 1886).

confidence that one turns to a comparison of landed gentlemen sitting in this House and their locations on the scale. Here the strongest case can be made for a relationship between the social background of Members and their politics. By this evidence, nearly three-quarters of the landed gentlemen who could be fitted on the scale held positions on the right, and more than half of these Members who were unconnected to the landed classes held positions to the left. Social class, here, predicts the political behaviour of Members of the House of Commons. It is a point which finds further confirmation in the figures at the bottom of Table 4.7. These show the relationship between political position and the listing of Members in Walford's *County Families of the United Kingdom*, a standard guide of the time to respectability and status. Again, the test is positive. Two-thirds, or nearly, of all Members so listed are found on the rightward extremity of the scale, and nearly two-thirds of the Members who are not listed in Walford are found on the left side of the scale.

While on the face of it satisfactory, these findings break down under further analysis. Partisan affiliation masks important counter-trends in the evidence, and once party affiliation is controlled for, the strong positive results in Table 4.7 prove to be very much less than they appear to be. Since the Irish Nationalists and the Tories were highly unified and cohesive, as Chapter 3 has shown, the social position of the members of these parties had virtually nothing to do with the locations they held on the great parliamentary voting dimension which describes the nature of ideological behaviour in this House of Commons. In fact, after controlling for political party, the social background of Members accounts for scale position in only three of every ten cases.

Rarely riven anyway, the Irish Nationalists and the Conservatives were even more infrequently internally divided along social lines. In fact, the present study has discovered only six instances in which the Irish Nationalist Party and only three instances in which the Conservative Party had internal disputes whose character included a social dimension.[83] These materials can be used only with the greatest caution. The social groups voting in these parliamentary divisions were numerically very small. Most of these parliamentary divisions failed to fit the major voting dimension in 1886 and were, consequently, distant from the centre of political attention. They are, consequently, implausible materials for the construction of social conflict theories.

For the Liberals, however, a quite different aspect of the matter appears. The Liberals in 1886, as Chapter 3 showed, were distributed along the ideological dimension described by the great voting scale. This chapter shows the Liberals to be distributed along a status dimension with landed gentlemen at one extremity and Liberal MPs without the characteristics of landed status at the other. These two dimensions, in a crude sort of way, corresponded. No case for this can be made in the analysis of the scale positions of Liberals in the professions: they are located along the dimension in similar proportions. The scale positions of Liberals with active and substantial business interests show little either, except that the percentages are in the expected direction. For the working classes and the landed gentlemen in the Liberal party, on the other hand, there is a strong association between their social positions and their political positions. Though there were not many working-class MPs to talk about, those that can be tended strongly to the left. Non-working-class Liberals tended slightly to the centre and to the right. The ideological stances of landed gentlemen, on the other hand, were found at the median, or to the right of the median, and strongly so (70 per cent). Liberals without landed status, in sizeable proportions (60 per cent) are found to the left. This political dimension represents

---

[83] The Compensation for Damages Bill, which divided social groups within the Conservative Party, is one of the most interesting of these, and it is examined in my article 'The Class Struggle and the House of Commons: The Parliamentary Response to the London Riots of 1886', *Histoire sociale–Social History*, 18 (May 1985).

TABLE 4.8 *Social Class and the Dimensional Positions for Liberals Only on the Major Parliamentary Voting Dimension*

	Dimensional positions			No.
	7-5 (%)	4* (%)	3-1 (%)	
Landed classes[†]	24	38	38	97
Non-landed classes	60	29	11	171
Landed classes with active business interests	23	46	31	26
Landed classes without active business interests	24	35	41	71
Active and substantial business men	52	31	17	111
Not active and substantial business men	43	33	24	157
Active and substantial business men who belonged to the landed classes	23	46	31	26
Active and substantial business men who did not belong to the landed classes	61	27	13	83
Professional men	48	33	19	135
Not professional men	46	31	23	133
Working classes	80	10	10	10
Not working classes	46	33	21	258
Listed in Walford[‡]	29	40	31	146
Not listed in Walford	69	22	9	122

*Indicates the median dimensional position.
[†]This reckoning of the landed classes includes all Liberal MPs who were connected to landed society through the male and female lines and through marriage.
[‡]Walford, *The County Families of the United Kingdom*.

the traditional parliamentary agenda: political reform, social policy, Irish issues,[84] and votes on foreign, imperial, and military policy.

These were issues which had been around a long time. On the dimension which includes these, therefore, Liberal Members took positions which corresponded to their social positions. Liberals without connections to landed society tended to support radical policies. Landed gentlemen tended to be more conservative elements in the Liberal party. Orientated toward the centres of power, they

[84] The division on the Government of Ireland Bill fits the major dimension of parliamentary voting for the House of Commons as a whole (see Chapter 2), but when dimensions are established using the votes of Liberals alone in this House it fails to fit a scale relationship with the other items in the political agenda. This is the meaning of the great separation in the Liberal party, and it is discussed at length in Chapter 6. See also Lubenow, 'Irish Home Rule and the Great Separation in the Liberal Party in 1886'.

supported positions taken by Gladstone's Government, and in consequence opposed radical policy adventures.

Table 4.8 also reveals the way in which connections to the landed classes, rather than active business interests, influenced political behaviour. When the figures for landed gentlemen are controlled for active business interests, not very much happens: 77 per cent of landed gentlemen with active business interests, as opposed to 76 per cent of landed gentlemen without active business interests, held ideological positions at the centre or to the right of centre.[85] But when active business interests are controlled by membership in the landed classes, quite a sharp difference emerges: only 23 per cent of the active business men who were also landed gentlemen are found on the leftmost fringe of the party, as opposed to 61 per cent of the active business interests but without landed status who are found there. Connections with the landed classes pulled active business men decidedly to the right in parliamentary politics.

As in the case of the distribution of dimensional positions for the whole House, the relationship between Liberals' political and social position finds confirmation in the figures at the foot of Table 4.8. Sixty-nine per cent of the Liberal party in the House of Commons who are not listed in Walford's guide to the great county families are found at the left of the dimension; 71 per cent of those listed are found at the centre or to the right. If further evidence for this point is wanted, figures could be produced comparing the dimensional positions of Liberal with the indicators of social status used earlier in this chapter: public school educations, connections to the landed classes through the maternal line or marriage, the possession of substantial landed territories, commissions in local militias or yeomanries, and the patronage of Church livings. In each case, these confirm the patterns described by Table 4.8. A majority of those without them are found on the left; those Liberals with them are found at the centre or on the right.

The pull of social background in the Liberal party was stronger because the pull of party was weaker. But even on questions having explicit social or economic content, as in the case of the Manchester Ship Canal Bill,[86] party could override the interest of personal

[85] However, as it will be noted in Table 4.8, the proportion of landed gentlemen with active business interests in the three rightwardmost dimensional positions is separated from landed gentlemen without active business interests in those ideological positions by 10%, an indication of some powerful grip by business interests on landed gentlemen, at least in the most moderate sections of the party.

[86] Armytage, 'The Railway Rates and the Fall of Gladstone's Third Ministry'; Lubenow, 'Home Rule, the Great Depression, and the Railway Rates', p. 208.

background. For the Liberals, the Ship Canal Bill was a party question. Thirty-four Liberal railway directors participated in the division on this Bill, and twenty-four (71 per cent), contrary to their apparent economic interest, voted for it. On the Compulsory Purchase of Land Compensation Bill, the debate on which was strewn with references to class and class interest,[87] the votes of Members defy a class interpretation, and, again, party told. When the thing came to a decision, the Land Compensation Bill fell along party rather than social lines: 97 per cent of the Conservatives opposed it, 97 per cent of the Liberals favoured it.

Voting on the Crofters Bill illustrates the twisted role of class and the controlling influence of party in parliamentary politics. Throughout the many divisions on this question, social class meant nothing for Conservatives who voted continuously and unanimously against Amendments designed to enlarge the Bill. In the early days on this question, it was also a partisan matter for the Liberals. However, as the long day wore on in divisions on the Crofters Bill, as radicals' patience became thinner when they faced their leaders' obdurate resistance to extending Amendments (and Gladstone's Government enjoyed support in this from the Conservatives), party influence declined. Then social influence found itself freed. This is illustrated in the analysis of Liberal voting in two divisions on the Crofters Bill found in Table 4.9. In the first of these, the vote on McLaren's Amendment taken on 29 March, the force of party was stronger: 26 per cent of the party, by voting for the Amendment, dissented from the party position. In the second division, one taken on an Amendment proposed by Macfarlane on 5 April, party influence was less: 48 per cent of the Liberals dissented from the position of the party leaders. In the first of these divisions the social background of Liberals says nothing about their votes, and the matter did not turn on class. A large majority of all social groups opposed the Amendment and supported the Government. In time's fullness, however, Liberal voting on Amendments to the Crofters Bill took a social cast. In the division on Macfarlane's Amendment on 5 April, large proportions of landed gentlemen continued to oppose the radicalizing Amendment. On the other hand, while working-class members divided themselves equally on the matter, a large proportion of MPs without landed connections, men of substantial business interests and the professions, broke with their party and supported the Amendment. In this division the votes of Liberals reflected their social background.

---

[87] Hansard, 305: 855–69; Temple Letters, 12 May 1886, BL Add. MS 38916, f. 80–80ᵛ.

TABLE 4.9 *Class Voting Among Liberals on the Crofters Bill*

	% +	% −	No.
C. B. B. McLaren's Amendment to the Crofters Bill, 29 March 1886:			
Landed classes*	16	84	81
Non-landed classes	34	66	116
Active and substantial business men	25	75	77
Not active and substantial business men	28	72	120
Professional men	25	75	106
Non-professional men	27	73	91
Working classes	17	83	6
Non-working classes	28	72	191
D. H. Macfarlane's Amendment to the Crofters Bill, 5 April 1886:			
Landed classes*	27	73	63
Non-landed classes	61	39	99
Active and substantial business men	55	45	60
Not active and substantial business men	43	57	102
Professional men	49	51	84
Non-professional men	46	54	78
Working classes	50	50	6
Non-working classes	47	53	156

*This reckoning of the landed classes includes MPs having connections with landed society through the male and female lines and through marriage.

As these votes on the Crofter measure show, social background came to count for something only when the influence of partisanship became reduced. In a perverse way, therefore, social background still cannot be regarded as the shaping force in the voting behaviour of Members. The shaping force, in these cases, was the reciprocal of partisan influence; its absence or reduction, which accounts for the disposition of Liberals in scale positions away from the centre and toward the extreme. This point can be pushed further by considering the votes of Liberals on two very different measures: Labouchere's Motion against the House of Lords, and Richard's Motion against foreign involvements. The feature of voting which both of these divisions share is a high proportion of Liberals, in their support for the Motions, opposing the position of the party's leadership. In these, as in later divisions on the Lords' Amendments to the Crofters Bill, large proportions of non-landed MPs in the Liberal party supported these policies, and found themselves opposed by large proportions of Liberal landed gentlemen. Patterns of social

TABLE 4.10 *Class Voting Among Liberals on Radical Initiatives and Foreign Policy*

	% +	% −	No.
Labouchere's Resolution on representative government, 5 March 1886:			
Landed classes*	39	61	59
Non-landed classes	81	19	108
Active and substantial business men	80	20	74
Not active and substantial business men	56	44	93
Professional men	62	38	82
Non-professional men	71	29	85
Working classes	100	0	6
Non-working classes	65	35	161
Richard's Motion against foreign involvements, 19 March 1886:			
Landed classes*	32	68	41
Non-landed classes	70	30	88
Active and substantial business men	67	33	49
Not active and substantial business men	53	47	80
Professional men	54	46	74
Non-professional men	64	36	55
Working classes	75	25	8
Non-working classes	57	43	121

*The landed classes by this reckoning include MPs connected to landed society through the male and female lines as well as through marriage.

voting emerged only when it became clear on the back benches that the front bench was impervious to the views of those supporting these Amendments and Motions. At that point the support for the position of the Liberal Government, in social terms, came from Liberal landed gentlemen. Table 4.10, which shows the relationship between social class and Liberal voting on the Motions offered by Labouchere and Richard, represents two of those few occasions on which a majority of the Liberal party stood against the policy of their leaders, or, more exactly, when the leadership opposed the policy advances of a majority of their back-benchers. These particular political circumstances — a revolt against the party leadership by a majority of the Liberal rank and file in the House of Commons — released the forces of class voting. They were the instances in which the Liberal party failed to sustain its integrative function and could not contain the forces for radical change within the party. But this did not happen often in 1886, for which reason it is rare to find in particular divisions a relationship between voting and the social background of Members.

The Social Background of the Great Separation in the Liberal Party

The great political event of the 1880s was the Home Rule split in the Liberal party. The figures on the social background of Liberals and its relationship to their votes, found above, might lead to the presumption that their social background was also related to Liberal voting on Mr Gladstone's Government of Ireland Bill. Certainly this is what past and current scholarship on the question holds. For one historian of the Liberal split, ' a striking feature of modern British history has been the class alignment of political parties'. As he goes on to argue, 'the Liberal Unionist party . . . was a half-way house, which entertained for a time much of the wealth and territorial influence which had been Liberal and was to be Conservative.'[88] One of the most influential historians of these matters puts it in broader terms. The origins of Conservative dominance after 1886, R. C. K. Ensor proposes, as well as the leakage of the landed and business classes to the Conservative party, are to be found in the undermining of British agriculture by the invasion of prairie wheat from North America. This produced in its turn agrarian revolution in Ireland, and the rejection of Irish political demands by a British ruling élite made conservative by its fear and abhorrence of terrorism.[89] Another historian attributes the fall of Gladstone's third Ministry to a general revolt on behalf of propertied interests led by railway directors.[90] Thus the application of class conflict interpretations of politics to the Home Rule crisis.

Their flaw is that there is virtually no evidence to support them. As Table 4.11 reveals, the army officers and railway directors in the Liberal party were the only groups who supported Unionism. Majorities of every other group supported the Home Rule Bill and the position of Gladstone's Government. Landed gentlemen in the Liberal party supported the Bill. Depending upon how one reckons their composition, 55 per cent or 58 per cent held to Gladstone's position. To be sure, the percentage of Liberals with connections to the peerage are slightly inflated in this vote—fifteen of the thirty-two Liberals belonging to peerage families (47 per cent) became Liberal Unionists—but this difference is slight, and the detailed figures support only the conclusion that to belong, or not to belong, to peerage families meant nothing in determining how Liberals voted

[88] Gordon L. Goodman, 'Liberal Unionism: The Revolt of the Whigs', *Victorian Studies*, 2.2 (1959), pp. 173, 190.
[89] Ensor, 'Some Political and Economic Interactions in Later Victorian England'.
[90] Armytage, 'The Railway Rates and the Fall of Gladstone's Third Ministry'.

TABLE 4.11 *Social and Economic Stratification and the Great Separation in the Liberal Party*

	Gladstonians		Unionists		Others*		No.
	No.	%	No.	%	No.	%	
Landed gentlemen:[†]	77	58	46	35	9	7	132
Landed gentlemen with active business interests	21	64	10	30	2	6	33
Landed gentlemen without active business interests	56	56	36	36	7	7	99
Landed gentlemen with professions	42	62	21	31	5	7	68
Landed gentlemen without professions	35	55	25	39	4	6	64
All professional men:	118	72	41	25	5	3	164
Professional men who were also landed gentlemen	42	62	21	31	5	7	68
Professional men who were not also landed gentlemen	76	79	20	21	0		96
Army officers	2	14	11	79	1	7	14
Naval officers	6	100	0		0		6
Lawyers	70	72	23	23	4	4	97
Newspaper proprietors or editors	15	94	1	6	0		16
All business men:	107	62	55	32	11	6	173
Active and substantial business men only	94	66	38	27	10	7	142
Active business men who were landed gentlemen	21	64	10	30	2	6	33
Active business men who were not landed gentlemen	73	67	28	26	8	7	109
Bankers	11	58	8	42	0		19
Brewers	6	60	2	20	2	20	10
Merchants	30	71	9	21	3	7	42
Textile manufacturers	17	74	4	17	2	9	23
Railway directors	23	42	31	56	1	2	55
Working class	12	100	0		0		12

*Indicates those Liberals who for reason of death, health, expulsion from the House, or elevation to the House of Lords, or for unknown causes, did not vote on the second reading of the Government of Ireland Bill.
[†]According to this reckoning, landed gentlemen in the Liberal party were those Members who belonged to the peerage–baronetage–landed gentry through the paternal line, the maternal line, or marriage.

on the question. Lower proportions of Liberals with connections to the baronetage and the landed gentry, 36 per cent of the former and 32 per cent of the latter, became Liberal Unionists. Still, the slightly inflated proportions of Liberals connected to the peerage–baronetage–

landed gentry give some support to the notion that the landed classes revolted against Gladstone on this occasion. Substantial elements of landed society had been Liberal before 1886, and this general pattern was unchanged by the Home Rule crisis. As these figures show, the Home Rule issue did not drive Liberal landed gentlemen, at least those sitting in the House of Commons, into the waiting arms of the Conservatives through the mediation of the Liberal Unionist faction. The evidence will not bear the weight of this contention.

And similarly for other social groups in the Liberal party. So far as the fact that army officers and railway directors tended to become Liberal Unionists is concerned, Table 4.11 shows the former untypical of Liberals with professions and the latter untypical of Liberal business men. Naval officers and, more tellingly, lawyers strongly pronounced for Home Rule. Bankers, brewers, and, with great proportions, merchants and textile manufacturers supported Gladstone's Government. To control the figures for landed gentlemen by business interest or profession, or to control the figures for business men or professional men by landed status, yields not quite nothing, but little more. Aside for the slightest tendency for business men or professional men with landed status to be more Unionist, or a similarly slight tendency for landed gentlemen with active business interests or professions to be more Gladstonian, these figures are not convincing evidence for a social or economic interpretation of the Home Rule conflict in the Liberal party. From top to bottom the weight of the various social groups in the Liberal party rested with the Gladstonian, the Home Rule faction.

Moreover, as Table 4.12 indicates, Members with status did not desert the Liberals in this crisis. Since these qualities have a high degree of association with the landed classes, and since the proportion of landed gentlemen in the Liberal Unionist faction increased slightly, it is not surprising to find a similar increase in Unionist proportions for these groups. However, there are no substantial differences between these factions in the matter of status, and these indicators are divided nearly equally between both groups. The Gladstonians held the largest proportion of every status group, save one. Therefore, no matter where one turns, the analysis of the social background of Liberals, or the analysis of status groups within the parliamentary Liberal party, shed virtually no light on the Home Rule disruption in the Liberal party in 1886.

This conclusion should be pushed to a point of further resolution because the role of the Whigs in this crisis has excited so much attention. One historian has gone so far as to call the great separation in the Liberal party 'the revolt of the Whigs'. As Donald Southgate

TABLE 4.12 *Indicators of Social Status in the Gladstonian and Liberal Unionist Factions*

	Gladstonians		Unionists		Others*		No.
	No.	%	No.	%	No.	%	
Public school education	55	60	30	33	6	7	91
Patronage of Church livings	13	48	13	48	1	2	27
Commission in yeomanry or militia	19	45	22	52	1	2	42
Mother peerage–baronetage–landed gentry	32	54	21	36	6	10	59
Wife peerage–baronetage–landed gentry[†]	35	57	21	34	5	8	61
Personal land in excess of 3,000 acres	25	48	23	44	4	8	52
Family's land in excess of 3,000 acres	43	53	32	40	6	7	81

*Indicates those Liberals who for reason of death, expulsion from the House, or elevation to the House of Lords, or for other reasons, did not vote in the division on the Government of Ireland Bill.
†Indicates first marriages only.

has written, 'the meeting of the new Parliament at the beginning of 1886 was to see the definitive divorce between the mass of Whiggery and the official Liberal party.' And still another historian takes the view that the Home Rule crisis removed from the party 'the more opportunistic radicalism of Chamberlain and . . . almost all the Whigs'.[91] Chamberlain himself believed Home Rule would drive the Whigs out. As he wrote to Harcourt, 'you will, if you succeed, drive away from the Liberal party all the "classes" so graphically described by Mr Gladstone in his manifesto. The remnant will be "kittle cattle" to drive, especially as the G.O.M. will no doubt be employed in making his peace with his Maker and leave to Mundella and Morley and you the task of resisting irreconcilable demands.'[92] It would be an elementary, but important, advance to know how many Whigs defected in 1886. But who were they? Social nomenclature is always slippery, and the indefiniteness and elusiveness of this term renders its usefulness particularly limited in detailed research. W. S. Blunt described a Whig of whom he though thoroughly approved. 'Of all the people in the world I like Henry Cowper the best. He represents the Whig tradition in its most attractive form, that of the cultured

[91] Goodman, 'Liberal Unionism', *passim*; Southgate, *The Passing of the Whigs, 1832–1886*, p. 382; Peter Stansky, 'Review of Michael Barker's *Gladstone and Radicalism*', *Victorian Studies*, 19.2 (Dec. 1975), p. 267.
[92] Chamberlain to Harcourt, 5 May 1886, Chamberlain Papers JC5/38/160.

politician of a hundred years ago, partly humane, partly sceptical, full of dignity and profoundly immoral.'[93] But just before the onset of the Home Rule crisis, in quite another mood, Blunt described a Whig dinner, at Brooks's, a Whiggish club. Henry Brand, Lord Richard Grosvenor, and Courtney Boyle

> talked about liberty in a way to make C. J. Fox turn in his grave. They are all for blood & iron in Ireland. They are going to support Lord Salisbury if he goes for martial law. They are for disenfranchising the whole country, suppressing habeas corpus, & dragooning the people all round. . . . They are all Whigs of the old school, who are a bloody race, — & are maddened with the thought of losing property to Ireland. Hartington, Harry says, will go with them for he has great possessions.[94]

Even statements of individuals normally assumed to have been Whigs have not always been helpful in efforts to define either social position or political policy. The Duke of Argyll, for example, denied he was a Whig:

> I was born and brought up in a house on which the Flag was hoisted every day when news came of a Whig defeat in Parliament. People on Clydeside used to say when they saw the flag flying 'Hech sure! What's happened to the Whigs NOO!'
> So that I never had special sympathy with the Whigs as a section.
> I began as a Peelite and I remain of that complexion — holding to what you call 'an enlightened spirit of administration'; and to 'all elementary principles of Government'.[95]

Only two Members of this House of Commons consciously styled themselves as Whigs, Henry Wyndham West and Sir Mathew Wilson, Bt. To go on the basis of their social and political experience alone in an effort to define the concept of Whiggery would not take the discussion far.

By the early twentieth century the term Whig had come to mean any moderate Liberal.[96] In the 1880s, however, it retained, in addition to the note of political moderation, the tone of social exclusiveness and an association with the landed classes. As one observer of parliamentary politics put it, 'in the English House of Commons . . . the Left Centre includes not only Whigs, but men . . . who have nothing in common with the Whigs except the general

[93] Blunt Diary, 19 Aug. 1885, Blunt MS 333-1975, f. 125.
[94] Ibid., 30 Dec. 1885, Blunt MS 333-1975, ff. 227–8.
[95] Argyll to Gladstone, 2 Oct. 1885, BL Add. MS 44106, ff. 11–12.
[96] Trevor Wilson, *The Downfall of the Liberal Party, 1914–1935* (London: 1968), p. 16.

moderation of their views and a sense of political responsibility.'[97] Alfred Milner, Goschen's private secretary in 1884, was even more explicit about the differences between the Whigs and other moderates in the Liberal party. 'The moderation of the Whig is the result not of moderate principles but of the accident of birth and of having no principles at all.'[98] Moderates such as Goschen wished no association with the Whigs, because it implied a traditionalism and a connection with privilege they found repugnant.[99]

It is possible, despite the indefiniteness of social language, to assemble the evidence of social background and political position used for this study in such a way as to isolate those members of the Liberal party who by virtue of their political moderation and their connection to the landed could be considered Whigs. One hundred and forty-two Liberals were moderate in the sense that they held scale positions at the median or to the right of the median on the great parliamentary voting dimension. Of these moderates, seventy-four were also landed gentlemen. These, for the purposes of this discussion, were the Whigs. Some were the sons of peers and included the sons of the Duke of Devonshire, Lord Edward Cavendish and the Marquess of Hartington, the sons of the Third Earl Minto, A. R. D. Elliot and H. F. H. Elliot, and the son of the Sixth Earl of Fitzwilliam, William John Wentworth Fitzwilliam. Some were baronets or their sons, including Sir Thomas Dyke Acland and two of his sons, Sir Saville Brinton Crossley, and Sir Ughtred James Kay-Shuttleworth. Representatives of gentry families included Henry Allen, John Glencairn Carter Hamilton, Edward Heneage, the Howard brothers, Miles MacInnes of Rickerby, and Thomas Tertius Paget. Some of these gentry members, such as William Coare Brocklehurst of Butley Hill and Tytherington and Miles MacInnes, have the appearance of *nouveaux*, but others claimed distinguished family histories. R. F. F. Campbell, of Craigie House, Ayrshire, claimed descent from William Campbell, who acquired a fortune in India and purchased the Craigie estate in 1783. William Henry Grenfell, of Taplow Court, Buckinghamshire, traced his ancestry to the Grenfells of Cornwall in the seventeenth century. Robert Thornhagh Gurdon, of Woodbridge and Brantham Court, Suffolk, located his origins with Brampton Gurdon, High Sheriff for Suffolk

---

[97] G. C. Broderick, 'Liberals and Whigs', *Fortnightly Review*, 29 (May 1879), p. 738.

[98] Milner to Goschen, 21 Aug. 1884, Viscount Milner Papers, Bodleian Library, Box 182, quoted in Cooke and Vincent, *The Governing Passion*, p. 100 n.

[99] Cooke and Vincent, *The Governing Passion*, p. 100 n.

in 1645 and MP for Ipswich from 1640 to 1654. Edward Heneage, of Hainton Hall, Lincolnshire, derived his ancestry from Sir Robert de Heneage who lived during the time of William Rufus. Heneage and Acland claimed to hold land in unbroken succession since the fifteenth century. In general these moderate landed gentlemen held those qualities most often associated with the landed élite. A majority had attended public schools and sat for county constituencies, and of these last some were beneficiaries of the last remnants of territorial electoral influence.

But to turn to the point, there is no foundation in the evidence for the notion that the Home Rule crisis in the Liberal party turned on social conflict in which these moderate landed gentlemen revolted and bolted from the party. As an inspection of Table 4.13 will show, Whigs with active and substantial business interests or with professions were most likely to remain Gladstonian; Whigs with connection to the peerage were most likely to become Liberal Unionists. However, the Whigs divided themselves on both sides of the Home Rule question. The crisis in the Liberal party over Home Rule reflected a crisis in the regime, not in society. Political characteristics, not social characteristics, go furthest in explaining the great separation in the Liberal party.

Conclusion

Evelyn Waugh, speculating upon the decline of the gentleman, believed 'American marriages in the 90s and the lady shopkeepers in the 20s . . . made all the trouble'.[1] Whatever its fate or nostalgic

TABLE 4.13 *The Whigs and the Great Separation in the Liberal Party in 1886*

	Gladstonians		Unionists		Others		No.
	No.	%	No.	%	No.	%	
Peerage	7	44	9	56	0		16
Baronetage	13	62	8	38	0		21
Landed gentry	16	57	10	36	2	7	28
Connected to PBG through the maternal line or marriage	7	78	2	22	0		9
All Whigs	43	58	29	39	2	3	74
Whigs with active and substantial business interests	9	75	3	25	0		12
Whigs with professions	15	65	7	30	1	5	23

[1] Waugh to Nancy Mitford, 8 Jan. 1952, *The Letters of Evelyn Waugh*, ed. Mark Amory (New Haven and New York: 1980), p. 364.

function in the twentieth century, status which was associated with the landed classes stood for something in political circles during the 1880s. Uniting people by education, moral values, marriage, property, and a sense of political and social responsibility, it separated those with connections to landed society from those attached to the worlds of business and the professions. Yet, this social cleavage did not translate itself into political conflict. The social background of Conservatives and Irish Nationalists had virtually nothing to do with the policy preferences of these parties, because their members voted with virtual unanimity on the questions coming before this House of Commons. The social background of Members, it is true, revealed itself in a slight, though not significant, preference for partisan affiliation, and, for the Liberals alone, distinguished between those who supported and those who opposed radical measures. When the Liberal party could not contain the excessive radical spirits in its ranks (that is to say, when extremist dissent rose to half the party voting) on questions fitting the radical agenda, political behaviour found itself expressed in such a manner as to correspond to the social background of Liberals. This did not split the party, however. It is a paradox, which makes it none the less true, that social stratification in the Liberal party was associated with parliamentary voting on those occasions when policy differences did not rupture the party, and that social stratifications had no great consequence on that great occasion of conflict when Home Rule split the party. The social background of Liberals had utterly nothing to do with the stances Liberals struck on the Irish government question. This was a political matter which did not turn on questions of social or economic interest. Home Rule was politically disruptive because it was unconnected to a social grouping of political values. Had it been, social association could have mediated conflict, making the Liberal disruption and the Liberal Unionist–Conservative alignment unnecessary. Since the distribution of social groups in the Liberal party remained consistent throughout the Home Rule crisis, it is clear that social differences did not cause the Liberal split. It is evidence, on the other hand, that the party could contain social differences and prevent them from becoming political differences.

Irksome findings such as these, pointing in different directions simultaneously, surprise only those who have not soiled themselves in the materials of social and political research; they merely reveal the limitations of social class as an independent variable. Moreover, they go to show that social class is not structured naturally into political experience. Social class, as Giovanni Sartori has pointed out, is an ideology.[2] It is what Disraeli called a 'cry', a device for the rallying and defeating of majorities. As a consequence, like other ideologies, social class is subject to the transforming power of intervening variables which may modify them. Parties, even Parliament itself in this case, served this intervening function.

Parties in the nineteenth century (and this remained true in 1886) were not economic or social groupings. In fact, a strong body of opinion sought to prevent them from so becoming, their function being to contain or reconcile social differences. This was part of Disraeli's argument for electoral reform in 1867, for the participation of working-class members in the Liberal party, just as it was part of Lord Randolph Churchill's attempt to assert his leadership in the Conservative party. As Churchill put it, shortly before the Home Rule crisis developed:

The principles of political organization which animate the Council [of the National Union of Conservative Associations] are the encouragement, extension, & formation of popular associations combining all classes & electing a representative and responsible executive in electoral districts for the carrying on of all business relating to parliamentary elections. This is the form of political organization which has been widely and successfully adopted by the Liberal party, which is the only political combination suitable to the present vast electorate, but which, as far as the Conservative party is concerned, is solely confined to some of the most populous constituencies.[3]

Such was the function of partisanship for some Liberals, as they themselves recognized. John Morley was once asked how he enjoyed country house weekends. They were pleasurable, he responded, but blighted his democracy.[4] Edward Hamilton described a parliamentary dinner at Herbert Gardner's home in the spring of 1886. There, at table, the Marquess of Breadalbane, the owner of vast estates, sat next to Joseph Arch, the agricultural labourer. Hamilton commented on the remarkable sight of a landowner 'chumming' with the labourer MP.[5] Such was the way social mechanisms, within parties, drew together those of differing backgrounds, serving as bridges to cross social distinctions, allowing social distance and permitting political intimacy. Parties were more than channels for

[2] Giovanni Sartori, 'From the Sociology of Politics to Political Sociology', *Politics and the Social Sciences*, ed. Seymour Martin Lipset (New York and Oxford: 1968), pp. 83–5.
[3] Lord Randolph Churchill to M. Satchell Hopkins, n.d. but late Nov. 1885, Lord Randolph Churchill Letters 1/9/1043.
[4] Earl of Midleton, *Records and Recollections*, p. 51.
[5] Edward Hamilton Diary, 14 Apr. 1886, BL Add. MS 48643, f. 86.

interests and policies. As others have shown for other legislatures,[6] they did not eliminate internal differences, but transcended and transformed them; they produced the kind of co-ordination within the political system which made it possible to develop the ideological policy fronts which appear in the form of parliamentary voting dimensions.

Parties, moreover, as the history of the Labour and Conservative parties in the twentieth century would prove, could induce class feeling. Social class, like other ideologies, expresses what individuals want; it serves as an over-simplification of a political sort to manage conflict. Labouchere, for example, regarded the Home Rule crisis as an opportunity to ditch the Whigs, to 'shunt' them aside and to reconstruct the Liberal party along more radical lines.[7] Gladstone himself, in his classes and masses manifesto, used class language to mobilize electoral support behind his Home Rule policies. Edward Hamilton recognized that social class was not naturally structured into political experience, and that the language of class could produce undesirable consequences. He described the ways in which Gladstone's allusion to class had 'been fixed upon with avidity by his opponents and [had] shaken many a weak knee'. Hamilton believed this was a bad turn. After the Home Rule crisis, he remarked, 'the last thing one wants to see stirred up in this country is class hatred or a war of classes'.[8]

From this it follows that the language of class conflict in 1886 did not refer to objective social conditions nor to their consequences for political action. Rather the reverse. The language of class conflict was moral and prescriptive; it referred to social conflict as the consequence of political action. An objective toward which political action directed itself, class conflict was often the consequence rather than the cause or the explanation of political behaviour. Political conflict became social only when parties and the parliamentary system failed to accommodate the diverse forces at work in the House of Commons.

[6] Smith and Turner, 'Legislative Behaviour in the German Reichstag, 1898–1906', pp. 14–16; Ballard Campbell, *Representative Democracy, Public Policy and Mid-western Legislatures in the Nineteenth Century* (Cambridge, Mass.: 1980), Michael Less Benedict's review of *Representative Democracy* in *Journal of Interdisciplinary History*, 13.1 (Summer 1982), pp. 170–1.

[7] Labouchere to Chamberlain, 31 Mar. 1886, Algar Labouchere Thorold, *The Life of Henry Labouchere* (London: 1913), pp. 289–90.

[8] Edward Hamilton Diary, 6 May 1886 and 29 June 1886, BL Add. MS 48643, f. 110, and 48644, f. 49.

5

The Constituency Basis of Politics
in the House of Commons

My electioneering experience in Cumberland and elsewhere leads me
to the conclusion that no creature which God has created is so difficult
to understand as the English elector. You never can safely predict what
he will do under any circumstances.

Sir Wilfred Lawson[1]

I am furious at the possible chance of finding no seat for you [Reginald
Brett] up here — unless death clears out someone or insanity in the case
of Havelock-Allan. That is the worst of the new scheme, small expense
& single member constituencies will bring forward any idiot who fancies
he is a politician.

The Earl of Durham[2]

I wish all the counties had followed the example of Hertfordshire
and am grieved that my own prophecy has come true, namely that
we should do well in the boroughs and that the rural districts would
be radical.

Baron Dimsdale[3]

The 'Cow' has done well in the agricultural districts and would have
done better but for the fear as to the secrecy of the Ballot. The labourers
will gain confidence by experience but we are dreadfully in want of an
'urban Cow'. The boroughs do not care for our present programme
and I confess I do not know what substitute to offer them.

Joseph Chamberlain[4]

In my own division I was terribly handicapped by the hostile presence
& influence of Derby & Burton, & of the most Radical towns in
England, the former only relieved of the charitable debauchery of
Bass Senior to fall prey to the political corruption of Sir W. Harcourt:
the latter saturated with the streams (both of beer & money) set
in motion by Sir Arthur Bass. Though things are going badly, I hope

---

[1] G. W. E. Russell (ed.), *Sir Wilfred Lawson*, pp. 147–8.
[2] The Earl of Durham to Reginald Brett, 9 Jan. 1885, Esher Papers 10/7. For
the influence of Lambton Castle see Henry Pelling, *The Social Geography of British
Elections, 1885–1910* (London, Melbourne, Toronto, and New York: 1967), pp. 335,
338.
[3] Baron Dimsdale to Lord Salisbury, 7 Dec. 1885, Third Marquess of Salisbury
MSS Class E.
[4] Chamberlain to Sir William Harcourt, 6 Dec. 1885, Chamberlain Papers
JC5/38/152.

209

we may still be spared of the shame of another period however short
of Gladstonian rule.

George Curzon[5]

Introduction

Albert Grey must have felt a kinship with Lawson. His electors in
the Tyneside division of Northumberland returned him with a very
safe majority in the general election of 1885. He believed he had
triumphed completely over the caucus there, and they suspected he
would be a 'thorn in the side of any Liberal Govt. which proposes
Liberal measures'.[6] In the fever of the Home Rule crisis he asked
his election agent to call together his friends and supporters. Grey's
agent wrote back, 'you have no supporters and I am your only
friend.'[7] Lewis Harcourt was much amused at Grey's efforts to rally
constituency support when only thirteen of 1,000 men gathered at
a Newcastle meeting voted for his anti-government resolution.[8] If
Members such as Grey have had difficulties assessing their relationship
to their constituents, how much more difficult must it be for students
of these matters, who cannot interview the dead, to chart the
connections between electors and those they returned to Westminster.
One wag has called electoral sociology the *vice anglais*, and the most
distinguished student of elections has spoken of his 'melancholy
experience with the eccentricity' of their data. But the importance
of constituencies and the significance of local research into them is
great, and, much to the disadvantage of some distinguished research
in parliamentary history, these elements have sometimes been overlooked.[9] Unfortunately, much of the richness of constituency information[10] is rendered inaccessible in studies such as the present one.

---

[5] Curzon to Salisbury, 6 Dec. 1885, Third Marquess of Salisbury MSS Class E.
(This is George Nathaniel Curzon, the heir of Lord Scarsdale, who stood unsuccessfully
for the Southern division of Derbyshire in the general election of 1885, and who was
elected for the Southport division of Lancashire in 1886, not George Richard Penn,
Viscount Curzon, the son of Earl Howe, who was returned for the Wycombe division
of Buckinghamshire in 1885 and 1886.)

[6] Lewis Harcourt Journal, 12 Jan. 1886, Harcourt dep. 376, f. 52.

[7] Edward Hamilton Diary, 9 May 1886, BL Add. MS 48643, ff. 118–19. In
1885 Grey had been returned with a majority of 25% of the poll. The Tyneside
division, however, was not a safe seat for Liberal Unionists. In the general election
of 1886 the official Liberal candidate, Wentworth Blackett Beaumont, defeated Grey,
and it remained a Liberal seat, though marginally, until 1900.

[8] Lewis Harcourt Journal, 3 May 1886, Harcourt dep. 378, f. 117.

[9] J. H. Plumb, 'The True Voice of Clio', *The Times Literary Supplement*, 2 May
1980, p. 485.

[10] Pelling, *The Social Geography of British Elections*; Peter Clarke, 'Electoral
Sociology of Modern Britain', *History*, 57 (1972), pp. 31–55.

The histories of local disputes and wrangles, of doubtless importance in shaping the relations of representatives and electors, cannot be reported in a form comparable for all elections and in all constituencies. It is difficult to know which is typical and which is sport. Consequently, the information used in the following pages is about neither elections nor the motivations of electors. Rather, it takes certain comparable features of constituencies and seeks to determine whether or not they were related to the partisan preferences[11] and the political behaviour of Members of the House of Commons as measured by their positions on parliamentary voting dimensions. These data include the size and type of electorates, the regions of constituencies, and the degree to which electors returned their Members with safe majorities. These first two are crude indicators of the urban–rural character of the electorate. The third is an indicator of ethnicity and sectionalism in British politics. The fourth estimates the degree of security with which Members held their seats, an indicator of the extent to which they might be expected to be returned again.

As modern research on the subject shows, legislators may only imperfectly understand the preferences of their constituents, but they invariably vote in ways they conceive to be consistent with those preferences.[12] There is ample evidence to document the assiduity with which some Members of the House of Commons in 1886 concerned themselves with their constituents' views. Forty volumes of letter-books in the Balfour Papers testify to Balfour's involvement in the local affairs of his constituency during the years he represented the Eastern division of Manchester.[13] Colonel George Salis-Schwabe, a business man, told Gladstone that, eager as he personally was to support the Government's Irish policy, 'the pledges on which I won the Middleton Div. of S. E. Lancashire, would I fear not be compatible with voting for a Legislative Assembly in Dublin for the whole of Ireland'.[14] All Lancashire Liberals, he believed, were bound by a similar pledge. Sir Richard Temple expected the votes of the Members on the Home Rule question, and especially those of the 'waverer Liberals', to turn on constituency

---

[11] For another study using the structural characteristics of constituencies, but different ones for the twentieth century, see Jorgen Rasmussen, 'The Impact of Constituency Structural Characteristics Upon Political Preferences in Britain', *Comparative Politics*, Oct. 1973.

[12] Warren E. Miller and Donald E. Stokes, 'Constituency Influence in Congress', *American Political Science Review*, 62 (1963), pp. 51, 56.

[13] BL Add. MSS 49838–58, 49870–91.

[14] Salis-Schwabe to Gladstone, 6 Mar. 1886, BL Add. MS 44495, f. 153.

opinion.[15] Salis-Schwabe paid close attention to the opinions of his electors. He had won pretty handily in 1885 and his seat was a safe one, but after voting against the Home Rule Bill he stood down in the elections of 1886.

One of Salis-Schwabe's Lancashire colleagues in the House, Lord Cranborne, had even greater reason to heed the opinions of his electors. In 1885 Cranborne had gained his seat in the Darwen division by merely five votes. He retained his seat in the general election of 1886, but the swing to Toryism and Unionism was insufficient to convert it into a safe seat. Still, he did considerably better, and his majority exceeded 6 per cent of the poll. In the period between these elections Cranborne attended to his electors diligently, and his papers are full of correspondence on constituency matters during the months of January, March, and, especially, June of 1886. L. W. Wraith, the chief agent for the Darwen Conservative Registration Association, wished particularly to have Cranborne broaden his circle of support. As Wraith put it concerning an invitation to speak to the Darwen Society, 'it is a good [opportunity] of becoming better known to the opposition [while] appearing in a non-party character to your constituents in general and may give you an opportunity to state your readiness to be of service to all alike. . . . You will forgive me for saying that I think your position will be strengthened in proportion as you find opportunities to speak to the enemy.'[16] Some Members found a closer connection with their electors necessary; some more than others had an interest in developing such a connection. For John Edward Ellis, for example, the value of a democratic election lay in an association between himself and his constituents which would 'enable him to represent their views faithfully'.[17]

One cannot say how far Ellis's colleagues, whether Conservative or Liberal or Irish Nationalist, shared his attitudes on the subject of representation. What can be said, however, is that under certain circumstances the social and economic characteristics of constituencies influence the political choices electors make in choosing their representatives.[18] Moreover, for British politics in the nineteenth

---

[15] Temple Letters, 14 and 20 Apr. 1886, BL Add. MS 38916, ff. 60ᵛ, 73ᵛ.

[16] Wraith to Cranborne, 18 Jan. 1886, Fourth Marquess of Salisbury MSS Bundle 1.

[17] A. T. Bassett, *The Life of the Rt. Hon. John Edward Ellis, M.P.* (London: 1914), p. 57.

[18] Duncan MacRae, Jr., 'The Relations Between Roll Call Votes and Constituencies', *Legislative Behaviour: A Reader in Theory and Research*, ed. John C. Wahlke and Heinz Eulau (Glencoe, Ill.: 1959), pp. 197–203.

century there was a close association between the extent to which constituencies had an urban or rural character and the political affiliation or political behaviour of Members of the House of Commons.[19] The history of the relations between electors and Members after 1884–5, it can be shown, was different. The reforms of those years created a new political world in which the ancient distinction between town and country, in a political sense, meant considerably less than it once had done. By destroying one set of electoral structures and establishing others, constituencies were increased in numbers and size, and this freed electoral energies. Organization, in the constituencies and in the House of Commons, became more important than ever before. Forces of partisanship, consequently, grew both inside the House and without it. Other forces released themselves as well; the forces of Welsh, Scottish, and Irish Nationalism, forces which were alike cultural and ethnic.

The Reforms of 1884–5

Sir William Harcourt regarded the reforms effected in 1884 and 1885 as a social as well as a political revolution. 'Since the conversion of the Franks there has never been seen such a moral transformation as that which has come over the party aspect of the eastern, western, the southwestern and some of the midland counties . . . The influence of the peer, squire, and the parson has vanished.'[20] Harcourt's partisan enthusiasm may be excused, perhaps; but by admitting to the franchise adult males in the counties the reform Bill vastly expanded the electorate. The redistribution legislation was even more remarkable. Its principal features were two. The redistribution Bill established single-Member constituencies and worked toward an equalization of their sizes. Twenty-five exceptions were allowed to the creation of single-Member constituencies, and these only in large towns. More constituencies, in consequence, were created. The House was increased from 658 Members to 670, but the number of constituencies was increased from 413 to 643. The legislation achieved greater equality of electorates by removing representation from boroughs having populations of less than 1,500 and by combining these with adjacent counties. The counties and the larger cities were divided into single-Member electoral divisions. This freed

[19] W. O. Aydelotte, 'Constituency Influence on the British House of Commons, 1841–1847', *The History of Legislative Behaviour*, pp. 229–30, 233–6; Hugh W. Stephens and David W. Brady, 'The Parliamentary Parties and the Electoral Reforms of 1884–1885 in Great Britain', *Legislative Studies Quarterly*, 1.4 (Nov. 1976).

[20] Sir William Harcourt to the Editor of *The Times*, 11 Dec. 1885, p. 8.

142 for redistribution. The consequences of redistribution, therefore, were two. Small boroughs virtually disappeared from the political life of the country. Seven cities (London, Birmingham, Leeds, Liverpool, Manchester, Sheffield, and Edinburgh) held better than 14 per cent of the representation of the United Kingdom. The electoral weight of the country shifted to the industrial north from the agricultural south.

Some electoral fashions continued, and status was one of these. Sir Richard Temple wished to be raised to the Privy Council because 'it would give me additional weight in my county at a time when we need all the moral strength obtainable in order to sustain our position'.[21] Wilfred Scawen Blunt wanted peers to canvass for him in the Northern division of Camberwell in 1885, and Lord Randolph Churchill sent him, not peers, but the sons of peers.[22] Yet, as electoral forces, the Rothschilds, the Barons Egerton of Tatton, the Dukes of Devonshire, and the Earls of Verulam, if not wholly spent, represented a dying breed. The Earl of Selborne, having the defeat of Lord Henry Cavendish-Bentinck by Joseph Arch specifically in mind, believed the new electoral conditions had driven the sons of peers from constituency politics.[23] He neglected to remember his own son sitting for the Petersfield division of Hampshire, or the son of Lord Salisbury sitting for the Darwen division of Lancashire. Strictly speaking, landed patronage had become a thing of the past, and only twelve landlords controlled seats in the old style.[24]

The decline of landlord control over elections, of course, is one of the great stories of the nineteenth century, but it can be overdone. Selborne's closeness to the situation tempted him in the overdoing. It would be more accurate to speak of the transformation of landed influence rather than its disappearance. Studies of local politics in Northamptonshire and Warwickshire show the ways in which formal and direct mechanisms for the control of elections were replaced by informal and indirect techniques of election management. Prominence in local constituency associations and substantial contributions to party funds allowed landowners to have considerable say in the selection of candidates. Their desire to have considerable say was prompted in the 1880s and 1890s by the character of the policy agenda of the period, especially by the prominence given over to land

[21] Sir Richard Temple, Bt. to Salisbury, 6 Dec. 1885, Third Marquess of Salisbury MSS Class E.

[22] Blunt Diary, 4 Aug. 1885, Blunt MS 333-1975, f. 104.

[23] Earl of Selborne, *Memorials, Part II, Personal and Political 1865–1895* (London: 1898), pp. 188–9.

[24] Hanham, *Elections and Party Management*, p. 405.

reform. The demands for the ransom of property and for 'three acres and a cow' and other attacks on territorial influence provoked a landlord counter-attack in which they found new and more flexible ways to set forward and maintain their local political authority between 1885 and 1914. Landed gentlemen continued to have an electoral advantage because they were natural leaders. Because of their status and reputation, though no longer because of their patronage of seats, they continued to influence the fortunes of their parties.[25]

Though to such an extent landlord influence remained, the electoral world after 1885 changed mightily. The constituency Sir Richard Temple fought in 1885, the Evesham division of Worcestershire, 'comprised a goodly portion of the area I had contested in 1880, which was nearest my home, and which had Evesham for its head-quarters'. However, he had to increase his electoral exertions in 1885 because, instead of dealing only with electors of local substance, 'the upper section of rural society, with the farmers and freeholders', Temple had to concern himself with the newly enfranchised. A meeting had to be held in every village for this purpose, and in Temple's case this required more than eighty meetings.[26] It was not far different for Murray Finch-Hatton, the son of the Earl of Winchilsea, in the Spaulding division of Lincolnshire. Because of the election's uncertainty and the increased number of meetings, the contest began early. On 1 July 1885, Finch-Hatton wrote to Lord Salisbury, 'I began my own campaign in the Spaulding division yesterday with a successful meeting at Spaulding, and I have others every day this week.'[27] William Tyssen-Amherst, the leading land-owner in the Southwest division of Norfolk, reported similar activity. 'On the eve of the battle I must write you a line to tell you what our prospects are. We have two more meetings, tonight and tomorrow, which will complete some 54 that we had open to all Electors. 45 of them have been held in different places. We thought it advisable to visit the larger towns twice.'[28] Nor were the Tories alone in being concerned about the demands new electoral conditions imposed.

---

[25] Janet Howarth, 'The Liberal Revival in Northamptonshire, 1880–1895: A Case Study in Late Nineteenth Century Elections', *Historical Journal*, 12.1 (1969), pp. 91–2; Roland Quinault, 'Landlords and Parliamentary Politics' (unpublished Ph.D. dissertation, University of Oxford: 1975), p. vii and *passim*.

[26] Sir Richard Temple, *The Story of My Life*, vol. 2, pp. 103, 105.

[27] Finch-Hatton to Salisbury, 1 July 1885, Third Marquess of Salisbury MSS Class E.

[28] Tyssen-Amherst to Salisbury, 2 Dec. 1885, Third Marquess of Salisbury MSS Class E.

Edward Hamilton described the efforts of the Hon. Charles Robert Spencer, recently risen from his sick-bed after a 'frightful illness', in Northamptonshire, a division—the most rural in the region—which his brother's influence and acres should have made safe for him. 'He is just entering on his election campaign. He had to *stump* the whole of his Division. He has got over 40 meetings already arranged and there will be some 20 others to follow.'[29]

If peers could not chivvy votes, if vastly increased numbers of electors and the equalization of electoral districts increased the work of candidates and their canvassers, the multiplication of the number of constituencies offered new opportunities for parliamentary service to political outsiders. No longer could local communities produce the talent required for Parliament. The crofter districts, the large cities, and even the rural divisions had the advantages, and the banes of representatives who came from elsewhere. This was not received with satisfaction by many, and the Earl of Durham, whose thoughts on this are found at the head of this chapter, could refer to the way in which single-Member constituencies and reduced election expenses produced intellectually negligible candidates. The Earl of Selborne distrusted the tendencies of the newly enfranchised who were prepared 'to listen to adventurers or theorists who professed to have special interests at heart'. The new electoral conditions brought candidacy, for the first time, 'within reach of men of moderate means, or of no means at all if they represented any cause in aid of which a subscription could be raised'.[30]

As participants in these events recognized, the redistribution features of these reforms did the most to alter the relations between electors and Members. In London, Sheffield, Leeds, Bristol, Birmingham, and the Lancashire towns, the boundary commissioners could construct socially homogeneous constituencies. This was not possible everywhere. In the drive to create constituencies of comparable sizes the commissioners constructed constituencies which were socially artificial. Thrusting together rural and town electors, they often liquidated the more natural electoral demarcation between town and country.[31] South Northamptonshire, for example, was a rural

---

[29] Edward Hamilton Diary, 28 Sept. 1885, BL Add. MS 48641, f. 88. The Hon. C. R. Spencer held his seat with a safe majority in 1886, took it with another safe majority in the general election of 1886, and held it with a diminished and vulnerable majority in 1892. He lost the Mid-Northamptonshire seat in 1895, but regained it, though with a vulnerable majority, in 1900.

[30] Selborne, *Memorials, Part III*, pp. 188–9.

[31] H. J. Hanham, *The Reformed Electoral System in Great Britain, 1832–1914* (London: 1968), p. 25.

constituency which contained market towns such as Brackley and
Daventry. From 1885 it included more villages from the south
which were strongly Liberal.[32] Consequently, the constituency was
Conservative in 1885 and 1886, but only marginally so. It fell to
the Liberals in 1892 and only became strongly Conservative in 1895
and 1900. In Cardiganshire, the reforms absorbed the borough seats
and merged four contributory boroughs with the county division.
Accordingly, the most prominent student of modern Wales has
noted, 'the more static politics of the county were injected with the
more complex tensions and the more radical passions of the urban
voters.'[33]

The significance of redistribution was lost on no one, and, as
T. H. Sidebottom noted, franchise extension without a favourable
redistribution policy would be 'political suicide' for the Tories.
The particular manifestations of redistribution could be worked to
partisasn advantage. Sidebottom knew how fraught Derbyshire
would be if the Cardiganshire example were followed there. 'The
position of each [of the] counties near here is practically urban
and in any redistribution Bill the Boroughs round about can be so
manipulated by attaching a portion of the county as to [render?]
them sure Radical seats.'[34] Similarly, Reginald Mcleod, Salisbury's
agent in Scotland, realized a mingling of town and country electors
would work to the disadvantage of the Conservative party there.
He wanted the amalgamation of towns into electoral burghs in
order to 'prevent our strength being everywhere overwhelmed by
an illogical and unfair distribution of representation'. The real
point of importance, Mcleod went on to note, 'is the addition
of populous places to existing groups of boroughs. If this is con-
ceded as shown in the enclosed brief memorandum the prospects of
our party are materially improved in *ten* county divisions.'[35] The
interpenetration of town and country in the election in the Frome
division of Somersetshire was also decisive. Here, close enough to
Longleat for the Marquess of Bath to have limited influence, the
towns had been the traditional enemies of the Fourth Marquess's
brother. When Lord Weymouth, the heir to the marquisate, stood

---

[32] Peter Gordon, 'Lady Knightley and the South Northamptonshire Election
1885', *Northamptonshire, Past and Present*, 6.5 (1981–2), p. 266.

[33] Kenneth O. Morgan, 'Cardiganshire Politics: The Liberal Ascendancy, 1885–
1923', *Ceredigion, The Journal of the Cardiganshire Antiquarian Society*, 5.4 (1967),
p. 313.

[34] T. H. Sidebottom to Salisbury, 8 May 1884, Third Marquess of Salisbury MSS
Class E.

[35] Mcleod to Salisbury, 19 Feb. 1885, Third Marquess of Salisbury MSS Class E.

for the seat in 1885 he was defeated by the number of colliers there.[36] In 1885 and after, artificial constituencies of this sort became creatures of Westminster politicians rather than of local communities. National and regional political issues rather than local ones would decide election results.[37]

The Nature of Constituencies and their Relation to Political Behaviour[38]

The consequences of the electoral separation of town and country before 1885 can be shown by the fact that before the reforms of the 1880s the behaviour of Members of the House of Commons was related to the size of electorate and the type of constituency they represented. In the House of Commons which sat between 1841 and 1847, these characteristics, more than any other feature of the background of Members, were related to their partisan preferences. Members for counties in England, Scotland, and Wales tended to belong to the Conservative party. Boroughs in England and Wales returned Tories and Liberals almost equally, but when these constituencies are controlled for size the smaller seats tended to return the Conservatives and the larger returned Liberals. Members for Scottish boroughs, on the other hand, were overwhelmingly Liberal. And when the positions of Members on voting dimensions in the 1840s are compared with these aspects of their constituencies, the same results are found. These features predict the breaks within parties as well as the breaks between parties. Counties and small boroughs returned Members who fitted positions toward the right, and larger boroughs returned Members who can be located in positions on the left.[39] These indicators measure the degree to which constituencies

---

[36] The Marquess of Bath to Edward Hamilton, 6 Dec. 1885, BL Add. MS 48624B, ff. 160–1.

[37] Hanham, *The Reformed Electoral System*, p. 26.

[38] The analysis in this section is based upon evidence concerning the types of constituency for which Members sat (whether they were county divisions, parliamentary boroughs, or university seats), and the sizes of the electorates of those constituencies. The median of electorate sizes is found in the interval of between 9,000 and 9,500 electors; and the threshold of 9,000 electors is taken here, therefore, as the dividing line between small and large electorates. Sources from which this evidence was drawn: Charles Dod, *Parliamentary Companion* (London: the two editions for 1886); *The Constitutional Yearbook, 1887* (London: 1887); *The Liberal Yearbook, 1887* (London: 1887); F. W. S. Craig, *British Parliamentary Election Results, 1885–1918* (London: 1974); Frederick M. McCalmont (ed.), *The Parliamentary Poll Book of All Elections from the Reform Act of 1832 to February 1910*, 7th edn. (London: 1910).

[39] Aydelotte, 'Constituency Influence on the British House of Commons, 1841–1847', pp. 229–30, 233–6.

were urban or rural. The more rural the constituencies—that is, if it was a county or small borough—the more it was likely to return a Liberal. Ireland was the exception to this in the 1840s, where region was the most salient feature of its constituencies. Members for Ulster, irrespective of the size of the electorate which returned them or the type of seat, were Conservatives. Members from the south voted as a faction within the Liberal coalition on the left.

The power of these constituency characteristics sustained themselves across the threshold of franchise reform in 1867 and into the early 1880s. A positive association emerged between constituency characteristics and partisanship in the House of Commons which sat from 1880 to 1885 in a study which calculated the population density and the types of constituency.[40] Clear majorities of boroughs and constituencies with high population densities returned Liberals. A majority of county seats and a bare majority of constituencies with low population densities returned Conservatives. Until 1885, therefore, the degree to which a constituency was urban or rural had a great deal to do with the kind of Member it returned to Westminster.

All this changed after the general elections of 1885, as the evidence for the new House of Commons indicated in Table 5.1 shows.[41] Tests for the relation between the urban–rural character of the seats Members held and their political behaviour in the House of Commons in 1886 are negative. The facts are these. Small constituencies returned both Conservatives and Liberals, and large constituencies did as well. The proportions of Conservatives holding large and small seats were, in fact, identical (37 per cent). A slightly larger proportion of Liberals held large seats, it is true, but they also held a large proportion of small seats. Indeed, the news in these data is a picture the reverse of which was found for earlier parliaments. The size of electorates had nothing to do with the political character of the Members they returned. Similarly with regard to whether constituencies were county or borough seats. In contrast to the period before 1886, a large proportion of Liberals sat for counties and a large proportion of Conservatives sat for boroughs. The type of constituency made as little difference as the size of its electorate in the shaping of partisanship in the House of Commons in 1886.

---

[40] Stephens and Brady, 'The Parliamentary Parties and the Electoral Reforms of 1884–1885', pp. 497–8.

[41] The figures for the size of electorates in Table 5.1 total 671 rather than 680 because Members sitting for university seats, for which the size of the electorates made little difference, are excluded.

TABLE 5.1 *Constituency Size and Type and Partisan Affiliation in the House of Commons in 1886*

	Irish Nationalists (%)	Liberals (%)	Conservatives (%)	No.
Size of electorate:				
0–4,999	13	42	45	55
5,000–7,499	36	36	28	118
7,500–8,999	15	44	41	149
9,000 +	4	59	37	349
Summary:				
0–8,999	22	41	37	322
9,000 +	4	59	37	349
Type of constituency:				
County	19	49	32	382
Borough	4	53	43	289
University	0	11	89	9
Type of constituency controlled for the size of electorates:				
Counties:				
0–8,999 electors	44	33	24	147
9,000 + electors	4	59	37	235
Boroughs:				
0–8,999 electors	4	48	48	175
9,000 + electors	4	60	36	114

Redistribution had worked to the advantage of the Conservatives in 1886. They gained in electoral strength and made a strong showing in constituencies with large electorates and in boroughs. This was the continuation of an electoral tendency which Labouchere acknowledged when he congratulated Lord Randolph Churchill on Tory successes in urban areas.[42] Sir Algernon Borthwick, who stood for the Chelsea seat in 1880, found 'hosts of Radicals in Chelsea but a steadily increasing force of Conservatives'. In 1885 he won the contiguous borough seat of South Kensington, which Charles Booth had described as 'verging on fashion and wealth',[43] by a very safe majority. 'It shows the very different state of feeling which obtained

---

[42] Labouchere to Churchill, 30 Nov. 1885, Lord Randolph Churchill Letters 1/10/1116. James Cornford, 'The Transformation of Conservatism in the Late Nineteenth Century', *Victorian Studies*, 7 (1963–4), pp. 35–66; Marsh, *The Discipline of Popular Government*, pp. 83–4.

[43] Quoted in Pelling, *The Social Geography of British Elections*, p. 31.

six years ago when I first contested the old Borough of Chelsea', he wrote. 'I found it then very uphill work.'[44] Even Hammersmith, which was more mixed, fell to the Tories, as General W. T. Goldsworthy predicted it would in the spring of 1885.[45]

The Liberals were worried about urban constituencies, and even in the north of England. Sheffield, Mundella wrote to Chamberlain, 'is the very political antipodes of Birmingham and indeed of almost every other large industrial centre. Unitarianism & Wesleyan Toryism abounds, and even Congregationalists have gone over to the enemy since 1874. All owing to the long reign of Roebuck and the ultra Jingo tendencies of the people.'[46] James Mackenzie Maclean was not wholly confident of Oldham, and the electors in this two-Member constituency returned a Conservative and a Liberal in 1885. 'The Irish did not vote straight, and their strength had been considerably exaggerated, while Mr S. R. Platt, the great employer of labour, though a churchman himself, used all of his influence to secure Lyulph Stanley's return.' Yet, as Maclean observed, 'Conservatism is steadily gaining ground in Oldham', and the electors returned Maclean and another Conservative in the general election of 1886.[47] As Salisbury recognized, Lord Randolph Churchill's challenge to John Bright's Liberal stronghold in Birmingham was an important showing of Tory colours. 'If we succeed it will give the tone to the very many of the thickly populated county divisions in the middle and the North of England.'[48]

But redistribution helped the Liberals as well. By drawing increased support from counties and small constituencies, they broadened their base of electoral support. Conservatives complained of the difficulties they faced. Sir Edmund Lechmere's opponent in the Bewdley division of Worcestershire was 'a strong man, though a stranger from the neighbouring county of Warwick, but [?] being a disciple of Chamberlain, he was a colleague of Mr. Arch & was supported by all the staff & the press of the National Labourers' Union'.[49] Walter Long believed the situation was sufficiently serious in Wiltshire to

---

[44] Borthwick to Salisbury, 29 Sept. 1882, 15 July 1886, Third Marquess of Salisbury MSS Class E.

[45] Goldsworthy to Salisbury, 23 May 1885, 26 Nov. 1885, Third Marquess of Salisbury MSS Class E.

[46] Mundella to Chamberlain, 18 Dec. 1883, Chamberlain Papers JC5/55/4.

[47] J. M. Maclean to Salisbury, 6 Dec. 1885, Third Marquess of Salisbury MSS Class E.

[48] Salisbury to Churchill, 20 Nov. 1885, Third Marquess of Salisbury MSS Class D/15/133.

[49] Lechmere to Salisbury, 1 Dec. 1885, Third Marquess of Salisbury MSS Class E.

require a visit from Lord Salisbury. 'It is impossible to say how things are going, but undoubtedly the labourers are much taken with the idea of getting land & much flattered at this second visit of Mr. Chamberlain.'[50] The Earl of Kimberley happily reported favourable Liberal prospects in Norfolk where meetings and demonstrations showed marked support for disestablishment. 'The non-conformists have evidently got the hearts of the labourers with them.'[51] John Edward Ellis thought 'the assault on the County divisions has on the whole been successful — & it has simply confirmed what I have always held, that the county householder ought to have been enfranchised in 1867 — It is the *slums* of London, & Sheffield & c & the outlying villadom we have to fear.' The triumph was one of policy, not personality. 'The victory was the more satisfactory because it was due to a robust & thoughtful Liberalism rather than the merits of the candidates.'[52] Ellis Ashmead Bartlett regarded Liberal strength in counties with a strong mining element as '*sui generis*', but this did not lead him to minimize their importance. They represented what Ashmead Bartlett estimated as a loss of forty seats or more,[53] and Sir William Harcourt called the mining districts 'a great reserve of the Liberal party'.[54] In Scotland Sir James Fergusson attributed the defeat of Major General Alexander, the Conservative candidate for South Ayrshire, to the large mining vote which by the end of the century amounted to a third of the electorate.[55] Salisbury, in contemplating the Conservative losses in Devonshire, where 'the majorities adverse to us were unhappily large', could only hope that 'the revolt of the agricultural labourer' could be taken as 'analogous to similar events which took place after the enfranchisements of 1832 and 1867, & as being probably destined like them to disappear'.[56] Though the numbers of votes obtained and the numbers of seats won varied, both parties extended their bases of electoral support in 1885 in terms of the kinds of community they represented.

Though there is no relationship between electoral size or type of constituency and partisan preference, the labels of party affiliation

[50] Long to Salisbury, 12 Oct. 1885, Third Marquess of Salisbury MSS Class E.

[51] Kimberley to Lord Ripon, 10 Oct. 1885, BL Add. MS 43526, ff. 10ᵛ–11.

[52] Ellis to Chamberlain, 16 Dec. 1885, Chamberlain Papers JC5/29/2.

[53] Ellis Ashmead Bartlett to Salisbury, 6 Dec. 1885, Third Marquess of Salisbury MSS Class E.

[54] Harcourt to Gladstone, 4 Feb. 1886, BL Add. MS 44200, f. 20.

[55] Fergusson to Salisbury, 9 Dec. 1885, Third Marquess of Salisbury MSS Class E.

[56] Salisbury to W. J. Harris, 11 Dec. 1885, Third Marquess of Salisbury MSS Class C/6/236.

TABLE 5.2 *Constituency Characteristics and Ideological Position in the House of Commons in 1886 (whole House of Commons)* *

	Scale positions (%)			No.
	7–5	4[†]	3–1	
Size of electorate:				
0–4,999	30	14	57	37
5,000–7,499	54	12	34	101
7,500–8,999	38	16	46	123
9,000 +	34	18	48	269
Summary:				
0–8,999	43	14	43	261
9,000 +	34	18	48	269
Type of constituency:				
County	43	14	42	305
Borough	32	19	49	225
Type of constituency controlled for the size of electorates:				
Counties:				
0–8,999 electors	58	12	29	130
9,000 + electors	32	16	52	175
Boroughs:				
0–8,999 electors	28	16	56	131
9,000 + electors	38	22	39	94

*These tallies do not include MPs who sat for university seats.
[†]Median position

have been known to obscure significant political differences. Therefore, it would seem wise to push this analysis further to see if the size of electorates,[57] or the type of constituency, was related to the behaviour of Members reflected in their positions on the major voting dimension of the House of Commons in 1886. This test, as Table 5.2 shows, is also negative. Constituencies with large and small electorates returned Members who distributed themselves across the voting dimension in virtually identical proportions. As to the type of constituency, counties and boroughs also returned Members who held positions on the continuum described by the dimension with near-equality.

[57] Figures for electoral size will total fewer than the total number of Members who can be classified on the great voting dimension, because Members sitting for university seats, about which electoral size means little, are excluded.

What deviations there are emerge at two points, neither of which fits the pattern which existed before 1885: 54 per cent of the constituencies with between 5,000 and 7,499 electors and 43 per cent of the county seats returned Members located in the leftwardmost positions on the voting dimension. The reason for this is clear, and it is partisan. Conservatives, who voted with absolute consistency on the right, were often returned by larger constituencies and boroughs. It is Irish Nationalists, whose numbers enlarge the figures on the left, who were returned by small electorates and county constituencies. And the same pattern emerges at the bottom of Table 5.2 when the type of constituency is controlled for by the size of the electorate. The only elevated proportion worth calling attention to is the 58 per cent of the more radical Members returned for the smallest county seats, and this elevation can be accounted for, also, by the fact that most of these were Irish Nationalist Members who sat for small county seats in southern Ireland.

The general import of this evidence cannot be missed. Before 1885 the size of electorate and the type of constituency predicted the partisanship of Members and their positions on parliamentary voting dimensions, but not afterwards. Before 1885 counties and small electorates tended to return Conservatives and boroughs and large electorates tended to return Liberals, but not afterwards. Liberals, it is true, held large constituencies with the most heterogeneous electorates. What is true for the House of Commons in 1886 is also true for the House which sat from 1886 to 1892. The type of constituency and the density of its population were unrelated to the partisan preference of the Member it returned.[58] All of this is evidence for a changed relationship between constituencies and the kinds of Member they elected. Parliamentary politics, in electoral terms, came to cut across traditional constituency cleavages. Members no longer represented homogeneous electoral interests. And since the character of representation changed, the means for mobilizing support changed as well. As MacRae has pointed out, when the association between constituency characteristics and voting is low, it indicates that legislators did not represent local interests.[59] The effect of the 1884–5 reforms was to reduce and nearly eliminate the biases of electoral size and constituency type from parliamentary politics. To remove these was to remove one source of conflict and cleavage. But conflict and cleavage never disappear, and these

[58] Stephens and Brady, 'The Parliamentary Parties and the Electoral Reforms of 1884–1885 in Britain', pp. 497–8.
[59] MacRae, *The Dimensions of Congressional Voting*, p. 256.

reforms merely reordered them. This created the opportunity for a new stability around new forms of organization. At such a transitional moment, with the waning of local forces and influences, it is not paradoxical for regional characteristics and sectional politics, which had never been unimportant, to carry greater power and force. And that is what happened. The new stabilities and new organizations would shape themselves along regional and sectional lines, and would reflect national and ethnic ideals.

Regionalism and Political Behaviour[60]

To compare the region in which constituencies were located with the partisan affiliation and the positions Members held on parliamentary voting dimensions in 1886 is to construct a measure of regionalism. For this purpose the analysis which follows uses the scheme for classifying regions adopted by Dr Pelling from the work of Professor C. B. Fawcett. Fawcett, using data drawn from the 1911 census, sought to devise regions which would be the most suitable for purposes of administrative devolution. Each, in terms of its residential and occupation patterns, was self-contained. Each had an obvious urban centre. Each had a substantial population.[61] No system for classifying constituencies according to their regions is unflawed; neither is this one. These regions are not homogeneous wholes; smaller units would reveal more marked characteristics. Yet, as one scholar using these materials observes, this system is clear and convenient, and these units are large enough to assume a consistency of class composition, unmarred by migration, for the period it describes.[62] Table 5.3 describes the representation of each of these regions according to the number of Members returned for each party in 1885.

[60] The evidence on regionalism in British elections is organized into the regional patterns used by Pelling in *The Social Geography of British Elections*. This study uses another distinction — that between northern and southern England. The usual means for making this distinction, a line drawn from the Wash in the east to Bristol in the west, bisects Bristol, Peterborough, and the Northern, Middle, Eastern, and Southern divisions of Gloucestershire. But for purposes of convenience, and because a more specific classification of constituencies did not yield substantially different results, I have considered Bristol and Peterborough and all of Northamptonshire and Gloucestershire to be southern English constituencies. The figures on electoral swings and descriptions of constituencies in what follows are from Pelling, *The Social Geography of British Elections*, a book to which all students of these matters are indebted.

[61] C. B. Fawcett, *The Provinces of England* (London: 1919). See Pelling, *The Social Geography of British Elections*, pp. 3–4.

[62] J. P. D. Dunbabin, 'British Elections in the Nineteenth and Twentieth Centuries, A Regional Approach', *English Historical Review*, Apr. 1980, p. 246.

TABLE 5.3 *The Regions of the United Kingdom and their Representation in the House of Commons in 1886*

	Irish Nationalist (%)	Liberal (%)	Conservative (%)	No.
London	0	39	61	59
South-eastern England	0	12	88	56
Wessex	0	44	56	18
Devon–Cornwall	0	65	35	20
Bristol	0	64	36	22
Central England	0	65	35	23
East Anglia	0	56	44	27
East Midlands	0	75	25	32
West Midlands	0	76	24	42
Peak–Don	0	75	25	12
Lancastria	1	37	62	78
Yorkshire	0	68	32	41
North England	0	82	18	33
Wales	0	89	11	35
Scotland	0	89	11	71
Ulster	50	0	50	34
Southern Ireland	100	0	0	68
University	0	11	89	9
Summary:				
Northern England and Celtic fringe	19	54	26	446
Southern England and universities	0	41	59	234

These findings define the regional character of partisanship in British parliamentary politics.[63] But it is a point made more directly in the summaries at the foot of the table. Members sitting for southern English seats, together with those holding university seats, tended, by a small majority, to be Conservatives. Members sitting for northern English, Welsh, Scottish, and Irish constituencies, on the other hand, tended strongly toward the parties of the left. Their decided preference was for the Liberal or Irish Nationalist parties. This configuration of evidence, since it is derived from the election results of 1885, pre-dates the entry of the Irish Home Rule question into the parliamentary scheme of things. The Liberal party, it is sometimes argued, was relegated to the electoral periphery of the United Kingdom because it adopted Home Rule in 1886. As these figures show, however, the Liberals were already strongest in those regions toward the north and the west in the Celtic fringe. As

[63] Pelling, *The Social Geography of British Elections*, p. 418; Dunbabin, 'British Elections in the Nineteenth and Twentieth Centuries', pp. 264–6.

E. N. Mozley put it in 1910, 'few Liberal members can lead a settled life within an hour or two's train journey from London'.[64]

It is only in northern English regions that the size of electorate makes a difference in the partisan preferences of Members. The regional pattern dominated in southern English regions which, irrespective of size of electorate or type of constituency, tended to be Conservative. In Wales and Scotland, irrespective of size of electorate or type of constituency, MPs tended to be Liberal. In northern English regions, however, counties and boroughs with smaller electorates were nearly all equally divided between Liberal and Conservative Members, while in counties and boroughs with larger electorates the Members tended to be sharply Liberal.

The figures for partisanship and region tend to exaggerate the strength of the Liberal party in the south. Liberals, to be sure, made gains in southern counties in the election of 1885 because of the enfranchisement of the agricultural workers and the talk of 'three acres and a cow'. However, in some ways this was an urban cow; talk designed to appeal to urban radicals. Liberals on the spot were not always confident about the capacity of their party to sustain itself in these rural districts. Francis Allston Channing, who took the Eastern division of Northamptonshire in 1885, believed the Liberal advantage there would 'melt away like the snow in summer' if the party failed in its sedulous concern for agricultural questions. 'Instead of the sweeping victory expected in the counties, we have but staggered through — by the help of the Franchise cry — to a qualified and unstable success.'[65] Channing was not fooled by the election results, and recognized a more conservative political complexion in southern England than the numbers of Liberals and Conservatives returned there would suggest.

Channing might have been thinking of the narrowness of the Liberals' electoral victory in the south, as opposed to the north.[66] Whatever that might be, however, and whatever the numbers of Liberals returned for southern constituencies, the ideological disposition of those Members was more moderate than that of their colleagues from the north. This becomes clearer if the evidence for a relationship between region and the political behaviour of Members

----

[64] E. N. Mozley, 'The Political Heptarchy', *Contemporary Review*, 97 (Apr. 1910), p. 405.

[65] Francis A. Channing to Gladstone, 15 Dec. 1885, BL Add. MS 44493, ff. 225–6.

[66] The average Liberal proportion of the poll in southern constituencies was 50.8%. The corresponding figure for the north, Wales, and Scotland, was 56.8%. For northern English constituencies alone it was 55%.

TABLE 5.4 *Region and the Ideological Positions of MPs in the House of Commons in 1886*

	Dimensional positions			No.
	7–5 (%)	4* (%)	3–1 (%)	
London	32	8	60	50
South-east England	8	0	92	39
Wessex	8	25	67	12
Devon–Cornwall	18	18	65	17
Bristol	20	20	60	15
Central England	20	27	53	15
East Anglia	25	25	50	20
East Midlands	40	20	40	25
West Midlands	36	25	39	28
Peak–Don	22	33	44	9
Lancastria	15	12	73	59
Yorkshire	33	33	33	33
North England	41	26	33	27
Wales	53	27	20	30
Scotland	39	26	34	61
Ulster	57	0	43	28
Southern Ireland	100	0	0	62
Summary:				
Northern England, Wales, Scotland, and Ireland	47	18	35	362
Southern England and universities	19	12	68	177

*Median dimensional position

is examined in another way, through a comparison of the regions of Members' constituencies and the positions they held on the great parliamentary voting dimension for the House of Commons. In the first place, as Table 5.4 shows, the Members returned for constituencies in southern England were more conservative than their designations of party affiliation indicated. Nearly two-thirds of the parliamentary representation of Devon and Cornwall, the Bristol region, and central England came to Westminster as Liberals, yet the ideological position of a majority of these Members (65 per cent for those returned from Devon and Cornwall, 60 per cent from the Bristol region, and 53 per cent from central England) was toward the right. In the second place, this effect is even more pronounced if the dimensional positions of Liberals alone, rather than of the whole House, is consulted. Of the Liberal Members for these regions, 72 per cent held ideological positions at the median or to the right of the median on the great parliamentary voting dimension. It is another way of saying that, although the constituencies in these regions may have returned Liberals, the Liberals they returned were decidedly on the moderate wing of the Liberal party. Indeed, to look at the summaries at the foot of Table 5.4, 68 per cent of the Members returned for the regions of southern England held the most conservative ideological positions, positions to the right of the median. This *The Times* recognized:

The counties, it is true, have returned a Liberal majority, over which Liberal partisans may exalt as much as they please. From a national point of view it is important to ask what manner of Liberals they are whom the counties have returned. In the majority of cases they are men who for national purposes are just as satisfactory a barrier against the retrograde policy of modern Radicals as the Conservatives they have beaten. It is a significant fact that, notwithstanding sanguine anticipations of a great victory in the counties, few extreme men have adventured themselves as county candidates, and those who have made the attempt have generally failed. A sound instinct has probably taught them that if a victory was to be won in the counties it would have to be won by the type of Liberal to which the counties are accustomed, not by the class that bear the hallmark of Birmingham.[67]

The other news in Table 5.4, of course, has to do with the support for the political left in parliamentary politics. This came from northern England, with the exception of Lancastria, and the Celtic fringe. Even Ulster, because of the inroads of Parnellite candidates there, was tilted in the direction of the left. By this showing, 47 per cent of the Members of the House of Commons in 1886 who were elected from constituencies for these districts fit the most radical ideolotical positions on the major voting dimension.

The south was the bastion of the Conservative party. Their strength was most pronounced in the south-east region, bolstered by the organization put in place by Lord Abergavenny and the Kentish gang to which Akers-Douglas and Captain Middleton were connected,[68] in Wessex, and in London. In contrast, the parliamentary representation of the Devon and Cornwall, Bristol, and central England regions were very much more Liberal. However, the West Country Liberals held ideological positions very much unlike those of their more radical London brethren. Only 27 per cent voted in such a manner that they could be regarded as radicals. The same point can be made for Liberals sitting for central English constituencies. Though

[67] *The Times*, 8 Dec. 1885, p. 9.
[68] Pelling, *The Social Geography of British Elections*, pp. 63–5, 73; Marsh, *The Discipline of Popular Government*, pp. 154, 186.

their number included Channing, Bradlaugh, and Labouchere, only 27 per cent, these three in fact, held positions toward the left on the major voting dimension. The parliamentary forces from East Anglia were more evenly divided. Marginally Liberal in 1886, this region remained so for the remainder of the century. The by-elections in 1886, however, allowed the Conservatives to improve their position slightly. When the two sitting Liberals for Ipswich, Jesse Collings and Henry Wyndham West, were unseated on petition, the electors returned two Conservatives, Lord Elcho and Charles Dalrymple, in their place. Norwich's representative, as a result of the election of 1885, was divided between Jeremiah Colman, the Liberal mustard manufacturer, and Harry Bullard, the Tory brewer, but when Bullard was unseated on petition, another Tory, Samuel Hoare the banker, was returned.

If Members sitting for constituencies south of a line drawn from the Wash to the mouth of the Severn tended to be Conservatives, those sitting for constituencies in the north tended to be Liberals. Members from the East Midlands were solidly so. They held all the parliamentary boroughs and dominated the largest county divisions, except for the Bassetlaw division which William Beckett Denison had won. The only section of the region to return Conservatives in any proportion was in the eastern county divisions, where they claimed seven of the twelve seats. The West Midlands was just as Liberal. More than 75 per cent of the constituencies in Joseph Chamberlain's 'Duchy' and stronghold[69] returned Liberals, and these voted in such a manner that 50 per cent of them held positions at the leftwardmost part of the parliamentary voting dimension. The Conservatives claimed not a single seat in Birmingham, and only two constituencies in the Black Country. Wednesbury, which returned Wilson Lloyd the iron-master, and the Kingswinford division of Staffordshire, which returned Alexander Stavely Hill the lawyer, sent Conservatives to Westminster. Tories did better, but only marginally so, in the outer urban and industrial districts and in the agricultural sections of the West Midlands. Henry William Eaton, who was in the silk trade, took Coventry in the general election of 1885, and G. H. Allsopp, the brewer, won Worcester. Conservatives took three agricultural divisions: Stanley Leighton the Oswestry division of Shropshire; Sir Richard Temple, Bt. the Evesham division of Worcestershire; and Sir Edmund Lechmere, Bt. the Bewdley division of Worcestershire.

[69] Michael Hurst, *Joseph Chamberlain and West Midland Politics* (Oxford: 1962).

Liberals dominated the representation of the Don–Peak region, and this tendency continued into the twentieth century. The Liberal proportion of the poll exceeded 58 per cent in the election of 1885 and the average Liberal percentage remained high (56 per cent) in the elections which followed. Conservatives sat for only three of the region's seats, all of them in Sheffield, in the House of Commons in 1886: Charles Vincent, the Central division; Stuart-Wortley, the Hallam division; and Ellis Ashmead Bartlett, the Eccleshall division. Of these, the Hallam and Eccleshall divisions were middle-class constituencies with smaller electorates.

Yorkshire was Liberal as well, and its Liberal MPs tended to be radicals. Twenty-eight of the forty-one men sitting for Yorkshire constituencies were Liberals, and nearly half of these can be classified on the leftward side of the major parliamentary voting dimension. Conservative strength, such as it was, was located in boroughs with small electorates. For example, the Hon. Rowland Winn, the eldest son of Lord St Oswald, held Pontefract, and Edward Green, the engineer and patenter of the fuel economizer, held Wakefield. But these constituencies had among the smallest electorates of the country, the former with 2,465 electors and the latter with 4,801. In Leeds and Kingston-upon-Hull the Tories held four of eight seats. Sir James Kitson, intimating class voting, described one of these, the Northern division of Leeds, as 'villadom'.[70] The only substantial Conservative showing in Yorkshire was in the strongly agricultural districts, and even here the Liberals held half the seats.

And so it was in the North England region. Liberals held 82 per cent of the seats, and nearly half of these held radical positions on the major parliamentary voting dimension. Conservatives held only three boroughs (Thomas Milvain in Durham, George Augustus Cavendish-Bentinck in Whitehaven, and R. S. Donkin in Tynemouth), and these constituencies had very small electorates.[71] Furthermore, Conservatives sat for only three of the nineteen county divisions, and one of these, the Appleby division of Westmorlandshire for which William Lowther, the kinsman of the Earl of Lonsdale, sat, was said to be in the Lowther interest.[72]

Lancastria was the exception to the Liberal trend in the north. Of its seventy-eight Members, forty-nine were Tories. While the Conservatives held a majority of both borough and county seats,

---

[70] Pelling, *The Social Geography of British Elections*, p. 292.
[71] Durham had 2,302 electors, Tynemouth had 6,669 electors, and Whitehaven had 2,687.
[72] Pelling, *The Social Geography of British Elections*, p. 339.

they were strongest in the boroughs, and especially in those which were small and homogeneous. In so far as the Liberals succeeded in Lancastria, they did so in the county divisions. For example, the Liberals did not return a single Member in Merseyside, and they returned only two (Caleb Wright, the cotton-master, and John Brunner, the chemical manufacturer) in the heavy industrial district. Wright's constituency, the Leigh division, had a large mining population, and Brunner's constituency, the Northwich division, had many of its electors employed in the chemical industry. Henry Seton-Karr, the Conservative who sat for St Helens, with its large working-class electorate, regarded his political support as 'naturally Conservative'.[73] The representation of the Manchester district was more strongly Liberal, and their support in the pottery district of north Staffordshire was stronger yet. Here Liberals held all the seats in the House of Commons in 1886. Even with this said, however, the electors of Lancastria returned only a minority of their representation as Liberals, and only a minority of these, about a third, held safe seats. The Conservative character of Lancastria has been put down to a number of things: class voting, Tory democracy, a reaction against Home Rule policies. Even though opposition to Irish devolution had been present before (even among Liberals such as Hartington, who sat for the Rossendale division), the strong Conservative showing in the region pre-dated Gladstone's Irish government plan. Even though the Conservatives had clear working-class support, this arose as much from religious proclivities and tensions in the region as it did from class concerns. The presence of Irish immigrants in the towns, living cheek-by-jowl and restively amongst the population, produced nativist tendencies which became the strength of Conservatives there,[74] as it would also do in Ulster.

Strongly Liberal, in this Wales resembled northern England. Thirty-one of its thirty-five Members were Liberals. That these were amongst the most radical Members of their party is shown by their places on the principal voting dimension, where 62 per cent can be classified in the leftwardmost ideological positions. Liberal candidates, on average, took 60 per cent of the Welsh vote in the general election of 1885, and they sustained this proportion in the period from 1886 to 1910. Conservative strength located itself in the smaller boroughs, where George Kenyon, the heir of

[73] Henry Seton-Karr to Lord Randolph Churchill, 2 Apr. 1886, Lord Randolph Churchill Letters 1/12/1445.

[74] P. F. Clarke, *Lancashire and the New Liberalism* (Cambridge: 1971), pp. 33, 37, 38, 53, 63, 74-5.

Lord Kenyon, held the Denbigh district, and Pryce Jones, the merchant and woollen manufacturer, won the Montgomery district. Pryce Jones, aware of Conservative weakness, advised Salisbury to postpone the Welsh polling until after the poll in England had been taken.[75] If the Conservatives were weak in the boroughs, so also was their condition in the counties. Frederic Courtney Morgan, the brother of Baron Tredegar, and Arthur H. J. Walsh, the heir of Lord Ormathwaite, were the only Conservatives to hold county seats, and these with narrow majorities. As Lord Ormathwaite put it, 'as all the neighbouring English constituencies of Herefordshire & Shropshire have also gone wrong, [*sic*] Radnorshire is like a little Conservative oasis in a great Radical desert.'[76]

The distinctive feature of Welsh politics in 1886, a feature it shared with most of northern England, was the support it gave in Parliament to the most advanced section of the Liberal party. It had not always been so. In the 1840s and before, Welsh representation in the House of Commons had been Conservative,[77] but from mid-century, certainly from 1868, it became increasingly Liberal. It was assisted in this transformation by the presence in Wales of heavy industry, mining, and nonconformity. These, of course, continued as political forces, as John Puleston observed in his remarks to Salisbury on the condition of Welsh politics in 1885.[78] However, nationalism further assisted the transformation of Wales to liberalism.[79] This gave a new edge to Welsh politics, an edge shown by the support Lewis Llewelyn Dillwyn and Stuart Rendel gave to Welsh disestablishment, and an edge which was responsible for the support Welsh Liberal Members gave to Irish Home Rule. When he was first returned for Montgomeryshire in 1880 Rendel knew nothing of the province, its language or its literature. Ill at ease in the House of Commons, Rendel moved with confidence in London society and in the cottages and farmhouses of Wales. He gained a poet's vision of the province,

[75] Pryce Jones to Salisbury, 14 Oct. 1885, Third Marquess of Salisbury MSS Class E.

[76] Second Baron Ormathwaite to Salisbury, 5 Dec. 1885, Third Marquess of Salisbury MSS Class E.

[77] Dunbabin, 'British Elections in the Nineteenth and Twentieth Centuries', pp. 258-9, 261; Aydelotte, 'Constituency Influence on the British House of Commons, 1841-1847', p. 229.

[78] J. H. Puleston to Salisbury, 4 Oct. 1885, Third Marquess of Salisbury MSS Class E.

[79] Kenneth O. Morgan, *Wales in British Politics, 1869-1922* (Cardiff: 1970), p. 75; 'Welsh Nationalism: The Historical Background', *Journal of Contemporary History*, 6 (1971), pp. 153-72; *Rebirth of a Nation: Wales, 1880-1980* (New York: 1981).

coming to appreciate its culture and religion, and the sacrifices the Welsh had made for education. To consolidate the Welsh Liberals into a meaningful political force Rendel turned to questions of policy, especially disestablishment, as a means to express the claims of Welsh nationalism. In so doing he became more Welsh than the Welsh themselves, and became known, both within as well as without the province, as 'the Member for Wales'.[80]

'Scotland with its dead weight over powers us', Carnarvon wrote in his bleak assessment of Conservative affairs north of the Tweed.[81] Though Liberals were wildly divided there during the general election of 1885 and during the Home Rule crisis, the political tendency in Scotland was the same as for northern England and Wales. The Liberals held sixty-three of the possible seventy-one seats. When Gerald Balfour, the other nephew of Lord Salisbury, sought a new seat in the general election of 1886 he was advised against seeking one in Glasgow. 'If you want to spend money for the cause go to Glasgow', he was told. 'If your object is to get into Parliament steer clear of it. It is 10 to 1 against any Conservative candidate there.'[82] The Tories had political strength in the western counties, and there alone. Aware of their traditional strength there, they used the politics of distribution reform in 1885 to preserve it.[83] Even here Liberal strength was not negligible because they held nine of the sixteen seats, five of them with safe majorities.

If Parnellite control was absolute in southern Ireland, it was not insubstantial in Ulster. Indeed, Irish Nationalists held half of the northern Irish seats in the House of Commons of 1886. This is no slight matter and shows the degree to which Ulster had swung in terms of its parliamentary representation since the 1840s, when it had been overwhelmingly Conservative.[84] There is an aspect of this evidence which is particularly revealing because it is possible to

---

[80] F. E. Hamer (ed.), *The Personal Papers of Lord Rendel* (London: 1931), pp. 278–87, 290–1, 292–3.

[81] Diary of Lord Carnarvon, 30 Nov. 1885, BL Add. MS 60925, unbound and unfoliated.

[82] Gerald Balfour to Salisbury, 26 Mar. 1886, Third Marquess of Salisbury MSS Class E.

[83] 'Sir Stafford Northcote informs me that Lord Bute has written to you urging most strongly the preservation of Buteshire. Having just come up from Scotland permit me to represent at the direct request of our candidate Mr. Robertson the great importance of preventing any departure from the "Redistribution of Seats Bill" as it stands, in the matter, the constituencies not being interfered with.' Reginald Macleod to Salisbury, 19 Feb. 1885, Third Marquess of Salisbury MSS Class E.

[84] Aydelotte, 'Constituency Influence on the British House of Commons, 1841–1847', p. 229.

distinguish between Conservative and Nationalist Members in the north by the kinds of constituency which they represented. Sixty per cent of Ulster's county constituencies returned Nationalists, and 86 per cent of its borough constituencies returned Conservatives. Political support for Ulster Unionism was urban and industrial; the support for nationalism in the north, as in the south, was rural and agricultural. To put it another way, by 1886 the Liberal party had disappeared from Ireland, and the peculiar social and cultural cleavages in Ulster made it possible for urban and industrial groups to join forces in the Tory party, which became the political expression of Unionism.[85] By 1886 the situation in Ulster was already highly polarized: 75 per cent of both Conservative and Irish Nationalist Members for northern Irish constituencies either held their seats with safe majorities or took them without a contest.

In sum, the partisan affiliation and voting behaviour of Members of the House of Commons in 1886 reflected the regions in which their constituencies were located. Edward Hamilton understood this: 'Mr. G.', he wrote, 'has no doubt a still very powerful hold on the constituencies, especially in the North of England.'[86] Holmes Ivory, Gladstone's election agent in Scotland, captured the same thought in appraising the election of 1886:

the reports from the English Burghs & counties are heartrending. It is evident that it is to be Scotland, Wales, & Ireland against the prejudices & slow power of understanding political truth & justice of England & above all of London.[87]

It reminds one of Lloyd George's remark when he contrasted the 'progressive north' with the 'semi-feudal south'.[88] When Lancastria shifted to the left, as it did in 1906, the Liberals would come out of the wilderness for their last day in the sun.

This is a finding which defies interest and social class theories of political behaviour, and the broad body of modernization theory which incorporates them. Patterns of regional cleavage of the sort discovered here are manifestations of peripheral–central conflict through which regional fringes resisted the centralizing and integrating efforts of strong political centres. It was, consequently, no new thing, but

---

[85] For a discussion of this subject see Peter Gibbon, *The Origins of Ulster Unionism: The Formation of Popular Protestant Politics and Ideology in Nineteenth Century Ireland* (Manchester: 1975), ch. 5. and pp. 144–5.

[86] Edward Hamilton Diary, 9 May 1886, BL Add. MS 48643, ff. 118–19.

[87] Holmes Ivory to Gladstone, 10 July 1886, BL Add. MS 44498, f. 174.

[88] Clarke, *Lancashire and the New Liberalism*, p. 8.

a political consequence of events involved in the medieval formation of the English State. This traditional territorial structure had been established through a process in which the central offices of State established control over outlying regions by indirect means while at the same time providing for the direct representation of regional élites at Westminster. The Irish Act of Union in 1800 was the most recent expression of this strategy. Inherent in such a system were persistent tensions between the regions and Westminster. At times in the nineteenth century these tensions had a class content, but only in the sense that they were about class issues; conflict was not fundamentally between class interests, and class politics had to fit itself into this older political style.[89] Territorial conflict was not merely the persistence of anachronism in modern politics; nor was it a reactionary force. It was — and is — a radicalizing element, enhanced by romantic culture in an industrial age, which gets its bonding power from its capacity to draw on sentiments and feelings at odds with the machinery of industry and the machinery of the modern State. If these territorial conflicts were not new in Britain in the nineteenth century, neither were they unique to Britain, and expressions of the same cleavages can be found in German and French legislative politics.[90]

Something, however, was new in the 1880s. Regional forces were released, almost paradoxically, by processes such as industrialization, urbanization, and electoral reform, processes which had political integration as their function. The political reforms of the nineteenth century, of which the franchise and redistribution reforms of 1884–5 were the most recent and the most powerful, acted as forces for political organization and mobilization. One aspect of this was integrative: they brought new political elements into the political system. Another aspect of this, however, was disintegrative, at least in its potential. Because these reforms coincided with an increase of central government activities, they stimulated a debate on the existing territorial structure and the relations between the regions and Westminster. Additionally, they provided the political means for mobilizing this debate.[91] The Irish nationalist party and the election

---

[89] Derek W. Urwin, 'Territorial Structures and Political Developments in the United Kingdom', *The Politics of Territorial Integrity*, ed. Stein Rokkan and Derek W. Urwin (London, Beverly Hills, and New Delhi: 1982), pp. 43, 54, 65.

[90] Best, 'Biography and Political Behavior', pp. 20–1, 30.

[91] Urwin, 'Territorial Structures and Political Developments in the United Kingdom', pp. 40–1, 55, and 'Towards the Nationalisation of British Politics: The Party System, 1885–1940', *Wählerbewegung in der Europäischen Geschichte*, ed. O. Busch (Berlin: 1980), pp. 225–58. T. J. Nossiter, in 'Recent Work on English Elections, 1832–1935', *Political Studies* 18.4 (Dec. 1970), pp. 525–8, and Dunbabin, in 'British

of members to express the grievance of Scottish crofters were two expressions of this kind of mobilization.

But these effects of political reform are only superficially paradoxical. The association of region with party in which the Conservatives expressed the impulses of the centre and the Liberals expressed the grievances of the territorial peripheries blunted centrifugal energies. Wales and Scotland did not follow Ireland into devolutionism. They benefited from the Industrial Revolution, they could look with optimism to the development of the British Empire, and neither had experienced the kind of direct intervention expressed by the Dublin Castle regime and the settler ascendancy. It was too late for the Liberal party in Ireland in the 1880s, but not too late for them in Wales and Scotland. And because the Liberal party became strongly rooted in Wales and Scotland it could express for these regions their characteristic reservations about the territorial constitution, disestablishment in Wales, land reform of the Crofter sort, and the Scottish Office in Scotland. When Gladstone took up Irish Home Rule on behalf of the Liberal party he was seeking to preserve an integrationist, a Unionist strategy for the Liberal party. By 1886, however, the only value the Irish could find at Westminster was liberation. For the Welsh and Scots and the English of the north, on the other hand, representation at Westminster could retain its political value.

Safe and Vulnerable Seats and Political Behaviour[92]

The size of a Member's electoral majority, an indication of electoral support, is a measure of political security. As George Leveson-Gower

Elections in the Nineteenth and Twentieth Centuries', have had interesting things to say on these subjects. See also Keith Robbins, 'Core and Periphery in Modern British History', *Proceedings of British Academy*, 1985.

[92] The question of what constituted a safe seat in 1886 is an extremely difficult one. Since the election of 1885 was the first held under the new electoral conditions, no seat was safe in the sense that a Member, or his agents, had the experience of finding it safe in a historical sense, in the sense of winning it consistently several times. Yet the size of a Member's electoral majority might be taken as a measure of the ease with which he might win it again. After experimenting with thresholds of 5% and 20% of the total poll, I settled on 10% of the total poll as the threshold above which a seat could be considered safe. I checked this by taking the mean of the six-election average majorities for the twelve seats which were still controlled by patrons after 1885 (see Hanham, *Elections and Party Management*, p. 405). If any seats were safe in 1886, they must have been these. Their mean was 8.1%. An electoral criterion of 10% of the total poll, then, would seem to be a reasonable measure for the test of a safe seat. The data on electoral security in this was obtained and confirmed in Craig's *British Parliamentary Election Results, 1885–1918*, McCalmont's *Parliamentary Poll Book*, and Dod's *Parliamentary Companion*.

pointed out,[93] it was naturally something which preoccupied the attention of the whips. It was a matter about which Members could not be certain, and occasioned a good deal of discussion and speculation. Some Members of the House of Commons in 1886 had the impression their electoral majority had been sufficient to give them political security. Baron Henry de Worms wrote to Lord Randolph Churchill disavowing any intention of returning to his former constituency at Greenwich. 'I have not the remotest idea of doing anything of the sort. My present seat is quite safe.'[94] The West Toxteth division of Liverpool, indeed, was. De Worms held it in 1886 with a majority of 16 per cent, and in the summer of 1886 his electors returned him without a contest. James Bryce's seat, the Southern division of Aberdeen, was also, and correctly, regarded as safe.[95] John Compton Lawrence, the barrister, made the Stamford division of Lincolnshire a safe constituency.[96] He sat for south Lincolnshire from 1880 to 1885, and then won the new Stamford division with a majority of 14 per cent of the total poll. In the election of 1886 he was unopposed.

Others worried about their seats. James Maclean who held one of the Oldham seats, the other going to a Liberal, hoped to avoid another contest, at least at an early date, but believed the Tories could carry both seats 'if I have a strong local candidate associated with me'.[97] Sir Savile Brinton Crossley, Bt. held his seat, the Lowestoft division of Suffolk, uncertainly because 'there are a large number of fisherman voters who hate Chamberlain and like Birkbeck and the promises he had made if the Tories come into Office'.[98] William Tyssen-Amherst reported on the electoral uncertainties in Norfolk: 'And now what can I say about our prospects, where I have an opportunity of judging. . . . I believe mine is safe and I cannot help thinking that Henry Bentinck has a very good chance for Arch is certainly losing ground, but it is a very terrible fight for so young a candidate. We are quite astonished at the increase of the Electorate! Under the old Franchise both seats would have been

[93] Leveson Gower, *Years of Content*, p. 236.

[94] De Worms to Churchill, 31 Aug. 1886, Lord Randolph Churchill Letters 1/15/1738.

[95] Lord Acton to Herbert Gladstone, 30 Jan. 1886, BL Add. MS 46052, f. 11.

[96] The Eleventh Earl of Winchilsea and Nottingham (who had sat in the House of Commons in 1886 as the Hon. Murray Finch-Hatton) to Salisbury, 10 Oct. 1886, Third Marquess of Salisbury MSS Class E.

[97] J. M. Maclean to Salisbury, 6 Dec. 1885, Third Marquess of Salisbury MSS Class E.

[98] Lewis Harcourt Journal, 7 Dec. 1885, Harcourt dept. 374, f. 43.

certain.'[99] Joseph Chamberlain did not think the West Newington constituency of London would be safe for his brother Arthur.[1] According to Lewis Harcourt, James Lowther, in the Louth division of Lincolnshire, Edward Harcourt, in the Henley division of Oxfordshire, Sir Richard Cross, in the Newton division of Lancashire, and Lord Elcho, in Haddingtonshire, were likely to be defeated. Evan Charteris, Elcho's brother and like him a Tory, 'laid 20 to 10 on Liberals being a majority at the election'.[2]

In 1886 Oldham's two seats were divided between Liberals and Conservatives. The Conservatives took both seats in the general election of 1886, but only with a vulnerable majority (50.4 per cent). Crossley held the Lowestoft division of Suffolk with a majority of 7 per cent of the total poll, but in the rush of Unionist sentiment took the seat again in the next election without a contest. In Norfolk Tyssen-Amherst held his seat with a vulnerable majority (4 per cent of the total poll) but Bentinck lost his contest to Arch. Chamberlain was correct about West Newington: a Tory held it with a narrow majority in 1886, and it went Tory again in the general election of 1886. The Louth division of Lincolnshire went against Lowther, and a Liberal held it with a safe majority in 1886. Edward Harcourt held the Henley division of Oxfordshire with a narrow majority in the House of Commons in 1886. Haddingtonshire was hopeless for the Conservatives. Haldane, the Liberal, defeated Lord Elcho in the election of 1885 with a majority of 28 per cent of the poll. Haldane took the seat again in the election of 1886, with a majority reduced to 22 per cent. These were cases where the electoral anxieties of candidates and Members were well deserved.

While whips and Members found themselves preoccupied with the degree of electoral security in 1886, it remains to be seen whether parliamentary behaviour varied according to the strong or weak support for Members in the constituencies which returned them. What follows, then, is a comparison, first, of the electoral security of Members and their partisan affiliation, and second, of their electoral security and their ideological position on the great parliamentary voting dimension. As these results show, Liberals and Conservatives divided the vulnerable seats between them, but the parties of the left, the Liberals, and the Irish Nationalists dominated

---

[99] Tyssen-Amherst to Salisbury, 12 Oct. 1885, Third Marquess of Salisbury MSS Class E.

[1] Joseph Chamberlain to Arthur Chamberlain, 12 May 1886, Chamberlain Papers JC/11/7.

[2] Lewis Harcourt Journal, 6 and 15 Nov. 1885, Harcourt dep. 373, ff. 18, 36.

TABLE 5.5 *Safe Seats* and Political Behaviour in the House of Commons in 1886*

	Irish Nationalists (%)	Liberals (%)	Conservatives (%)	No.
Safe seats	15	53	31	378
Uncontested seats	47	31	22	45
Vulnerable seats	2	49	49	257
Dimensional positions	7–5	4	3–1	No.
Whole House:				
Dimensional positions	7–5	4	3–1	No.
Safe seats	46	17	37	308
Uncontested seats	54	14	32	37
Vulnerable seats	22	15	63	194
Liberals only:				
Dimensional positions	7–5	4	3–1	No.
Safe seats	51	32	18	165
Uncontested seats	30	50	20	10
Vulnerable seats	42	31	27	93
Liberals who had no previous parliamentary experience:				
Dimensional positions	7–5	4	3–1	No.
Safe seats	72	21	7	82
Uncontested seats	—	—	—	0
Vulnerable seats	46	32	21	56

*I have considered any seat to be safe if the electors of that constituency returned their Member by a majority attaining or exceeding 10% of the total poll.

those seats whose electors returned their Members with safe majorities. Conservative Members held less than a third of the safe seats. Even if the Irish Nationalists are excluded from the calculations, the Liberal proportion of safe seats attained 53 per cent. A finer point can be placed on this by comparing the ideological positions of Members with their electoral security. As the figures for the whole House indicate, Members who can be classified in the most extreme ideological positions on the left of the great parliamentary voting dimension held nearly half of the safe seats in 1886. Members who can be classified in the most extreme ideological positions on the right held nearly two-thirds of the vulnerable seats.

In other words, those on the left in this House of Commons tended to be returned by safe electoral majorities, and those on the right tended to be returned by marginal or vulnerable majorities. This is a finding which is worth brooding about. One reason why the Conservatives were so cohesive and united in 1886 was that they had to be. All things being equal, with the consequences of Gladstone's Irish Home Rule policies unknown, and with the reception of those policies in the constituencies uncertain, the Conservatives were least likely to do well if there was a new election. Because of their electoral insecurity, the Tories had to stick together and to their leaders in resistance to policies advanced from the other side. Electoral vulnerability does not favour political experimentation. As for the Liberals, they could afford fragmentation and political dissent. Though their majority in the House of Commons in 1886 was slight if one subtracts the weight of the Irish Nationalists from their forces, the seats they held were secure. This is a reason, perhaps, why Gladstone dared advance an Irish initiative. The parliamentary forces supporting him, it was plausible for him to suspect, were electorally safe.

There is some evidence for this speculation if one consults the dimensional positions of Liberals alone. These figures are divided with some evenness in all the cells of the comparison found in Table 5.5. However, if one examines the ideological positions of those Liberals returned for the first time in 1886, the safest constituencies returned Members who can be classified on the extreme left of the party. Those who were the least socialized at Westminster were at one and the same time the most radical and the most secure in their seats. These Members could afford political adventures, and the security of their seats gave no little encouragement to their own initiatives. Furthermore, these very constituencies may have encouraged radicalization within the Liberal party; at least, this is what some Liberals believed. At a dinner given by Reginald Brett in March 1886, a dinner attended by Arthur Balfour, Albert Grey, Joseph Chamberlain, and Nathaniel Rothschild, those present discussed the forthcoming election. Chamberlain wondered why he had been approached by moderate Liberals who wished to be sheltered behind the position he was taking on the Home Rule question. 'There is your Whig all over', he said. 'They dare not follow out the dictates of their own conscience, except under the shadow of a Radical.' To this Albert Grey responded, 'The reason is that they know that the majority of their constituents are Radical.'[3] As recent research on party cohesion indicates, Members with sizeable margins of victory are those exposed to local party sanctions.[4]

---

[3] Balfour to Salisbury, 24 Mar. 1886, in Arthur J. Balfour, *Chapters of Autobiography* (London: 1930), p. 218.

[4] Deselection', *British Politics Group Newsletter*, no. 31 (Winter 1983), p. 3.

Liberals with safe electoral majorities could make claims on their party's leadership, time, and patience in 1886 because they represented their party's future. It was not an immediate future, of course. Home Rule, the power of Unionism in the country, and the alliance of the Liberal Unionists with the Conservatives would delay all this when the Liberal party went into the wilderness in the summer of 1886.

The Nature of Constituencies and their Relations to the Political Behaviour of Liberals and the Great Separation in the Liberal Party

If the size and type of constituencies had little effect in 1886 on inter-party conflict, it remains to be seen whether these constituency characteristics were more significant for disputes within the Liberal party, and especially for the split in the party over Irish Home Rule. As Table 5.6 shows, the relations between constituency attributes and the political behaviour of Liberals as reflected in their positions on the great parliamentary voting dimension was stronger than for

TABLE 5.6 *The Constituency Characteristics of* Liberals only *and their Ideological Positions**

	Dimensional positions			No.
	7–5 (%)	4[†] (%)	3–1 (%)	
Size of electorate:				
0–8,999	44	34	21	108
9,000 +	49	31	20	159
Type of constituency:				
County	42	30	28	145
Borough	53	34	12	122
Type of constituency controlled for the size of electorates:				
Counties:				
0–8,999 electors	33	37	30	43
9,000 + electors	46	27	26	102
Boroughs:				
0–8,999 electors	52	32	15	65
9,000 + electors	54	37	9	57

*These tallies do not include Sir John Lubbock, Bt., who sat for London University.
[†]Median dimensional position

the House of Commons considered as a whole, but these relations varied according to the location of constituencies. As the figures at the top of the table reveal, Liberals sitting for larger constituencies and boroughs tended to be more radical than Liberals sitting for smaller constituencies and counties. However, when the type of constituency is controlled for by the size of electorates, the greatest divergence is among those Liberals sitting for counties. There is not much to distinguish between Liberals sitting for large and small boroughs, but Liberals holding larger county seats tended to be more radical than Liberals sitting for the smaller county divisions. In this complex manner the type of constituencies and the size of electorates shaped the ideological organization of the Liberal party on those questions which had long been in dispute amongst them. The reform settlements of 1884–5 created a situation in which larger, less homogeneous constituencies returned Liberals who tended toward the radical wing of the Liberal party.

It requires another test, however, to see if this same pattern occurred in connection with the great separation in the Liberal party over Irish Home Rule. When this proposition is put to the figures in Table 5.7, quite a different picture emerges. The relationship between the attributes of constituencies and Liberal factionalism is negative. Predominant majorities of Gladstonian Members sat for constituencies of all types, having electorates of all sizes, and these proportions remain constant. A sharp elevation in these figures occurs only when the type of constituency is controlled for by the size of the electorate, and then the Gladstonian proportion for borough seats with larger electorates increases to 81 per cent. To put the matter another way, the relative weights of Gladstonian and Liberal Unionists was constant in constituencies of all sizes and types except in large boroughs, whose representatives supported Gladstone even more extensively than their other colleagues. The same kinds of seat which returned the more radical Liberals tended to be the seats who returned Liberals more likely to be supporters of a Home Rule policy for Ireland. But this is only a slight tendency in the evidence, and this is the only connection between these attributes and the split in the Liberal party.[5]

Regionalism had greater consequences for the split in the Liberal party over Home Rule. Liberals returned for constituencies in southern

---

[5] For a different view of this question, argued differently, see Stephens, 'The Changing Context of British Politics in the 1880s: The Reform Acts and the Formation of the Liberal Unionist Party', *Social Science History*, 1.4 (Summer 1977), pp. 486–501.

TABLE 5.7 *Constituency Characteristics and the Great Separation in the Liberal Party in 1886*

	Gladstonians %	Liberal Unionists* (%)	Other Liberals (%)	No.
Size of electorate:				
0–4,999 electors	70	26	4	23
5,000–7,499 electors	63	32	5	43
7,500–8,999 electors	61	31	8	66
9,000 + electors	70	25	4	206
Summary:				
0–8,999 electors	63	31	6	132
9,000 + electors	70	25	4	206
Type of constituency:				
Counties	66	29	5	186
Boroughs	70	25	5	152
Type of constituency controlled for the size of electorates:				
Counties:				
0–8,999 electors	67	31	2	48
9,000 + electors	65	29	6	138
Boroughs:				
0–8,999 electors	61	31	8	84
9,000 + electors	81	18	1	68
Location of constituency:				
Southern England	64	31	4	90
Northern England	71	23	6	154
Wales	71	23	6	31
Scotland	60	37	3	63

*These tallies will total 93 rather than 94 because they exclude Sir John Lubbock, Bt., who sat for a university constituency.

England had a greater tendency toward Unionism than their colleagues sitting for constituencies in northern England. However, Devon and Cornwall was the only region in the south which had a majority of Liberal Members who became Liberal Unionists. That Devon and Cornwall were in fact the hotbed of Liberal Unionism in the south is also shown by the fact that seven of the eight of these Liberals held their seats in 1886 by safe majorities. But aside from Devon and Cornwall, a majority, though a diminished majority, of Liberals returned for constituencies in southern England were Gladstonians. Liberals sitting for Welsh and northern English seats were strongly Gladstonian, in a pattern which reiterates the strong Liberal control which existed in these regions. All regions in northern England returned Members among whom the proportion of Gladstonians of the total number of Liberals exceeded 70 per cent, except for the West Midlands. This region, as one would expect, which was under the powerful influence of Joseph Chamberlain, returned Liberals who were nearly equally divided between Gladstonian and Liberal Unionists. (Fifteen Liberals supported Gladstone in the Home Rule crisis; twelve became Liberal Unionists; five did not vote in the parliamentary division on the Government of Ireland Bill.) Unionism's hold over Liberals even in the West Midlands was not wholly secure, as the figures for electoral security in this region reveal. Fully half of the Liberal Unionists sitting for seats in the West Midlands held their seats with only vulnerable majorities. And this is in contrast to the Gladstonians who had been returned for this region, 67 per cent of whom held their seats with safe majorities. Scotland is a special case. Divided amongst Liberals in the elections of 1885, Scotland was also divided in the Home Rule crisis. According to Rosebery, Unionism was strong amongst Liberals in Scotland 'because the Bill is not understood there, and because it is supposed, a similar fate would be meted out to them. Scotland, it seems, has no wish to become a province or dependency.'[6] Whatever the reasons for Liberal Unionism in Scotland, its electoral support, in contrast to Devon and Cornwall, for example, was weak: 61 per cent of the Liberal Unionists sitting for Scottish seats had vulnerable majorities; 63 per cent of the Gladstonians sitting for Scottish seats had safe majorities. Consequently, in the general election of 1886, the Gladstonians recovered many of these seats.

The question of electoral security, in the light of a soon-to-be-called general election, cut through the Home Rule crisis. Supporters of Gladstone's Irish policy tried to turn this to his advantage in accumulating support for the Home Rule Bill by threatening Liberals with vulnerable majorities with a new election. Sir Joseph Pease, Bt. had a list of twenty-five Liberals who could be got to abstain. If 'the dread of dissolution' would have this effect, Labouchere argued, 'it will not be a difficult matter to get a half dozen to go a step further, and to vote for the Bill. This would give us a majority.'[7] But this could work the other way, as the problem of funding contests in the next election shows.

Nathaniel Rothschild told Reginald Brett that Albert Grey's Liberal Unionist Committee had unlimited funds. 'This circumstance, and

[6] Journal of Reginald Brett, 24 May 1886, Esher Papers 2/8.
[7] Labouchere to Herbert Gladstone, 3 June 1886, BL Add. MS 46016, ff. 83^v-84.

the poverty of the Ministerialists', Rothschild believed, 'procures the Seceders adherents.' ('It may be so', Brett commented, 'but I should doubt these hangers on of money bags numbering many.')[8] How far this went it is diffficult to say, but the fear of Liberal defections was evident among their Irish Nationalist allies. As William O'Brien observed on 27 May 1886, after the Foreign Office meeting where Gladstone agreed to withdraw the Home Rule Bill after the second reading, and to reconsider clause 24, the Gladstonians were 'even more rejoiced than the kickers. They dread a General Election more abjectly than any school boy of spirit would dread flogging. Their hearts are only half in their votes.' Five days later O'Brien went further. 'Long-headed Liberals like Henry Wilson are sure we are in for a General Election, and that, as the Party have no candidates and no money, the smash will be phenomenal, even in Yorkshire.'[9] These anxieties might have accounted for a great deal; anxieties usually do. However, the facts were something else again. Gladstonian Liberals in the House of Commons in 1886 were more secure than the Liberal Unionists. Two-thirds of the Gladstonians held safe Liberal seats compared with 54 per cent for the Liberal Unionists. In Yorkshire, about which contests Henry Wilson and William O'Brien were so concerned, the Gladstonians maintained a decided advantage: 60 per cent of the Liberal Unionist seats there were at risk, and 76 per cent of the Gladstonian seats in Yorkshire were safe. This, however, is merely a manifestation of traditional Liberal strength in the north, and the figures for the country as a whole give little support to the notion that fear of losing their seats affected the break-up of the Liberal party over Irish Home Rule.

When the fateful day came, and when the split in the party became manifest, local Liberal associations rallied round Gladstone. Not a single constituency organization, save in Birmingham, rejected a Gladstonian candidate. They stuck as one with Gladstone and the Liberal leadership.[10] As Sir William Harcourt put it to Chamberlain, 'as far as I can judge the great majority of the Liberal constituencies will go with Gladstone. Loulou on his return from Derby reports that my constituency is distinctly in that frame of mind.'[11] The

---

[8] Journal of Reginald Brett, 24 May 1886, Esher Papers 2/8. (The portion of this entry indicating the attactiveness of election funding for the Liberal Unionists, and Brett's suspicion that this might not amount to much, is crossed out in the typescript of Brett's journal (Esher Papers 2/8), but is clear enough in the autograph (Esher Papers 1/3)).

[9] O'Brien, *Evening Memories*, pp. 125, 128.

[10] Griffiths, 'The Caucus and the Liberal Party in 1886', pp. 192–3, 194–5.

[11] Harcourt to Chamberlain, 19 Apr. 1887, Chamberlain Papers JC/38/48.

Rossendale Three Hundred thrust aside Hartington by a vote of 138 to 45. In Bury, Sir Henry James suffered defeat by 118 to 64. The Scots, rebuffing Goschen and Trevelyan, were no more tolerant of Liberals who had become Unionists. Even family influence counted for little, as Henry Charles Howard learned when he was rejected in the Penrith division of Cumberland. Gladstone and Gladstone's version of Liberalism, now converted to Home Rule for Ireland, dominated the Liberal party in the countryside as it was to dominate the Liberal party in the House of Commons. Differences in constituencies, therefore, did little to institute the cleavage between Gladstonian Liberals and Liberal Unionists. Policy on Ireland, like other policy, had its origins at Westminster, not in constituency pressure. Therefore it is in the parliamentary Liberal party in 1886 that the origins of the great separation in the party are to be found.

Conclusion

It was rare in the House of Commons in 1886 for Members' votes to reveal direct constituency interests. In fact, there are only two instances of such voting in this House of Commons: on an Amendment to the Labourers Acts Amendment Bill for Ireland, and on the Manchester Ship Canal Bill. In the former, Ulster Conservatives voted with the Parnellites, and, in the latter, irrespective of party, Liverpool Members opposed Manchester Members. But this concatenation of votes was a pattern of political behaviour so untypical of politics in this House of Commons as to show that Members did not regard these measures as part of the political agenda of the period. To pursue the role of constituency influence in the House of Commons in 1886 by following these leads would be to chase red herrings. Indeed, as this chapter has shown, and as other research has revealed,[12] the conditions of electoral contests often override the socio-economic characteristics of constituencies.

The conditions of the electoral contests of Members sitting in the House of Commons in 1886 had been established by the reforms of 1884–5. Earlier, the rural or urban characteristics of constituencies, as measured by the size of their electorates or by their type, counted for a great deal in shaping the behaviour of Members at Westminster. These were the most important qualities for predicting the party affiliation of Members or their placement on parliamentary voting dimensions. This was not true in the House of Commons in 1886, and this for the first time. What made the difference was the reforms

[12] MacRae, 'The Relations Between Roll Call Votes and Constituencies', pp. 202–3.

of 1884–5, and especially the redistribution features of those reforms. Rather than their rural or urban character, the constituency attributes which weighed the most in this House of Commons was the region of their constituencies and the size of the electoral majority by which Members held their seats. These characteristics shaped the relative radicalism or conservatism of Members. Regionalism and the importance of large majorities called forth new political energies and organizations. The energies were those of nationalism; the organizations were those which, in the House of Commons and in the constituencies, would direct policy and ideology. Both parties responded to these energies and organizations, and in so doing made futures for themselves.

6
The Great Separation in the Liberal Party

I went to Mentmore on Sunday and from the tone of the conversation there I gathered that there is very little doubt that Mr. Gladstone is coming out again & that the Liberal party are to be presented with a new revised edition of their Koran.

George Curzon to Salisbury, 16 September 1885[1]

I presume however that Mr. Gladstone will not swerve from his opinion, so we are within view of a temporary break up of the Party. This would not, in my judgment, be a bad thing, as we require time in order to draft our stud of cripples.

Reginald Brett to Rosebery, 21 December 1885[2]

My father went to the Reform Club today and saw Henry James & Labouchere there. The former is depressed and the latter elated at the situation.

He said Labby had a number of lies of various kinds but they did not come to much.

Lewis Harcourt Journal, 24 December 1885[3]

At present I see nothing for it but the temporary break up of the party, but this is an evil altogether less than patching up a makeshift agreement in order merely to turn the Tories out without having a remedy for Ireland, less also than Dilke's preposterous notion of sitting in opposition with hands folded.

Herbert Gladstone to Edward Hamilton, 4 January 1886[4]

There is no wound yet made which cannot be healed but if you once begin to turn a jagged sword round in the flesh [it] is a different thing.

Sir William Harcourt to Chamberlain, 19 April 1886[5]

The Home Rule Bill seems doomed. This combination against it by Whigs and Radicals is I think too powerful to be resisted, unless at the last moment Gladstone sd by some ingenious artifice outgeneral his opponents. The position is a very curious one.

Carnarvon Diary, 15 May 1886[6]

---

[1] Curzon to Salisbury, 16 Sept. 1885, Third Marquess of Salisbury MSS Class E.
[2] Brett to Rosebery, 21 Dec. 1885, Esher Papers 2/7.
[3] Lewis Harcourt Journal, 24 Dec. 1885, Harcourt dep. 375, f. 50.
[4] Herbert Gladstone to Edward Hamilton, 5 Jan. 1886, BL Add. MS 48611, f. 181–181ᵛ.
[5] Harcourt to Chamberlain, 19 Apr. 1886, Chamberlain Papers JC5/38/48.
[6] Carnarvon Diary, 15 May 1886, Carnarvon Papers, BL Add. MS 60926, f. 71.

> G. is meditating surrender. Except Spencer he has not a man ready to
> face the panic in the party.
>
> William O'Brien, 25 May 1886[7]

Introduction

In the early hours of 8 June, Gladstone's third Government fell
when ninety-four Liberals voted with the Conservatives against
the second reading of the Government of Ireland Bill. For weeks
before the event there was great uncertainty about the numbers
who would defect. On 2 May Chamberlain claimed to have a list
of 119 Liberals who had promised to vote against the Bill. Of these
he judged seventy to 'have publicly committed themselves', and
twenty-three of the remainder were 'absolutely safe'.[8] On 4 May,
in a letter to Hartington, Chamberlain claimed to have a list of 133
Liberals who at one time or another had promised to vote against
the Home Rule Bill, and he regarded the Bill as doomed.[9] But
three days later, in a letter to his brother, he was more modest.
'The members against 2nd R continue to increase. They are now
93.'[10] And this turned out to be almost on the mark. W. S. Caine,
Chamberlain's whip, who did his counting for him on this occasion,
estimated on 27 May that 112 would vote against the Bill. By 31
May twelve of these had gone over to Gladstone. Of the remaining,
sixty-nine were 'stalwart' and thirty-one were 'still doubtful'.[11] Of
the thirty-one whom Caine considered 'ours' but 'shaky', seventeen,
in the event supported Gladstone. As the debate on Home Rule came
to its conclusion, as the ground for disagreement narrowed to the
position Liberals would take on clause 24 (the provision excluding
Irish Members from Westminster), the line separating Liberal
Gladstonian from Liberal Unionist became increasingly difficult to
draw, and it shifted constantly. Edmund Verney expressed the
ambiguity fully:

---

[7] O'Brien, *Evening Memories*, p. 124.

[8] Chamberlain to Sir William Harcourt, 2 May 1886, Chamberlain Papers JC5/
38/159.

[9] Chamberlain to Hartington, 4 May 1886, Chamberlain Papers JC5/22/45.

[10] Chamberlain to Arthur Chamberlain, 7 May 1886, Chamberlain Papers JC5/
11/6.

[11] Among the 'shaky' Chamberlain followers, Caine listed the following: Blades,
Bolton, Brinton, Baker, Compton, Cozens-Hardy, Crossley, Ferguson, Milnes Gaskell,
Ker, Green, Grove, Hobhouse, Ingram, Jacks, Johnson Ferguson, Kitching, McIver,
MacInnes, McLagan, Menzies, More, Moulton, Otter, Sir Joseph Pease, Quilter,
Rathbone, Ruston, Salis-Schwabe, Seely, Verney, Wason, and John Wilson. Caine
to Chamberlain, 27 and 31 May 1886, Chamberlain Papers JC5/10/2–3.

There is no doubt that I entirely disapprove of the Government Bills in the present shape, and therefore I propose to attend your [Chamberlain's] conference this afternoon.

At the same time, and the Government only ask that their Bills may be still-born, I shall probably vote for the second reading, and in doing so shall not forget that it is owing to your courageous and self-denying policy that I am able to go on with the bulk of my party.[12]

Verney could disapprove of Home Rule, but because of Gladstone's concessions he refrained from becoming a Liberal Unionist. Even after the Home Rule division was taken, there was some debate about who was a Liberal Unionist and who was not. Lewis McIver, for example, accepted 'the postulate that Home Rule is inevitable', and he believed the division on the second reading of the Government of Ireland Bill would turn on the question of 'the maintenance or the destruction of the Supremacy of Parliament'. He regarded Chamberlain's position as the one which 'more closely represent[s] my views on the Irish question than any other' leader's. Yet McIver was satisfied by the concessions Gladstone made at his Foreign Office meeting with the parliamentary Liberal party, and professed himself prepared to give a 'sterile' vote on the bill. 'You will have won for us not only a vindication of our opposition', he wrote to Chamberlain, but also 'six months time where in to put the country right on this question.'[13] But McIver voted against the second reading of the bill.

Some Liberals cannot be considered Liberal Unionist in any strict sense because they did not vote in the parliamentary division on the Government of Ireland Bill; but because of their views on the question they might be easily so considered. Jesse Collings, for example, did not vote in the Home Rule division because he had been expelled from the House for electoral corruption. Had he voted, he would surely have been in the division lobby with Chamberlain and Hartington. Hamar Bass abstained in the Home Rule division, but stood as a Liberal Unionist in the general election of 1886 for the Western division of Staffordshire, where he was returned as a Liberal Unionist in every succeeding election until his death in 1898. A. W. Peel, the younger son of the great Prime Minister sitting in this House where he was also Speaker, expressed himself as a Liberal Unionist, but, because he was Speaker, of course, could not vote. Peter McLagan is another such case, though he finally came round to the Gladstonian position. McLagan, who sat for Linlithgowshire,

---

[12] Verney to Chamberlain, 31 May 1886, Chamberlain Papers JC8/5/3/41.
[13] McIver to Chamberlain, 7 and 27 May 1886, Chamberlain Papers JC8/5/3/19 and 37.

did not vote in the division on the Home Rule Bill. Because of his churchmanship and his unwillingness to be stampeded by Scottish disestablishers, the Tories treated McLagan with kid gloves in the general election of 1885.[14] For this reason as well as his failure to support the Government on Home Rule, John Sinclair, lately a Free Church minister, declared himself in opposition to McLagan in the run-up to the election of 1886. McLagan, consequently, became serious about the Home Rule issue and desisted from his trimming, and the local Liberal association adopted him as their official candidate in 1886.[15]

Abstainers, cutters and fillers, trimmers and waverers, all make it difficult to identify with certainty the line between Gladstonian and Liberal Unionist in 1886, and voting in the parliamentary division on the second reading of the Government of Ireland Bill is the closest guide to the membership of these two principal factions as one is likely to get. Therefore, this study takes the Gladstonians to be those Liberals who supported the second reading of the Home Rule Bill, and takes the Liberal Unionists to be those Liberals who opposed it. (See Appendix I for a discussion of these classifications.) Those Liberals who did not vote in the Home rule division are classified separately. What follows traces the divide between Gladstonian Liberals and Liberal Unionists in 1886. It examines the issues on which they were disagreed, and shows the extent to which conflict over Home Rule was related to other policy disagreements in the party. By exploring the dimensional structure of Liberal disunity in 1886, this analysis reveals two things. First, there was an extensive pattern of ideological voting within the Liberal party in 1886. Second, the Home Rule division does not fit this voting dimension. Consequently, the cleavage in the Liberal party did not cut very deep, nor was it extensive in terms of the number of issues it touched. And this has great implications for the future of the Liberal party after 1886, and for the alliance of the Liberal Unionist with the Tories. In the controversy[16] between the inevitabilists, those scholars who date the inexorable decline of the Liberal party from the Home Rule crisis, and the accidentalists, those scholars who establish the decisive decline of the party very much later, the evidence recited below very much favours the latter. The Home Rule crisis in 1886 ended with

[14] Archibald Orr Ewing to Salisbury, 29 July 1885, and Charles Dalrymple to Salisbury, 31 July 1885, Third Marquess of Salisbury MSS Class E.

[15] *The Times*, 30 June 1886, p. 10.

[16] For a summary of this controversy see Geoffrey Hosking and Anthony King, 'Radicals and Whigs in the British Liberal Party, 1906–1914', *The History of Legislative Behavior*, ed. W. O. Aydelotte (Princeton: 1977), pp. 137–8.

Gladstone in command of a defeated parliamentary force, but a force competent to fight another day.

The Dimensions of Parliamentary Liberalism

Gladstone, from the beginning, dominated all social groups in the parliamentary Liberal party during the Home Rule crisis. In the end he would also control Liberal constituencies having characteristics of all kinds. The great separation in the Liberal party, therefore, was not the parliamentary reflection of a social crisis, nor was it a matter of constituency pressure. It was a matter of policy. It remains to explain whether or not this crisis in the affairs of the Liberal party was a power struggle, a dispute over strategy, or whether or not it found its ground in substantial policy disagreements within the party, and, if so, on which issues. For the high politics scholars, the great separation in the Liberal party was a power struggle, a contest between Gladstone, Chamberlain, and Hartington for the leadership of the Liberal party. As Cooke and Vincent put it, 'the problem of how his lieutenants were to displace Gladstone was solved in 1886 by Gladstone displacing his lieutenants.' For Cooke and Vincent the Home Rule crisis marked 'the most successful party purge in British history'. Irish policy was the occasion for schism, not its cause. In this way of looking at things, Irish policy was a triviality:

. . . the cabinet did not regard Ireland as its collective business in the sense that it did so regard such questions as the enfranchisement of the police, the promotion of the Duke of Connaught, or the situation in Bechuanaland. Unless a politician was actually required to administer Ireland, he would see no reason to think about it as a country presenting problems of government, unless he saw himself as an entrepreneur of party tactics who could turn substantive questions of government into the gold of party gain . . . The 'Irish question' was the temporary and particular name given in the 1880s to a continuous and permanent existential problem which party managers inflict upon themselves.[17]

Other scholars, harping very much less on the question of seizing power, view the Irish question in 1886 as a matter of strategy, as a device for the unification of a Liberal party which was divided on policy questions. For some, disunity by itself was a bad thing. Party leaders required a single issue, one of magnificent magnitude, to forge party unity. Home Rule in 1886, according to this view, was such a unifying issue. Other scholars do not agree. For these, factionalism was a source, not of political weakness, but of strength. Ideological

---

[17] Cooke and Vincent, *The Governing Passion*, pp. 15–18.

diversity allowed the Liberal party to face a bright future in 1886 because, by allowing new elements into the party, it reflected a responsiveness within the Liberal party leading to social and agrarian reform, nationalism, trade unionism, disestablishment, and, ultimately, to the Liberal revival in 1906. According to this view of things, Irish Home Rule was not essential to Liberal politics in the 1880s, nor was it the only policy or approach the Liberals possessed. Gladstone was not preoccupied with Ireland alone, but he was open to the other, more radical policy initiatives.[18]

The interpretation of the high politics scholars and the controversy over the role of Irish Home Rule as a unifying force in Liberal politics admit of a systematic and formal test through the examination of the voting of Liberal Members in 1886. If the high politics school is correct, the record of Liberal voting will reveal few voting dimensions, and those which existed should be extremely narrow, consisting of few legislative items. If, as they claim, the politics of the period can be explained by the competition among party leaders for the command of the Liberal party in 1886, voting patterns will be limited and fragmented because ideological considerations would have been absent. Furthermore, if Irish Home Rule served as a unifying force, consolidating a Liberal policy agenda, Liberal voting on the Home Rule question should show it to have been related to other Liberal initiatives; the Home Rule division should fit a common ideological dimension with the other issues exciting Liberal action in the 1880s.

When Lady Frederick Cavendish spoke about the 'innumerable hobby-riders and crotchetmongers'[19] in the Liberal party, she was referring to the divisions which haunted its history; and, as an early chapter has shown (see Table 3.5 and the discussion about it), in 1886 the Liberals continued to be internally divided by questions of land reform, the empire, foreign policy, and the Church. To find some clear thread to guide one through the rubble of Liberal policy disagreements is no easy matter. However, by analysing the

---

[18] For their respective views on this question, see Hamer, *Liberal Politics in the Age of Gladstone and Rosebery*, esp. pp. 110, 117; Barker, *Gladstone and Radicalism*; Emy, *Liberals, Radicals, and Social Politics*, pp. viii–xiv, 5, 54, 70–1; H. C. G. Matthew, *The Liberal Imperialists*, pp. 265 ff. For a wide-ranging debate on this question see Kenneth O. Morgan, 'The Liberal Regeneration', *The Times Literary Supplement*, 22 Aug. 1975, p. 941, and letters to the editor of the *TLS*, in 1975 from D. A. Hamer (9 Sept., p. 1024), from Michael Barker (26 Sept., p. 1094), from Hamer again (31 Oct., p. 1294), and from Morgan (14 Nov., p. 1361).

[19] J. Bailey (ed.), *The Diary of Lady Frederick Cavendish* (London: 1927), vol. 2, p. 168.

TABLE 6.1 *Liberal Voting on the Major Liberal Policy Agenda and Irish Home Rule*

	18	24	27	38	48	124
18. Labouchere's Motion on representative government	—	.96	.87	.87	1.0	.56
24. Dillwyn's Motion for Welsh disestablishment		—	1.0	.83	1.0	.79
27. Motion to reduce the estimate for royal palaces			—	.93	.82	.58
38. Richard's Motion against foreign involvements				—	.88	.25
48. MacFarlane's Amendment to cl. 1 of the Crofters Bill					—	.52
124. Government of Ireland Bill						—

dimensional structure of Liberal voting in the House of Commons it is possible to assess the general character of Liberal disunity, and to examine the place of the Irish Home Rule dispute in the larger patterns of Liberal ideological cleavage. Table 6.1 is drawn from those parliamentary division lists which show Liberal dissent achieving or exceeding 10 per cent of the party voting. The pattern revealed here is compelling and complete, and could be illustrated with many other examples. Three points are so important that they deserve all the emphasis which can be placed upon them.

First, Table 6.1 reveals a pattern of Liberal voting behaviour so regular and coherent that it is inconsistent with interpretations of political motivation which rest solely on manoeuvre, ambition, and the quest for power. Liberals disagreed on policy questions in 1886, but those disagreements rested upon ideological differences in the party, differences among Members on the grounds of political beliefs and values. On the questions which fit a common voting dimension in this table, Liberals of the more radical tendency voted consistently in the affirmative, and Liberals of a more moderate political stripe voted consistently in the negative. Between these ideological extremes rested those Liberals who voted for some measures and opposed others, but rarely in such a manner as to vote for more radical questions if they had opposed issues of a more moderate character.

Second, this Liberal voting dimension, like the great parliamentary voting dimension discussed in Chapter 2, cuts across questions having very different kinds of legislative content. It includes questions of land reform, disestablishment, the reform of the House of Lords, foreign policy, the empire, and demands for budgetary retrenchment. This was the traditional Liberal programme, an agenda for radical reform which had divided the party for no little while. As surprising as it may superficially appear, Chamberlain and Hartington had not dissimilar views about divisions in the party on such questions.[20] Chamberlain wrote, 'I do not think it worth while to accentuate the differences between us & Mr. Gladstone. In the first place he is squeezable & will probably give way to our views. . . . It is possible to read between the lines in his manifesto & to find in it allusions to all our points, which are treated as matters for consideration and in some cases of probably adoption.' Lord Hartington, speaking at Mansfield during the general election of 1885, and in an approving tone, also commented upon internal Liberal disagreements:

> The Liberal party included, generally speaking, not a section only, but the whole of those who were in favour of measures of progress and reform. (Cheers.) There were some who wanted to advance more quickly; there were those who wanted to proceed more slowly; there were those who desired more sweeping and immediate change; there were others who desired that those necessary changes should be made in a more cautious manner.

As these quotations may serve to show, Liberals disagreed about questions on the Liberal agenda, but the nature of their disagreement revealed that they had common assumptions about these issues. They were not disagreements of fundamental principle, consequently, but disagreements about the rate of reform, its timing, and the degree and the amount of reform which they judged to be appropriate.

Third, Table 6.1 shows that Liberal voting behaviour in 1886 was multi-dimensional: the Irish Home Rule Bill did not fit the major Liberal voting dimension. Indeed, Home Rule fits a dimensional relationship with only two items in the general Liberal voting pattern. Home Rule was *sui generis*, and an understanding of it serves as no

---

[20] Hartington's speech was quoted in *The Times*, 4 Dec. 1885. Chamberlain to Collings, 25 Sept. 1885, Chamberlain Papers JC5/16/108.

guide to understanding Liberal voting behaviour on the other questions which had long preoccupied them. Therefore, not only was
the Home Rule crisis something more than a power struggle among
the leadership in the Liberal party, but the Home Rule Bill could
not provide, as some have argued it could,[21] an ideological basis
for party unity. A significant number of Liberals in the House of
Commons did not consider the question of Irish nationalism as being
related to the other issues with which they were associated. Various
visions of a Liberal version of Ireland reigned. Some, like Chamberlain,
considered Ireland a province; some, like Gladstone, were learning
to consider Ireland a nation. Consequently, a purge, if Gladstone
and his lieutenants intended a purge, would have to include more
than other political rivals. It would have to include those on the
Liberal back benches who could not conceive of a place for Irish
nationalism in the traditional Liberal agenda. The great efforts
Gladstone made in 1886 to reconcile all factions around his Home
Rule policy indicate his unwillingness so to do. To purge and to
slough off was too direct and purposeful for a man who has been
characterized as 'imprecise and guarded'[22] in his plans and strategies,
a manner which many within and without his circle deplored.
Gladstone's movement towards Home Rule had been of a piece with
the rest of his career, the career of a conservative constantly adjusting
his principles to political necessities and forging his liberalism from
the accidents and emergencies he faced. Such a man is not, by nature,
a purger or a slougher.

The reasons for the failure of Liberal voting on Irish Home Rule
to square with voting on the main Liberal agenda is an important
question, one to be addressed shortly. For the present it is enough
to indicate that radicals had long been reluctant and cautious on
the question of Irish nationalism. As one historian of Liberal factionalism has put it, 'the commitment of a substantial majority
of Radicals to Home Rule was due more to a realization that
Ireland was beyond Radical understanding and capabilities than to
an application of Radical precepts to Ireland. Home rule never
became an integral part of Radicalism.'[23] On 1 February, when he
kissed hands and accepted the seals of office, Gladstone himself

[21] 'And in Gladstone's thinking on the political situation it was Ireland that began
to emerge as the great cause that might control and subordinate all other political
questions and thus create order out of the prevailing chaos.' Hamer, *Liberal Politics
in the Age of Gladstone and Rosebery*, pp. 110 and 117.
[22] Michael Lynch's review of Perry Butler's *Gladstone: Church, State, and Trac-
tarianism*, in *Victorian Studies*, 26.3 (Spring 1983), p. 352.
[23] Heyck, *The Dimensions of British Radicalism*, p. 233.

represented his Irish policies as something distinct from other Liberal considerations.[24]

To be sure, radicals on the back benches had pressed Gladstone to seize an Irish initiative, but the tone of their pressure shows them to have been at least as concerned with other radical objectives as they were with Ireland. Before he joined Gladstone's third Administration, Henry Broadhurst wrote: 'it appears to me that no effective public work can be done while the Irish question remains before the country. The Tories have everything to gain by this.' And Henry Cobb, the radical banker and solicitor who had been recently returned for the Rugby division of Warwickshire, wrote in a similar vein: 'For seven months the new voters have been fighting to turn out the Tories. . . . I am perfectly sure that you will have the support of the Country in a bold, plain policy, and the sooner the better, while the steam is up.'[25] Home Rule would get radical support, Labouchere confidently announced to Chamberlain, but not because the radicals were enamoured with Irish nationalism. The radicals 'do not love the Irish, but hate them, & would give them Home Rule on the Gladstone or Canada pattern to get rid of them'.[26] W. S. Blunt was also afraid of weak links between radicalism and nationalism. 'Home Rule in Ireland', he confided to John Morley and John Dillon, 'did not lie quite on the tracks of English Radicalism.' As Blunt seems to have realized, democracy was consistent with radicalism in 1886, but nationalism was not.[27]

So long as Gladstone faced the opposition of radicals, such as Chamberlain, and Liberals for whom nationalism was unacceptable, Home Rule would not fit the major Liberal voting dimension. The multi-dimensionality of Liberalism in 1886 was something some Liberals had an intimation of. Schnadhorst warned Chamberlain about his position on the major questions of the day. Those issues fitting the major Liberal voting dimension were inconsistent with his position on Home Rule, and other radicals would not follow him.

[24] Queen Victoria's Diary, 1 Feb. 1886, cited by Cooke and Vincent, *The Governing Passion*, p. 357.

[25] Broadhurst to Gladstone and Cobb to Gladstone, both writing on 22 Dec. 1885, Gladstone Papers BL Add. MS 56336, unbound and unfoliated.

[26] Labouchere to Chamberlain, 31 Mar. 1886, Chamberlain Papers JC5/50/69.

[27] Blunt Diary, 13 May 1886, Blunt MS 334-1975, ff. 186–7. On 24 Mar. 1886 Blunt had met T. D. Sullivan, the Lord Mayor of Dublin and the Member for the city's College Green division, who convinced him that the Irish members had no confidence in Chamberlain. 'He is a democrat, not a Nationalist, [and] wants to make use of Ireland for democratic purposes & his own & was at heart opposed to all their views except regarding the land.' Ibid., 24 Mar. 1886, Blunt MS 334-1975, f. 84.

'The people who supported you on the "Three Acres & C" would be against you on Ireland & those who agreed with you on the latter would be against you on the former.'[28] Consequently, as Gladstone and the party leaders increasingly drew the radical back benches behind them, they isolated Chamberlain and his immediate followers. Joseph Leicester, the glass-blower MP, told Blunt, 'Our Joe has gone completely off the rails.'[29] The way in which Home Rule cut across previously existing ideological divisions is shown in a story told about Francis Mildmay, who became a Liberal Unionist but who abstained in the division on Collings's Amendment. He had been staying with the Fitzwilliams, who also became Unionists, in Yorkshire and returned to London for the division on 'three acres and a cow'. But Lord Ebrington, who also became a Liberal Unionist, got to him and persuaded Mildmay to stay out of the division lobbies. Collings, who had spoken for Mildmay in Devonshire during the general election of 1885, was furious.[30]

The findings in Table 6.1 can be pushed further in examining the form and structure of Liberal dissent in 1886. Judging dissent by the relative positions taken by leaders and back-benchers, it is possible to chart both the direction and the intensity of the various cleavages in the Liberal party. When members of the rank and file rejected the position taken by the Treasury bench, forcing the leaders to join in voting alliances with the Tory Opposition, these rebellions took the form of extremist or radical revolts. When dissidents voted with the Tory Opposition themselves, these rebellions took the form of cross-bench or centrist revolts.[31] As the following analysis will show, the measures dividing the Liberal party and which fit a common voting dimension, as in Table 6.1, those belonging to the traditional Liberal programme, were radical revolts. The Irish Home Rule Bill and the few additional divisions which join it in a common voting dimension were centrist revolts. When instances of Liberal dissidence in 1886 are tabulated against this scheme of things, the clear direction of Liberal rebellion was toward the left: 85 per cent of these were radical revolts against the Liberal leadership, and only 15 per cent were centrist revolts across the cross benches in which Liberal rebels joined the Conservative party in voting coalitions.

[28] Schnadhorst to Chamberlain, 13 Feb. 1886, Chamberlain Papers JC5/63/9.
[29] Blunt Diary, 13 May 1886, Blunt MS 334-1975, f. 188.
[30] Harcourt Journal, 28 Jan. 1886, Harcourt dep. 377, f. 48.
[31] This analysis follows Hugh Berrington, 'Partisanship and Dissidence in the Nineteenth Century House of Commons', p. 343.

Radical Revolts in 1886

As Gladstone was not unaware, revolts by the parliamentary extreme in the party he commanded were no new things but a part of the history of the Liberal party. In a holograph dated 7 March 1874 he wrote:

The habit of making a career by & upon constant active opposition to the bulk of the party, and its leaders, has acquired a dangerous predominance among a portion of its members. This habit is not checked by the action of the great majority, who do not indulge or approve of it; & it has become dangerous to the credit & efficiency of the party.[32]

Radical revolts occurred on questions of Irish policy (with the exception of Irish government), foreign and imperial policy and defence, land reform, and radical initiatives directed against the House of Lords and other institutions of privilege. Some of these disagreements cut deep into the Liberal party, sufficiently deep for some of these radical rebellions, such as in a division on Henry Richard's Motion to require parliamentary consent for certain foreign policy questions, to be temporarily successful. Alfred Pease described the occasion:

I voted with Richard, and to my horror we defeated the Government on the motion 'that Mr. Speaker do now leave the chair [and] to leave out the words after *That*' by 112 to 108, so that when it came to substituting the Resolution for the words left out I voted the other way for the Government and [with] 4 Liberals 'going out', a majority of 6 was secured for the Government.[33]

It was a question of the Liberal Government and its immediate supporters being assisted by the Conservatives in opposing radicals within the Liberal party and the Irish Nationalists. Sir Richard Temple described a similar parliamentary situation in divisions on the Crofters Bill.

The Liberal Government very properly take their stand and won't move an inch further in the direction of unsound principle. In this resolute attitude they are half deserted by their followers, the Liberals proper, and Opposed by the English Radicals, and the Irish—stand it out, in sufficient numbers to give the Govt (with their particular followers) a good majority. This entirely destroyed the little game of the Radicals, notably Macfarlaine, Clark

---

[32] Gladstone's holograph, 7 Mar. [1874], BL Add. MS 44762, f. 37, quoted by H. C. G. Matthew (ed.), *The Gladstone Diaries with Cabinet Minutes and Prime Ministerial Correspondence* (Oxford: 1982), vol. 8, p. 472.

[33] Pease's Diary, 19 Mar. 1886, in Pease, *Elections and Recollections*, p. 114.

and Barclay, who as they themselves said, looked on the Bill as a pitiful installment of what they mean to get someday and 'as a framework to hang amendments'.[34]

Henry Chaplin wrote to Salisbury the same evening. 'We finished the Committee last night on the Crofter Bill, and the persistently large majorities against the Radicals & Home Rulers until last night when most of the men had gone home, have been satisfactory. [But they have got?] no concessions worth having except one relating to deer forests.'[35]

Radical revolts of this sort, naturally, troubled those responsible for dragooning Liberals into the division lobbies. Arnold Morley, who became whip in 1886, was among these. 'I had serious misgivings' about accepting the position of whip, he wrote to Edward Hamilton, 'and they are by no means removed now that I have done so. At the best times the post must be difficult, but especially now when men on our side are unpledged, and it is impossible to tell how they will go.'[36] The Tories, of course, took no little delight in Liberal disarray, and, in so doing, exaggerated the extent, and meaning, of Liberal disunity. Cranborne wrote to his father that the Liberal Government 'have no control and without us I don't know what they would do'. As Lord Harrowby reported to Carnarvon, then at Portofino, 'the tone of the present H. of C. is very revolutionary. Much more so than appears in the papers, & . . . for the present the moderate Liberals appear cowed & fear to vote.' Hicks Beach agreed in these assessments. 'Labouchere could carry any revolutionary proposal against them any night, if we did not take some trouble on such occasions to help them.' Sir Richard Temple observed, '*this* Govt has no moral power atall [*sic*] over its supporters and drifts about.'[37] Resistance to radical revolts by the Liberal Government, consequently, 'had a Conservative tendency'. 'It is important that Conservative Members should support Mr Gladstone in well-doing, when he and his were thus deserted by a portion of their own followers.' Consequently, a certain comradeship came to be built up between Liberals and Conservatives who found themselves on these occasions in the same division lobby. 'Sir R. T. [Temple] is

[34] Temple Letters, 20 Apr. 1886, BL Add. MS 38916, ff. 70ᵛ–71.

[35] Chaplin to Salisbury, 20 Apr. 1886, Third Marquess of Salisbury MSS Class E.

[36] Arnold Morley to Edward Hamilton, 1 Feb. 1886, BL Add. MS 48625, f. 3-3ᵛ

[37] Cranborne to Salisbury, 11 Mar. 1886, Third Marquess of Salisbury MSS Class E; Harrowby to Carnarvon, 23 Mar. 1886, BL Add. MS 60863, unbound and unfoliated; Hicks Beach to Salisbury, 27 Mar. 1886, Third Marquess of Salisbury MSS Class E.; Temple Letters, 12 May 1886, BL Add. MS 38916, f. 89ᵛ.

TABLE 6.2 *The Strength of Liberal Dissent in Radical Revolts*

	No. of Divisions	%
Divisions in which 50% or more of Liberals voting dissented from the party position	8	18
Divisions in which 49% or fewer of Liberals voting dissented from the party position	37	82

very fond of Marjoribanks [another Liberal whip] and begins to feel as if he were a regular dog under his Whip, and says the Liberals night after night leave Gladstone in the lurch; also "we always hum affectionately when Hartington comes into the House; we like him, but we fear he does not like us".'[38]

The strength of dissent in radical revolts can be judged by the proportion of the Liberal party engaging in them. As Table 6.2 indicates, on eight occasions (18 per cent) among these radical revolts a majority of the Liberal party voting rebelled against the positions taken by the Treasury Bench. These included the two divisions on Richard's Motion against foreign engagements without parliamentary consent and Labouchere's Motion to reduce the estimate for royal parks. This amused the Tories, who, Cranborne reported to his father, 'roared with laughter'.[39] Sir Richard Temple, who took a more sober view of the matter, believed Labouchere's motivation arose from 'a spirit of mischief to embarrass the Govt'. It was, he held, shocking bad tactics and management and 'the result [was] calculated to bring the House into contempt'.[40] (In a week's time the Government got the House to revote this supply estimate on the understanding that the London parks which were not royal parks would be placed under the management of the Metropolitan Board of Works, a compromise which Edward Hamilton, in his observations on this parliamentary débâcle, regarded as fair.[41]) Labouchere's Resolution on Representative Government, which was directed against the political authority of the House of Lords, was nearly as successful in the division lobbies as his efforts to reduce the estimate

---

[38] Temple, *The Story of My Life*, vol. 2, p. 229; William Johnson Cory to Reginald Brett, 22 Mar. 1886, Esher Papers 9/11. (There is an autograph of this letter in the Esher Papers 9/19. Neither is foliated.)

[39] Cranborne to Salisbury, 11 Mar. 1886, Third Marquess of Salisbury MSS Class E.

[40] Temple Letters, 12 Mar. 1886, BL Add. MS 38916, ff. 41–2.

[41] Edward Hamilton Diary, 19 Mar. 1886, BL Add. MS 48643, ff. 46–7.

for royal parks.[42] A voting coalition of the Liberal leadership and their followers, joined by the Conservative party, defeated Labouchere and the rebels by only thirty-six votes. Finally, these radical revolts, which were among the strongest examples of extremist dissent in 1886, included two divisions on the Crofters Bill when it came back to the House of Commons with additional limiting Amendments from the House of Lords. These Amendments, of course, further irritated agrarian reformers, who had been frustrated at every step of the Bill's progress. According to W. A. Hunter, the Government had restricted the scope of the measure, reducing its value, and the Lords had rendered it a nullity.[43]

These rebellions represent the high tide of radical feeling in the House of Commons in 1886. A point wants making here. These indications of radical sentiment do not support the widely held view that the left wing in the Liberal party was roughly damaged when Chamberlain, and radicals of his ilk, left the party as Unionists,[44] because radicalism persisted without 'Our Joe'. Though the value of Chamberlain's leadership — and the lack of it after 1886 — should not be minimized, radicalism survived and came into its own. On the other hand, the Liberal party could restrain its radical section. If 18 per cent of the radical revolts were sufficiently attractive to garner the support of a majority of the Liberal party, it obviously means that, on the remaining 82 per cent of these tilts toward the left, the Liberal party maintained its hold over a majority of its members. This larger proportion of radical revolts does not seem to justify the partisan glee of Cranborne and Hicks Beach. The Liberal leadership was dependent upon a voting coalition with the Conservatives to defeat radical adventures only on those occasions in which radical dissidents had sufficient support from the Irish Nationalists to pose a threat to the combined Liberal and Conservative parties.

The substantive outline of Liberal Unionist–Gladstonian cleavage on radical revolts in 1886 can be charted by constructing simple indices of likeness, comparing these two factions, and by summarizing them in the form of averages for each of the several voting

[42] Ibid., 7 Mar. 1886, BL Add. MS 48463, f. 34.

[43] Hansard, 306: 960.

[44] See, for example, E. J. Feuchtwanger: '[T]he loss of the Radical Unionist followers of Chamberlain undoubtedly damaged Liberal prospects for many years to come.' Introduction to A. V. Dicey, *England's Case Against Home Rule* (Richmond: 1973), pp. ii–iii.

TABLE 6.3 *Likeness Scores Comparing the Relationship Between Gladstonians and Liberal Unionists on Liberal Voting Dimensions**

	Average Likeness Score
General Liberal voting dimension	80
Voting dimension of Irish issues	80
Voting dimension of foreign policy and imperial issues	81
Voting dimension of divisions on the Crofters Bill	80
Voting dimension of division on radical initiatives	72

*Q threshold for these dimensions = .80

dimensions discovered in these materials.[45] The average likeness score for Gladstonians and Liberal Unionists on the general Liberal voting dimension sets a bench-mark against which the scores for specific policy dimensions can be judged. While not agreed, the principal Liberal factions acted in a similar manner in radical revolts. The great separation in the Liberal party, therefore, was no yawning chasm involving many matters of policy; it was very much more limited, restricted to policy questions which do not fit these dimensions of Liberal ideological behaviour. In fact, it suggests that factionalism in the Liberal party took some time to develop, and was not markedly present earlier in the session when many of these parliamentary divisions were taken.

These conclusions are confirmed in the average likeness scores comparing the behaviour of Gladstonians and Liberal Unionists on specific policy questions. The average scores are roughly similar, and the Liberal party in 1886 seems not very much more vulnerable on one as compared with others. All elevated, these averages hover about the average derived for the general Liberal ideological voting dimension. The score for issues fitting the Irish policy dimension is especially suggestive, because it reveals that the depths of disagreement between Liberal Unionist and Gladstonian factions on Home Rule did not communicate itself to other matters of Irish policy. On these the behaviour of these two factions was pretty similar. Moreover, the elevated score for factional voting on the Foreign Policy and Imperial Dimension indicates that Rosebery had misjudged the

[45] A Likeness Score is given by the formula L = 100 − (% of Liberal Unionists voting positively − % of the Gladstonians voting positively). A score of 100 represents perfect likeness, and a score of 0 represents perfect dissimilarity. Likeness scores for each legislative item in each Liberal voting dimension were averaged together to produce an Average Likeness Score.

situation when he believed these questions to be as important as Home Rule in the Liberal breach of 1886.[46] The likeness score for the voting dimension of radical initiatives alone is deflated, but not by enough to suggest that these policies lay behind the great separation in the Liberal party.

The similarity of Gladstonian and Liberal Unionist voting on radical revolts may be shown in somewhat more detail in the tallies for all items in one of these dimensions. As Table 6.4 shows, similar proportions of Liberal Unionists and Gladstonians opposed radical criticisms of the foreign and imperial policy of their own party. And this is particularly true for the most radical proposals, those located at the top of the dimension at the top of the table. The proportions of Liberal Unionists voting in the nay lobby are slightly thicker throughout, and they enlarge toward the bottom of the dimension, on those questions which were increasingly moderate and which gained, increasingly, a larger proportion of the party's support. At the bottom of the dimension, among these more moderate proposals, Gladstonians, by a slight majority, came to support these radical revolts, and the Liberal Unionists were nearly evenly divided. And this increasing Gladstonian support and Liberal Unionist opposition to radical proposals would have consequences for the positions members of these factions held on the various parliamentary voting

TABLE 6.4 *Unionist and Gladstonian Voting on the Liberal Foreign-Military-Imperial Policy Dimension*

		Gladstonians		Unionists	
		% +	% −	% +	% −
10.	Healy's Motion to reduce the supply estimate for the salaries of colonial governors	16	84	5	95
9.	Hunter's Amendment against expenses for military operations in Burma	39	61	11	89
12.	Bradlaugh's Motion to reduce the supply estimates for embassies and missions	47	53	21	79
39.	Richard's Resolution against foreign and imperial involvements without the consent of Parliament	60	40	45	55
38.	Richard's Resolution against foreign and imperial involvements without the consent of Parliament	61	39	45	55

[46] Matthew, *The Liberal Imperialists*, p. 132.

dimensions. Generally speaking, Gladstonians tended toward the left wing of the party and Liberal Unionists toward the right wing.

There, however, is another point which should not be overlooked. Some Liberal Unionists consistently supported radical revolts. Since these were among the more radical measures to come before the House, it is obvious that the more radical members of the Liberal Unionist faction would be those to support them. But not always. Sixteen Liberal Unionists, nearly half of the Liberal Unionists voting, supported Labouchere's Motion against the House of Lords. These included Lord Wolmer, and Albert Grey was believed to have paired in support of the measure. Both were amongst the more prominent Liberal Unionists, and neither could be regarded as a radical.[47]

Radical revolts, such as the division of Labouchere's Motion against the House of Lords, almost all of them, were more radical than the Home Rule revolt in the sense that a greater proportion of the Liberal party opposed them than the proportion opposing Home Rule. Consequently, the opposition of certain Liberal Unionists to the Home Rule Bill, after the fairly consistent support some of them had shown for radical revolts, prevented the Home Rule Bill from fitting a dimensional relationship with the measures which made up the traditional Liberal agenda. Radical revolts were numerous in 1886, and some of them cut deep into the Liberal party, but they did not predict the great separation in the Liberal party over Irish Home Rule.

Centrist Revolts

The rebellion in the Liberal party over the Government of Ireland Bill was a revolt by centrists in a voting alliance with the Conservatives. Some Tories had hoped for a general Liberal alliance along these lines for no little while. As one correspondent put it to Sir Stafford Northcote in the middle of 1885, 'I trust we shall be able to form a permanent coalition between ourselves and the moderate Liberals without which it will be difficult to resist the Irish and Radical attacks.'[48] And in December 1885 the Duke of Manchester believed many Liberals wished the Conservative Government would be preserved in power, and would vote for its measures, if they were not forced into the party line by a vote of

---

[47] For Albert Grey's pair in support of Labouchere's Motion against the House of Lords, see Gladstone to the Queen, 6 Mar. 1886, in Guedalla, *The Queen and Mr. Gladstone*, vol. 2, p. 396.

[48] Samuel Aker to Northcote, 23 June 1885, BL Add. MS 50042, ff. 117ᵛ–118.

confidence.[49] Even after resigning office the next month, Salisbury regarded the strength of the anti-Conservative alliance as insufficient to cause what he was pleased to call 'lasting mischief'. 'Except Mr. Gladstone', Salisbury wrote to the Queen, 'the forces of subversion have no dangerous champion.'[50] The accuracy of these prognoses would rest in the extent and strength of centrist revolts in the Liberal party.

The division on the Government of Ireland Bill was the occasion of the most notable centrist revolt. However, as the comparison of Liberal voting in Table 6.1 showed, it was quite a unique political creature. Irish nationalism, an expression of populist romanticism, was inconsistent with the traditional agenda of the Liberal party. It was the special approach of Gladstone and his lieutenants, an approach they had adopted before in dealing with the Irish Church and Irish land. It was designed to limit sharply the imperial implications of their actions through a pluralistic policy which sought to integrate the Home Rule question into liberalism's mainstream. Those who would become Liberal Unionists were not deceived by this tactic, and, by itself, this manner may have disturbed them. Home Rule, for the Liberal Unionists, threatened national power and imperial unity, and they justified their alliance with the Conservatives as the formation of a national bloc to protect the national interest. Gladstone's Government, for these Liberals, had departed from Liberal orthodoxy. As one Whig put it to a radical, 'Mr. Gladstone & Mr. J. Morley have formed a fresh Party and have deserted Liberal Principles now!! it is on this assumption we ought to act and combine amongst ourselves here and in the country.'[51] The Liberal Unionists, in this, stood in a tradition of their own, a tradition of resistance to nationalist impulses. Nine years before, on Isaac Butt's annual Motion for Home Rule, only one English Liberal spoke for the Motion (Sir Wilfred Lawson), and only eight voted for it. Now, with Home Rule taken up by the Liberal leadership, dissenting Liberals prepared themselves to go to the Tories and to the country.

In this, the Liberal Unionists were nearly a single-issue faction, a point Salisbury recognized. 'There seems to be no obstacle to our acting together to resist Home Rule', he wrote to Goschen, 'but any

[49] The Duke of Manchester to H. J. B. Manners, 23 Dec. 1885, Third Marquess of Salisbury MSS Class D/47/63.

[50] Salisbury to the Queen, 31 Jan. 1886, Third Marquess of Salisbury MSS Class D/87/339.

[51] Edward Heneage to Chamberlain, 14 Mar. 1886, Chamberlain Papers JC5/44/2.

further co-operation is not within the field of practical politics at present.'[52] However, there are policy intimations which suggest that the great separation in the Liberal party went beyond Home Rule, and these are found in the other centrist revolts which occurred in 1886. These occurred in the voting on a question of local taxation, in a division on the Irish Labourers Amendment Acts Bill, in the division on the Dundalk Gas Bill, and in divisions on disestablishment for Wales and Scotland, and the greatest of these were centrist revolts over disestablishment.

A connection between disestablishment and Home Rule went back to the general election of 1885. In Scotland, the Church question stimulated political co-operation of the sort Home Rule stirred the following year. Peter McLagan, who had sat as the Liberal Member for Linlithgowshire since 1865 and whose ambiguous position on Home Rule has already been noted, had the support of Tories because he resisted disestablishment.

Mr. McLagan has been [pressured] for the past three months to pledge himself for the disestablishment of the church. . . . The Conservatives intend starting a Conservative agst. Mr. McLagan at the next elections, which I think most unwise. They have not the least chance of gaining the seat and in my opinion no Conservative should contest the seat of a Liberal Churchman unless they are sure of winning.

How can we expect Liberals to vote for Conservatives because they are churchmen if we Conservatives vote agst such a man as Mr. McLagan who is so strong a Churchman?

So wrote Archibald Orr Ewing,[53] and in terms which would be duplicated in the Tory–Liberal Unionist electoral pact in 1886. Charles Dalrymple wrote, 'I need not trouble you by saying anything as to the policy of sparing Liberal candidates, but Mr. McLagan's case is exceptional.'[54] Others grasped the religious connection between Home Rule and disestablishment. A. B. Forwood advised Salisbury to solicit Roman Catholic support: 'The Ulster & Loyal question should not be treated simply as Protestant matters.'[55] Lord Harrowby warned Carnarvon, still at Portofino, 'the depth & intensity of feeling excited by the Separatist scheme is beyond anything we have seen.

---

[52] Salisbury to Goschen, 4 Mar. 1886, Third Marquess of Salisbury MSS Class D/26/32.
[53] Orr Ewing to Salisbury, 29 July 1885, Third Marquess of Salisbury MSS Class E.
[54] Dalrymple to Salisbury, 31 July 1885, Third Marquess of Salisbury MSS Class E.
[55] A. B. Forwood to Salisbury, 16 June 1886, Third Marquess of Salisbury MSS Class E.

An Anti-Roman feeling is on the verge of rising.'[56] Taking his information from Miss Catherine Walters (who had it from the Prince of Wales), W. S. Blunt attributed the Queen's opposition to Home Rule to her religious views. 'Her Majesty is a violent partizan on the other side, principally on Protestant religious grounds.'[57] He also put down Gladstone's defeat in the general election of 1886 to 'the No Popery cry [which was] almost as strong an argument with the Radicals as with the Tories'.[58] Himself a Roman Catholic, Blunt ascribed his personal political problems to his religion. 'It is almost an absolute bar just now, as the Irish quarrel has enflamed all Protestant minds; and Wyllie at the Liberal Office told me as much today. "We have a good many Catholic candidates on our list" he said, but the constituencies say "give us a Jew if you like but not a Catholic".'[59]

How far the great separation in the Liberal party may be regarded as a broad-based voting alliance with the Tories can be judged by using the division lists for these centrist revolts to see if voting was ideological, if the likeness scores for Liberal Unionist and Gladstonian factions are low, and if large numbers of Liberals participated in them. As these reckonings show, Liberal voting in centrist revolts was highly volatile because this was the cutting edge of the split in the Liberal party, and these were the sorts of issue likely to produce the most partisan anxiety. The story they tell, therefore, is highly complex.

Table 6.5 compares the votes of Liberals alone in these centrist revolts, and reveals dimensional voting of a very limited and fragmented sort. The largest dimension which can be constructed with these materials with a minimum Q threshold of .80 consists of only four questions (Barclay's Amendment to the Address to the Queen's Speech, which was concerned with land reform, two divisions on Welsh disestablishment, and the division on the second reading of the franchise Amendment to the Belfast Main Drainage Bill). The division on Home Rule does not fit this dimension when $Q = .80$. Home Rule not only failed to fit the dimension consisting of the major Liberal agenda (see Table 6.1), it fails to fit this one. Home Rule, consequently, while central to party politics, was not central to the

---

[56] Harrowby to Carnarvon, 21 Apr. 1886, BL Add. MS 60863, unbound and unfoliated.

[57] Blunt Diary, 13 May 1886, Blunt MS 334-1975, f. 185.

[58] Ibid., 17 July 1886, Blunt MS 335-1975, f. 147.

[59] Ibid., 16 June 1886, Blunt MS 335-1975, f. 107–9. Blunt's Catholicism is a consistent theme in his diary; see the entries for 7 July 1885, 18 and 19 June, and 5 July 1886, Blunt MS 333-1975, ff. 62–3; 335-1975, ff. 111, 113, 139.

TABLE 6.5 Dimensions of Liberal Voting on Divisions Which Were the Occasions of Centrist Revolts

	1	24	25	30	41	53	100	124	140
1. Barclay's Amendment to the Address on the Queen's Speech	—	.88	.87	-1.0	.83	.76	.68	.85	.85
24. Dillwyn's Motion for Welsh Disestablishment		—	1.0	.55	.81	1.0	.37	.79	.85
25. Grey's Motion for the reform of the Welsh Church			—	.86	.77	.97	.46	.72	.81
30. Labourers (Ireland) Acts Amendment Bill				—	.80	.80	.88	.36	1.0
41. Incidence of local taxation					—	.70	.39	.85	.77
53. Scottish disestablishment						—	-.37	.75	.83
100. Dundalk Gas Bill							—	.62	.94
124. Irish Home Rule								—	.91
140. Belfast Main Drainage, Franchise Amendment									—

ideology of parliamentary Liberalism. Moreover, it was only imperfectly related to voting on other questions which, in 1886, it resembled most closely in terms of its structural characteristics.

If, however, a more generous statistical test is allowed and the Q threshold is reduced to .70, a dimension of Liberal votes emerges which includes the division on Home Rule, three divisions on disestablishment motions, one on land policy, one on local taxation, and the franchise question for the Corporation of Belfast. Disestablishment appears to be the other major question to which Home Rule, albeit in an imperfect statistical way, was related. This is a point worth some consideration because, as Table 6.1 indicated, disestablishment (in the form of Dillwyn's Motion for the disestablishment of the Church in Wales) was also related to the mainstream of Liberal politics. Disestablishment in 1886 cut in both directions. It had been around a long time; it had been widely disputed in and out of Parliament; it was a part of the discussion of public policy. Despite Gladstone's caution, its support upon the back benches was being matched by support among Liberal leadership. Lewis Harcourt gave insider's gossip on the development of disestablishment sentiment among Gladstone's colleagues:

Gladstone in bed with a cold & home rule fever. Sent down word to the Cabinet that Chex [Sir William Harcourt] is to oppose Dillwyn's motion for the Disestablishment of the Church in Wales on Tuesdasy. Whereupon all the commoners in the Cabinet said that if they did not vote *with* Dillwyn they certainly would vote against him.[60]

In the event two-thirds of those who held, or had held, government office supported Dillwyn's Motion. (Seventy-seven per cent supported Scottish disestablishment and 63 per cent supported Grey's Motion for the reform of the Church in Wales.) When Harcourt spoke against Dillwyn's Motion he gave the clear impression that he 'admitted the case for disestablishment'.[61] Consequently, even as disestablishment was coming to fit the major Liberal voting dimension, indeed perhaps for this reason, nascent Liberal Unionists saw it as the kind of question which went beyond their ideological limits, and by their voting on it put it into the same class of question as Home Rule. This is confirmed by an average likeness score calculated for the Liberal Unionist and Gladstonian factions on these three disestablishment votes and the remaining four centrist revolts which fit a common ideological dimension when Q = .70. This score (57) is much lower

---

[60] Harcourt Journal, 8 Mar. 1886, Harcourt dep. 378, ff. 5–6.
[61] 10 Mar. 1886, *The Diary of Gathorne Hardy, Later Lord Cranbrook*, p. 600.

than the average likeness scores for questions fitting the major Liberal agenda. These questions, therefore, come closest to predicting the Liberal break in 1886 because these are the closest to the Home Rule question.

How dangerous for the Liberal party these centrist revolts were may be indicated by their frequency and strength. Centrist revolts were a very small minority (15 per cent) of the rebellions within the Liberal party on the divisions fitting the great parliamentary voting dimension in 1886. Moreover, if radical revolts in the party were weak on the whole, centrist revolts were yet weaker. Few achieved support approaching 30 per cent of the party voting (in the division on the Home Rule Bill, 28 per cent of the party defected). In 78 per cent of these centrist revolts, less than 20 per cent of the Liberal party participated. There is a clear and distinct basis for Liberal separation on grounds of ideology and policy, but Home Rule did not fragment the fundamental basis of parliamentary Liberalism. Consequently, the Gladstonians and Liberal Unionists entered separate wildernesses after the fall of Gladstone's Government in 1886. Gladstone retained control over his party (and this is quite different from Sir Robert Peel's situation in 1886, primarily because the Corn Laws question fitted the major Conservative voting dimension for the 1840s and the Home Rule Bill in 1886 did not), and it was a party strengthened by its most powerful ideological elements. The Liberal Unionists, on the other hand, while talented and eminent, were a political faction whose basis in policy was very narrowly constructed. They had more in common with Liberals than they had with their new Conservative allies. Goschen was the first to go into a Tory Cabinet, and he was the only one of the original Liberal Unionists to declare himself, formally, as a member of the Conservative party. The remainder held themselves aloof, co-operating with the Conservatives to retain the Act of Union with Ireland, and only slowly assimilated themselves into the Unionist party.[62]

The Basis of Liberal Voting Behaviour in 1886

Therefore, in 1886 the Liberals were divided in two directions. One division separated radicals from moderates; the other separated Gladstonians from Liberal Unionists. These dimensions of voting

[62] Dr Gregory Phillips has examined the votes of Liberal Unionists in the House of Lords, and finds that they acted rather as a swing group, independent of the Tory leadership, and continued to support Liberal policies, especially those associated with land reform, until the Liberal leadership adopted the more radical positions of the Newcastle Programme in 1891. See Phillips, 'The Whig Lords and Liberals, 1886–1893', *Historical Journal*, 24 (1981), p. 167.

behaviour were unrelated to each other, and only the latter produced the great separation in the Liberal party. It remains to consider the structural conditions in parliamentary life, those having consequences for political assimilation, on these cleavages. It is commonplace in legislative studies that membership in a parliamentary institution forges bonds of common interest and *esprit de corps*. A study of the United States Senate recognized the importance in its folk-ways of modesty, hard work, courtesy, personal reciprocity, and institutional loyalty as guides to legislative success and as buttresses for continuity.[63] Three political characteristics may serve as indicators of assimilation. The first of these is previous parliamentary experience, an essential precondition to any kind of assimilation because, as one scholar observed, it is the aperture which establishes political opportunities and shapes the perceptions of the politically ambitious.[64] The second is the governmental experience of Liberals, whether or not they held offices at the Cabinet or sub-Cabinet level, an indicator of their experience in policy formation and government responsibility. The third is membership in London's clubs, which was jealously and carefully guarded. It indicates the degree to which Liberals penetrated the more informal world of Westminster ruling circles.[65]

The test comparing these characteristics with the radical–moderate cleavage in the Liberal party was largely positive. That is, Liberals with these characteristics tended to be moderates; those without them tended to be radicals. However, the test comparing these characteristics with the Gladstonian–Liberal Unionist cleavage was largely negative. That is, there is no tendency in the evidence to indicate that Liberals with previous parliamentary experience, with experience in Liberal administrations, or with club memberships were likely to be either Gladstonians or Liberal Unionists. Whether Liberals possessed these characteristics or not had nothing to do with voting on the Home Rule Bill, the dimension on which the party was broken. This is another way of saying that the issues which involved the party in radical revolts had been assimilated into the

---

[63] Donald R. Matthews, 'The Folkways of the United States Senate: Conformity to Group Norms and Legislative Effectiveness', *American Political Science Review*, 53.4 (Dec. 1959), pp. 1064–73.

[64] Mogen N. Pedersen, 'The Personal Circulation of a Legislature: The Danish Folketing, 1849–1968', *The History of Legislative Behavior*, ed. William O. Aydelotte (Princeton: 1977), p. 65.

[65] The principal Liberal clubs, of course, were the Reform Club, Brooks's Club, and the Devonshire Club, but since I am describing a general culture here, and since Members frequently belonged to other clubs, I include all club memberships in these tallies.

Liberal agenda and into the repertoire of political behaviour in the Liberal party, whereas Home Rule had not.

The weight of previous parliamentary experience can be shown first. Of the 339 members of the parliamentary Liberal party, 163 (48 per cent) sat for the first time following the general election of 1885. As Table 6.6 shows, nearly two-thirds of these fit dimensional positions to the left of the median; they were radicals. More than two-thirds of the Liberals with previous parliamentary experience held dimensional positions at the centre or on the right; they were moderates. New initiatives came from new Members, and it is in the recruitment and replacement of Members that it is possible to account for radical policies, and for the support of those policies, in the Liberal party. The resistance to those initiatives came from the old parliamentary hands, a phrase by which Gladstone styled himelf during the debates on foreign policy in 1886. To put this another way, previous parliamentary experience forged commitments beyond particular policies and toward larger partisan goals. Whether by encouraging greater caution, or wisdom, or respect for the party's leadership, previous experience in the House of Commons limited support for advanced policies in 1886. Those without this experience, those without regard for their careers, in Liberal Governments or in the House of Commons, could be crocheteers riding off on their legislative hobbies.

The importance of political experience, and the lack of it, can be pushed further by examining the matter of the relationship between Government office-holding and ideological position. Ninety-eight per cent of those Liberals who in 1886 had held Cabinet or sub-Cabinet

TABLE 6.6 *Political Assimilation in the Liberal Party and Voting on the Major Parliamentary Voting Dimension*

Scale positions	7–5 (%)	4* (%)	3–1 (%)	No.
Previous parliamentary experience	31	40	29	131
No previous parliamentary experience	62	25	13	137
Held government offices	2	59	39	41
Had not held government offices	55	27	18	227
Members of clubs	39	36	25	197
Not members of clubs	69	23	8	71
Age in 1886:				
Under 40	38	29	33	52
41–60	47	35	18	146
61 +	55	29	16	55

*Median dimensional position.

offices were moderates in the sense that they occupied dimensional positions at the centre of the party or to its right. A mere 2 per cent of those Liberals who had fought their way to the top supported advanced policies, and, in so doing, were radicals. This point, it is important to observe, is not a manifestation of party leaders choosing their colleagues from among those members of the Liberal party known to have moderate views. The process, as some fragmentary evidence from the manuscript sources shows, was the reverse. Since the days of Palmerston the front bench had been open to radicals, and the list of men holding advanced views and taking their places amongst the party's leadership is an extensive one. It is another of those ironies of British political history that radicals enjoyed an advantage, so far as the opportunities for their entrance to the front bench was concerned, during those years in which the Whigs dominated the party. During this period of Government service the ideological qualities of radical MPs changed. From extremists, with little regard for the detailed consequences of their policies, they became politicians.[66] In short, advanced Liberals assumed positions of leadership, but not because they were moderate. They became moderate in coming to hold positions of power and influence.

This is a point of some importance, and it is therefore necessary to develop it. In general, the assumption of office required the defence of Government policy and the rejection of radical initiatives, but this was not an invariable rule. Gladstone permitted absences in the case of certain consciences made tender. On a division dealing with Scottish disestablishment, he allowed G. O. Trevelyan, his Scottish Secretary, to follow his own inclinations.[67] Disestablishment enthusiasm was rife in Scotland, and Trevelyan sat for Hawick, a Scottish constituency, which would show considerable Unionist sentiment in the very near future.[68] Moreover, in March of 1886 Trevelyan was preparing to bolt from the Cabinet with Chamberlain over Irish Home Rule. Gladstone may have felt the need for mollifying kid gloves for a Cabinet minister in a delicate political situation. There is evidence of a more comprehensive sort in a Cabinet memorandum in the Gladstone Papers which shows the number of occasions on which members of the Administration participated on the Government side. The whips, Arnold Morley, Edward Marjoribanks, and George Leveson-Gower, as one might expect, participated in the greatest

---

[66] Vincent, *The Formation of the Liberal Party*, pp. 17–18.
[67] Gladstone to Trevelyan, 12 Mar. 1886, BL Add. MS 44548, f. 60.
[68] Pelling, *The Social Geography of British Elections*, p. 392.

number of these. However, seven members of the Ministry—and these included Gladstone, Sir William Harcourt, and Henry Campbell-Bannerman—participated in half, or less. In contrast, Liberals belonging to the Ministry, but well-known for their advanced views, voted in a very large number of these: Henry Broadhurst, seventy-six; James Bryce, fifty-five; Henry Harley Fowler, fifty-four.[69]

The formative power of political office can be illustrated in the careers of Bryce and Fowler, both of whom had considerable reputations as radicals,[70] and both of whom took office in Gladstone's third Ministry, the former as Under-Secretary of State for Foreign Affairs and the latter as a Secretary to the Treasury, Sir George Campbell criticized Bryce in a debate on Egyptian policy for having failed his radical principles. 'It is sad to see how a Radical, when he accepts office, gets into the official groove', Campbell said. 'Formerly', he went on, 'there was no man who was more robust in his sympathy with people struggling to be free.'[71]

Some Liberals recognized the danger office offered to principle, and refused Gladstone's request to serve in his Government. Alfred Illingworth, the Member for Bradford West, had been offered a place at the India Office. He declined, because, as he recognized, to assume office would require a defence of the Government's military policy in India, and for this he was unprepared. Illingworth believed he could best fulfil his parliamentary functions as a private Member.[72] The effect of office-holding on political behaviour is shown by an anecdote told by Sir Algernon West. On 2 February 1886, following Mary Gladstone's wedding, Gladstone, who was then forming his Government, invited a group to a luncheon. There, Gladstone asked West about his views concerning who should be the new Chancellor of the Exchequer. West proposed Joseph Chamberlain. Gladstone thought this would horrify the City in the light of Chamberlain's speeches in the recent election calling for the ransoming of property. 'A few weeks of official experience', West responded, 'would soften the crudeness of his views.'[73] Administration, participation in the executive, the wielding of power, and the shaping of policy are

[69] Cabinet Minutes, n.d. but June 1886, BL Add. MS 44647, f. 130.

[70] That their early radical reputations were reflected in their previous voting behaviour is shown by the historian of the radical section of the Liberal party. See Heyck, *The Dimensions of British Radicalism*, pp. 242–3, 249.

[71] Hansard, 303: 1892.

[72] Illingworth to Gladstone, 10 Apr. 1886, BL Add. MS 44496, ff. 210–11.

[73] Sir Algernon West, *Recollections, 1832–1886*, 2nd edn. (London: 1899), vol. 2, p. 261.

aspects of a socializing process in which the good opinion of colleagues welds bonds of solidarity. Granville spoke of the Cabinet as 'a great bond between him and those with whom he has served'. Government requires loyalty to policy jointly formed, but such loyalty is forged by more than merely the premier's coercive authority to cast dissenters into the darkness. It rests upon personal and informal bonds as well.[74]

Previous parliamentary experience and the holding of Government offices, therefore, were institutional aspects of political life in the 1880s which modified the behaviour of Members. Membership in London's political clubs was a third. In the period from 1867 to 1885 the numbers both of clubs and of club members increased.[75] It was an expression of political polarization and exclusiveness which was important to political leaders and followers. In 1881 there were 1,223 candidates on the waiting list for the Carlton Club, and under the rules then current, which called for the election of ten members a year, it would not be until 1910 before these candidates could be admitted. Consequently, Rowland Winn proposed reforms to increase the numbers which could be advanced for membership. 'The club was originally established more for political than social objects', he wrote, and 'it was believed that great jeopardy is being done to the party by the length of time now required to get a candidate into the club.'[76] When W. S. Blunt decided to contest the general election of 1886 as a Home Rule Liberal he resigned from the Carlton, but he was not yet ready to join the Reform Club. 'I do not intend to join any other club at least till I see my way clearer. My headquarters are now the Travellers.'[77]

Clubs combined society and politics. It is difficult to get at the ways in which this was achieved, but Sir Almeric Fitzroy described the process at work in his history of the Travellers' Club. 'The unity of club life resides in the assimilation of contrasts, the insensible approach by a graduated series of mutual impressions to a common standard of appreciation.'[78] This was not accomplished easily, and clubs could not be free of rivalry and conflict. Joseph Chamberlain resigned from the Reform Club in 1883 after his brothers had been

[74] Vincent, *The Formation of the Liberal Party*, p. 19. See *The Journals and Letters of Reginald Viscount Esher*, ed. Maurice V. Brett (London: 1934), vol. 1, p. 60.
[75] Hanham, *Elections and Party Management*, pp. 100–1.
[76] Rowland Winn's memorandum to Salisbury, 14 Mar. 1881, Third Marquess of Salisbury MSS Class E.
[77] Blunt Diary, 12 June 1886, Blunt MS 335-1975, f. 100.
[78] Sir Almeric Fitzroy, *The History of the Travellers' Club* (London: 1927), p. 150.

rejected.[79] During the Home Rule crisis Sir William Harcourt uttered some objectionable comments against the Liberal Unionists one night at Brooks's Club. When his son, Lewis, came up for election to the club he was promptly blackballed. Shortly afterwards, Lord Wolmer, himself a Liberal Unionist in this House of Commons, was put forward for election to Brooks's, and Gladstonian members directly administered the blackball to him.[80] 'The circle of carnage', as the historian of this incident puts it, widened until Lord Granville restored peace there.[81] However, even Herbert Gladstone could not be certain that his Home Rule views would not earn him the blackball at Brooks's, and he had Edward Hamilton withdraw his nomination before it could be brought to a vote.[82]

Club members believed that conciliation and accommodation, though not accomplished easily, were accomplished in clubs. A nineteenth-century historian of the Reform Club described the process:

The party has experienced of late years more than one period of internal strife, yet the Reform Club has not reproduced these dissensions—it has continued to shelter 'Adullamites' and 'Radicals,' 'Liberal Unionists' and 'Gladstonians'. Hence the members of the various sections into which a great party is from time to time necessarily divided, meeting constantly on common ground, have learned to know and to understand each other better than they would have if no such place of *reunion* had existed. It would be difficult to exaggerate the importance of the Club as a place where all shades and grades of Liberalism are brought together in friendly intercourse. . . . [The Club is] a stronghold of unity and a healer of division.[83]

Another example of political ecumenism in nineteenth-century club life can be found in Lord Blythe's recollections of the founding dinner of the Devonshire Club. On that occasion Gladstone sat between Lord Cork and Sir Joseph Pease, and the three of them became the subjects of Sir Wilfred Lawson's doggerel:

---

[79] For letters relating to the blackballing of the Chamberlain brothers, see Chamberlain Papers JC6/5/1/1-24.

[80] Henry S. Eeles and the Earl Spencer, *Brooks's, 1764-1964* (London: 1964), p. 124. The authors made use of Lord Crewe's recollections in relating this incident.

[81] Fitzmaurice, *The Life of Lord Granville, George Leveson Gower, Second Earl Granville, K.G., 1815-1891*, vol. 2, pp. 494-5.

[82] Herbert Gladstone to Edward Hamilton, 5 Jan. 1886, BL Add. MS 48611, ff. 181ᵛ-180.

[83] Louis Fagan, *The Reform Club: Its Founders and Architect* (London: 1887), p. 137.

This dinner must Mr. Gladstone well please,
In eating and drinking and talk;
On his left I see him devouring his *Peas*
On his right he is drawing out *Cork*.[84]

Table 6.6 shows the effect of club membership for the ideological positions of Liberals on the major parliamentary voting dimension.

As with the other characteristics of political assimilation in the Liberal party, club membership is negatively associated with radical policies and those who supported them. Sixty-nine per cent of the Liberals who can be classified on the major parliamentary voting dimension and who were not members of clubs are found in the leftwardmost ideological positions; 61 per cent of the Liberals with club memberships can be assigned to positions either at the centre or on the right. Club membership, like previous parliamentary experience and government office-holding, was a socializing mechanism which provided access to power and influence. Having less access to these mechanisms, radicals were left with the floor of the House of Commons and its division lobbies as arenas for the expression of their views and the development of their policies. The general pattern which Table 6.6 expresses remains if one holds previous parliamentary experience constant for club membership. That is, it might be supposed that Liberals who had held seats at Westminster previously were more likely to have club memberships than newcomers to parliament. This is true. Of the Liberals holding club memberships, 123 were old hands and eighty-four were new Members. Nevertheless the proportion of Liberals with no club memberships in the radical portion of the voting dimension was significantly higher, by 17 per cent, than the proportion of Liberals belonging to clubs, irrespective of their previous parliamentary experience. The positions Liberals took on the issues forming the principal Liberal agenda in 1886, those on which radical revolts occurred and which establish the general ideological dimension described in Table 6.1, in short, can be predicted by whether or not they possessed the characteristics of political assimilation.

The voting dimension consisting of those issues which separated the Liberal Unionists from the Gladstonians, however, is quite another matter. On this dimension the characteristics of political assimilation do not predict Liberal voting. This finding stands in sharp contrast to the existing scholarly orthodoxy on the split in the Liberal party over Irish Home Rule, according to which the Liberal

---

[84] Lord Blyth's recollections are quoted in H. T. Waddy's *The Devonshire Club — and 'Crockford's'* (London: 1919), pp. 27, 32.

TABLE   6.7 *Political Assimilation in the Liberal Party and the Great Separation over Home Rule*

	Gladstonians (%)	Liberal Unionists (%)	Others (%)	No.
Previous parliamentary experience	59	34	6	177
No previous parliamentary experience	76	20	4	162
Held government office	67	22	12	51
Had not held government office	67	29	4	288
Members of clubs	64	30	6	253
Not members of clubs	76	21	3	86
Age in 1886:				
Under 40	75	25	0	64
41–60	65	30	5	187
61 +	67	24	9	82

Unionists were 'a vast army of militant amateur[s]' who 'needed the crisis more than the crisis needed them'. Their behaviour belonged 'to the pathology of political virginity'.[85] In so far as language such as this has any precise meaning at all, Liberals with the least administrative service, with the least parliamentary experience, and who did not belong to the clubs of St James should have had the greatest propensity to bolt from the party and become Liberal Unionists in their rejection of Gladstone's Irish Home Rule policies.

When the figures for these characteristics for the Gladstonian and Liberal Unionist factions are consulted, as in Table 6.7, no such pattern emerges. A clear majority of Liberals with experience in Liberal Governments, with previous parliamentary service, and with club memberships were Gladstonians. Similar proportions of Liberals without these characteristics were also Gladstonians. Nothing here predicts the great separation in the Liberal party. Though the differences are slight, sometimes trivial from a statistical point of view, there are some modest straws in the wind in the more detailed figures of this comparison. A larger proportion (33 per cent) of Liberals with Cabinet experience as opposed to those with sub-Cabinet experience only (17 per cent) were Liberal Unionists. Cabinet members, therefore, were slightly more independent of the party position on Home Rule than their junior colleagues, perhaps because they were less dependent on the party leadership for political advancement. They had advanced as far as they could, and therefore enjoyed the luxury of their political principles. Similarly, a greater proportion

---

[85] Cooke and Vincent, *The Governing Passion*, p. 16.

of Liberals with previous parliamentary experience (34 per cent), as opposed to those sitting for the first time in 1886 (20 per cent), were Liberal Unionists. This might be taken to mean that the disruption in the party can be traced back to policy disagreements in earlier Parliaments. This does not go very far, however. The only clearly Unionist group of Liberals, when judged by their previous parliamentary experience, was the small number who entered the House of Commons for the first time in by-elections during Gladstone's first Administration (1868–74). It is more likely that these differences reflect the greater obligation and vulnerability new Members, without an established position in their party, felt toward their leaders and their leaders' policy. The matter of club membership yields the same conclusions. Majorities of both club members and non-club members supported the Home Rule policies of the Liberal Government. A slightly larger percentage of club members (30 per cent), as opposed to Liberals who had not such memberships (21 per cent) were Liberal Unionists, but the only political club whose proportion of Unionist members tended to be elevated was Brooks's. (The only club a majority of whose members in the parliamentary Liberal party opposed Home Rule was the Travellers' Club.)

Indicators of political innocence in the Liberal party, therefore, in so far as they predict anything, predict support for, not opposition to, the Home Rule policies of the Liberal Government. And this finds support in the figures on age which are displayed at the bottom of Table 6.7. It is a point which contrasts with the observations of some contemporaries who saw Liberal Unionism as something for the young. Alfred Pease believed Arthur Elliot, G. O. Trevelyan, and Albert Grey were engaged in an effort to attract the young away from Home Rule. Albert Grey, Pease wrote, 'was one of the most irresistible and charming of men, with tact, temper, humour; he had a most happy disposition, and his ceaseless efforts told on the young, for he was always young himself.'[86] Yet strong majorities of Liberals of all ages supported Home Rule, and the youngest members had, in fact, a greater tendency to be Gladstonians than their elder colleagues. Perhaps for similar reasons, age had the same relationship to voting on items fitting the main Liberal agenda in 1886 as it did to the vote on Home Rule. Older members (see Table 6.6), were more radical—55 per cent of those who were sixty-one years of age or older held dimensional positions indicating that they tended to support radical revolts—while 62 per cent of the members who were forty-one years of age or younger held dimensional

[86] Pease, *Elections and Recollections*, p. 108.

positions at the centre or to the right, indicating that they opposed radical revolts and supported the Government position. The young tended toward loyalty on the Home Rule question and toward moderation on the major Liberal voting dimension, because their future lay with Gladstone and the Liberal party.

Previous parliamentary experience, service in Liberal Governments, and memberships in clubs predict support for the Liberal Government, and, similarly, fail to predict the split in the Liberal party over Home Rule. The traditional disagreements in the Liberal party in 1886 did not destroy it. Assimilating features of parliamentary life reinforced and supported partisan loyalty. With little institutional room in which to manoeuvre, consequently, the Liberal Unionists faced the political test with growing frustration and anxiety. This allowed greater scope for personal animosities in the crisis, and the drama of personal rivalries was played out on the edge of those institutional conditions which sustained partisanship.

It became a question of time. The Liberal Unionists complained that Gladstone had pressed the Home Rule issue on the party too quickly. Home Rule 'came before the House and the constituencies as a matter of surprise', W. S. Allen remarked. 'It had not been raised at the last election.'[87] Indeed, some Liberal Unionists believed that the point of the general election of 1885 had been to produce a Liberal majority in the House of Commons competent to resist Irish nationalism. Indeed, even Gladstonian loyalists pleaded for time. Samuel Whitbread opposed haste, and Sir Joseph Pease called for additional Cabinet deliberations to modify its policy.[88] Sir Thomas Brassey explained the importance of this:

From circumstances, on which I need not dwell, the usual process of tilling the land, and sowing before reaping the harvest, have in this case been reduced to the most simple expression. The speeches delivered at the election gave no indication of the great plan which has been proposed for Ireland. It would be unreasonable to claim from the average member of parliament, and still less from the average elector an instant apprehension of your novel, and elaborate plan. Patience and reiteration are necessary in exposition. With this essential preliminary, and with concessions to the popular opinion of the hour, which is not ripe for everything that might ultimately be proposed, you have an excellent prospect for the next session.[89]

---

[87] This is from W. S. Allen's speech against the Home Rule Bill, Hansard, 304, 1222.

[88] Whitbread to Gladstone, 11 May 1886, Pease to Gladstone, 14 and 20 May 1886, BL Add. MS 44497, ff. 199–200, 223–4, 246–8.

[89] Brassey to Gladstone, 24 May 1886, BL Add. MS 44497, ff. 269–70.

If members of the Liberal party had been surprised, and if time was necessary to educate and reconcile them, one solution to the problem of party management would be to grant time so that the Home Rule issue could be assimilated into the party's political agenda.

To this end, back-benchers threw up all species of advice and warning. Some Members hoped Gladstone would yield critical compromises in his second reading speech, and Herbert Gardner thought that the hedge-sitters, and even those opposed to Home Rule, would vote for its second reading. These hopes were doomed. After Gladstone's speech, sentiment shifted sharply against the Government and its Bill. 'Those who had been doubtful declared to me that they would vote agst. the Bill and those who had been certain to vote said they were doubtful.'[90] Sir Joseph Pease predicted the failure of the second reading unless 'some yet unknown, and difficult to conceive [of] alterations are made in the Irish measures'.[91] Pease urged Gladstone to withdraw the Bill and to substitute some resolution 'confirming general principles' of it. Brassey, Edward Heneage, and Sir Donald Currie also advised such an approach.[92] Alfred Illingworth, among others, called for a party meeting at which Gladstone could clarify his policy and provide concessions.[93] However, at his Foreign Office meeting on 26 May he failed to satisfy his critics, and W. S. Caine called the Prime Minister's performance a 'bewildering deliverance'. He 'surrenders the fort & armaments', Caine said derisively, 'but asks for a cotton pocket handkerchief & some old muskets, that he might please the women and children as he marches out.'[94] Time, as it always does, ran out. When it did Gladstone had failed to integrate his Home Rule policy into the Liberal agenda, and the Government fell.

Even when the Liberal Government fell, however, Gladstone held both wings of his party. Even with unpleasantness in society and in the clubs, institutional forces worked in support of party loyalty and for the limitation of rebellion. W. S. Caine was quite off the mark when he estimated the proportion of radicals amongst the rebels

[90] Herbert Gardner to Edward Hamilton, n.d. but May 1886, shortly after Gladstone's speech on the second reading of the Home Rule Bill, BL Add. MS 48625, ff. 11–12ᵛ.

[91] Pease to Gladstone, 14 May 1886, BL Add. MS 44497, ff. 223–4.

[92] Pease to Gladstone, 14 and 20 May 1886, Heneage to Gladstone, 18 May 1886, Brassey to Gladstone, 24 May 1886, Currie to Gladstone, 24 May 1886, BL Add. MS 44497, ff. 223–4, 246–8, 243–4, 267–73, 274–5.

[93] Illingworth to Gladstone, 12 May 1886, BL Add. MS 44497, ff. 201–2.

[94] Caine to Chamberlain, 27 May 1886, Chamberlain Papers JC5/10/2.

at 50 per cent.[95] The Liberal Unionists, as Alfred Pease pointed out, were a heterogeneous lot. 'Some were merely Liberals in name, others were Whigs; some were Liberals apart from the Irish Question, others were Radicals, others teetotal fanatics, and a small body was whatever Chamberlain was.'[96] Carnarvon and Gladstone judged the situation more shrewdly than did Caine. The Liberal Unionists, Carnarvon observed, were a coalition of moderates and 'a certain number of Radicals wh. is remarkable. It is I think anti-Irish—and perhaps also it is anti-Gladstone for there has been a fire smouldering for a long time against him which till now had not dared to break out.'[97] Gladstone described the Liberal Unionist defection as a rebellion of the moderates 'with a strange and unnatural addition of Mr. Chamberlain and the small parliamentary force at his command. (Mr. Bright's position is wholly different; he recommends nothing, and until his speech yesterday had abused nobody.)'[98] As Table 6.8 makes clear, the Liberal Unionist rebellion cost Gladstone neither his left nor his right wing. The clear majority of Liberal Unionists were moderates in the sense that 88 per cent of them were located at the centre or to the right of centre on the major parliamentary voting dimension in 1886. Yet the Gladstonian main force was divided between right and left. Fifty-eight per cent of those who remained loyal to Gladstone were radicals, and 42 per cent were moderates. When the positions of Liberal Unionists and Gladstonians are consulted on other voting dimensions, the proportions are different but the pattern remains the same. On land policy a larger proportion of Liberal Unionists held radical positions (43 per cent), but it is a proportion still exceeded by Gladstonians (67 per cent). The same can be said for the voting of the Liberal factions on foreign policy. In sum, the Liberal party which remained after the Liberal Unionist rebellion was more radical, but Home Rule had not shorn from it moderate elements. The Liberal party emerged from the Home Rule crisis with a political compositon which was similar to that with which it had entered the crisis. It remained, in Alfred Pease's description of the traditional Liberal party, 'an *omnium gatherum* of the fast and slow, of theorists and practical men, of aristocrats, plutocrats, and democrats, but it was a mixture of talents. It managed to keep step fairly well under trusted leaders and its banner of Peace, Retrenchment, and Reform.'[99]

[95] Ibid., 31 May 1886, Chamberlain Papers JC5/10/3.

[96] Pease, *Elections and Recollections*, p. 273.

[97] Carnarvon Diary, 17 Apr. 1886, BL Add. MS 60926, f. 57.

[98] Gladstone to the Queen, 2 July 1886, in Guedalla, *The Queen and Mr. Gladstone*, vol. 2, p. 416.

[99] Pease, *Elections and Recollections*, p. 41.

TABLE 6.8 *The Classification of Liberals on Various Voting Scales in 1886*

The major parliamentary voting dimension:

Scale positions	7–5 (%)		4* (%)		3–1 (%)		No.	
Unionists	11		35		53		62	
Gladstonians	58		31		11		198	
Other Liberals	50		38		12		8	
	No.	%	No.	%	No.	%	No.	%[†]
TOTALS	126	47	86	32	56	21	268	79

The land policy dimension:

Scale positions	5–3 (%)		2* (%)		1 (%)		No.	
Unionists	43		55		1		74	
Gladstonians	67		33		0		188	
Other Liberals	100		0		0		8	
	No.	%	No.	%	No.	%	No.	%[†]
TOTALS	166	47	103	38	1	0.4	270	80

The foreign policy dimension:

Unionists	8		88		6		49	
Gladstonians	34		43		23		122	
Other Liberals	20		80		0		5	
	No.	%	No.	%	No.	%	No.	%[†]
TOTALS	46	26	99	56	31	18	176	25

*Median dimensional position.
[†]of all Liberals.

Conclusion

Some might say that the Home Rule issue, as a result of the Liberal Unionists' *Anfechtungen*, revolutionized the party system in 1886. The evidence, however, points the other way. A greater case may be made for the conclusion that the party system revolutionized the Home Rule issue by domesticating it, by making it a creature of parliamentary politics, and by so containing it for thirty years. The Home Rule question stood at the periphery of Liberal party politics, since it was not a part of the major Liberal agenda. It was, since it fitted the major parliamentary voting dimension described in Chapter 2, central to party politics, and it was in the arena of party politics, rather than Liberal party politics, that its implications would be worked out. The great separation in the Liberal party was not grounded in social distinctions or constituency differences in the party (see Chapters 4 and 5), and the political distinctions discussed in the present chapter, similarly, had little bearing on this cleavage. The Home Rule question split the Liberal party, but did not destroy it.

The Liberal party which emerged from the Home Rule crisis was a diminished mirror of its former self. Any defection is damaging to a party, and the loss of a third of its parliamentary membership in 1886 could not be underestimated or shrugged off. But this was a numerical loss alone, and the strength of the party rested on additional qualities. It had always 'aspired to be classless but it was riddled with class; it hoped for interdenominationalism but it divided between Erastianism, sectarianism, and secularism'.[1] These were sources of strength which were not lost when oppugnant forces came into play in 1886. The liberalism over which Gladstone presided sought to stabilize the political system by drawing into its midst the policy goals of Catholics, Jews, Nonconformists, and, in 1886, the Irish, even when these elements seemed provocative and dangerous. These were Whiggish objectives, but presented with radical methods.[2] While the party was slightly more radical, Gladstone's party was not shorn of either political wing, nor did it lose major sections of social groups represented in the parliamentary party. Beyond this the Liberal party continued to represent constituencies of all types and sizes. This was a party put into the wilderness, but a party not incapacitated from returning, and from governing. Riotous disunity exhibited by the Liberals in 1886 is, superficially, a picture of weakness. The reality was damaged strength, but strength none the less.

The Liberal Unionist schism, so far as schisms go, was imperfect. Constructed on a narrow policy base, it was limited to the questions of Home Rule and disestablishment. Not very much separated the rebels from the main body of the Liberal party. Certainly their votes on issues fitting the major Liberal policy agenda were not very different from the votes of their former colleagues. Consequently, they were, in Harcourt's telling jibe, 'like a knot tied in a dilapidated mule's tail to keep the harness on; this was their use—they kept the Conservatives in power' from 1886 to 1892.[3] This made them restive; and when the separation came, therefore, the Liberal Unionists felt it keenly.

---

[1] Matthew, introduction to *The Gladstone Diaries*, vol. 7, p. xci.

[2] Brian Harrison, *Peaceable Kingdom: Stability and Change in Modern Britain* (Oxford: 1892), p. 326.

[3] Pease, *Elections and Recollections*, pp. 273–4.

Some returned to the Liberal party early, and one almost immediately. Christopher Rice Mansel Talbot, the father of the House, had voted against the Home Rule Bill, but during the weeks following found himself persuaded by Gladstone's explanations and modifications. In the run-up to the election of 1886 he satisfied the Glamorganshire Liberal Association on this point, and they duly adopted him as the official Liberal candidate. Other Liberal Unionists departed in 1886, only to return in time's fullness. G. O. Trevelyan came back in 1887. T. R. Buchanan came back in 1888. W. S. Caine, Chamberlain's whip in 1886, came back in 1890. In 1892 when Caine stood for Parliament as the Liberal candidate for the Eastern division of Bradford, Chamberlain wrote to explain how he was 'grieved and wounded' by Caine's return to the Liberal party. To which Caine responded, 'nine-tenths of what I want in politics I must get from the recognized Liberal party.' Caine was content, as he believed other Liberal Unionists were, with the modifications Gladstone had made in his Irish policy since 1886. '[T]he bondage of the Tory Alliance has become unbearable & their attack on the whole Temperance movement, which I could never subordinate to anything, gave me emancipation.'[4]

Sir Thomas Grove, Bt., William Jacks, Albert Kitching, Sir Henry Hussey Vivian, Bt., Sir Edwin Watkin, and Arthur Winterbotham returned to the Liberal party when they stood in the general election of 1892. A. R. D. Elliot remained a Liberal Unionist through every election between 1886 and 1900, but he broke from the Durham Constitutional Association (the official Unionist association in his constituency) in 1905 when they took exception to his views on free trade. While he did not rejoin the Liberal party, Elliot stood as a Free Trade candidate in the general elections of 1906, in opposition to a Liberal Unionist, and in this he had the support of the local Liberal association. Leonard Courtney began a process which would lead to his return to the Liberal party in 1895 when he stood as both a Liberal Unionist and an Independent Liberal. He did not contest the election of 1900, but in 1906 Courtney stood for the Western division of Edinburgh as a Liberal. Archibald Corbett stood as both a Liberal Unionist and an Independent in 1906, and as both an Independent Liberal and a Liberal in January of 1910. He completed his return to the party with which he had begun his career by contesting the Tradeston division of Glasgow, the seat he had held uninterruptedly since 1885, as a Liberal in December of 1910. After

---

[4] Chamberlain to Caine, 26 Mar. 1892, Caine to Chamberlain, 27 Mar. 1892, Chamberlain Papers JC5/10/10–11.

the general election of December 1910 only thirty-six Liberal Unionists sat in the House of Commons, and only four of these (Finlay, Mildmay, Meysey-Thompson, and Joseph Chamberlain) belonged to the original corps who bolted in 1886. Defeat, death, resignation, elevation to the House of Lords, succession to their fathers' titles, and reconversion to the Liberal party reduced and depleted Liberal Unionism's ranks. Only one of the original Liberal Unionists (Goschen) became a Conservative; thirteen (14 per cent) crossed back.

If the Liberal Unionist schism was imperfect on the back benches, where policy considerations dominated behaviour, it was also imperfect amongst the Liberal Unionist leaders, for whom tactics and manoeuvre, as well as policy, were important. When Lewis Harcourt met Hartington at Ascot the day after the division on Home Rule, he told him that, because the Liberal Unionists had been successful in contributing to the fall of Gladstone's Government, he could not expect success on the turf. Hartington responded, 'I would sooner win today than last night.'[5] Even Chamberlain, who would never belong fully to the Unionist party, just as he had never belonged fully to the Liberal party,[6] entered the wilderness with trepidation. He did not want to be the first to attack fellow Liberals in the general election of 1886, but he was prepared to fight them if put upon. If attacked, the Liberal Unionists 'must take off the gloves, but if they let us alone we must stand aside'.[7] With his eye always on the leadership of the party, Chamberlain awaited Gladstone's retirement, and this led him to avoid stressing differences between himself and the Liberal party. Consequently, he also avoided closer ties with his new Tory allies. 'All action intensifies differences which it is our object to remove and I believe we must "lie low" till the inevitable disappearance of G.O.M. from the scene.'[8] Voting alliances between the Liberal Unionists and the Conservatives during the lifetime of the House of Commons in 1886, as noted above, were extremely limited things; and the Liberal Unionist–Tory electoral pact during

---

[5] Harcourt Journal, 8 June 1886, Harcourt dep. 378, f. 165.

[6] As St Loe Strachey put it: 'the truth is that so English an Englishman from many points of view, [Chamberlain] is in other ways utterly unEnglish. Almost every Englishman has a touch of the essential Whig in him and a liking for moderation and the via media. Joe has none. Once a Jacobin always a Jacobin.' Strachey to Lord Rosebery, 26 Apr. 1910 (carbon copy), House of Lords Records Office, St Loe Strachey Papers 5/12/7/21. Quoted in Harrison, *Peaceable Kingdom*, p. 319.

[7] Chamberlain to Arthur Chamberlain, 9 June 1886, Chamberlain Papers JC5/11/14.

[8] Chamberlain to Jesse Collings, 29 July 1886, Chamberlain Papers JC5/16/117.

the general election of 1886, as noted below, suffered its own difficulties. Consequently, as Parliament prepared to reassemble after the election of 1886, the Liberal Unionist leaders were in a quandary about the seats they would take in the House. To Gladstone's amazement they decided to sit in their customary seats, on the Opposition front benches.[9]

[9] 'The place where we sit is not a matter of mere convenience or form. If we sit with the Tories we shall be of them.' Sir Henry James to Chamberlain, 22 July 1886. See also Chamberlain to Hartington, 28 July 1886, Chamberlain Papers JC5/46/6 and JC5/22/10. James Agg-Gardner described this episode in *Some Parliamentary Recollections* (London: 1927), p. 131. The Liberal Unionist peers faced the same problem in the Lords, and chose to settle it in the same way. Selborne alone wished to sit on the Government side. Derby Diary, 9 Aug. 1886, *The Later Derby Diaries*, p. 73.

7

The General Election of 1886 and the Consolidation of the Home Rule Settlement

> If the dissolution takes place the Tories will come in. The Unionist Liberals are almost every where sufficient to turn the scale. Take Stroud as an illustration. I heard from the *Gladstonian* side that the opposition to Brand is hopeless. There are 500 Unionist Liberals and the Tories in this case will not oppose.
>
> Chamberlain to Harcourt, 2 May 1886[1]

> I do not see much prospect of the next Prlt lasting any longer than this one as I don't think either party is likely to have a large majority.
>
> Harcourt Journal, 28 May 1886[2]

> [Churchill] prophecies of Tory majority, — and indeed a Tory rule for 20 years! So likely! My own belief is that the election will change the situation very little. I expect the Tories will come back stronger; that is, in lieu of 250 they will number 280 or 290; and that the Hartingtonians will muster about 40 or 50. These two parties combined will just about equal the Gladstonians & Parnellites. So we would be no nearer out of the fix.
>
> Hamilton Diary, 22 June 1886[3]

> Schnadhorst who was here is in good spirits about the election but I confess I do not see how we can win with our party divided as it is and not at all well off for candidates.
>
> Harcourt Journal, 26 June 1886[4]

> As far as I can learn the Party seems rather anxious & out of heart in going into the Election. There is more *popular* support of Gladstone than was expected. It may easily happen — as I first expected — that parties will come out as they went in — a very unfortunate result.
>
> Carnarvon Diary, 30 June 1886[5]

Introduction

The general election of 1886 had been long anticipated, and for a time all sides held uncertain, though high, hopes. In the midst of the Home Rule crisis Sir Richard Temple believed there would be time during the Easter recess for the electors to influence wavering

---

[1] Chamberlain to Harcourt, 2 May 1886, Chamberlain Papers JC5/38/159.
[2] Harcourt Journal, 28 May 1886, Harcourt dep. 378, f. 148.
[3] Edward Hamilton Diary, 22 June 1886, BL Add. MS 48644, f. 42.
[4] Harcourt Journal, 26 June 1886, Harcourt dep. 378, f. 189.
[5] Carnarvon Diary, 30 June 1886, BL Add. MS 60926, f. 94.

Liberals, and for the worm to turn against Home Rule.[6] Schnadhorst took soundings that spring and believed, initially, that Gladstone would be able to carry Birmingham, Chamberlain's stronghold. 'Whenever the National Liberal Association is called together', Labouchere told Herbert Gladstone, Schnadhorst 'thinks it will either go for Mr. G., or will be so hopelessly divided that it will be powerless'.[7] About Gladstone's earnest and steadfast supporters in the Liberal Association, this proved to be correct. About the electors, hope faded when the Gladstonians faced first a parliamentary deadlock and then defeat.

All manner of intrigue characterized the general election. Husbands and wives found themselves divided against each other. George Howard, who succeeded to the peerage as the Ninth Earl of Carlisle, was a Unionist Liberal and an artist. His wife, Rosalind, was a radical. She supported W. S. Blunt, who in the summer of 1886 contested Kidderminster as a Gladstonian Liberal; Howard opposed him. Hartington wrote to Howard urging him to stand for one of the Cumberland divisions, since Howard alone could carry it. Rosalind Howard hoped to keep her husband out of the way in Italy, where he had been staying. She did not forward Hartington's letter, and she did not give his address to the Liberal Unionist whips.[8] Much alarmed when he heard the rumour that Hartington would speak against him at Derby, Sir William Harcourt protested that former colleagues ought not to take such an active role against each other, and pointed out that Lord Edward Cavendish, Hartington's brother, was not being opposed in Derbyshire. (Hartington decided against going to Derby.)[9] Alarm of this sort spread elsewhere. There had been talk of Sir Robert Peel, the Tory maverick, contesting Bury against Sir Henry James. This prospect 'frightened James out of his senses though he would have been in no danger but Peel has a power of ridicule which James would not at all like'.[10]

The elections were conducted in a spirit of unrivalled bitterness and passion. At Doncaster Lady Mary Fitzwilliam, the wife of the Unionist candidate, the Hon. H. W. Fitzwilliam, was struck on the neck by a rock which was cast through her carriage's window. On July 13 there was rioting in the Newmarket division of Cambridgeshire.[11] On polling day in York, Alfred Pease and Frank Lockwood, the sitting

[6] Temple Letters, 14 and 20 Apr. 1886, BL Add. MS 38916, ff. 60ᵛ and 73ᵛ.
[7] Labouchere to Herbert Gladstone, 23 Mar. 1886, BL Add. MS 46016, f. 16ᵛ.
[8] Blunt Diary, 14 June 1886, Blunt MS 335-1975, ff. 102–3.
[9] Harcourt Journal, 27 and 29 June 1886, Harcourt dep. 379, ff. 1 and 1ᵛ.
[10] Ibid., 27 June 1886, Harcourt dep. 378, f. 190.
[11] *The Times*, 10 July 1886, p. 12, and 14 July 1886, p. 7.

Liberals, accompanied by Pease's son, Edward, toured the city. Bombarded with rotten eggs, the little party made its way in an open carriage. Young Edward was hit, full in the face, by a very large and very rotten pear. 'I was much amused at his indifference', Pease wrote, 'to the howling mob and the disturbed stolidity of his countenance as he sat covered with yellow ochre and rotten pear, without even raising a hand to wipe his face, as if he went about like this every day.' That night Lockwood and Pease made their way to Castlegate where 'a huge dirty Irishman' embraced Lockwood and covered his face with kisses. 'I should have preferred Edward's anointing or even a rotten egg to this', Pease recorded.[12] Chamberlain felt constrained by the dangers to maintain a bodyguard.[13] On 18 June, even before the House rose for the final time, a band of roughs rushed the platform at South Islington on the occasion of a meeting for Raymond Lleullyn, the Unionist candidate. Women were knocked about. The Duke of Norfolk, who was in the chair, had his throat seized and was pinned to the wall. The intruders assaulted the candidate, who died soon afterward of an inflammation of the lungs resulting from a chill he took after the meeting.[14] *The Times*, speculating about the incidents of electoral turbulence in the summer, observed that they might succeed in Ireland, but with Englishmen 'they will have an effect the opposite of that hoped from them'.[15]

In assessing this general election, a good deal has been made of the events of 1886 as a watershed in the history of the Liberal party, in the realigning of the party system, and in the history of the relationship between England and Ireland. Some scholars, using ideas formulated for American politics by V. O. Key and developed by Walter Dean Burnham, have seen this election as critical, as a realigning election. Others have disputed these claims.[16] The present study has not the data to contest the issues involved in this debate directly. None the less, it seeks to assess the significance of the general election in 1886 by examining the nature of the contest, its results, and the character of parliamentary politics which followed from it. By studying those who stood for re-election, those who were

---

[12] Pease, *Elections and Recollections*, pp. 144–5.

[13] *The Times*, 26 June 1886, p. 7.

[14] Ibid., 28 June 1886, p. 9; 9 July 1886, p. 9.

[15] Ibid., 28 June 1886, p. 9.

[16] V. O. Key, Jr., 'A Theory of Critical Elections', *Journal of Politics*, 17 (1955), pp. 3–18; W. D. Burnham, *Critical Elections and the Mainsprings of American Politics* (New York: 1970); Blewett, *The Peers, the Parties, and the People*, chs. 1–2; Stephens, 'The Changing Context of British Politics in the 1880s'.

defeated, those who were returned, those who were elected for the first time, and the relationships among the major coalitions, something can be said about the degree to which the House of Commons in 1886 stood on the precipice of a new political order. The important question, for purposes of this discussion, however, is the relationship of the general election in 1886 to the resolution of the parliamentary crisis of the 1880s. The picture which emerges is one in which the general election of 1886, rather than redefining and reshaping parliamentary politics, endorsed, ratified, and consolidated policy changes which had been made at Westminster.

The Election Contest in 1886

Of the Members who had sat in the House of Commons in 1886, 628 stood for re-election. Of these, 245 were Conservatives, eighty-one were Irish Nationalists, and 215 were Liberals who had supported Gladstone in the division on the second reading of the Home Rule Bill. Of the Liberal Unionists, those who had voted in the cross-bench revolt against Gladstone's Home Rule policy, seventy-nine stood for re-election. Among those not standing for re-election were the discouraged, the dead, and the sick. Francis Otter, a lawyer and private tutor at Oxford who held the Louth division of Lincolnshire, suddenly 'felt too ill to be nominated'.[17] Otter had taken Louth with a majority of 14 per cent of the poll in 1885, and his sudden illness allowed no time for the local Liberal Association to select another candidate. A Conservative was permitted a walk-over in a safe Liberal seat.

There is much in the election of 1886 which suggests a throw-back to an earlier period. Only the persistence of a strong regional pattern in the contests and in the election results provides a thread of continuity with the election of 1885. By way of contrast, the election of 1886 revealed a decline in partisanship. This is seen particularly in the vast numbers of uncontested seats in 1886. In contrast to 1885, when only forty-five were uncontested, 221 constituencies in 1886 returned Members without a contest.[18] Additionally, the number of straight-party fights declined in 1886. In the previous election, 80 per cent of the candidates had been returned after contests between Liberals and Conservatives, or between Conservatives and Irish Nationalists. In 1886 this proportion declined to 67 per cent of the

---

[17] *The Times*, 6 July 1886, p. 6.
[18] The figures I use here are those for seats fought by sitting Members of the House of Commons of 1886 only. It does not include candidates contesting seats who had not sat in this House of Commons.

contests. This decline of inter-party conflict in the election of 1886 can be put down to two interrelated aspects of electoral politics: the Liberal Unionist-Tory election pact, and the high proportion of occasions on which Liberal Unionists and official Liberal candidates opposed each other. Each of these must be considered in its turn.

There was some talk of electoral co-operation between Conservatives and those who would become Liberal Unionists during the election of 1885. Sir Edmund Lechmere claimed to have used his influence to secure John Corbett, who took the Droitwich division of Worcestershire uncontestedly in 1885, 'as an independent Liberal, [who is] in a great measure on our side'.[19] But there could not have been much of this, because the Liberal Unionist faction only fashioned itself in the spring of 1886. Serious discussions between Conservatives and Liberal renegades, or potential renegades, began with the formation of a Liberal Home Rule policy. An effort to place policy above partisanship, this compact, in which Conservatives agreed to support sitting Liberal Unionists and Liberal Unionists agreed to support Tory candidates, was essential to both. 'Without the compact to spare Unionists seats', Lord Rowton, a Tory, reported to H. W. Primrose, the Home Rule Bill would not have been defeated.[20] Having lost the Irish vote they had enjoyed in the previous election, the Conservatives needed the support of the Liberal Unionists. Salisbury doubted, early on, whether the Home Rule question would bring the Tories any popular advantage. 'The instinctive feeling of an Englishman is to wish to get rid of an Irishman', he wrote to Churchill. 'We may gain as many votes as Parnell takes from us: I doubt more. Where we shall gain is in splitting up our opponents.'[21] According to W. H. Houldsworth's estimate, two Manchester seats were put at risk and 'we require a definite Liberal vote in our favour to neutralize the Irish vote'.[22] For their part the Liberal Unionists, having lost the support of their local Liberal organizations, required the votes of Conservative electors. Letters exchanged between Peter Rylands, a Liberal Unionist, and Viscount Cranborne reveal the reciprocal nature of this relationship. In one letter Rylands wrote, 'the Conservative Unionists of Burnley

[19] Edmund Lechmere to Salisbury, 30 Jan. 1886, Third Marquess of Salisbury MSS Class E.

[20] Primrose to Gladstone, 7 July 1886, BL Add. MS 56445, unbound and unfoliated.

[21] Salisbury to Churchill, 31 Mar. 1886, Third Marquess of Salisbury MSS Class D/15/183.

[22] Houldsworth to Churchill, 21 June 1886, Lord Randolph Churchill Letters 1/13/1545.

have given me their loyal and earnest [support] and have set an example to Liberal Unionists in Darwen which I hope will stimulate them to record their votes in your favour.'[23] And it was this election pact which cast the results of the election into further doubt and uncertainty. As a Cabinet memorandum stated, shortly after the Home Rule division, 'the conditions under which the Election would take place are so exceptional that it is impossible to form a confident judgment as to the result.'[24]

The Conservative–Liberal Unionist alliance held. Amongst the higher politicians there was a good deal of co-operation and mutual understanding. When Jesse Collings, Chamberlain's client, decided to stand for the Bordesley division of Birmingham, Joseph Rowlands, Churchill's agent there, wrote to Churchill to notify him that a Conservative was preparing to stand against Collings. In response, Churchill observed that such an action would be impolitic. 'If Mr. Hawkes persists, [the] Cons. party should dissociate itself from candidature.'[25] On 19 June 1886, Churchill wrote to Hartington saying he would undertake to provide that 'all your Unionist candidates shall have the full support of our party'.[26] Upon hearing from Henry Houldsworth that Manchester Conservatives believed Hartington's personal position in the Rossendale division of Lancashire was at risk, Cranborne telegraphed, in his father's name, to Hartington's chairman saying that Salisbury was 'deeply sensible of the patriotic conduct of the Liberal Unionists in Lancashire and earnestly hoped that Conservatives in Rossendale would show equal patriotism and do their utmost to increase Lord Hartington's majority'. Hartington showed the telegram to the President of the Conservative Association there, who believed the Tories 'would poll up all right'.[27]

Cranborne's constituency, the Darwen division of Lancashire provides an example of the Conservative–Liberal Unionist alliance at work. Cranborne had won the seat in the 1885 election by only the merest of majorities. However, Cranborne gained the support of local Liberal Unionists in the general election of 1886. His former opponent in the election of 1885, J. G. Potter, who was enjoined

---

[23] Peter Rylands to Cranborne, 4 July 1886, Fourth Marquess of Salisbury MSS Bundle 2.
[24] Cabinet minutes, n.d., but around 9 June 1886, BL Add. MS 44647, f. 118.
[25] Rowlands to Churchill, 15 June 1886, Churchill to Rowlands, 16 June 1886, Lord Randolph Churchill Letters 1/13/1529.
[26] Churchill to Hartington, 19 June 1886, Lord Randolph Churchill Letters 1/13/1537a.
[27] Cranborne to Salisbury, 10 July 1886, Third Marquess of Salisbury MSS Class E.

by Hartington to do everything in his power for the Viscount, placed 'patriotism above party' and did not stand.[28] Additionally, W. T. Ashton, the former President of the local Liberal club, came over to Cranborne. Ashton told Slagg, who had become the official Liberal candidate, that, because of Home Rule, he would vote against him even if he had been his own son. 'I have done all I can on the Exchange, in the Railway carriage, & amongst my relations and friends to oppose Mr. Gladstone's schemes and I shall continue to do so.' Ashton expected Cranborne to collect some of the votes of Liberal electors; he expected many others to abstain in the polling; however, he confessed that he could not estimate the numbers of these. With all of this Ashton refused to appear on the platform with Cranborne. This reveals the reluctance of Liberal Unionist support for Tories, and indicates that the alliance rested more upon opposition to Gladstone than it did upon a positive attachment to Conservative policy. As Ashton put it, to appear publicly with Cranborne would give credit to the charge that he had become a Tory, and this 'will nullify my efforts in favour of the Union amongst Liberals'. Therefore, Ashton resigned his positions as president of the Liberal club and as a member of the Liberal council, and went to Oban.[29] W. H. Waith, the chief Conservative agent in Darwen, hoped for the active help of other local chieftains of the Liberal Unionist persuasion and 'that they won't all go off to Oban'.[30] Cranborne expected to lose the 400 votes held by Irish electors, as well as the votes of many English Roman Catholic sympathizers with the Irish. To make up the difference he reckoned on the votes of 500–750 Liberal Unionists to bring him home. In this wise he wrote to his father asking for money and for a 'Liberal swell' to speak for him.[31] Salisbury could deliver the money, but found the Liberal swell to be a more difficult problem.[32] At the end of the day Cranborne regained his seat by 726 votes, 6 per cent of the total poll.

But, as the Darwen contest reveals, the Liberal Unionist–Conservative alliance was not unfraught with peril. In the first place, so uncertain were

[28] Hartington to Cranborne, 27 June 1886, Fourth Marquess of Salisbury MSS Bundle 2.

[29] W. T. Ashton [writing from Oban] to Cranborne, 17 June 1886, 28 June 1886, Fourth Marquess of Salisbury MSS Bundle 2.

[30] L. H. Wraith to Cranborne, 10 June 1886, Fourth Marquess of Salisbury MSS Bundle 1.

[31] Cranborne to Salisbury, 20 June 1886, 22 June 1886, Third Marquess of Salisbury MSS Class E.

[32] Salisbury to Cranborne, 23 June 1886, Fourth Marquess of Salisbury MSS Bundle 2.

its numerical consequences, that no one could guarantee how much good electoral co-operation would do. Secondly, feelings of peril were enhanced by mutual mistrust between the partners. Both are illustrated in Henry Matthews's contest for the Eastern division of Birmingham. 'I can hardly bring myself to believe', he wrote, 'that any assistance which Chamberlain may be able and willing to give will add many votes to my poll, — although it may cause abstentions, — but these things are on the knees of the Gods.'[33] Joseph Rowland, the head of the Conservative organization in Birmingham, reported that he could get no assurance from Liberal Unionists about support for Matthews, and this despite Tory support for Jesse Collings in the Bordesley division. 'We must keep our hands perfectly free unless we can get a *quid pro quo*. Our people are desirous to fight Bordesley & if we restrain them & are also beaten in the East Division we shall look rather foolish.'[34] Chamberlain finally endorsed Matthews, on polling day, in a letter circulated to all electors. However, even Chamberlain could not guarantee the electoral permanence of his support. Matthews, he suspected, would lose his seat if he sought re-election upon taking a place in a new Salisbury Government.[35] When Matthews had to stand for re-election following his acceptance of office, the Tories demanded Liberal Unionist support. 'Mr. Chamberlain owes a great deal to us here. We have strained [the] allegiances of our rank and file to the utmost to allow the unopposed returns of himself & his four unionist colleagues from Birmingham & to permit Collings to carry Bordesley.'[36]

Another problem plaguing the alliance, as Salisbury's difficulty in procuring a Liberal swell for his son in Darwen shows, was the unwillingness of Liberal Unionists to appear jointly with Tories. This reputation for political haughtiness emerged very early in their dealings.[37] Salisbury wrote to Churchill on 16 March 1886: 'It was said of the Peelites of 1850 that they were always putting themselves up for auction & always buying themselves in. It seems to be the Whig idea at present.'[38] Some of this could be justified by political

[33] Henry Matthews to Churchill, 20 June 1886, Lord Randolph Churchill Letters 1/13/1539.

[34] Joseph Rowlands to Churchill, 17 July 1886, Lord Randolph Churchill Letters 1/13/1533.

[35] Chamberlain to Churchill, 16 July 1886, Lord Randolph Churchill Letters 1/13/1566.

[36] Sir James Sawyer, MD (President of the Birmingham Conservative Association) to Churchill, 4 Aug. 1886, Lord Randolph Churchill Letters 1/14/1633.

[37] Cranborne to Salisbury, 10 July 1886, Third Marquess of Salisbury MSS Class E.

[38] Salisbury to Churchill, 16 Mar. 1886, Lord Randolph Churchill Letters 1/12/1416a.

practicalities. Hartington refused to appear for Cranborne because 'on the whole I can do the most good by supporting Unionist Liberals'.[39] Conservatives were not unaware of the problems that joint meetings with Liberal Unionists might raise. 'I understand the Liberals are very much divided among themselves on the subject of Home Rule both in Darwen & Blackburn', Cranborne's election agent wrote. 'It is just possible that if we were to hold a large meeting it would help them heal their differences.' Excessive intimacy, as Salisbury realized, might jeopardize the solidarity of Tory–Liberal Unionist alliance in the division lobby against the Home Rule Bill:

I received from many Whig sources the warning that if the Conservatives are too prominent just now they will run the risk of spoiling the division. A good many of them think the meeting at the Opera House was a mistake. I am very anxious not to spoil the division. . . . Their view seems to be that in allying with us they are contacting a *mésalliance*: and though they are very affectionate in private they don't like showing us to their friends till they have had time to prepare them for the shock.[40]

Salisbury had received a letter from Goschen which advised the Tory leaders to 'practise the virtue of silence' during the parliamentary recess 'lest their voices should frighten the wary and timid Radical. . . . It is better to leave the matter in their hands until the second reading.'[41] Respectful distance, in the early days, therefore, might be regarded on both sides as helpful to their policy objectives, but, in later days, with the approach of the election and after the Home Rule Bill had been safely defeated, Hartington's statements about the difficulties of asking 'Unionist Liberals to appear on a purely Conservative Platform'[42] would become increasingly difficult to bear. Salisbury wrote to Hartington, pleading with him to make some declaration on behalf of Tory candidates.[43] With the election over, Salisbury attributed the defeat of Liberal Unionists at the polls to their own aloofness. As he wrote to Lord Cranbrook, 'it is a good deal their own fault—for they have so systematically snubbed us, that I have no doubt our own people voted rather languidly.' 'If they

[39] Hartington to Cranborne, 27 June 1886, Fourth Marquess of Salisbury MSS Bundle 2.

[40] Salisbury to T. W. Preston, 22 Apr. 1886, Third Marquess of Salisbury MSS Class D/23/15.

[41] Salisbury to H. J. B. Manners, 26 Apr. 1886, Third Marquess of Salisbury MSS Class D/47/71.

[42] Hartington to Salisbury, 21 June 1886, Fourth Marquess of Salisbury MSS Bundle 2. (Salisbury had forwarded this letter to his son.)

[43] Salisbury to Hartington, 21 June 1886, Third Marquess of Salisbury MSS Class D/13/166.

had spoken out like Chamberlain and J. Collings', Salisbury wrote to the Marquess of Bath, 'still more if they had deigned to let us appear on their platforms — our people would have supported them more strenuously.'[44]

For his part Salisbury supported Liberal Unionists, recognizing the while how infrequently they shared points of policy with the Conservatives. Though Sir William Crossman 'differs from us very gravely on some very essential matters', Salisbury expressed his gratitude to the Conservatives at Portsmouth for resisting the temptation to run a candidate against him.[45] Though Lewis Fry in the North division of Bristol 'does not agree with us on many important questions', Salisbury would vote for him if he were opposed by a Gladstonian Liberal.[46] Salisbury sought to comfort nervous Tory electors with the view that the new Parliament would be preoccupied with Ireland, not questions likely to require the expression of Fry's or Crossman's liberalism. If such questions arose, the House of Lords would be a reliable poodle. 'It appears to me', Salisbury wrote, 'that the ensuing Parliament is likely to deal with the Union question & that the danger of other burning questions being brought up, such as Church Disestablishment, is not very great. I think that on these you may trust the House of Lords to prevent any decision being arrived at until another opportunity of consulting the electors has been afforded.'[47]

While the Liberal Unionist–Conservative alliance was accomplished, it was not easily accomplished. Lord St Oswald warned Salisbury about the electors in Yorkshire: 'There are, in my opinion, hundreds who will never consent to vote for the colour which they have hitherto always been accustomed to oppose.'[48] Some rank and file Tories wanted sharp limitations placed on any agreement with the Liberal Unionists in order to free them for the prosecution of partisan advantages. Sir John Gorst, for example, appealed to Lord Salisbury, asking him to pay close attention to the agricultural constituencies in the West Country. 'The Whigs', he wrote, have no claim on the

[44] Salisbury to Cranbrook, 10 July 1886, Salisbury to Bath, 10 July 1886, Third Marquess of Salisbury MSS Class D/29/199, D/82/115.

[45] Salisbury to R. W. Ford, 9 June 1886, Third Marquess of Salisbury MSS Class C/6/275.

[46] Salisbury to G. S. Harvey, 22 June 1886, Third Marquess of Salisbury MSS Class C/6/278.

[47] Salisbury to Rev. G. L. Wilson, 15 June 1886, Third Marquess of Salisbury MSS Class C/6/274.

[48] St Oswald to Salisbury, 5 June 1886, Third Marquess of Salisbury MSS Class E.

Chippenham division of Wiltshire 'as it is properly a Conservative one & the sitting member is a Gladstonian. . . . I think we ought to pay a great deal of attention to these agricultural counties because with the split in the Liberal party & the indirect help of Mr. [?] and Mr. Jesse Collings we ought to win a great many of them which are not held by Unionist Liberals.'[49] William Buchan, past president of the Edinburgh University Conservative club, was even bolder. While appreciating the importance of mutual support between Liberal Unionists and Conservatives in the election, he opposed an arrangement which would prevent Conservatives from contesting seats held only marginally by Gladstonians. Describing such a situation as 'monstrous', Buchan predicted it would 'prove highly disastrous to the Conservative party' since it would ask the party to 'rest content with the present state of its representation in the House of Commons, that is to say, with a hopeless minority of 250 members. . . . Once the Home Rule question was defeated, there is no security that the Liberal majority would not unite on some revolutionary programme in regard to some other matter of vital importance e.g. Disestablishment, or the position of the House of Lords.'[50]

The alliance in Scotland, according to Reginald Macleod, the Conservative agent there, worked well. 'The sacrifices we have had to make', however, did not go down well with 'our more eager and zealous partisans'.[51] Pugnacious Conservatives wanted more than the Tory–Liberal Unionist compact would allow them. Consequently, in Greenock, John Scott, the defeated candidate in the 1885 election, and the local Conservative organization appealed to Macleod to allow them to make a fight. As they reasoned it, Thomas Sutherland, the sitting Liberal, though a Liberal Unionist, had become unpopular; the Conservative organization was strong; there was no need for the Unionists to stand together because there was no 'separatist' in the field against them; there was no local arrangement with Sutherland; Scott had gained ground fighting the seat in the three previous elections. Nevertheless, Macleod reported, Scott and the local Conservatives were fully prepared to do what 'they are told is right'. It was a seat, Macleod believed, that Conservatives could take in a straightforward fight under ordinary circumstances. He himself took the view that there was no reason to allow Sutherland

[49] Sir John Gorst to Salisbury, 14 June 1886, Third Marquess of Salisbury MSS Class E.

[50] William Buchan to Churchill, 12 May 1886 and 24 June 1886, Lord Randolph Churchill Letters 13/13/1499, 1547.

[51] Reginald Macleod to Salisbury, 28 June 1886, Third Marquess of Salisbury MSS Class E.

a walk-over. However, he concluded, 'in a view of the general situation I dread the effect the appearance of a Conservative Candidate might have as giving an excuse to the Liberals to say that we were not playing fair and so disturb the harmony and friendly co-operation what everywhere exists in Scotland between us—at least so far as the Leaders are concerned.'[52] Salisbury responded to Macleod by urging Scott to stand down,[53] and the Greenock Tories resisted the temptation of sending Scott forth against Sutherland. In the end an official Liberal candidate opposed, but was defeated by, Sutherland.

It was difficult, as these tensions reveal, for the Liberal Unionist–Conservative electoral compact to quell the forces of partisanship. And, as a few figures will confirm, the Conservatives did not easily relinquish their electoral advantages. Judged by the safety of seats taken in the 1885 election, as Table 7.1 shows, the Conservative–Liberal Unionist alliance was most in force in those seats taken and held by Liberals, either safely or uncontestedly. For the most part, the Conservatives tended to throw their support behind Liberal Unionists in those constituencies which they were least likely to win themselves. Salisbury stated this policy clearly:

TABLE 7.1 *The Conservative–Liberal Unionist Electoral Compact in the General Election of 1886* *

	Contests between Conservatives and Liberals (%)	Contests between Liberals and Liberal Unionists (%)
Safe or uncontested Liberal seats in the 1885 election	36	64
Vulnerable Liberal seats in the 1885 election	61	39
Safe or uncontested Conservative seats in the 1885 election	100	
Vulnerable Conservative seats in the 1885 election	99	1

*This table includes information for only those Members of the House of Commons of 1886 who stood for re-election in the 1886 general election. It excludes figures for uncontested elections in the 1886 general election.

[52] Macleod to Captain Middleton, 28 June 1886, Third Marquess of Salisbury MSS Class E.
[53] Salisbury to Macleod, 30 June 1886, Third Marquess of Salisbury MSS Class C/6/252.

In regard to constituencies where the sitting Member ought to be opposed, I think the general policy to be pursued is to run a Conservative if a Conservative has a fair chance of getting in; but to abstain from contests which do not rest in any confidence on success but which, under other circumstances, might fairly be taken for tactical reasons. Where a Conservative is not likely to be returned, & there is a better chance for the Unionist Liberal, I think it is clearly our duty under existing circumstances to support a candidate of the latter school.[54]

To give this the force of numbers, Liberals and Liberal Unionists contested each other in 64 per cent of the seats Liberals had taken in the 1885 election either with safe majorities or without contests. On the other hand, Conservatives opposed Liberals in 61 per cent of the seats Liberals had taken with only vulnerable majorities, seats in which the Tories could anticipate the greatest chance of success. None of the safe Conservative seats was opened to Liberal Unionists, and a Liberal Unionist fought only one vulnerable Conservative seat in the election of 1886. Conservatives, therefore, protected their partisan electoral advantages as much as possible, and co-operated with Liberal Unionists only in those constituencies in which the Tories were at a disadvantage.

The Conservative–Liberal Unionist electoral alliance failed to hold in only three constituencies: the Romford division of Essex, the Torquay division of Devonshire, and the Petersfield division of Hampshire. At Romford John Westlake, the sitting Liberal Unionist, fought a contest against J. H. Webster, the Gladstonian challenger, and James Theobald, a landowner and a Conservative. In this Theobald was 'in a state of open rebellion'[55] against his party's leaders. The leading Conservatives in the region felt obliged to support Westlake, but they were aware of Theobald's strong local support.[56] Conservative candidates in the region, such as W. H. Makins, who sat for the South-east division of Essex, feared Theobald's candidacy would both allow Webster in and damage the fortunes of Conservative candidates in adjoining constituencies.[57] Local leaders appealed to

[54] Salisbury to D. Clark (in Glasgow), 11 June 1886, Third Marquess of Salisbury MSS Class C/6/237.

[55] Salisbury to Goschen, 19 June 1886, Third Marquess of Salisbury MSS Class D/26/34–5.

[56] H. Holmes to Churchill, 29 June 1886; D. J. Morgan (the chairman of the local Conservative association) to Churchill, 30 June 1886, copy of a letter from D. J. Morgan to [?], 30 June 1886, Lord Randolph Churchill Letters 1/13/1553, 1556, 1557.

[57] Colonel Makins to Churchill, 27 June 1886, Lord Randolph Churchill Letters 1/13/1551.

Churchill, asking him to renounce Theobald. Lord Claud Hamilton, after trying to influence the situation against Theobald through the Great Eastern Railway officials, called upon Salisbury to act. 'Mr. Theobald is of no account and is a stupid man', Lord Claud wrote. Westlake, on the other hand, 'is a clever man and active politician. Neither he nor his more active partner Mrs. Westlake are likely to forget any consideration on our part at this crisis. Such men are sometimes very useful in the House when critical divisions are impending.'[58] Party leaders attempted arbitration; but though Westlake was willing, Theobald was not. In the end Theobald's defiance of local and national leaders, and of the Conservative-Liberal Unionist compact, succeeded. He romped home in the three-cornered contest, with 57 per cent of the total poll.

Lewis McIver, in the Torquay division of Devonshire, whom *The Times* described as a man 'who voted against Mr. Gladstone's Home Rule Bill while declaring himself a Home Ruler',[59] found himself opposed in the general election of 1886, as he had been opposed in 1885, by Richard Mallock. McIver, on Home Rule as well as on other questions, held a position close to Chamberlain's. However, he accepted the principle of Home Rule and had been conciliatory toward Gladstone. The London *Daily News*, with its Gladstonian sympathies, supported McIver's return, and the local Liberal organization at Torquay, tolerant of his independence on Home Rule, endorsed him. However, Torquay was a new constituency in 1885, with a delicate balance between Conservatives and Liberals.[60] In such a setting, Tory confidence in McIver's Unionism was as slight as their awareness of his radicalism was great. Even before the Home Rule crisis crested, Iddesleigh wrote to Lord Randolph Churchill asking him to visit Torquay in support of Mallock, 'our late and I hope future candidate'. 'Torquay ought to be rescued from the Radicals,' he went on, 'but it will only be by the infusion of a little spirit into the body of the people; and you would be particularly acceptable there.'[61] W. H. Mallock, in the midst of the campaign, on the same day wrote to both

[58] Lord Claud Hamilton to Salisbury, 8 June 1886, Third Marquess of Salisbury MSS Class E.   [59] *The Times*, 14 July 1886, p. 9.

[60] Brian William Rodden, *Anatomy of the 1886 Schism in the British Liberal Party: A Study of the Ninety-Four Liberal Members of the Parliament Who Voted Against the First Home Rule Bill* (unpublished Ph.D. dissertation, Rutgers University: 1968), pp. 513–14; W. H. Mallock, *Memoirs of Life and Literature* (New York and London: 1920), chs. 11 and 12.

[61] Iddesleigh to Churchill, 23 Mar. 1886, Lord Randolph Churchill Letters 1/12/1429.

Churchill and Carnarvon asking them to send letters in support of his cousin and against McIver, 'a vacillating adventurer'.[62] Claiming that he had limited influence with local Conservative bodies, Salisbury refused to intervene at Torquay. In his judgement, McIver would have been turned out with or without a Home Rule Bill. 'I cannot personally interfere in Devonshire. In the first place, it is Iddesleigh's country; in the second the Cons. have made (as they think) large sacrifices in that country already.'[63] Mallock defeated McIver in the general election of 1886, but McIver stood as a Liberal Unionist in every general election between 1886 and 1906. He finally resigned from the House of Commons in 1909, one of the last original Liberal Unionists remaining there.

In the Petersfield division of Hampshire the Tories ran William Nicolson against Lord Wolmer, the sitting Liberal Unionist. Nicolson, himself a renegade to the Conservatives, had represented the region from 1880 to 1885 and had lost the contest to Wolmer in the last general election. Wolmer's position on Home Rule, unlike McIver's, was unequivocal, and despite his opposition to Home Rule the local Liberals made no effort to run an official Gladstonian candidate against him in 1886. He had an advanced cast to his political views, as Lewis Harcourt pointed out, which separated him pretty clearly from his father, Lord Selborne, and Lord Salisbury.[64] In fact, Wolmer had voted for Labouchere's motion against the House of Lords, a vote which required some considerable explanation between the Cecil and Palmer households during the election campaign. Both Wolmer and Selborne wrote Salisbury on 2 July 1886. Wolmer, Selborne said,

intended no more than to express his opinion that it is desirable to strengthen the House of Lords by some reform which should modify the exclusive power in it of the hereditary element which (rightly or wrongly) he regards as a source of weakness; and that nothing was further from his mind than to vote for the abolition of our House.[65]

[62] Mallock to Churchill, 25 June 1886, Lord Randolph Churchill Letters 1/13/ 1548. Mallock to Carnarvon, 25 June 1886, BL Add. MS 60857, unbound and unfoliated.
[63] Salisbury to Goschen, 19 June 1886, Third Marquess of Salisbury MSS Class D/26/34–5.
[64] Harcourt Journal, 3 Nov. 1885, Harcourt dep. 373, ff. 4–5.
[65] Selborne to Salisbury, 2 July 1886, Wolmer to Salisbury, 2 July 1886, Third Marquess of Salisbury MSS Class E. The story of Lord Wolmer and the House of Lords does not quite end here. In 1894 Wolmer, Lord Curzon, and St John Broderick, these last heirs of Lord Scarsdale and Lord Midleton, brought in a Private Member's Bill to allow the heirs of peers sitting in the House of Commons to retain their seats

Salisbury, though 'hampered there by the relationship', acted on Wolmer's behalf, and tried to get Nicolson to stand down.[66] 'Willi's manifesto is capital', Wolmer's sister wrote, 'short, simple, manly. Despite Lord Salisbury's order about not opposing Unionists Mr. Nicolson here insists on standing—the Salisburys are furious.'[67] The local Tory leaders rejected Salisbury's advice. George Sclater-Booth, the Conservative Member for the neighbouring constituency, spoke for Nicolson, calling him a 'proper proponent of Conservatism', and regarding his claim as a 'legitimate one'.[68] In the general election of 1885, in a region long considered a Conservative stronghold, with only a partial Liberal organization, but with the advantages of personality, Selborne influence, and a Tory vote divided between two candidates, Wolmer came home with a majority of 161 votes. In 1886, against Nicolson alone, Wolmer's majority was reduced, but only slightly, to 111 votes.

The Results of the Election

The parties which had the greatest ideological coherence in 1886 maintained or expanded their parliamentary forces. The Irish Nationalists became one fewer; the Conservatives enhanced their numbers; Liberals of both Gladstonian and Unionist inclinations were depleted. While they had no absolute majority, Conservative numerical dominance was complete in the House of Commons between 1886 and 1892. They did not require Liberal Unionist votes, only their abstention, to remain in office because the combined votes of the Liberals and Irish Nationalists were insufficient to displace them. Consequently the threat to Tory mastery, about which they were none too confident, lay only in the possibility of Liberal reunion. Since this possibility was directly related to the prominence of the Home Rule issue, and so long as Gladstone and his party were pledged to it, such a reunion would remain unlikely.

The election results in 1886, just as the previous general election and behaviour in the House of Commons shows, had a regional character to it. The forces of Unionism were most successful in

upon their fathers' deaths. Furthermore, they took a compact that whichever of their fathers died first, the heir would test the situation by refusing to vacate his seat. Kenneth Rose, *Superior Person: A Portrait of Curzon and his Circle* (London: 1969), pp. 142-3.

[66] Salisbury to Goschen, 19 June 1886, Salisbury to Hartington, 21 June 1886, Third Marquess of Salisbury MSS Class D/26/34-5, Class D/13/166.

[67] Rodden, *Anatomy of the 1886 Schism in the British Liberal Party*, pp. 540-2; Lady Sophia Palmer to Sir Arthur Gordon, 18 June 1886, printed in *A Political Correspondence of the Gladstone Era*, p. 37.

[68] *The Times*, 9 July 1886, p. 10.

TABLE 7.2 *The Parties and the Results of the General Election in 1886*

	Irish Nationalists	Liberals	Liberal Unionists	Liberals (Others*)	Conservatives
Re-elected with a contest	17	116	37	4	143
Re-elected without a contest	63	40	25	4	88
Newly elected	5	31	12	0	84
TOTAL ELECTED	85	187	74	8	315

*Indicates those Liberals who did not vote in the division on the second reading of the Home Rule Bill. Those designated as Liberals here supported Gladstone in the division.

England where the Conservatives and their Liberal Unionist allies fared best. In southern English constituencies, the sitting Conservatives held 81 per cent of their safe seats either uncontestedly or with safe majorities. Even in the north, 60 per cent of the Conservatives got their seats on the same basis. In southern English constituencies, sitting Liberal Unionists held 74 per cent of their seats either without contests or with safe majorities. In northern England these proportions were reduced, but with less of a reduction than for the Conservatives there, to 69 per cent. Sitting Gladstonians fared far worse in southern England, where they were defeated in 41 per cent of their seats, and where only 26 per cent of their seats were regained without contests or with safe majorities. Their situation was better in northern English constituencies, but even here the Gladstonian position weakened.

The elections in the West Midlands are worth a closer examination as a means of testing Conservative strength in this formerly Liberal stronghold, and as a means of estimating the electoral power of Chamberlain and the radical wing of Liberal Unionism. Chamberlain's influence did not run far beyond Birmingham. In the city it was, however, absolute. Chamberlain and his clients kept their seats there and added Bordesley to their total. The Gladstonian Liberals lost their places there. Chamberlain got one, the Conservatives took the East division of Birmingham, and outside the city, in Aston Manor, they took another. Henry Matthews took the East division with a safe majority, and local Conservatives, unlike Chamberlain, anticipated that, when he stood for re-election on taking a place in Salisbury's next Administration, Matthews would have a walk-over. The Liberals in the East division were in disarray, and the

TABLE 7.3 *The Members of the House of Commons in 1886 and their Fortunes in the General Election of 1886 by Party and by Region*

	Uncontested (%)	Safe majority (%)	Vulnerable majority (%)	Defeated (%)
Conservatives:				
Southern English constituencies	40	41	18	1
Northern English constituencies	33	27	30	10
Wales	0	25	50	25
Scotland	0	22	44	33
Ulster	25	56	13	6
Liberal Unionists:				
Southern English constituencies	30	44	15	11
Northern English constituencies	46	23	12	19
Wales	50	0	0	50
Scotland	11	32	21	37
Liberals:				
Southern English constituencies	5	21	32	41
Northern English constituencies	21	36	14	30
Wales	41	32	18	9
Scotland	19	56	14	11
Irish Nationalists:				
Northern English constituencies	0	100	0	0
Ulster	31	44	19	6
Southern Ireland	94	6	0	0

Conservatives felt well placed.[69] Outside the Birmingham region the picture was different, and here radical Unionism brooked less large. In the Black Country the balance of factional forces remained the same in 1886 as it had been following the election of 1885: four Gladstonians, three Conservatives, and two Liberal Unionists. The Gladstonians were the big losers in the outer urban–industrial districts. The number of their seats shrank from seven in 1885 to two in 1886. However, it was the Tories, not the Liberal Unionists, who gained at the expense of the Liberals. From two seats in 1885 the Conservatives went to seven. The Liberal Unionists held the same seats, four. Similarly in the agricultural districts of the West Midlands. Where the Gladstonians had held three seats after 1885, after 1886 they held only one. The Liberal Unionists lost one seat

---

[69] William Barton (Secretary of the Birmingham Conservative Association) to Churchill, 31 July 1886, Sir James Sawyer, MD to Churchill, 31 July 1886, Lord Randolph Churchill Letters 1/13/1604, 1605.

here, with their numbers declining from three Members to two. The Conservative representation increased from three to six seats. As Lord George Hamilton pointed out, 'outside Birmingham and the big towns in its locality the actual voting power of the Liberal Unionist was small.' 'Did I not tell you that Chamberlain would be no where with the Rads?', Labouchere wrote to Churchill. 'He did not influence 50 votes out of Birmingham & the district [round?].'[70]

If the English heartland was the strength of the Conservatives, the reverse was true for them and their Liberal Unionist allies in Wales and Scotland. At the outset Fitzroy Steward, a Tory election manager, believed Scotland could become a 'stronghold of Conservatism,' but at day's end Salisbury confessed to disappointed expectations.[71] His party, which had emerged from the general election of 1885 weakened in these regions, found itself weakened further. The Tories held only a single seat in Wales with a safe majority. They held two seats with vulnerable majorities, and lost a third. In Scotland, 77 per cent of the seats held by Conservatives after the election of 1885 were lost or held by marginal majorities. The Liberal Unionist secession had been great in Scotland—twenty-three of the ninety-four original Liberal Unionists had been Scottish Members—but great also was Gladstonian vengeance. Here Liberal Unionist–Gladstonian rivalry was sharpest. In this rivalry the Gladstonians triumphed.[72] Half the sitting Liberal Unionists in Wales and a third of those sitting in Scotland were defeated. A further 21 per cent of the Scottish Liberal Unionists were returned by their electors with only vulnerable majorities. The Gladstonians in these regions held three-quarters of their seats either with safe majorities or without a contest. Sitting Gladstonians lost only four seats in Scotland and only two in Wales. In fact they captured Goschen's seat at East Edinburgh, a feat which surprised several. Campbell-Bannerman, when asked to contest the seat, had thought it hopeless. [Goschen] 'is in possession of the field; he has a strong and influential organization; we have *none*; and he beat Costelloe by 4,337 votes to 1,929. To pull up 2,408 votes out of 6,266 is a terrible task.' Campbell-Bannerman recommended contesting the seat, but without his candidacy, and avoiding the need to make the contest 'more conspicuous than is

---

[70] Hamilton, *Parliamentary Reminiscences and Reflections, 1886–1906*, p. 30, cited by Hurst, *Joseph Chamberlain and Liberal Reunion*, p. 43, n. 1. Labouchere to Churchill, 29 July 1886, Lord Randolph Churchill Letters 1/13/1588.

[71] Harcourt Journal, 27 June 1886, Harcourt dep. 378, f. 191; Salisbury to Cranbrook, 10 June 1886, Third Marquess of Salisbury MSS Class D/29/199.

[72] Kenneth O. Morgan, 'The Liberal Unionists in Wales', *The National Library of Wales Journal*, 1969.

necessary and risk a damaging and almost humiliating defeat'.[73] Campbell-Bannerman was incorrect. Dr Robert Wallace, a minister and sometime editor of the *Scotsman*, a professor of Church history and a lawyer, defeated Goschen with a swingeing majority which exceeded 24 per cent of the total poll. In Scotland, Home Rule and disestablishment came together. The connection between Home Rule and Church questions which the analysis of Liberal voting in the House of Commons in 1886 identified was carried out in the Scottish elections. Home Ruler and disestablisher knew each other as allies.[74]

The Irish elections were things unto themselves. Concerning those in Ulster the Unionist press engaged in exaggerated claims. It rejoiced in Healy's defeat by Thomas Lea, a Liberal Unionist, in South Derry, and applauded the efforts of local Conservative and Liberal Unionists to put partisanship behind them in order to advance loyalism. It hoped for similar consequences in South Tyrone, East Tyrone, and South Down.[75] *The Times* relished Sir James Corry's success over R. R. Gardiner in the Mid Armagh division 'by a largely increased majority'.[76] This was to say too much, because Professor McKane had taken the same seat with 61 per cent of the poll and Corry took it with only marginally more, 62 per cent of the poll, in the previous elections. This is an example either of a contemporary misunderstanding of the numbers or of Unionist relief. In Ulster, in fact, the Unionists and the Nationalists divided the political terrain between them and held their relative positions with relatively equal strengths. A slightly larger precentage of the Conservative seats were held with safe majorities, but a slightly larger percentage of Irish Nationalists held their seats without a contest. The Nationalists, indeed, were able to seize the Western division of Belfast when Thomas Sexton defeated James Horner Haslett, the Tory druggist. Salisbury expressed his regret at the situation in such a manner as to reveal its uncertainty. It 'is all Sauderson's fault — and Goschen's failure. How difficult it is to find a place for people who are neither fish flesh fowl nor good red herring.'[77] In the south, of course, all was nationalism. Ninety-four per cent of the sitting Nationalists were returned to Westminster in the summer of 1886 without having to face an opponent.

---

[73] Campbell-Bannerman to Gladstone, 11 June 1886, BL Add. MS 44117, ff. 55–6.
[74] Kellas, 'The Liberal Party and the Scottish Disestablishment Crisis', p. 40.
[75] *The Times*, 12 July 1886, p. 6.　　　　　[76] Ibid., 9 July 1886, p. 10.
[77] Salisbury to H. J. B. Manners, 7 July 1886, Third Marquess of Salisbury MSS Class D/47/73.

As this regional appraisal of the election of 1886 shows, the shift to Unionism, and the Tory victory, were English events. The chief gains for the Tories and their Liberal Unionist allies were taken in the south. These findings, then, confirm the figures for the election results of 1885 and the calculations of regional constituency influence on parliamentary voting. Members for English constituencies tended to be Conservative, and these were the seats for the right wing of the Liberal party. Gladstone, and the left wing of the Liberal party, held their own in other regions. Since the regional outlines of electoral politics remained constant in the elections of 1885 and 1886, another point becomes clear. The Home Rule question did not alter the regional character of politics. It fitted into and could be accommodated by the existing regional basis of political behaviour.

Support for the parties in the general election varied according to region, but not according to the type of constituency for which MPs were returned. The Tories and Liberal Unionists did well in both counties and boroughs. Even with the Irish vote, as *The Times* remarked, Gladstone barely held his own in the boroughs, which had 'always been the main support of Liberalism'. Gladstone, *The Times* concluded, 'had alienated the Democracy' and had been rejected by the 'masses'.[78]

But the plainest and greatest lesson to be gathered from a study of the electoral map is that the traditional hearth and centres of Liberalism will not espouse the doctrine of Home Rule as taught by Mr. Gladstone. In the favourite homes of free trade, in the cities which were the staunchest friends

TABLE 7.4 *The General Elections of 1885 and 1886, the Parties, and the Types of Constituencies They Held*

	Irish Nationalists (%)	Liberals (%)	Liberal Unionists (%)	Liberals Others (%)	Conservatives (%)
After the general election of 1885:					
County seats	19	49	—	—	32
Borough seats	4	53	—	—	43
University seats	0	11	—	—	89
After the general election of 1886:					
County seats	19	26	12	1	41
Borough seats	4	31	10	1	54
University seats	0	0	11	0	89

[78] *The Times*, 3 July 1886, p. 11; 8 July 1886, p. 9.

of all movements which the Liberal party had inspired, he is stubbornly and successfully opposed.[79]

As the detailed figures for the elections of 1885 and 1886 show, the Irish Nationalists claimed the same proportion of borough seats in the two elections. The Liberals held better than half the boroughs after the 1885 election, but the proportion for sitting Liberals slumped to less than a third in the 1886 election. Even if, for purposes of making a comparison between the two elections, the Liberal Unionist returns in 1886 are counted with those of the Gladstonians, they took together 41 per cent of the borough seats. In contrast, the Conservatives claimed 43 per cent of the borough seats in 1885, and increased this to 54 per cent in 1886. Salisbury corresponded with Cranbrook on this turn of events: 'When you and I were first in the House of Commons how little we should have expected that you should even be able to write "London is really the base of Tory principles".'[80] If the Conservatives and Liberal Unionists are classed together in this analysis, the Unionist forces were able to claim nearly two-thirds of the borough constituencies. Unionism, therefore, was broadly based in 1886, and deeply rooted in urban centres.

The counties, according to *The Times*, did not pronounce against Gladstone as strongly as the boroughs, perhaps because 'the education of the newly enfranchised labourers proceeds somewhat more slowly than that of their better trained fellow-citizens in the towns'.[81] Salisbury, however, was not as dissatisfied. 'A sufficient number of the newly enfranchised voters', he wrote, 'appear to be satisfy [*sic*] with their first kick last November—and are now content to jog along reasonably.'[82] The Liberals were aware of their sharp losses in English counties. 'The county returns are so bad', Henry Primrose wrote to Gladstone, 'that we must expect a considerable loss in that quarter.'[83] The Irish Nationalists held a similar proportion of county seats after the two elections. On the other hand the Liberal share declined sharply, to only 26 per cent in 1886 from nearly half in 1885. Their reduced position in the counties was in fact greater than their reduction in the boroughs. The Liberal decline is even reflected in the figures if the Liberal Unionists are counted with the

[79] Ibid., 10 July 1886, p. 11.

[80] Salisbury to Cranbrook, 10 July 1886, Third Marquess of Salisbury MSS Class D/29/199.   [81] *The Times*, 10 July 1886, p. 11.

[82] Salisbury to the Marquess of Bath, 10 July 1886, Third Marquess of Salisbury MSS Class D/82/115.

[83] Primrose to Gladstone, 7 July 1886, BL Add. MS 56445, Unbound and Tunfoliated.

Gladstonians. What this means is that the election of 1886 was not a victory for Unionist policy with regard to Ireland alone; it was additionally a shift to the political right, an advance for the Conservatives. The Conservative share of the county seats increased from less than a third in 1885 to 41 per cent in 1886. If the Liberal Unionist share is added to this, the combined Unionist proportion becomes 53 per cent. Strong rural support accompanied urban support for the Unionist majority.

There is another way of estimating the shift toward the Conservatives and Liberal Unionists in the general election of 1886, and this by going beyond tallies of seats won or lost and by considering the size of the majorities by which seats were held. This involves a comparison of seats safely or marginally held after the general election of 1885 with the result of the election for sitting Members during the following summer. By seeing if constituencies were converted from safe to marginal seats, or from marginal to safe seats, and by seeing which parties or factions held those seats, it is possible to judge the volatility of the election and the partisan groups which came to be favoured by it. If Members were uncertain about their electoral fortunes, they were even more uncertain after the Home Rule crisis in the House of Commons. William Grenfell at Salisbury, Pascoe Glyn, a younger son of Lord Wolverton, at the Eastern division of Dorset, and Henry Broadhurst, the junior minister in Gladstone's Government, who fled the Bordesley division of Birmingham for an easier time in the Western division of Nottingham, all felt their electoral situations at risk.[84] Salisbury and East Dorset were vulnerable seats after 1885, but Western Nottingham was safe. In the election of 1886 Grenfell and Glyn lost their seats; Broadhurst won his, against the sitting Liberal Unionist (Charles Seely), though with a very much diminished Liberal majority. But in general, it may be said, the electoral system was highly stable in 1885–6. When the seats safely held after the 1885 election are compared with the results of the next election, it is clear there was little erosion. Eighty-two per cent of the seats held with safe majorities in the 1885 election continued to be held, either uncontestedly or safely, in the next election. The shift occurred among the marginal seats: 41 per cent of the seats which were held with marginal majorities either became safe or were taken without a contest in the election of 1886.

Table 7.5 shows the way the Conservatives and Liberal Unionists benefited from this shift. The Tories continued to hold, in the election

[84] Harcourt Journal, 8, 13, and 26 June 1886, 1, 10 and 15 July 1886, Harcourt dep. 378, ff. 165, 173, 189; 379, ff. 9, 27, 33.

TABLE 7.5 *Shifting Patterns of Seat Security in the General Elections of 1885 and 1886*

Election of 1885	Election of 1886			
	Uncontested (%)	Safe seats (%)	Vulnerable seats (%)	Defeated (%)
Conservatives:				
Uncontested	60	30	10	1
Safe seats	56	38	3	3
Vulnerable seats	15	34	43	9
Liberal Unionists:				
Uncontested	40	40	0	20
Safe seats	28	38	15	20
Vulnerable seats	35	24	18	24
Liberals:				
Uncontested	71	29	0	0
Safe seats	24	44	18	14
Vulnerable seats	4	14	19	62
Irish Nationalists:				
Uncontested	94	6	0	0
Safe seats	78	22	0	0
Vulnerable seats	0	0	50	50

of 1886, 94 per cent of their safe seats either by safe majorities or without a contest. Moreover, 49 per cent of the seats Conservatives had held with vulnerable majorities were converted to safe or uncontested seats. The Liberal Unionists held two-thirds of their safe seats by safe majorities or without a contest. Furthermore, they were able to convert 59 per cent of their vulnerable seats to safe majorities or to seats held in 1886 without a contest. For their part, the Liberals were able to retain 68 per cent of their safe seats with safe majorities in 1886, but were defeated in 62 per cent of their marginal seats and in 14 per cent of their safe seats.

When this shift from vulnerable to safe seats is examined regionally, the importance of region, which has been referred to earlier, is again confirmed. The Conservatives held their safe seats, and gained still more, in English constituencies. Of the marginal Conservative seats in southern England, sixty-three became safe or uncontested. Doing less well in northern England, the Tories, even here, retained 88 per cent of their safe seats, either safely or uncontestedly. However, in the north the conversions from vulnerable majorities to safe or uncontested seats were less, only 39 per cent. The Liberal Unionists also did their best, and made their greatest advances in southern English constituencies. Even in the north, 82 per cent of the vulnerable Liberal Unionist seats became safe or uncontested. On the other hand, in this region the Liberal Unionists lost twenty-nine of their safe seats, and a further 14 per cent of their seats became vulnerable.

The pattern for Liberals was the reverse. The shift against them was strongest in the south, where they lost 19 per cent of their safe seats, and where a further 41 per cent of seats once safely held became marginal. In the north the Liberals held 75 per cent of their safe seats, or held them without a contest, but they lost 70 per cent of their marginal seats. In Wales and Scotland they scored far better. They held 92 per cent of their safe seats in the former, and in the latter 71 per cent of their safe seats, either by safe majorities or without a contest. Further, in Scotland the Liberals transformed 75 per cent of their marginal seats to safe ones. The Conservatives, in 1886, therefore, found success in the English heartland, in boroughs, to some extent in counties, and in the consolidation of their electoral strength. Not only did they win Liberal seats, the Tories were also able to convert seats held marginally to seats held safely.

In the literature on critical and realigning elections, much has been made of increased intensity of electoral involvement and volatility as characteristics of these events. On this point, there is thought-provoking evidence for the election of 1886 indicating an absence of increased intensity and volatility. The far smaller number of election contests in 1886, as opposed to 1885, is one such piece of evidence. Another has to do with the cost of elections. Elections are always expensive enterprises, and one would have expected the elections in 1886, if they were stimulated by exceptional volatility, to be exceptionally costly. The problem of cost was a great problem for Liberals. Rosalind Howard wanted W. S. Blunt to stand as a Home Rule Liberal if only because the Liberals were 'terribly hard up for candidates who pay their own expenses', and Blunt could pay his. Moreover, Albert Grey discovered the £10,000 of Secret Service money available to the Government whips at election time 'made a row abt this & the sum will not be available'.[85] Lord Wolverton and Rosebery each contributed £5,000 to the election fund and Wolverton planned to spend an additional £5,000 in Dorset and Wiltshire, where he and his son, who sat for the Eastern division of Dorset, had interests.[86] But the excitement of Home Rule did not drive up the costs of elections, and in fact, the total election costs

---

[85] Blunt Diary, 1 June 1886, Blunt MS 335-1975, f. 75.
[86] Harcourt Journal, 19 June 1886, Harcourt dep. 378, f. 179.

in 1886 were less than in 1885. In 1885 they had been £1,026,645; in 1886 they were £624,086.[87]

Legislative replacement and turnover is another indicator of electoral intensity. One would expect, if there were increased volatility, increased turnover. In the general election of 1885 a House of Commons was returned in which 48 per cent of its members were sitting for the first time, a high level of turnover. In fact, in 1886, this turnover rate became sharply reduced. Only 136 MPs (20 per cent) had not sat in the House of Commons of 1886, and, of these a smaller number—103 or 15 per cent—had never sat in any previous House of Commons. The low number of sitting Members defeated in the general election of 1886 indicates a further point. Incumbency, which one would not expect to be high in a highly volatile election, favoured sitting Members to such a strong degree that constituency variations were simply absorbed in it. For the whole House, 85 per cent of the sitting Members, if they stood, sat again in the House of Commons of 1886-92. The type or size of constituency did not make much difference in estimating the chances for return, for the county constituencies returned 88 per cent of their sitting Members and boroughs returned 81 per cent. Small constituencies (those with fewer than 8,999 electors) returned 86 per cent of their Members, and larger constituencies returned 85 per cent.

One might be tempted to the view that the Home Rule issue did not matter very much in this election, that electoral choices were not based upon it; that electors were prepared to return the same MPs because they had already taken into account, in their votes in 1885, the way their MPs would go on the Home Rule question. This is improbable, however, because the Irish question entered but little into the electoral politics of 1885. It surfaced only after the election was over. It is more probable that election behaviour in 1886 was responsive to processes of political institutionalization in the same way parliamentary behaviour was. When new issues emerged, as they did in the case of Irish Home Rule, they emerged in the world of Westminster, the world of party leaders and rank and file. Electoral choice was less fixed upon specific policy choices, which issues had to be considered in relationship to partisanship, the social status of MPs, and the relationship of MPs to their local constituencies.

To put the matter another way, British elections were not critical to the development of policy in the same way that American elections were. Critical election theory argues that elections, and especially certain elections (realigning elections), manage tension between

---

[87] Gwyn, *Democracy and the Cost of Politics in Britain*, p. 55.

elastic social conditions and rigid political institutions. The general election of 1886 did not mediate, in this way, processes of social and political change. In the first place, the Home Rule issue did not arise from social conditions in Ireland, though it was exacerbated by them. The nationalist movement was political and became cultural. The Liberal response to this emerged out of political considerations, and the split in the Liberal party was based upon two issues, Home Rule and disestablishment. Second, the structures of British politics were not rigid, and were not made so by a system of checks and balances dividing power from authority. The obstacles in Gladstone's way rested upon resistance within his own party; it was a matter of insufficient political support. Furthermore, the Home Rule crisis ended and was resolved by the parliamentary alliance of Tories and Liberal Unionists, an alliance which put the resistance to Home Rule on a partisan basis.

Turn-out, which one would expect to be high in a critical or realigning election, fell also, from 81 per cent in 1885 to 74 per cent in 1886. While turn-out figures for the country as a whole must undoubtedly be related to the increase in uncontested elections, turn-out was reduced beneath the 1885 levels even in constituencies in which there were contests. In London seats, for example, the turn-out in 1885 had been 74 per cent of the electorate, and this was reduced to 65 per cent in contested constituencies during the next election. Turn-out was greater in 1886 in only four constituencies, all English boroughs (Chelsea, Boston, the Scotland division of Liverpool, and Wednesbury), and then only by minuscule proportions. (In the Western division of Wolverhampton the turn-out remained constant in the two elections, at 86.9 per cent). The Liberals feared a decreased turn-out would work against the Home Rule coalition. In Derby, Sir William Harcourt's constituency, this was an issue Lewis Harcourt watched carefully. 'Our only danger is want of interest in the contest', he wrote on 24 June. On polling day there was a 'decided apathy amongst the people and they are not coming up to vote as quickly or as thickly as I should like'. At the end the 'majority [was] as good in proportion as that of last year though the poll was very much lighter'.[88] Chamberlain, knowing that the leaders of local Liberal associations were with Gladstone, realized that 'they consist of the most active & thorough going partisans'. A decreased turn-out, therefore, was part of his fondest dream, because 'it is the men who stay away who turn elections & there

[88] Harcourt Journal, 24 June 1886, 3 July 1886, Harcourt dep. 378, f. 186; 379, ff. 12,14.

TABLE 7.6 *The Political and Social Composition of the House of Commons Elected in the General Election of 1886*

	% of the re-elected	% of the newly elected	% of the whole House
Conservatives	43	63	47
Liberal Unionists	12	9	11
Liberals	29	25	28
Other Liberals*	2	0	1
Irish Nationalists	15	4	13
Peerage–baronetage–landed gentry	47	49	48
Active businessmen	30	27	30
Professional men	54	48	53
Working class	2	2	2
Public school educations	32	37	33
Elected after 1885	46	76	52
Served before 1885	54	24	48

*Did not vote in the Home Rule division.

will be a larger abstention on this Irish question than we have ever had before in the history of the Liberal party'.[89]

The general election of 1886, then, sustained the realignment of political forces which had taken place in the House of Commons, but without the kind of electoral volatility associated with critical elections in the United States. The realignment of political forces in 1886 arose less from constituency pressure and electoral influence than from the features of political behaviour in the House of Commons. Change emerged in Parliament, not in electoral cycles.

The House of Commons, 1886–92

The election did not alter the social composition of the House of Commons in any fundamental manner. In an incidental way, which would not affect the trend of Parliament's composition in the long run, the newly elected Members were slightly more landed than their colleagues who had sat in the last House. Sixty-six (49 per cent) were connected to landed society through their fathers, their mothers, or their wives. This increase in the proportion of landed gentlemen sitting in the House is small beer, but it serves as a reminder that our thinking about the relationship between social change and politics is frequently the reverse of what the facts teach. Social change need not produce political reaction or

[89] Chamberlain to Labouchere, 30 April 1886, Chamberlain Papers JC5/50/84.

advance. In this case, the House of Commons in the summer of 1886 became more landed because it became more Conservative. Social composition did not dictate political change; partisan and policy change led to change, if only in the slightest degree, in social composition. While the proportion of business men among the new recruits remained constant, or was slightly less (27 per cent), the proportion of professional men among them was reduced to 48 per cent. Of the new Members, 37 per cent had been to public school, in contrast to the slightly lower proportion (31 per cent) for the House of Commons in 1886. Slightly more than a quarter (28 per cent) of the new Members had mothers connected to the landed classes, and 21 per cent had wives so connected. A slim proportion (7 per cent) were themselves large landowners, in the sense that they owned 3,000 acres or more, but 26 per cent belonged to families owning such landed properties. The newcomers were, on average, younger than Members of the previous House. In that House 27 per cent of the Members had been forty years of age, or less, and 49 per cent had been fifty-one years old or more. The newly elected had 36 per cent of their number who were forty years or younger, and 32 per cent who were fifty-one or older. Youth in 1886 was associated with the forces of Unionism and reaction rather than with the liberalism of the Gladstonian tradition. As might be expected, because it was necessarily so, these men had less political experience than Members of the former House. However, 24 per cent had sat in previous Parliaments, though not in the Parliament of 1886. Only two of the newly elected had experience in previous Governments (Henry Matthews and Thomas Salt). While they lacked parliamentary and governmental experience, many of the newcomers had experience on the hustings. Eighty-six (65 per cent) had contested constituencies, but lost their contests, in the general election of 1885.

The significance of the election comes out in the figures for the various partisan groups in Table 7.6. The Liberals, after the election of 1886, the Liberal Unionist defections and Gladstonian electoral losses, found their proportion of seats halved. From 49.8 per cent of the House after the 1885 election, the Liberals had been reduced in 1886 to 28 per cent of the House. Contemporaries sought to explain the Liberal defeat in 1886 in a number of ways. Some called attention to the drop-off in the vote during the summer's election, and believed that Liberal electors had been the abstainers. 'Quite as suggestive as the Unionist gains is the almost unvarying reduction in the majorities by which the Separatists hold their own. This feature is noticeable even in Wales. . . . On the other hand, the Unionist majorities show large increases'.[90] Edward Hamilton also detected a falling-off in Liberal electoral strength. Some of this, he knew, could be attributed to an erosion of the electoral register since 1885, but not all. 'The Conservatives are winning more seats than was expected, and where they have held seats they have held them by largely increased majorities, [and] the seats held by Ministerial candidates have been held by largely reduced majorities.'[91]

The Unionist alliance which was returned to the House in 1886 had a combined majority of 117 over the combined Liberal–Irish Nationalist coalition. Without the Liberal Unionists the Conservatives had an overall majority of 128 over the Liberals alone, and forty-three over the Liberals and Irish Nationalists together. The Conservatives, in the long and short of it, needed Ireland at least as much as the Liberals did. Ireland had to stay central to the political agenda for the Conservatives to retain the support of the Liberal Unionists. Therefore, the Tories and the Liberal Unionists developed a policy position on Ireland which captured support going beyond party and beyond class. Later in the year Salisbury could remind Churchill that the basic support for the Conservatives came from the 'classes', but in August he accounted for their success in the election by their capacity to draw upon the support of the full scope and spectrum of society. Differences of opinion, he observed — and this is supported by figures this study provides — were regional rather than social.[92] Even earlier *The Times* clothed the same thought in words: 'The main dividing lines of opinion run from top to bottom of English society, and the maintenance of the Empire is as dear to the working man of West Ham as it is to the masses who work in other ways in Kensington or Marylebone.'[93]

The Home Rule crisis, therefore, created a polarization of the political nation along ideological, rather than social, lines. And this can be confirmed, as in Table 7.7, by calculations of the dimensional positions of sitting Members in 1886 who were returned to the House of Commons for the period between 1886 and 1892. The totals at the foot of the table indicate what one would expect from what has already been said about this election. The effect of the election of 1886 upon the ideological composition of the House created a slight

[90] *The Times*, 5 July 1886, p. 6. See also *The Times*, 3 July 1886, p. 7; 4 July, p. 6; 5 July 1886, p. 9.

[91] Edward Hamilton Diary, 5 July 1886, BL Add. MS 48644, f. 56.

[92] Salisbury's speech at the Lord Mayor's dinner, *The Times*, 19 Aug. 1886, cited in Hurst, *Joseph Chamberlain and Liberal Reunion*, p. 50.

[93] *The Times*, 8 July 1886, p. 9.

TABLE 7.7 *Ideological Position and Party Affiliation of Members of the House of Commons of 1886 Who Were Returned in the 1886 General Election*

	Scale positions		
	7–5 (%)	4* (%)	3–1 (%)
Conservatives	0	0	100
Liberal Unionists†	10	30	60
Liberals	55	37	8
Liberals (others)	50	38	12
Irish Nationalists	100	0	0
TOTALS	36	15	50

*Median scale position.
†Liberal Unionists are those Liberal MPs who voted against Gladstone's Home Rule Bill, and Liberals are those who supported it. Liberals (others) are those who did not vote in the Home Rule division.

shift to the right. In the House which had sat during the previous six months, something less than half the House held dimensional positions to the right of the median. However, of the Members who had sat in that House and who were returned, 50 per cent held positions to the right. This slight tendency, of course, was accentuated by the election, which returned eighty-four additional Conservatives and twelve new Liberal Unionists to the House. The shift to the right in the House as a whole was accompanied by a shift to the left in the Liberal party. Of the Gladstonian Liberals who were returned in the 1886 election, 55 per cent held scale positions to the left of the median, compared with 47 per cent of the Liberals holding such positions in the previous House of Commons. There was, in other words, an erosion of moderate forces in the Liberal party as a result of the election. Of the Liberal Gladstonians who fit the scale and who were defeated in the general election or who did not stand for it, 34 per cent held scale positions to the right of the median. To these moderate losses in the Liberal fold must be added the defection of twenty-four Liberal Unionists who were returned to the House of Commons of 1886–92 who held positions to the right of the median, and who, after 1886, supported the Tory Government for reason of its Irish and ecclesiastical policy.

These figures for partisan affiliation and dimensional position reveal a polarization of partisan politics and the drifting apart of political groups. Of the returned Conservatives and Liberal Unionists, 93 per cent held scale positions to the right of the median, and

70 per cent of the Liberals and Irish Nationalists held positions to the left. The tendency of the Liberals to hold dimensional positions to the left of the median in the House of Commons from 1886 to 1892 would, in fact, be increased, since there was no need to keep a Liberal Government in office. The number of Liberals at the median would be reduced because these scale scores in the 1886 House of Commons reflect the votes of Liberals who opposed left-wing revolts. The parliamentary Liberal party, therefore, was radicalized in 1886, but it was the elections of 1885 and 1886, rather than the split in the Liberal party over Home Rule, which so radicalized it. The election of 1885, as this study has shown, introduced large numbers of new radicals into the House. The election of 1886, while pruning some moderates from the party, favoured radicals in the Liberal party. Radicals retained 64 per cent of the Liberal safe seats in the election of 1886. Though their numbers were reduced, the Liberal party in the period from 1886 to 1892 was more cohesive and more unified ideologically than it had been before. And these Liberals faced a Conservative–Liberal Unionist alliance which, despite its electoral victory, lacked confidence in its own future.

From an ideological point of view, the Liberal Unionists held to a precarious position. Their political wilderness was an uncertain one. Their sole object, according to Jesse Collings, was to 'prevent the possibility of a revival of the Gladstone Irish policy.'[94] As W. H. Houldsworth expressed it, 'Liberal Unionist opinion which though it exists, is not at all robust' in certain constituencies, such as Manchester's.[95] The uncertainty of the Liberal Unionists arose, in part, from a sense of electoral insecurity. Sir Henry James and R. B. Finlay, for example, felt their chances for re-election would be slim if they joined a Cabinet coalition.[96] But other uncertainties developed because they could separate themselves only with difficulty from their former colleagues on policy grounds. As Chamberlain admitted, 'many of the rank and file among the Unionists were uneasy and anxious to know what were really the points of difference between themselves and the Gladstonians.'[97] The consequence was to make the Liberal Unionist–Conservative alliance an uneasy one.

[94] Collings to Churchill, 8 Aug. 1886, Lord Randolph Churchill Papers 1/14/1645.
[95] Houldsworth to Churchill, 21 June 1886, Lord Randolph Churchill Letters 1/13/1545.
[96] Churchill to Fitzgibbon, 22 Aug. 1887, Lord Randolph Churchill Letters 1/21/2633.
[97] Chamberlain to W. H. Smith, 12 Aug. 1887, Hambledon Papers, quoted in Hurst, *Joseph Chamberlain and Liberal Reunion*, p. 49.

Despite its numbers, its strength in both boroughs and counties, and the shift and consolidation of safe seats in 1886, the position of the Conservative Government was not a sure thing, as the pessimistic reflections of Lord Randolph Churchill show. He had some appreciation of what he was up against:

The Opposition, consisting of ex-Ministers, independent Radicals, and the followers of Mr. Parnell, present a phenomenon never before seen in Parliament. For purposes of Opposition, they number 120 to 150. The Irish is really the only section which is under any control; they number about 70 in regular attendance; but their one object is to hamper the Govt. on every other question, and to degrade Parliament, & to render the transaction of public business impossible. In this they are out done, if possible, by the independent Radicals, such as Mr. Labouchere, Mr. Illingworth etc. It is really easier to deal with the Irish than with the Radicals. The ex-Ministers exercise no control & do not appear to be possessed by any sense of responsibility; they feebly follow & support all extravagance of Parliamentary behaviour. Mr. John Morley, no doubt, in his heart deplores & might deprecate aggravated & open obstruction; but he is only influential when he identifies himself with the Irish. Lord Randolph Churchill cannot trust himself to describe the actions of Sir W. Harcourt; it is sufficient to say that even the Irish, whom he is ready to countenance to any extent, regard him with contempt. But though this is the general characteristic of the opposition, it is important to point out that as such it is vastly more formidable than would be the action of regular, united, responsible opposition. The Govt. have to contend against a kind of guerilla warfare, sustained by different bands under different chiefs, but all under loose control and restraint, and none of them ever expecting to be called to a responsible position.[98]

Balfour sought out Chamberlain to gain assurance about Liberal Unionist support for the Conservative Government, and got it, but only informally. 'There ought to be no difficulty', Chamberlain told him, 'in obtaining a sufficient army of action by means of Consultations behind the Speaker's Chair.'[99] Churchill was not sanguine. The Liberal Unionists could not be trusted. They 'have melted away', he wrote to the Queen. 'For a very critical occasion about half of them might be counted upon by Ministers as a party

[98] Churchill to the Queen, 31 Aug. 1886, Lord Randolph Churchill Papers 1/15/1739.
[99] Memorandum of a discussion between Balfour and Chamberlain written at the end of June or the beginning of July 1886, BL Add. MS 49839, f. 270. This memorandum is also quoted in Blanche E. C. Dugdale, *Arthur James Balfour* (London: 1936), vol. 1, pp. 105–6, which gives the identities of the participants in these discussions.

of any value'.[1] He did not even feel that the Tories could count on their own natural supporters. This practical numerical weakness, he believed, arose from 'the time of the year, the attractions of the country, the great heat, the fatigue of public matters arising from electoral exertions'. These made it 'almost impossible for the Ministers to count upon more than two-thirds of their full strength, even on an emergency, and for regular attendance, much less'.[2] From within the Conservative party, some questioned the ability of their own front bench. Henry Howorth, who was newly elected in the summer of 1886, criticized the 'fossils' sitting there.

They are weak as debaters, weak in suggestiveness and weak especially as administrators . . . take Colonel Stanley for instance what in the world has he or can he do to strengthen our party. It is openly said that Lord Iddesleigh is to be Foreign Minister. Can anything be more ridiculous . . . Sir Michael Hicks Beach is a good administrator but he cannot lead our party. He is very [?] & very cold. He has no tact and is very shy.[3]

Thus ended the event. Edward Hamilton, as the quotation from his diary at the head of this chapter shows, suspected that the election would not change much of a fundamental character. The Home Rule crisis clarified, however, the political situation. Power was transmitted from one Administration to another, and responsibility for sustaining that Administration was transferred from the Liberals to the Conservatives. For the future, as for the past, the workings of power at Westminster would require the careful accommodation by party leaders to the policy preferences of their respective supporters.

Conclusion

Both Edward Hamilton and Lord Randolph Churchill saw something new in the hedgerows of parliamentary politics in 1886: an increased polarization of partisan positions. The election of 1886 ratified and endorsed polarization; it did not initiate it. The general election of 1885 had introduced new social and political elements to the parliamentary world, accompanied by their political objectives, and Gladstone's Government in 1886 introduced the question of Irish government. The House of Commons in 1886 found ways to domesticate these new forces into established patterns of political behaviour. The general election of 1885 displaced normal and

---

[1] Churchill to the Queen, 31 Aug. 1886, Lord Randolph Churchill Letters 1/15/1739.
[2] Ibid., 31 Aug. 1886, Lord Randolph Churchill Letters 1/15/1739.
[3] Henry Hoyl Howorth to Churchill, 27 July 1886, Lord Randolph Churchill Letters 1/13/1583.

expected electoral patterns, and the election following the Home Rule crisis marked a return to traditional electoral habits. A decline of partisanship, encouraged by Conservative–Liberal Unionist electoral co-operation, a decline in contested elections and turn-out, a decline in parliamentary turnover and recruitment, and even a slight decline in the cost of the elections, indicate a re-establishment of constituency behaviour along lines which had existed before 1885.

The incautious might be tempted to argue that this means that policy, even the dramatic policy changes of Irish Home Rule, meant nothing; that all was merely a matter of getting elected, or re-elected, to the House of Commons. This would be wrong. The meaning and significance of these features of politics is found in precisely the reverse; on policy everything turned. The chief interest of the political crisis of 1886 is that parliamentary politics could find ways of accommodating radical and divergent approaches to policy so that the terms for the resolution of crises of this character could be defined at Westminster rather than in the constituencies. Parties won and lost power, Governments changed hands, but in such a way that guidance in political change spread from Westminster to the constituencies, rather than from the constituencies to Westminster. Crisis definition and resolution was a parliamentary, not an electoral, matter.

CONCLUSION

If Gladstone brings forward an Home Rule Bill and passes the second reading by a narrow majority there will be such a row in Ireland as never was. Randolph will be bound to go over and lead Ulster to the last ditch. I hope somebody will string up Aberdeen.

Lord Salisbury[1]

Govt in this country has been carried on hitherto by 'tradition'. By men trained from their youth in the methods of ruling. In this way they have kept in view precedence and what was due to minortion [*sic*]. Mr. G. is the last link in this race of rulers.

The danger of democracy is that Govt is entrusted to men without this training and experience, men who are inclined to go rough shod over difficulties or to ignore them, both grave dangers.

Reginald Brett[2]

Although the House resembles those tropical seas where calm generally prevails, but where tornadoes suddenly supervene — still it has a wonderful power of restoring order after boisterous scenes and tumultuous excitement. As a corporate body it never loses its head, however wild some individuals or even some sections of its Members may be for a moment. There are ever abiding with the faculty of self-discipline, the sense of collective responsibility, the self-consciousness appertaining to an assembly that has no superior save the Crown. Thus, even after the most critical disturbances, order rapidly reasserts itself.

Sir Richard Temple, Bt.[3]

I also saw little Baumann in the Lobby who was rather disconsolate as he will pretty surely lose his seat at the Elections. It is pretty hard, he said, after having been six months in heaven to be pitched out.

Wilfred Scawen Blunt[4]

Gladstone will get a heavy fall and will finally disappear; but after him, probably, the deluge.

Lord Randolph Churchill[5]

THESE observations, with their references to inclusion and exclusion, call attention to the question of political integration. Walter Bagehot, with whom the study of British politics begins and ends for many

---

[1] Salisbury to H. J. B. Manners, 24 Mar. 1886, Third Marquess of Salisbury MSS Class D/47/66.

[2] Reginald Brett to Hartington, 19 Feb. 1886, Esher Papers 2/7.

[3] Sir Richard Temple, *Life in Parliament, Being the Experience of a Member in the House of Commons from 1886–1892 Inclusive* (London:. 1893), p. 376.

[4] Blunt Diary, 4 June 1886, Blunt MS 335-1975, f. 84.

[5] Churchill to his mother, 21 June 1886, Lord Randolph Churchill Letters 1/13/1531.

people, in one of his telling phrases, spoke of those 'ruling but unenacted customs' which forge a political culture.[6] Reginald Brett, in a letter to Lord Granville at the time of the Home Rule crisis, also referred to such a process. 'There are evident signs that the new democracy will insist upon its ceremonial and social duties no less than the regimes of old times.'[7] Processes of political integration do not prevent change, but they shape its direction and character. In the hedgerows of parliamentary politics, in the interstices and precincts of Westminster, the worlds of the landed élite, of large and small business men, of the professions, and of country houses, clubs, and the military services touched. How they touched is a matter of enormous interest, but it is a matter not easily penetrated by statistical tests and correlations. The memoirs and letters of Members of the House of Commons, however, though they provide but mere impressions, contain suggestive clues about political and social integration.

Sir Richard Temple described the House of Commons as a club where Members gathered from late afternoon until early next morning. 'They must work, read, write, and take their meals there day after day, for weeks together.' There, especially among Members of the same party, they 'developed bonds of mental affinity, of sympathy, of association'. 'Thus many friendships, many valued acquaintanceships are formed, which might never be begun but for the association within the House of Commons.' A highly regulated, highly ordered world, the House made and remade the behaviour of its Members because 'every personal movement in the Chamber is regulated by an unwritten code', understood by all no matter how new. 'There is a rule as to where and when a Member may sit or stand, when he may take his hat off, or put it on, when he should bow to the Chair as he quits his place.'[8] Lord Derby observed something obsessive in the situation. 'Some live at the House altogether, using it as a club, and having only a bedroom in some lodging house near.'[9]

In describing these parliamentary relationships, Justin McCarthy likened the House to a great public school, where, thrown together, Members developed an intimacy of a political if not a social sort.[10]

---

[6] Walter Bagehot, *The English Constitution* (London: 1872), introduction to the 2nd edn., pp. xxv–xxvi, xviii.

[7] Brett to Lord Granville, 22 May 1886, Esher, *Letters and Journals*, vol. 1, p. 128.

[8] Temple, *Life in Parliament*, pp. 7–8, 11, 12, 28–9.

[9] Derby Diary, 15 Mar. 1886, *The Later Derby Diaries*, p. 63.

[10] Justin McCarthy, *Reminiscences* (London: 1899), vol. 2, p. 92.

T. P. O'Connor also compared the House of Commons to a school. 'It is a wonderful demonstration of crowd psychology', he wrote. 'Its emotions rush from breast to breast with lightning rapidity; a small joke, which in private would scarcely raise a smile, leads to a hurricane of laughter.'[11] It is not without interest that these Irish Members, often regarded as outsiders violating the House's rules, should feel and express the emotional pull of parliamentary life. None the less it is true, and Justin McCarthy and his colleagues felt acutely the requirements imposed by Parliament. Taking the point of honour strongly, they did not divulge the confidences made to Parnell during the Carnarvon affair as it emerged in the debate on the Home Rule Bill.[12]

The club-like, school-like organization of belief and behaviour in the House was connected to partisanship, just as it was affected by it. Justin McCarthy and Lord Randolph Churchill did not know each other well, as McCarthy explained, because they sat on different sides of the House. This 'as most people know accounts for a great deal — men sitting on different sides are not thrown together in a casual way'.[13] The same was true for Sir Richard Temple and his relations with the Irish Members because his 'acquaintance among them is necessarily very limited'.[14] Temple also attributed different seating arrangements at dinner in the House to partisanship. 'There is a fine dining room in which Members of the Radical and National Parties usually dine. Probably a Conservative would not be welcome, nor would he feel at home if he dined there.'[15] In this setting Members shaped and moulded their colleagues' views. Sir John Mowbray, Bt., in his memoirs, gave an extended account of the House's capacity for socialization and domestication:

There is, and always has been a very real feeling for fraternity within the walls of the House. If a man is willing to learn and willing to work, he is recognized as a real recruit, and is welcomed accordingly. He comes in contact with other men, he respects their opinions, he discards some of his old prejudices, he gradually falls into line, and is ready to associate himself with his compatriots in the great work of legislation.

Mowbray went on to pay tribute to Charles Bradlaugh, with whose

---

[11] T. P. O'Connor, *Memoirs of an Old Parliamentarian* (London: 1929), vol. 1, pp. 42–3.
[12] T. M. Healy, *Letters and Leaders of My Day* (London: 1928), vol. 1, pp. 257–8.
[13] McCarthy, *Reminiscences*, vol. 1, p. 433.
[14] Temple Letters, 20 Apr. 1886, BL Add. MS 38916, f. 73.
[15] Temple, *Life in Parliament*, pp. 11–12.

political view he could not have disagreed more. Bradlaugh 'earned the respect of all by his constant labours and the honest and independent expression of his views'.[16]

As this implies, the folk-ways of the House of Commons influenced behaviour without the heavy hand of whipped coercion. William White, who had been the principal door-keeper of the House a generation earlier, pointed to the importance of organization, rather than oratory, in the conduct of the House's business. He attributed the power of the whips to 'mysterious arts and incantations'. 'Exactly what these circean arts are no one knows but the initiated, but that they are of wondrous power is certain and not to be disputed. Many a fond dream of independence has been dissipated, and many an indignant patriotic feeling have they damped down, and how it is done must ever remain a mystery to all but those who are behind the scenes.'[17]

It is unsurprising to find in this House, with large numbers of untested and untried Members thrust into the turmoil of a constitutional crisis, a preoccupation with the rules of tacit behaviour. It was a point to which James Agg-Gardner called attention when he portrayed his new colleagues after the election of 1885 as men having 'a somewhat excited and turbulent disposition'. These were men who had not been in the House long enough to become acclimatized to the atmosphere of parliamentary institutions.[18] Leaders and inexperienced men alike were aware of the difficulties they would face in shaping the opinions and moulding the behaviour of unruly parliamentary recruits. 'The composition of the new H. of C. is not promising on closer inspection', Lord Randolph Churchill observed. It would 'take a lot of training before they attain even the appearance of respectability'.[19] Edward Lyulph Stanley, who had been defeated while standing in the Liberal interest at Oldham in 1885, called attention to the 'newer and possibly cruder elements' in Parliament.[20] One March evening Sir Richard Temple was at the tea-table of the House with Sir Thomas Brassey and Sir William Harcourt, and afterward confided in one of his parliamentary letters 'it is evident

[16] Sir John Mowbray, *Seventy Years at Westminster*, ed. Edith Mowbray (London: 1900), pp. 106–7.

[17] William White, *The Inner Life of the House of Commons*, ed. with a preface by Justin McCarthy and a new introduction by E. J. Feuchtwanger (Richmond, Surrey: 1973), vol. 1, p. 27.

[18] Agg-Gardner, *Some Parliamentary Recollections*, p. 63.

[19] Churchill to Lord Dufferin, 14 Jan. 1886, India Office, Eur. F. 130/6/1. I owe my thanks to Dr Roland Quinault for this quotation.

[20] Stanley to Gladstone, 29 Nov. 1885, BL Add. MS 44493, f. 156.

that Harcourt thinks [it] is a very difficult House to lead, and so no doubt it is'.[21]

Members of this House of Commons were not unaware of formative associations at work there. As George Leveson-Gower realized, one of his functions as whip was to attend 'political gatherings of a social nature'.[22] There were not only evening receptions or garden parties but also 'gatherings held to welcome provincial delegates whenever some occasion brought them to town'. The political function of these gatherings was the same as that of London's clubs. Here leaders and the led met together to define policies and, what is very much the same thing, political objectives. Back-benchers wished for such meetings. Sir John Henniker Heaton, a new Member in 1886, asked Salisbury for a party meeting and for an address 'on our duty in the present crisis'. Such a meeting 'would have a most exhilarating effect on the party—many of whom have not yet had the honour of meeting you'.[23] Less formal occasions provided the same opportunities. Frank Lockwood described two dinners attended by leaders and back-benchers where politics and society mixed freely. At one of them (Mundella, Lord Kilcoursie, Sir John Lubbock, Sir Erskine May, and Dr Vaughan were present), Lockwood and Gladstone discussed local and constituency politics, a division forthcoming in the House of Commons, Gladstone's sleeping and drinking habits, and whether or not he read Greek at night. At another Gladstone reminisced about the history of the House of Commons, about Daniel O'Connell, about three men who wore pigtails in the House, John Bright's illness, and, once again, his own sleeping habits.[24] Henry Broadhurst described a dinner such as this after the great separation in the Liberal party as 'a golden bridge by which the two sections of the Liberal party might be reunited'.[25]

As this serves to show, the history and traditions of the House figured large on these occasions, and Gladstone was unusually sensitive to such matters. At a dinner party on 15 January Gladstone had a long talk with Lady Dorothy Stanley about manners and customs in the House. When Gladstone first entered some Members

---

[21] Temple Letters, 19 Mar. 1886, BL Add. MS 38916, f. 50ᵛ.

[22] Leveson Gower, *Years of Content*, p. 239.

[23] Henniker Heaton to Salisbury, 2 Feb. 1886, Third Marquess of Salisbury MSS Class E.

[24] Lockwood to his father, 20 Mar. 1887 and 24 Nov. 1888, quoted in Augustine Birrell, *Sir Frank Lockwood, A Biographical Sketch* (London: 1898), pp. 131–2, 132–3.

[25] Broadhurst, *Henry Broadhurst, M.P.*, p. 304.

wore pony-tails. 'There was only one M.P. a Mr. Sibthorpe, known as "the man with the beard", which was quite sufficient to designate him.' Beards came in with the militia in 1852, and Gladstone said there had been discussion in the Cabinet as to 'whether Sir Arthur Peel, as Speaker, could keep his beard. "Indeed", said Gladstone with a twinkle of fun in his eyes, and amusement beaming over his face, "I am not sure there was not some understanding come to that Sir Arthur should circumscribe and retrench that hairy abundance on his face, and yet, I do not see that he has complied in any way with the requisition of his office. The dress of a Speaker forbids a beard".' Gladstone went on to describe the greatest change in the House of Commons: ' "the want of reverence. I notice with alarm the growing irreverence and not in the House alone, but throughout society. I say with *alarm*, because the decline of reverence means the decline of liberty. Reverence is a barrier, a check upon licence, but once Reverence [is] gone, then that licence runs riot and liberty is necessarily curtailed".' Gladstone was not referring to the Irish Nationalists here. These he expected to be disruptive. It was the wider spreading of indignity he deplored.[26]

In defending himself against the Queen's charge that he had been insufficiently vehement in his support of the House of Lords during the debate of Labouchere's motion on representative government, Gladstone criticized the Tories for using the Lords as a poodle, and for their inadequacies as Conservatives in upholding political traditions. 'In cherishing a love of liberty Mr. Gladstone has always desired to cherish also his sympathy with antiquity; and it is a matter of grief to him to see that sympathy declining in the Conservative as well as the Liberal party.'[27] These thoughts had consequences for the constitutional crisis over Home Rule. Gladstone was unable to gain the support of those who would become Liberal Unionists, at least in part, because the compromises they demanded were inconsistent with Gladstone's regard for the dignity and reverence of government.

This is revealed in an exchange of letters between Edward Hamilton and Sir Henry Hussey Vivian, Bt. On 16 May Hamilton wrote that Gladstone 'would make any sacrifice in order to settle the question short of compromising the dignity of the Govt., *because* its authority (as you will be the first to admit yourself) depends on its dignity, and without the aid of its authority a settlement of this question cannot be made'. Hussey Vivian and others wanted the withdrawal

---

[26] Lady Dorothy Stanley's Diary, 18 Jan. 1886, Chamberlain Papers JC8/2/2.
[27] Gladstone to the Queen, 6 Mar. 1886, in Guedalla, *The Queen and Mr. Gladstone, 1880–1898*, vol. 2, p. 396.

of the Bill before the second reading division. To this Hamilton replied, 'I doubt if such a course is possible without too great a sacrifice of dignity.'[28] As Gladstone himself put it, he would not withdraw the Bill and substitute a Resolution in its place because such an action would be 'a distinct condemnation of the Bill set aside'. A Government, he went on, 'cannot afford to degrade itself by the confession of errors it had not committed'.[29] The demands of Liberal Unionists would violate parliamentary customs and traditions in such a manner as to remove the authority Gladstone deemed necessary for government. How far this went in Gladstone's mind is shown in an anecdote told by John Henniker Heaton. One evening during this session, in a nearly deserted House, Henniker Heaton and Sir John Commerell, another new Member, sat directly across from Gladstone, who was showing every sign of displeasure. At length, Gladstone rose from his place and approached the Speaker, who sent the Sergeant-at-Arms to Commerell calling him to order. Commerell had been sitting with one foot curled up under him and the other partially on the bench. This, for Gladstone, was a breach of the House's order.[30] For him this was not a triviality. Order of this sort domesticated social and political differences, and in so doing served to integrate issues and policy.

Salisbury was aware that Parliament functioned in such a manner. In 1886 he advised the Queen twice on the question of the dissolution of Parliament. On those occasions he conceived of the situation as a constitutional crisis which required threshing out in Parliament. In January, after the fall of his Government, Salisbury cited a series of policy and electoral arguments which told against the dissolution of Parliament. Dissolution would not favour 'the Constitutional section' of the House; the agricultural labourer had not yet discovered 'the hollowness of the promises made to him'; to dissolve presently 'would expose us to the extreme hostility of the Irishmen without having gained to us any other class'. As Salisbury observed, 'Gladstone's designs are still wrapped in mystery.'[31] It would take the parliamentary session to unwrap these and to clarify the political agenda. This is what happened between January and June of 1886. With the defeat of Gladstone's Government in the division on the second reading of the Home Rule Bill, Salisbury recommended

[28] Edward Hamilton to Hussey Vivian, 6 and 18 May 1886, BL Add. MS 48625, ff. 5^v, 9.

[29] Gladstone to Pease, 21 May 1886, BL Add. MS 44497, ff. 258–9.

[30] Porter, *The Life and Letters of Sir John Henniker Heaton*, p. 19.

[31] Salisbury to the Queen, 29 Jan. 1886, Third Marquess of Salisbury MSS Class D/87/337.

dissolution. Now it was an advantage to his party and his Unionist policy, which were the same things in his mind. Moreover, with the Liberal designs exposed and made public by the parliamentary session, to refuse to dissolve would be dangerous to the regime.

If Mr. Gladstone is refused leave to dissolve, the fact will certainly be known. His *entourage* is far from discreet; and they are very bitter. The consequence must be that those who are in favour of Home Rule—the Irish, and the more Radical English—will think, and say, that the action of the Queen is keeping them from Home Rule. A great deal of resentment will be excited against the Queen: and if tempestuous times should follow, the responsibility will be thrown at her. This is undesirable, to say the least; especially if no object is to be gained by it. Whether it would diminish her influence seriously or not, it is difficult to determine: but the risk of such a diminution ought not to be lightly incurred. Her influence is one of the few bonds of cohesion remaining to the community.[32]

The same concern for the stability of regime, the development of policy, and its integration was displayed on the other side of the House. Late in life, in commenting on the functions of the whip, Herbert Gladstone attributed the Liberal defeat in 1886 to the failure of parliamentary reciprocity, the failure of Members to consort together. When he allied himself with the Tories in the general election of 1885, Parnell made the 'greatest mistake of his political life' because the Irish Nationalists made attacks on the Liberal party and provoked leading Liberals into a premature opposition to Home Rule. Consequently, one of those Liberals, Sir Richard Grosvenor, failed to consult and negotiate with Parnell, functions which were essential to the development of policy and the resolution of conflict.[33]

The habitual ruling of unenacted customs such as these had the effect of creating a separate world at Westminster, insulating Members from the constituencies and from their previous experiences. This was a matter of bitter complaint to some outsiders. James Anthony Froude and Wilfred Scawen Blunt, spending New Year's Day together at Naworth, the home of the Howards, regarded Gladstone as 'a mere parliamentarian, to whom the politics of the world have no true existence and are, with his principles, only a means to parliamentary ends'.[34] But Blunt wanted to be an insider because he recognized the House as the centre of political action

---

[32] Memorandum of Salisbury to the Queen, 15 May 1886, Third Marquess of Salisbury MSS Class D/87/348–9.

[33] Herbert Gladstone, 'The Chief Whip in the British Parliament', *American Political Science Review*, 21.3 (Aug. 1927), pp. 524–5.

[34] Blunt Diary, 1 Jan. 1886, Blunt MS 334-1975, ff. 2–3.

where he would have openings on every side. If he had been elected he could have influenced the course of events 'if only by my presence'. 'Now I am helpless, voiceless, and powerless.'[35] Even more than the hustings, the House was the place for shaping decision. In February, Hicks Beach wrote to Churchill to say that they should not both plan to be in Belfast at the same time. 'There may be nothing in this House, but it is impossible to tell.' If Gladstone should seek to change the paragraph on the legislative union in the Queen's speech, 'we should surely do more good by fighting that than we could do anywhere else'.[36] It remains to describe the ways in which political behaviour in the House of Commons in 1886 squared with this culture.

For most of the nineteenth century, electoral arrangements, and indeed the Industrial Revolution, failed to have much effect on the social composition of the House of Commons. All of this changed in 1885 in the first general election following the reform legislation of 1884–5. Walter Bagehot believed that a full generation of electors would have to live under the conditions of a reformed electoral system before their behaviour would reflect those reforms. This was not true in 1885. Fuelled by high levels of turn-out, high levels of contested seats, and high levels of partisanship, the general election in 1885 returned a House of Commons to Westminster with a new social character. For the first time landed gentlemen were in a minority in the House, and additional numbers of businessmen and men of the professions, even a small cadre of working-class Members, sat there. This was, in addition, a very inexperienced House. Almost half had had no previous parliamentary experience. Consequently, it was a legislative assembly characterized by grave uncertainties.

Gladstone made this already uncertain political world even less certain when he interrupted its agenda with his Irish Home Rule policy. Contemporaries, especially those outside Parliament, despaired, seeing rack and ruin and desolation around them. Rather than political dislocation, however, the division lists of the House of Commons reveal quite a different picture. They show the taming and containing of wild and unruly political elements, even the forces of Irish nationalism. Voting was highly regular and consistent on all forms of policy. And this regularity and consistency was so extensive it could not have been produced randomly or by accident. These voting patterns describe how, in the midst of constitutional crisis, Members responded to policy questions along ideological lines

[35] Ibid., 13 Jan. 1886, Blunt MS 334-1975, ff. 15–16.
[36] Hicks Beach to Churchill, 12 Feb. 1886, Lord Randolph Churchill Letters 1/12/1376.

and in accord with ideas and values rather than individual, social or economic interests. Members with radical proclivities voted consistently for economic, social, and political reform, for Welsh and Scottish disestablishment, and for a foreign and imperial policy based upon principles of justice and international morality. Members of a conservative persuasion opposed these reforms, and supported a foreign and imperial policy based upon national and imperial interest. Between the extremes of radicalism and conservatism rested the many Members of the House who supported what they could support, who opposed what they felt had to be opposed, but who rarely voted in such a manner as to violate the powerful left–right ideological forces at work in the House.

It is a finding of the greatest importance that the general parliamentary voting dimension contains legislative items touching on all aspects of policy formation: the character of the electoral system, the state of society, the land question and the Church, and foreign affairs and the empire. Dimensional regularity and voting consistency of such a dramatic sort tells against arguments ascribing political motivation to the simple quest for power. Perhaps more than any other, this finding reveals why the approach of the high politics historians cannot be easily extrapolated from the study of Cabinets and imposed upon the study of Parliaments. If it could be so extrapolated, the dimensional patterns discovered in the division lists would be fundamentally different. There would be many more voting dimensions, and they would be less inclusive, containing fewer items, a reflection of interest voting rather than ideological behaviour. This finding points to the working of powerful centripetal forces in the House of Commons, integrating elements which transcended local and personal considerations.

The Home Rule crisis of 1886, because of the defection of the Liberal Unionists to the Conservatives, is sometimes taken to be an occasion of party weakness and partisan decomposition. The facts, however, are quite to the contrary. The Conservatives and the Irish Nationalists were highly unified, and the Liberals, though divided on many questions, were for the most part divided in a single, leftward direction. The major pattern of internal Liberal dissent was one in which radicals acted against their leadership. This meant that there was a powerful dispersion of Liberal votes toward the left. Rather than Liberals supporting a Conservative position, the Conservatives frequently supported the Liberal Government in moderate policies in order to restrain the more radical elements on the Liberal back benches. Consequently, the parties' relationship to each other remained adversarial. There is only one exception to this pattern of partisanship: voting on foreign and imperial policy. Here the broad body of the Liberals and Conservatives were largely agreed. On other questions, however, though the Tories supported moderates in the Liberal party, the respective positions of the major parties pushed in different directions. Parties were the vehicles of policy commitment which diverged from each other, and the willingness of the Tories to support the Liberal Government in opposing the more extreme positions of the radicals and Irish Nationalists cannot be seen as a form of ideological consensualism. As for the Parnellites and the radicals in the Liberal party, they were not ideological nomads, loose parliamentary cannons. They fit their appropriate positions on the various voting dimensions of this House of Commons, consistently on the left wing. There was, in consequence, a profound association between partisan position and voting on issues in the House of Commons in 1886. Parties were organizations devoted to policy, not machines to engineer elections alone. The association of party with vote was produced by informal forces of ideological integration, not the crude coercive power of party discipline, or the blind devotion to various bodies of party leaders. Members accepted the whip of one party, as opposed to others, because of shared political values.

When Wellington complained of the 'shocking bad hats' in the first reformed Parliament, he referred to a political conception present then and present now: that individuals' social background shapes their behaviour. Despite the conventional wisdom, however, social class does not account, in any total way, for political cleavage in the House of Commons in 1886. Though Irish Nationalists were very much less landed than Conservatives, and though the Liberals were slightly less so, there is only a mild association between social background and partisan preferences. All parties recruited their memberships from all social groups. Similarly, the Liberal Unionists and the Gladstonians were not divided in their Irish government policy by social differences. Landed gentlemen, business men, men of the professions in the Liberal party, and Whigs were on both sides of the question. And a majority of each group supported Gladstone. Evidence such as this cannot be used to show a defection of those Gladstone called 'the classes' in the parliamentary Liberal party to Toryism. In short, the Home Rule crisis did not produce a social polarization in the British party system. As for internal divisions in the various parties, the social background of Conservatives and Irish Nationalists accounts for little. It is only in the Liberal party, in voting on issues which fit the traditional political agenda (not Irish Home Rule, that is to say), that the social attributes of Liberals were associated with the political positions they assumed. Liberal landed gentlemen, on these issues, tended to be moderates, and those without connections to landed society tended to be radicals. Of these social attributes, landed status, rather than business interests or professions, apparently made the most difference. It mattered not whether a Liberal landed gentleman was a business man, but if a Liberal business man was a landed gentleman he was much more likely to be a moderate than a Liberal who was solely a business man.

The electoral reforms of 1884–5 effected a revolution not only in the social composition of the House of Commons but in the relations between constituencies and Members of Parliament. Until this time the urban or rural character of constituencies was important in shaping the behaviour of MPs. Conservatives had been returned by the more rural constituencies. After 1885 this was no longer the case. In this House of Commons many Liberals sat for rural constituencies and many Conservatives, continuing a pattern which had been initiated earlier, sat for boroughs. This change exposed a strong relationship between the region in which a constituency was located and the actions of Members. Southern English constituencies returned representatives who tended to be Conservatives, and if they were Liberals they tended to be moderate Liberals. Northern England and the Celtic fringe, except for Ulster, returned representatives who were members of the parties of the left. A regional pattern of this kind had always been present, but masked by urban–rural forces at work. With the urban–rural distinction removed, regional impulses had greater play. In the event this aided both major parties because each established a new base of support, the Tories in the towns and Liberals in the counties. This transformation also strengthened the forces of party because regional impulses, except for those in nationalist Ireland, came to be represented by the major partisan groups. The Conservatives held the English heartland and political centre and the Liberals held the ethnic fringe and political periphery. Because of the association of party with region (again, with the exception of nationalist Ireland), partisanship prevented Scotland and Wales from following Ireland into separatism. Temporarily at least, the configuration of associations between constituencies and Members produced by the reforms of 1884–5 gave an advantage to the forces of the political left. A majority of the safer seats, the constituencies held with safe electoral margins, was in the hands of more radical Members of Parliament. More than this, a majority of the safe seats held by Liberals were held by radicals who had been returned for the first time in the general elections of 1885. These Members had a boisterous time of it as they took adventurous positions on questions of political reform, land, and foreign policy which were often to the left of their own leaders.

The liberalism which the general election of 1885 delivered into the House of Commons was highly charged and divided. Conventionally, these internal divisions are taken to be indicators of the disruption of the Liberal party over Home Rule. This was not the case. For the most part, these Liberal divisions were radical revolts which did not threaten the Liberal party or the Liberal Government because on these occasions the Conservatives supported the Government. Moreover, the institutionalizing pressures in the party—parliamentary experience, Government office-holding, club memberships—encouraged internal agreement. It was only in a small number of centrist revolts, principally over Irish government and disestablishment, that the Liberal party and the Liberal Government were threatened. And this because the Liberal rebels, who were quite distinct from the Liberal rebels who participated in radical revolts, voted with the Conservative Opposition. In these instances, which were both numerically small and weak, the Government and the party were at risk, but not threatened in a fundamental way because the institutionalizing agencies at work pressed in the direction of partisanship. That is not to say that centrist revolts were unimportant. They were. Because Chamberlain could conceive of Ireland as a province while Gladstone and the Liberal party considered it a nation, they were separated powerfully. And the defection of one-third of the party was not trivial either. But it is to say that the rupture was not irreparable. And it is to say further that the centre which the Conservative party shared with the Liberals was extremely narrow. Any alliance, therefore, between Liberal Unionists and Conservatives would be fragile, and they would have to pay extremely close attention to electoral matters.

Because of the fragility of parliamentary alliances in 1886, the electoral matter which required the closest attention in the general elections of 1886 was the Conservative–Liberal Unionist electoral pact. This agreement depressed the level of partisanship, though even in these efforts to raise policy above party the Conservatives protected their partisan interests. The results worked to the Tories' advantage. Though they could not dominate the House of Commons without Liberal Unionist support, they increased their numbers. The Irish Nationalists retained their position almost exactly, and by way of contrast both Gladstonian Liberals and Liberal Unionists lost Members. Additionally, the Conservatives were able to convert vulnerable seats to safe ones, while the Liberals lost marginal seats and some of their safe seats became vulnerable. This conversion, from vulnerability to security for the Conservatives and from security to vulnerability for the Liberals, marks one of the most important transformations in 1886 and suggests one reason, at least, why the Conservatives could hope for an extended period of Government in the years to follow. The Tories gained in both county and borough seats, but the regional pattern of constituency relationships established in the previous general election remained. The Conservatives and their Liberal Unionist allies retained their hold in English constituencies, and the Liberals remained strong in the north, in Wales, and in Scotland. The effect of the Home Rule crisis was to polarize the House of Commons along ideological and regional lines rather than social lines. This was achieved not by the thrust of popular influence from the electorate but by electoral abstention. The turn-out in the general elections of 1886 was less than in the previous general election. There was a lower turnover in the House of Commons. The social composition of the House remained largely unchanged. The electors in the general election ratified a political settlement which had been made at Westminster.

A political culture such as this consists of several elements: a strong party system, a belief in the sovereignty of Parliament, Cabinet responsibility, a foundation of trust based upon the mutual respect of social status. Such a culture prevents the proliferation of interest groups, and brings them together in such a manner as to deal with their policy demands in an orderly fashion. Deference to the authority of this culture and confidence in political reciprocity prevents political fragmentation, political impotence, and the collapse of belief in the system as a whole. It has clear disadvantages. It is often isolated from the worlds of ordinary and practical experience. It is too far removed from the mental lives of people who are unprepared to compromise, or who are unprepared to accept political solutions to problems. And this may explain the difficulties some English politicians had in dealing with the Parnellites, and may also account for the intensity of the Home Rule crisis. On the other hand, this civic culture had pronounced advantages. It was pragmatic and unbound to dogma, features of behaviour shared by Liberals, Conservatives, and even Irish Nationalists in 1886. It discouraged selfish ambition by basing action upon discipline, duty, principle, and service, rather than upon interest. And all these qualities suggest reasons why politicians such as Captain O'Shea, and even Churchill and Chamberlain, failed to find true places in this world. This is the stuff which makes ideologies and ideological behaviour.

This is not high politics, nor is it the direct push and pull of social and constituency forces upon the political behaviour of Members of the House of Commons. It is more than these, and more complex. Where high politics scholars ascribe political action to ambition and the quest for power, this analysis points to the importance of ideology, to political and constitutional values, in the Home Rule crisis. Where students of social class and class conflict ascribe political action to the differences in social background, this analysis points to the moulding influence of parties and partisanship. Where students of critical elections ascribe political action to the forces of electoral influence, this analysis points to the importance of what happens to Members at Westminster when they are faced with policy choices. Marxists sometimes feel that if they are not grounded in a social base, political values are somehow false; that they are mere fictions. However, since political values and ideologies are always responses of human beings, they are always inventions. Members of the House of Commons constructed this parliamentary culture, based on ideology and forged by parties and partisanship at Westminster, within which the Home Rule crisis was born and resolved. Resolved not in the way one would wish, perhaps, knowing what we know about the history of Ireland since 1886, but resolved in such a manner as to transmit both the power and the authority to govern from one ruling élite to another.

THE CLASSIFICATION OF MEMBERS' PARTY AFFILIATIONS

The partisan affiliations of Members are obtained from their political biographies in Dod's *Parliamentary Companion*, the constituency returns for 1885 also published in Dod, the election returns found in *The Times* and the *Pall Mall Gazette*, and in McCalmont's *Parliamentary Poll Book of All Elections, 1832–1910*. Even when Dod listed no party affiliation for MPs, and this is true for only four Members (G. H. Allsopp, William Ambrose, F. G. B. Duncan, and Sir Richard Everard Webster), these other sources readily supply the missing information. In short, the record of party affiliation is complete, posing few taxonomic problems, and all Members can be assigned readily to one of the three partisan groups in this House of Commons. However, since the biographies which Dod published consist in MPs' self-designations of their political colours, and since these other sources provide certain rich variations on political themes, it is useful to call attention to some of the qualifications Members made to their political pledges.

Some Members expressed an independence from partisan connections, a tradition which had lost much of its meaning earlier in the century. Colonel Francis Charles Hughes-Hallett considered himself a 'firm but independent supporter of Lord Salisbury's Government', Sir Rainald Knightley was a Conservative but 'not pledged to any party', C. E. Lewis held 'Conservative principles, but considers that the maintenance to the Union in its integrity stands before all party combinations', and J. F. Hutton regarded himself as a 'moderate and independent Conservative'. R. U. P. Fitzgerald, Alfred Hickman, H. T. Knatchbull-Huggessen, and H. J. Trotter simply called themselves 'independent Conservatives'. Then there is the case of Sir Robert Peel, Bt., the son of the great Prime Minister and the brother of the Speaker of the House. Peel had been made a junior Lord of the Admiralty in 1855 by Palmerston, and was considered a Liberal. He became Chief Secretary for Ireland in 1861, also in a Liberal Government. By 1874 Peel had come to regard himself as a Liberal–Conservative, and he opposed Gladstone's Near Eastern policies. In 1884 he was returned as a Conservative for Huntingdon. Peel sought office in Salisbury's first Administration,[1] but he found himself frustrated in this. Peel was 'concerned and grieved' to think he had 'incurred the heavy displeasure of the Queen' so that he was barred from Government, and put himself in Salisbury's hands.[2] In 1885, the electors of Blackburn returned him as a Conservative, and Peel wrote to Salisbury to congratulate him on Cranborne's success at Darwen.[3] Unable

[1] Peel to Salisbury, 6 June 1885, Third Marquess of Salisbury MSS Class E.
[2] Peel to Salisbury, 29 June 1885, Third Marquess of Salisbury MSS Class E.
[3] Peel to Salisbury, 4 Dec. 1885, Third Marquess of Salisbury MSS Class E.

to find a place for himself in Tory ruling circles, Peel's relations with Salisbury and Churchill eroded during the spring of 1886. He abstained in the division on the Home Rule Bill, the only Conservative to do so. In the general election of 1886 Peel stood as the Liberal candidate for the Inverness Burghs, with the support of Gladstone, against Robert Finlay, the sitting Member and a Liberal Unionist, whom Gladstone described to Peel as 'one of the keenest and most vehement adversaries to the policy which you and I think to be recommended by the broad principles of justice and by clear dictates of expediency'. In the same letter, Gladstone went on to describe Finlay's political position in such a way as to shed light on both Peel's and Gladstone's assessments of their partisan relationships. Finlay 'calls and thinks himself a Liberal Unionist but this is Toryism of the worst type, the Toryism which breaks up Empires, the Toryism of George III and Lord North, not the Toryism which will ever stand associated with the name of Robert Peel'.[4] As his biographer observed of Peel, 'the want of moral fibre in his volatile character, an absence of dignity, an inability to accept a fixed political creed, prevented him from acquiring the confidence of his associates or the public.'[5] In these classifications I have counted Peel as a Conservative in the election of 1885 and for the lifetime of this House of Commons, but as a Liberal in the election of 1886. Backing and filling of Peel's sort is rare, though I am aware of one other relatively recent shift of political loyalty. William Thackeray Marriott accepted the Chiltern Hundreds in February 1884 after incurring the displeasure of his Liberal supporters in Brighton. He sought an interview with Lord Salisbury 'to communicate on political matters which I do not care to put on paper. Please consider this private.'[6] Whereupon he was re-elected by the Conservative electors of the borough in opposition to a nominee of the Liberal party.

On the Liberal side of the House, John Corbett and Sir Edward Watkin, Bt. list themselves in Dod as independent Liberals, and McCalmont ascribes independence to Joseph Cowen, though this may refer more to Cowen's relationship to the Liberal caucus than to his acceptance of the Liberal whip in the House of Commons. William John Fitzwilliam, fifth son of the sixth Earl of Fitzwilliam, stood as an independent Liberal for Peterborough in 1885. He had obtained the support of the local Conservative Association, and the adopted Conservative candidate withdrew when the Fitzwilliam family agreed not to oppose the Conservative candidates in the county.[7] A Liberal, S. C. Buxton, opposed Fitzwilliam in this election. His brother, W. C. Wentworth-Fitzwilliam, fought the Hallamshire division of the West Riding of Yorkshire in 1885 as a Conservative, the first member of this old family so to do.[8] In the election of 1885 Charles Conybeare contested, and

---

[4] Gladstone to Peel, 23 June 1886, Peel to Gladstone, 26 June 1886, BL Add. MS 44548, f. 103, 44498, f. 64.

[5] *Dictionary of National Biography*, vol. 44, p. 223.

[6] Marriott to Salisbury, 21 Feb. 1884, Third Marquess of Salisbury MSS Class E.

[7] James Morse Carmichael to Gladstone, 11 Dec. 1885, BL Add. MS 44493, ff. 206–8.   [8] *The Times*, 3 Dec. 1885, p. 9.

won, the Camborne division of Cornwall against the official Liberal candidate, A. P. Vivian, as an independent Liberal.

In addition to claims of independence, some Conservatives asserted other qualifications to their political allegiance. Five indicated sentiments which place them toward the right of their party. Major-General Sir Lewis Pelly, for example, described himself as a 'Constitutionalist', and Thomas Waring put himself forward as a 'Constitutionalist and an Imperialist'. Eight Conservatives considered themselves moderates, and thirteen as progressives. Harry Bullard's characterization of himself as a Conservative of the 'modern school' squares easily with none of these positions. What is important is the 223 Conservatives (88 per cent) qualified their political loyalties in no way.

The same point may be made about Liberals in the House of Commons in 1886. Two Members, Henry Wyndham West and Sir Mathew Wilson, Bt. described themselves as Whigs; eight claimed to be ardent, sincere, earnest, or decided Liberals; two considered themselves moderate Liberals; two as progressive Liberals; five as reformers; thirty-six as advanced Liberals; twenty-one as radicals; and one, George William Latham, considered himself an advanced radical. Even such richness of personal self-consciousness, however, cannot obscure the fact which remains: 262 Liberals (77 per cent) offered no qualifications to their political affiliation.

Materials for the period, other than Dod, indicate additional instances of differentiation in the Liberal party. McCalmont, for example, lists William Abraham, William Crawford, Joseph Leicester, Benjamin Pickard, and John Wilson as labour Members. He does not have the whole of it, however, for a social analysis of this House of Commons reveals an additional nine Members who had their origins among the working classes. As I have indicated in the narrative, Joseph Arch and Thomas Burt had ambiguous ties to the Liberal party,[9] but on the whole no evidence can be found for an independence of labour Members in 1886. Their self-designations in Dod, and their voting records, show these working-class MPs to be unequivocal adherents to the Liberal party, if on its left wing. Whatever their importance for the history of the labour movement, these men were not independently organized in the House of Commons.

The story of the Crofter MPs in 1886 is more complex. While Dod's biographies give no indication of some Liberals having a special association as Crofter representatives, McCalmont does. He lists five Members (J. MacDonald Cameron, Dr G. B. Clark, Charles Fraser-Macintosh, Dr Roderick McDonald, and D. H. Macfarlane), who, at least on the question of a fair-rent, fixed-tenure measure for the Scottish crofters, conducted their affairs independently of the Liberal party. As the historian of this 'party' puts it, 'Most of the "Crofters", however stood quite independently of the Liberal party; and the group possessed its own organization, quite unconnected with the Liberals.'[10] Doubtless these Crofter MPs felt at

---

[9] Arch, *Joseph Arch, the Story of His Life*, pp. 355, 358–9; Burt, *Thomas Burt, M.P.*, pp. 287, 289.

[10] Crowley, 'The Crofters' Party, 1885–1892', p. 110.

odds with the Liberal front bench, and their supporters, as a result of the official Liberal resistance to the enlarging Amendments they, and other radical MPs, put forward on the Crofters Bill in the spring of 1886. However, these Members did not ascribe a special independence to themselves in their biographies, nor is there evidence in the voting record that they disassociated themselves in some special way from the Liberal party on other issues, save for the fact that they voted consistently on the left flank of the party.

The most important faction in the Liberal party consisted of those Members who voted with Conservatives in the division on Gladstone's Government of Ireland Bill on 8 June, the Liberal Unionists. It is usual in the historical literature for the period to judge their number at ninety-three: see, for example, the list of Liberal Unionists which Arthur Elliot, himself a Liberal Unionist in the House of Commons, published as an appendix to his life of Goschen.[11] Most historians have followed this lead, and in so doing they have ignored Sir Edward William Watkin, Bt., who sat in this House of Commons for the borough of Hythe. Watkin exercised a vigorous political independence, so much so that W. S. Caine, another Liberal Unionist sitting in 1886, described him as a 'Tory of the worst type masquerading in worn out Liberal clothes. He only seeks a seat in Parliament so that he may further the railway interests. It is men like Watkin who write Liberal after their names in the Parliamentary lists and then stab the party in the back.'[12] Lord Richard Grosvenor, in his election reports to Mr Gladstone, counted Watkin for the Tories and Lord Fitzwilliam for the Liberals.[13] However, as Caine noted, Watkin considered himself a Liberal, and he is so listed in Dod's *Parliamentary Companion*. Moreover, he is listed as an Independent Liberal for the election of 1885 and as a Liberal Unionist for the election of 1886 in *The Constitutional Year Book for 1887* (London: 1887), pp. 204–205. As Pelling observes, while Watkin may have been originally returned to the House as a Conservative, and while he had few pronounced partisan views, the electors of Hythe returned him as a Liberal in 1885. There may have been local reasons for this, since Watkin's most prominent interest was to gain support for the Channel tunnel project, a scheme of no little importance for Hythe's electors.[14] Whatever Watkin's ambiguous attachment to the Liberal party, his Unionist sympathies are clear: he is listed as opposing Home Rule in the official list of House of Commons divisions as well as in the list published in Hansard.[15] With Watkin included, the number of Liberal Unionists becomes ninety-four.

Parnell's Irish Nationalist party has the reputation, a deserved one, as the most tightly disciplined partisan group in this House of Commons. Seventy-two Irish Nationalists (84 per cent) indicated an unqualified attachment to

---

[11] Elliot, *Life of Lord Goschen*, vol. 2, pp. 280–2.

[12] *Folkstone News*, 31 Oct. 1885, quoted in Rodden, *Anatomy of the 1886 Schism in the British Liberal Party*, p. 674.

[13] Grosvenor to Gladstone, 7 and 9 Dec. 1885, BL Add. MS 44316, ff. 143, 139ᵛ, 140.

[14] Pelling, *The Social Geography of British Elections, 1885–1910*, pp. 79–80.

[15] Hansard, 306: 1244.

their party. Yet ten Parnellites called themselves Liberals, and for these it was necessary to adopt additional criteria to establish their political affiliation. I classed these Members as Irish Nationalists if, in their biographies in Dod, they pledged themselves to Home Rule, if they sat for Irish constituencies, and if they are designated as Nationalists in the constituency returns published in Dod. Even these additional taxonomic criteria failed to solve all problems. Thomas Power O'Conner sat for an English constituency, the Scotland division of Liverpool. This constituency was unique because it was the only one in England in which the Irish–Catholic voters constituted a numerical majority.[16] Captain William O'Shea's case is complicated by Parnell's affair with his wife, Mrs O'Shea's political intrigues, and O'Shea's career as a political maverick. In the fall of 1885 Mrs O'Shea believed her husband's old seat in County Clare was threatened by a plot hatched by Davitt, Healy, and O'Brien. The O'Sheas entered into a complex conspiracy of their own, with Lord Richard Grosvenor and Gladstone, to gain the Mid Armagh seat, O'Shea running as a Liberal. These connivances made Grosvenor restive. He wrote to Gladstone, 'I'm very much afraid that they have made a fearful mess, as they always do with anything of this kind in Ireland.'[17] In the event, O'Shea stood as a Liberal for the Exchange division of Liverpool in the election of 1885. On his defeat there, Parnell allowed him to stand for Galway City without taking the Home Rule pledge expected of all Irish Nationalist Members. O'Shea was returned for Galway, as a Nationalist, on 11 February 1886. Nearly on the eve of the Home Rule division in the House of Commons, and under threat of assassination if he opposed Home Rule, O'Shea wrote to *The Times* saying that he would not vote against the Bill.[18] He abstained in only the most recent of several bizarre episodes which would mark his life and career. Because he held the Galway seat as a Nationalist, O'Shea is counted as a Nationalist here.

[16] Pelling, *The Social Geography of British Elections*, p. 249.

[17] Katherine O'Shea to Grosvenor, 23 Oct., Gladstone to Grosvenor, 24 Oct., William O'Shea to Grosvenor, 25 Oct., Grosvenor to Gladstone, 26 Oct., Grosvenor to Gladstone, Tuesday (n.d.), Gladstone to Grosvenor, 27 Oct., Grosvenor to Gladstone, 28 Oct. 1885, BL Add. MS 44316, ff. 63–7, 69, 70–1, 72–3, 74–74ᵛ, 75–6, 77–8, 79–80.

[18] O'Shea to Chamberlain, 16 May 1886, Chamberlain Papers JC8/8/1/71.

The Construction of Dimensions and the Classification of Members According to Their Positions on Them

The Division Lists

The official division lists of the House of Commons in 1886 are located in the library of the Institute for Historical Research. These lists contain the votes of MPs, in so far as they voted, on 143 legislative items. These include measures on Ireland and Irish government, social and political reform, the Crofters Bill, a motion to extend the parliamentary franchise to women, a motion to abolish capital punishment, disestablishment Motions for Wales and Scotland, and many more. The number of Members participating in these divisions varies. The largest was on the second reading of the Government of Ireland Bill (8 June) in which 655 MPs voted, and the smallest was on the Law of Evidence Amendment Bill (18 June) in which eighty-one Members participated. The average for this House of Commons was 255. Eight of the divisions (6 per cent) consisted of less than 100 votes. One hundred and twenty-five divisions (88 per cent) consisted of more than 100 votes, but less than 400. Ten divisions (7 per cent) consisted of upwards of 400 votes.

For this study all 143 divisions of this House of Commons were coded, recorded on punch-cards, eventually transferred to computer tape, and tabulated. In so doing it has been possible to avoid a common practice in investigations of this kind, namely sampling. To be sure, at certain points the use of sampling procedures might have been more economical. For example, twenty-nine divisions in which less than 150 MPs participated might have been excluded on the ground that they are too small to provide meaningful information. Further, several of the divisions of this House of Commons were on Bills of Supply. Generally, it might be argued, Bills of Supply were housekeeping questions, matters devoid of legislative content, and might for this reason suffer exclusion. As it happens, and as Chapter 2 shows, the debates on the supply estimates raised a number of highly significant and interesting political questions. These divisions were far from trivial. Finally, thirty-four items (23 per cent) were divisions on the Crofters Bill, and some of these might have been regarded as redundant, adding little to what might be learned from these data.

On the whole, however, there are some general reasons for tabulating all of the divisions. In the first place, as even the preliminary description of the division lists above indicates, absenteeism in the House of Commons raises problems both for the identification of subsets of issues and for the identification of partisan alliances. While annoying, absences are not an overwhelming problem. It is not, after all, a matter of missing evidence, which is perhaps the most serious barrier to historical research. The voting lists, even with the imperfections, constitute one of the most complete historical records one can expect to find. Containing, as they do, detailed statements about policy from the highest to the lowest in the political élite, the most important thing to emphasize is their value, not their defects. By using them it becomes possible to say as much as can ever be said about the positions taken by Members of House of Commons. Moreover, by using contrived items and rounding procedures, which I shall shortly describe, it is possible to overcome, to a very considerable extent, the difficulties imposed by absences. It seems wisest to use all of the available data, even when it has some limitations.

Secondly, all of the divisions are used for this study because, in addition to constructing scales along content lines, it is the intention of the project to construct scales on an empirical basis. This is a departure from the procedures used by Louis Guttman in his pioneering work. Guttman began by identifying the content variable underlying a dimension. By definition, for him, a dimension has two properties: it consisted in items having a common content, and it fitted a scale pattern. The universe of content, therefore, was defined not by the dimension but by the investigator. One reason, perhaps, for Guttman's emphasis on identifying a preliminary content universe is that he was less interested in defining issue subsets than he was in classifying respondents. Of course, Guttman's approach is attractive for many reasons. It would seem most efficient and economical for research to be guided by preliminary hypotheses, preliminary judgements about the organization of the evidence. These, then, may be tested by the facts at hand.

On the other hand, a more empirical approach, in this case at least, has much to recommend it. Whatever may be the preliminary identification of the content of a dimension, an examination of voting responses will suggest ways in which that identification should be modified. It is rare that preliminary research judgements can stand the test of evidence without adjustment. There is, as Thomas Kuhn has pointed out, a reciprocal relationship between theory and empiricism. Problems of paradigm articulation in normal research are simultaneously theoretical and experimental, for by matching theories with data a paradigm identifies what the significant facts are.[1] In this way, paradigms are fact-gathering apparatuses, guiding the collection of evidence at the same moment that they are developing theories. While advocating no strict Baconianism, a more empirical approach seems justified for this study. Historians have studied the politics of the 1880s in good detail, but other work remains to be done. Biographical studies of leading politicians have indicated much about their role in the parliamentary scheme of things, and work on the Irish question has done much to indicate its importance in the political life of the age. However, the study of major figures has not revealed the relationship between the Irish question and the other issues with which the House of Commons grappled.

---

[1] Thomas S. Kuhn, *The Structure of Scientific Revolutions* (Chicago: 1964), p. 33.

Consequently, I cast my net wider in this study by using all the items on which this House of Commons divided to explore wider patterns of political behaviour.

The Adjustment of Polarities

Before divisions of the House of Commons can be coded and recorded, it is necessary to make some preliminary classification to determine which position, the aye or nay, constituted the vote for, and which constituted the vote against, the issue or question contained in the motion. Procedural and substantive criteria can be used to make this assessment. For example, the division on the Parliamentary Franchise (Extension to Women) Bill on 18 February was taken on Sir Henry James's Motion to adjourn the debate. In this case the nays are recorded as positive responses to the issue and the ayes are recorded as negative because a vote for adjournment was a vote against the principle of the Bill. Similarly, Sir Joseph Pease's Motion 'That the Chairman do report Progress, and ask leave to sit again' during the debate on the Coal Mines Bill on 15 March was a Motion to postpone further action on the measure. In this case a positive vote opposed, and a negative vote favoured, the Coal Mines Bill. Substantive matters also bear strongly on decisions of this sort. The divisions on Dillwyn's Motion on the Church of England in Wales posed a choice between a radical and a moderate position. Dillwyn had moved that the continuation of the Church of England in Wales 'is an anomaly and an injustice which ought no longer to exist'. To this Albert Grey proposed an Amendment that 'this House is of opinion that the time has arrived for introducing, without delay, into its organization such reforms as will enable it to adapt itself more efficiently to the religious needs and wishes of the Welsh people'. The question proposed to the House was 'That the words proposed to be left out stand part of the Question'. An aye vote, therefore, was a vote for the more radical position and a nay vote favoured the more moderate proposal of Grey. In this case it was unnecessary to transpose polarities.

Adjusting polarities for the thirty-four divisions on the Crofters Bill presents a similar problem. The Bill was a Government measure extending land reform to the crofters of Scotland. During the progress of the Bill through the committee stage, Scottish members and English radicals proposed extending Amendments having the consequence of broadening and increasing the Bill's scope. These Amendments were, almost without exception, opposed by the Government and the Conservatives. Consequently, votes for the Amendments were recorded as positive responses and votes against the Amendments were recorded as negative. Additionally, a few Amendments were offered by Conservatives, limiting the nature of the Bill. In these cases votes for the Amendment were recorded as negative, since their purpose was directed toward a restriction of the Bill, and votes against these Amendments were recorded as positive. I retained the nineteenth-century understanding of these policies in adjusting the polarities on legislation for the local control and regulation of the liquor traffic, and positive votes stand as the more 'liberal' response.

Recording the Votes of Members

The data for this House of Commons are not altogether unambiguous in the identification of Members. Ernest William Beckett and William Beckett are alternatively referred to as Ernest William Denison and William Beckett Denison in different editions of Dod's *Parliamentary Companion*. Furthermore, there are various irregular listings of MPs in the division lists themselves. For example, Colonel Francis Charles Hughes-Hallett is listed as Colonel Hallett in the early division lists for the session. These lists contain also votes for John William Ellison Macartney and William Grey Ellison Macartney — never, however, in the same list. (Early lists record the votes of J. W. E. Macartney and later lists record those of W. G. E. Macartney.) Dod's *Parliamentary Companion* lists only W. G. E. Macartney (Conservative: Antrim), but indicates that he was the son of John William Ellison Macartney 'who was M.P. for Tyrone from 1874 to 1885'. Hansard lists only J. W. E. Macartney in its index for 1886, but indicates that he sat for Antrim. Hansard's return of Members for this session lists only W. G. E. Macartney, sitting for Antrim, but no J. W. E. Macartney sitting for Tyrone or anywhere else. Finally, F. H. McCalmont's *Parliamentary Poll Book of all Elections, 1832–1910* (London: 1910) lists only W. G. E. Macartney as sitting in 1886. Evidently, W. G. E. Macartney was the son of J. W. E. Macartney and all of the Macartney votes in 1886 are those of the former.

There are four instances in which the official division lists record a Member voting on both sides of a question. On Jesse Collings's 'three acres and a cow' Amendment, George Dixon is listed as voting both in the ayes and in the nays. Dixon did not speak in the debate on this Amendment, and it is not therefore possible to make an independent judgement of his position. However, his position is recorded with the ayes because of his advanced liberal political stance and his association with Chamberlain, Collings, and the Birmingham radicals. In a division on an Amendment to the Crofters Bill (Division 85), Lewis McIver is recorded with both the ayes and the nays. McIver did not speak in the debates on this occasion, but he opposed four of the six preceding Amendments to the Crofters Bill. (In one division he did not vote, and in a sixth he favoured the Amendment (Division 79).) Because of McIver's extensive opposition to extending amendments to the Crofters Bill, his vote is recorded in the negative here. E. A. Leatham is listed on both sides of Division 116, which was taken on the Registration of Voters (Ireland) Bill. His vote is recorded in the affirmative here because he voted in the affirmative in the immediately preceding division, which was taken on the same Bill. H. R. Farquharson is listed as present in both division lobbies on Healy's Amendment to the Parliamentary Elections (Returning Officers) Act (1875) Bill (Division 127). Since there were no additional divisions taken on this issue I recorded Farquharson with the nays, and this only because of his Conservative partisan affiliation. In addition, there are a few cases in which the tellers in divisions were difficult to identify. 'Dr. Hunter' is listed as a teller for Division 117. Is this William A. Hunter, who held an LLD, or Sir W. G. Hunter, who was an MD? This vote is recorded for W. A. Hunter because he is listed in Dod's constituency returns as Dr Hunter. 'Mr. Stevenson' is listed as a teller for Division 122. Is this F. S. Stevenson or J. C. Stevenson? This vote is recorded for J. C. Stevenson because the division was taken on an Amendment proposed by James Stevenson. In one case the records of the House of Commons show a correction for the division lists. In Division 95, H. J. Wilson's name was added to the list. Of course, this correction is accounted for in the coding of this division. Finally, to extract the greatest amount of data from these materials, the votes of both pairs of tellers are included in the tabulations. Because of these various corrections, the voting totals in some divisions differ here from those published in Hansard and in the official voting lists.

The Derivation of Dimensions

Dimensional research operationalizes the variable called 'liberal–conservative' and organizes the evidence of legislative voting in such a manner as to measure it.[2] That is to say, at one and the same time it ranks legislative items and the votes of legislators on liberal–conservative continua. Once the voting data are judged to be free of coding and punching errors they are processed, using a computer program, to produce fourfold comparisons in which each division in 1886 is compared with every other division. Each fourfold table, therefore contains the following information: (*a*) the number of Members voting in the affirmative in both divisions being compared; (*b*) the number of Members voting in the affirmative in the first division but who voted in the negative in the second; (*c*) the number of Members voting in the negative in the first division but in the affirmative in the second; and (*d*) the number of Members voting in the negative in both divisions. With voting information organized in this manner it is possible to begin building scales. And one begins by finding two divisions which stand in a scale relationship with each other. If the divisions are arranged in order from the most radical to the most conservative, in descending P − order (the divisions with the greatest proportion of negative votes first), a scale relationship may be said to exist if in the pairwise cross-tabulation the *b* cell—the cell containing the number of positive votes in the first division and negative votes in the second—is empty. This cell will be empty in a scale relationship because no Member will have voted in the negative on a less liberal item if he has voted in the positive on a more liberal item.

Since in practice few divisions stand in a perfect scale relationship with each other in the sense that the *b* cell in the fourfold cross-tabulations is absolutely empty, means have been found to measure these error responses and to establish criteria to judge tolerable levels for such responses in scale relationships. One procedure requires that the proportion of responses in the *b* cell should not exceed 10 per cent, squaring with the convention

---

[2] Lee F. Anderson, Meredith W. Watts, Jr., and Allen R. Wilcox, *Legislative Roll-Call Analysis* (Evanston, Ill.: 1966) pp. 89–121; Duncan MacRae, Jr., *Issues and Parties in Legislative Voting: Methods of Statistical Analysis* (New York, Evanston, and London: 1970), pp. 1–90.

established by Guttman that the reproducibility of a scale should be at least .90. However, this criterion is not completely satisfactory when comparing items which stand at opposite ends of the scale, items with extreme $P-$ values. An additional criterion, therefore, is necessary: that for a scale relationship, cell entries a and d must each be at least twice b. A modification of these procedures, used by Aydelotte and MacRae, and by me here, is the use of a coefficient developed by G. Udny Yule which satisfies all the conditions for scale relationships.[3]

This coefficient, given by the formula $Q = ad - bc / ad + bc$, attains the value of $+1.0$ when the scale relationship is perfect, that is, when there are no responses in the b cell. As the fourfold comparison departs from a perfect scale relationship, as the error responses in the b cell increase, the frequencies in the error cell are measured by the product bc in relation to the product ad. As the proportion of error responses increases, the Q value declines. Using Q as a searching statistic, set at a predetermined minimum value, it is possible to scan many fourfold comparisons quickly and determine which items fit a common dimension and which fail. What constitutes an acceptable minimum Q value, of course, is open to some debate. Professor MacRae suggests a minimum threshold of .80, and Aydelotte in his work on the 1840s has used a minimum value of .65. In some preliminary work on the House of Commons in 1886 I also used .65,[4] but here I have allowed my practice to vary, and have constructed scales at different Q thresholds. In fact, one of my objectives was to see how many items could be contained in a scale if the Q threshold is increased. Therefore, I began by using a minimum Q of .65, but then increased it. For the major parliamentary voting dimension for the House of Commons in 1886 I used a minimum Q of .80. Indeed, from time to time I was interested to see what might be obtained at higher levels and used .90.

Using Yule's Q, one begins by seeking two divisions which hold a scale relationship, and then one seeks a third which satisfies these conditions with the previous two, and then a fourth, and a fifth, until the population of items is exhausted. When a division fails to fit a scale relationship with one or more items which have been fitted into a scale, it is set aside, perhaps to be fitted in a separate scale with other issues failing to fit the scale being built. In this way scaling methods distinguish between subsets of legislative issues. Each subset, described by a separate cumulative scale, reveals the existence of a distinct attitude dimension. In this way the votes of legislators are used to define various left–right, liberal–conservative continua.

For this study, and using these methods, I constructed eight scales. Six consist of items having a common policy content.

(1) *Ecclesiastical policy.* Six items, five of which hold a scale relationship with a minimum Q threshold of .92, and six at .76. See Table 2.1.

---

[3] MacRae, *Issues and Parties in Legislative Voting*, p. 49.
[4] Lubenow, 'Ireland, the Great Depression, and the Railway Rates'.

(2) *Land policy.* If $Q = .65$, forty items concerning land policy fit a common dimension, and this remains unchanged if Q is elevated to .70. Thirty-seven items are associated at $Q = .80$, thirty-two at $Q = .90$, and sixteen at $Q = .95$. See Table 2.2 for some of the items fitting this dimension.

(3) *Imperial–foreign–military policy.* This dimension contains ten items, all of which hold a relationship when $Q = .78$. See Table 2.3.

(4) *Irish policy.* Twenty-three items, which fit a common dimension at $Q = .67$. See Table 2.4 for a description of voting on some of them.

(5) *Political reform.* Eighteen items scale together with minimum Q values of .80. The voting matrix for some of these is found in Table 2.5.

(6) *Social reform.* Fifteen items dealing with social policy fit together with common Q values in excess of .65, thirteen with Q values exceeding .70, five at $Q = .80$, and four at $Q = .90$. Table 2.6 indicates the voting relationships on this kind of question.

Additionally, and most importanatly, I sought to construct dimensions across content lines (see Table 2.7). This proved highly successful, and it was possible to establish a dimension consisting of eighty-one items with Q values exceeding .80. This, the major dimension of parliamentary voting, contains all the major issues of the age. It constituted the central ground of political action in 1886 — for which reason the analysis of its content, and the voting responses of MPs on it, provides evidence of the greatest importance to this project.

As will be observed, the cardinal value of scaling research lies in its empirical character. It provides the means for collecting a large volume of data, and, by putting these in a comparable framework, allows for a comprehensive analysis. It is not so much a matter of creating dimensions as it is one of testing for their existence. This has the intellectual satisfaction of subjecting all the votes of Members, in so far as they voted, to the same criteria and to the same standards of judgement. Dimensional research does not remove the necessity of historical interpretation, for, indeed as I have indicated, interpretations are imposed at every point in the investigation. And the results, the tabular descriptions of the evidence, do not explain themselves any more than any body of evidence explains itself. What it does, however, is to place the discussion of political issues, and politicians' responses to those issues, on a solid footing. Historians might not yet agree about the meaning of these phenomena, but at least they may have a clearer view as to the grounds of their disagreement. Moreover, the discussion of political behaviour may proceed on the basis of all the evidence available.

The Classification of Members on Voting Dimensions

I assigned Members to scale positions on the foreign policy, ecclesiastical policy, and land policy dimensions, as well as on the major dimension of parliamentary voting. Since the problem of absences is a grave one in legislatures, it is unrealistic to expect Members to have voted on every item in a scale. Therefore, adopting a convention in scaling research, I grouped items on the dimensions which fitted approximately the same points in the descending order of negative votes (that is to say, at the same P – points) to form aggregate or contrived items.[5] In this way, if a Member did not vote on one item at a certain point on the dimension he could have voted on others, and these provide the evidence for assigning him to a dimensional position. Additionally, to capture more Members into these classifications who might have been lost by reason of absence, I adopted standard rounding procedures for locating MPs on the various scales.[6] The following may serve as an example of the way this is done. For a scale of six contrived items, seven scale positions are possible (see table below). A pattern of

Dimensional positions	Contrived items (arranged in descending P – order)					
	1	2	3	4	5	6
1.	–	–	–	–	–	–
2.	–	–	–	–	–	+
3.	–	–	–	–	+	+
4.	–	–	–	+	+	+
5.	–	–	+	+	+	+
6.	–	+	+	+	+	+
7.	+	+	+	+	+	+
9.	Error response (e.g. + + – – + +)					
0.	Unclassifiable (e.g. 0000 – +)					

responses consisting of the following votes: – – – + + + unambiguously fits scale position 4, – – – – – – unambiguously fits scale position 1, and + + + + + + unambiguously fits scale position 7. Therefore, these cases require no rounding. However, patterns such as – – – 0 + + might fit either scale position 3 or 4, and – – – 00 + + might fit either scale position 4 or 5. Initially they would be given the raw scores of 35 or 45. Rounding takes place in the direction of the median. If the median position is position 4, the rounded scores for both Members would be scale position 4. In no case have I rounded the scores of Members across contrived items extending more than half the length of the scale. There is an additional pattern of response which these procedures do not accommodate, a pattern in which there is a potential, though not an actual, error response: for example, – – + 0 + +. I have sought to see if Members such as this might be saved by allowing rounding across a contrived item which contains a potential error response. In this case the Member would have the raw score of 35 and a rounded scale classification of 4. In the assignment of Members to positions on the scales, therefore, I have used three schemes: (1) one which allows for the classification of those cases which fit unambiguously, that is to say without

[5] Anderson, Watts, and Wilcox, *Legislative Roll-Call Analysis*, p. 106; MacRae, *Issues and Parties in Legislative Voting*, pp. 67–8.
[6] W. O. Aydelotte, 'British House of Commons, 1841–1847' (Iowa City: 1970), pp. 13–14.

any rounding whatever; (2) one which uses rounding procedures and allows the classification of cases in which there is a potential error response; and (3) a more astringent rounding scheme which does not admit potential error responses into the classification. Shortly I shall compare each of the schemes and consider which of them proves the most appropriate for this study.

The Major Dimension of Parliamentary Voting

With a minimum Q threshold of .80, eighty-one items fit the dimension. The items at the top of the scale, those dividing Liberals, were ranked according to their Liberal P − values (the proportion of Liberals voting in the negative); those toward the middle, on which straight-party voting occurred, were ranked according to their P − values calculated for the whole House; items at the bottom of the scale, those dividing Conservatives, were ranked according to their Conservative P − values. In this organization of the data there are seven contrived items: five consisting of items dividing Liberals, one consisting of straight-party votes, and one consisting of items dividing Conservatives. Eight scale positions, therefore, are possible. The median position is scale position 5, and roundings are made in that direction. Using the various classification schemes I have adopted for this study, the following assignments shown below can be made.

Unambiguous classifications:

Scale position	8	7	6	5	4	3	2	1	No.	
Members	93	17	20	24	14	4	25	70	267	(39%)

	Error responses	Unclassifiable	No.	
Members	21	392	413	(61%)

Rounded classifications
(including possible error responses):

Scale position	8	7	6	5	4	3	2	1	No.	
Members	93	20	23	41	23	4	128	70	402	(59%)

	Error responses	Unclassifiable	No.	
Members	21	257	278	(41%)

Rounded classifications
(excluding possible error responses):

Scale position	8	7	6	5	4	3	2	1	No.	
Members	92	21	22	37	19	4	123	70	388	(57%)

	Error responses	Unclassifiable	No.	
Members	35	257	292	(43%)

That such low proportions of the House can be classified is not a very happy matter. The reason, however, is clear if the dimension is considered a little. There are only two divisions in the last contrived item, the item dividing Conservatives and on which the Liberals and the Irish Nationalists were unified. This means that it was more difficult, given the problem of absences, to classify some Members on it. For the Conservatives, this was no serious matter, because if they failed to vote in both of these divisions they could still be classified on the scale using rounding procedures. A Member voting − − − − − − 0 could be classified 12 and rounded to scale position 2. However, this condition cuts particularly hard against the Liberals who, even if they could be classified on all other contrived items, but if they failed to vote in one of these two divisions, could not be classified through rounding procedures. One cannot round responses such as + + + + + + 0 or − − + + + + 0 without violating the principle that rounding should not occur across more than half the scale. These Members, therefore, are excluded from the analysis.

However, in an effort to save these data I used a second system of classification for the major voting dimension. In contrast to the former system with eight scale positions (called system A), this is system B. In it I assimilated the last contrived item in the scale—the item containing divisions on which the Conservatives alone were split—into the contrived item immediately above it—the item containing straight-party votes. This seems a reasonable course of action, since they were low-intensity issues; relatively few MPs participated in them. Yet, proportionately, they enjoyed widespread support in the House even among Conservatives; the P − values are very low. It is likely that Liberals, who voted positively on items toward the top of the scale, would have voted positively on these as well, if they had voted. Because of the wide support for these questions in the House, Liberals could enjoy the luxury of abstention knowing that the questions were certain to pass. The principal disadvantage of this system is that it obscures differences among Conservatives. However, since the Conservatives were divided on but two divisions in this scale, there are not all that many differences to obscure. The principal advantage of this system is that it allows the classification of a considerable number of Liberals. Using system A, and using the most generous rounding procedures, forty-one Members can be assigned to the median scale position, 136 can be assigned to positions to the left, and 225 can be assigned to positions to the right. Using system B, and using the most generous rounding procedures, eighty-six Members can be assigned to the median scale position, 205 can be assigned to positions to the left, and 248 can be assigned to positions on the right. The points on the scale on which the chief gains are made, therefore, are the median and the left. These gains seem worthwhile. Of course, using both systems, it is possible to obtain the advantages of both ways of doing things.

Using system B there are six contrived items and, consequently, seven scale positions. The median is position 4, and rounding takes place in that direction. Using system B the classifications shown below are possible.

Unambiguous classifications:

Scale position	7	6	5	4	3	2	1	No.	
Members	117	31	35	49	18	11	191	452	(66%)

	Error responses	Unclassifiable	No.	
Members	20	208	228	(34%)

Rounded classifications
(including possible error responses):

Scale position	7	6	5	4	3	2	1	No.	
Members	117	40	48	86	41	16	191	539	(79%)

	Error responses	Unclassifiable	No.	
Members	20	121	141	(21%)

Rounded classifications
(excluding possible error responses):

Scale position	7	6	5	4	3	2	1	No.	
Members	117	40	41	71	32	11	191	503	(74%)

	Error responses	Unclassifiable	No.	
Members	56	121	177	(26%)

In classifying Members on the major dimension of parliamentary voting, therefore, I used a scheme which allowed scale assignments if Members fitted the scale unambiguously, and two rounding schemes. Additionally, I used two different systems for organizing the contrived items. It may be useful, therefore, if some assessment is made of the reliability and justifiability of these schemes and systems. Such assessment provides a basis for choosing amongst them and to determine which identifies an organization of the evidence which proves most valuable for an analysis of political behaviour. In this assessment I use two criteria. The best system and scheme is that (1) which allows for the largest proportion of Members to be classified; and (2) on which the distribution on various attributes of Members most closely resembles the distribution of those attributes in the House as a whole. To give effect to this latter criterion I constructed a schedule of deviation scores for several political, social, and constituency attributes showing the degree to which MPs possessing each were either over-represented or under-represented on the scale. This schedule took the representativeness index for each attribute (given by the formula $R = \%$ of MPs on the scale having the attribute/% of the whole House having the attribute). I then calculated the deviations either $+$ or $-$ $(D = R - 1)$, indicating the extent to which MPs possessing each attribute were either over- or under-represented in the various classifications of Members on the dimension. I took a deviation score threshold of either $+.10$ or $-.10$ as the maximum value tolerable in making this test. For example, in this House of Commons 307 (45.1 per cent) landed gentlemen sat. On the great dimension of parliamentary voting, using contrived items organized in the form of system B, and using the most generous rounding procedures, 227 landed gentlemen (42.1 per cent) can be assigned scale positions. Therefore, R = 42.1/45.1, or .93. Consequently, D = .93 − 1, or − .07. All this is to say is that landed gentlemen were slightly under-represented on this scale by a value of − .07.

Schedule of Deviations from Representativeness of Various Political, Social, and Constituency Attributes on the Several Systems for Classifying Members on the Major Dimension of Parliamentary Voting

Classification system* % of House classified	ARS 39	ARO 59	ARE 57	BRS 66	BRO 79	BRE 74
Political attributes:						
Conservatives	− .06	+ .25	+ .29	+ .11	− .06	0
Liberals	− .21	− .28	− .32	− .18	− .01	− .07
Irish Nationalists	+ .96	+ .31	+ .36	+ .36	+ .15	+ .23
Social attributes:						
Landed class	− .19	+ .01	+ .01	− .10	− .07	− .08
Professions	+ .02	+ .04	+ .04	+ .04	+ .01	+ .02
Business men	− .03	− .09	− .08	− .09	− .03	− .06
Working class	− .15	− .43	− .43	− .10	+ .04	− .10
Family large landowners	− .26	− .04	− .04	− .13	− .12	− .12
Age attributes:						
20–40	+ .26	+ .13	+ .11	+ .07	+ .01	+ .02
41–60	− .14	− .02	− .02	− .05	− .02	− .03
60 +	− .39	− .38	− .37	− .18	− .17	− .16
Constituency attributes:						
County seats	+ .01	+ .01	− .01	− .01	0	+ .01
Borough seats	− .05	− .02	− .02	− .02	− .02	− .03
University seats	+ .69	+ .46	+ .53	+ .30	+ .23	+ .15
Electorate size attributes:						
0–4,999	− .35	− .16	− .13	− .17	− .14	− .13
5,000–7,499	+ .34	+ .16	+ .16	+ .12	+ .06	+ .07
7,500–8,999	− .01	− .01	0	+ .03	− .04	+ .02
9,000 +	− .12	− .05	− .06	− .05	− .03	− .03
Security of seats attributes:						
Safe seats	+ .03	− .01	− .01	0	+ .02	+ .01
Uncontested seats	+ .30	− .04	+ .01	+ .10	+ .03	+ .01
Vulnerable seats	− .11	+ .01	0	− .04	− .06	− .04
Region of constituency:						
London	− .19	+ .11	+ .11	+ .13	+ .05	+ .06
S. E. England	− .19	+ .18	+ .21	+ .04	− .13	− .07

Classification system*	ARS	ARO	ARE	BRS	BRO	BRE
% of House classified	39	59	57	66	79	74

Region of constituency cont.

	ARS	ARO	ARE	BRS	BRO	BRE
Wessex	− .31	− .08	− .12	− .16	− .16	− .20
Devon–Cornwall	− .25	+ .27	+ .24	− .04	+ .06	+ .13
Bristol	− .57	− .32	− .44	− .41	− .16	− .29
Central England	− .24	− .30	− .27	− .24	− .21	− .15
East Anglia	− .65	− .28	− .38	− .30	− .08	− .18
East Midlands	− .45	− .22	− .20	− .11	− .03	− .09
West Midlands	− .47	− .38	− .34	− .23	− .18	− .15
Peak–Don	− .39	− .23	− .17	− .17	− .12	− .17
Lancastria	− .03	+ .05	+ .06	− .03	− .06	− .09
Yorkshire	+ .11	− .02	− .02	− .02	+ .01	+ .01
Northern England	− .03	− .15	− .23	− .15	+ .02	− .05
Wales	− .14	− .34	− .30	− .02	+ .07	− .11
Scotland	0	− .03	− .07	− .03	+ .08	0
Ulster	+ .72	+ .24	+ .28	+ .22	+ .02	+ .10
Southern Ireland	+ .94	+ .31	+ .41	+ .34	+ .15	+ .23
University	+ .69	+ .46	+ .53	+ .30	+ .23	+ .15

Schedule of Deviations from Representativeness: Summary (shows average deviation for each group of attributes)

Classification system*	ARS	ARO	ARE	BRS	BRO	BRE
% of House classified	39	59	57	66	79	74
Political characteristics	.41	.28	.32	.21	.07	.10
Social characteristics	.13	.12	.04	.09	.05	.07
Age	.26	.17	.16	.10	.06	.07
Constituency type	.25	.16	.18	.11	.08	.06
Constituency size	.20	.09	.08	.09	.06	.06
Security of seats	.14	.02	.006	.04	.03	.02
Region of constituency	.35	.22	.24	.16	.10	.12
AVERAGE DEVIATION FOR ALL ATTRIBUTES	.24	.15	.14	.13	.06	.07
% of deviations which attain or exceed .10	75	53	50	56	31	44

*The following notations are used for these classification systems: ARS: Members who fit System A of the major voting dimension unambiguously; ARO: Members who fit System A of the major voting dimension but with roundings which include potential error responses; ARE: Members who fit System A of the major voting dimension but with roundings which exclude potential error responses; BRS: Members who fit System B of the major voting dimension unambiguously; BRO: Members who fit System B of the major voting dimension with roundings which include potential error responses; and BRE: Members which fit System B of the major voting dimension but with roundings which exclude potential error responses.

Additional notes: Landed gentlemen in this table are those MPs with connections to the landed classes through paternal and maternal descent as well as through marriage, though Members with foreign titles are not included. Large landowning families are those who held land in excess of 3,000 acres. A safe parliamentary seat is one in which the electors returned their Member by a majority which exceeded ten per cent of the total poll. A vulnerable seat is one in which the Member was not returned with a majority attaining or exceeding 10 per cent of the total poll.

As this deviation schedule, and especially the summary figures, shows, the organization of contrived items according to system B and the most generous rounding procedures (those which allow for the inclusion of potential error responses) provides the best rendering of the great dimension of parliamentary voting in the sense that it is the most representative. It has the defect of over-representing the Irish Nationalists, Members holding university seats, and Members for southern Ireland, and under-representing Members over sixty years of age, MPs sitting for the smallest constituencies, and Members whose constituencies were located in south-eastern England, Wessex, the Bristol district, central England, the West Midlands, and the Peak–Don regions. On the other hand, the deviation scores for all other attributes fall beneath a deviation threshold of .10. Indeed, the percentage of deviations attaining or exceeding .10 was the least (31 per cent), for this organization of the evidence. The average deviation for all attributes was also the least (.06), and these procedures allow for the classification of the largest proportion of Members (79 per cent).

Foreign Policy Dimension

With a minimum Q threshold of .80, nine items fit this dimension. (I did not use the division on Irish Home Rule in making these classifications.) On it the Conservatives were united consistently, and there were no straight-party votes. Therefore, I ranked the items in descending order according to their Liberal P − values (the proportion of Liberals voting in the negative) and grouped them into four contrived items. Five classifications, therefore, are possible. The median scale position is position 2, and rounding takes place in that direction. Members can be fitted on this dimension, using the various schemes I have described, in the manner shown below.

Unambiguous classifications:

Scale position	5	4	3	2	1	No.	
Members	32	7	6	7	66	118	(17%)

	Error responses	Unclassifiable	No.	
Members	16	546	562	(83%)

Rounded classifications
(including possible error responses):

Scale position	5	4	3	2	1	No.	
Members	32	21	21	182	66	322	(47%)

	Error responses	Unclassifiable	No.	
Members	16	342	358	(53%)

Rounded classifications
(excluding possible error responses):

Scale position	5	4	3	2	1	No.	
Members	32	16	15	165	66	294	(43%)

	Error responses	Unclassifiable	No.	
Members	43	343	386	(57%)

Ecclesiastical policy dimension

At Q = .76, this scale consists of six items which are segregated into three contrived items: one containing items dividing Liberals; a second containing a straight-party vote; and a third containing items dividing Conservatives. The P – values for Liberals alone were used to rank the first set of items, and the P – values for Conservatives alone were used to rank the third. With three contrived items, four classifications are possible. The median is position 2. Members can be assigned positions on this dimension in the following ways:

Unambiguous classifications:

Scale position	4	3	2	1	No.	
Members	66	3	37	19	125	(18%)

	Error responses	Unclassifiable	No.	
Members	0	555	555	(82%)

Rounded classifications:

Scale position	4	3	2	1	No.	
Members	66	20	172	19	277	(41%)

	Error responses	Unclassifiable	No.	
Members	0	403	403	(59%)

Note: On this dimension I rounded across no potential error responses.

Land Policy Dimension

This dimension consists of forty items at Q = .65. I segregated them into four contrived items consisting of 16, 12, 4, and 8 items respectively. On land policy questions the Conservatives found themselves consistently united throughout. Only the Liberals were divided, except for eight items at the bottom of the dimension on which both parties were unified, and ranged themselves in opposition to each other in straight-party votes. Therefore, in ranking divisions on land policy I used the P – values for the Liberals alone for the first three contrived items, and the P – values for the whole House for the items which divided the House along party lines. The median is position 2, and rounding for classification purposes is achieved in that direction. Since there are four contrived items, five positions are possible, and Members can be assigned to the scale in the following manner:

Unambiguous classifications:

Scale position	5	4	3	2	1	No.	
Members	131	20	35	26	183	395	(58%)

	Error responses	Unclassifiable	No.	
Members	3	282	285	(42%)

Rounded classifications
(including possible error responses):

Scale position	5	4	3	2	1	No.	
Members	131	30	83	124	183	551	(81%)

	Error responses	Unclassifiable	No.	
Members	3	126	129	(19%)

Rounded classifications
(excluding possible error responses):

Scale position	5	4	3	2	1	No.	
Members	131	24	68	101	182	506	(74%)

	Error responses	Unclassifiable	No.	
Members	47	127	174	(26%)

*Schedule of Deviations from Representativeness
of Political Attributes only on the Various
Systems of Classifying Members on the Foreign
Policy, Land Policy, and Ecclesiastical Policy
Dimensions*

Foreign policy dimension:

Classification system*	RS	RO	RE
% of House classified	17%	47%	43%
Conservatives	− .22	− .03	+ .03
Liberals	+ .05	+ .09	+ .07
Irish Nationalists	+ .40	− .32	− .33
AVERAGE DEVIATION	.22	.14	.13

Land policy dimension:

% of House classified	58%	81%	74%
Conservatives	+ .22	− .03	− .04
Liberals	− .32	− .02	− .04
Irish Nationalists	+ .54	+ .11	+ .22
AVERAGE DEVIATION	.36	.05	.10

Ecclesiastical policy dimension:

Classification system*	RS	RO
% of House classified	18%	41%
Conservatives	+ .15	+ .73
Liberals	− .22	− .51
Irish Nationalists	+ .39	− .20
AVERAGE DEVIATION	.25	.48

*The following notations are used in the preceding schedule: RS refers to the MPs who can be fitted to the various scales unambiguously and without rounding; RO refers to those MPs who can be fitted to the scale, but by procedures which allow rounding across a potential error response; RE refers to the Members who can be fitted to the scales, but without allowance for rounding across potential error response. RO is the most generous rounding procedure; RE is the most stringent rounding procedure.

So far as the number of Members can be classified on them, the dimensions discovered for foreign and ecclesiastical policy are much inferior to the major dimension of parliamentary voting. Only 47 per cent of the House can be classified on the foreign policy scale, and only 41 per cent of the House can be classified on the ecclesiastical policy scale, and this using the most generous rounding procedures. Moreover, they are not very representative. On the ecclesiastical policy scale there is an average deviation from representativeness for political attributes of .48. The average deviation from representativeness on the foreign policy scale is better, .14, but not totally satisfactory. For the land policy dimension, however, the picture is very much better. More Members can be classified on it using the most generous rounding procedures (81 per cent) than on even the major parliamentary voting scale. Moreover, this scale is highly representative when rounding allows the admission of a few possible error responses; the average deviation from representativeness for political attributes is .05.

Social Class and the Study of
Parliamentary Behaviour

'A DIRE VRAI', Marc Bloch said, 'ce mot de classe est un des plus équivoques du vocabulaire historique.'[1] And so it proves to be. Nevertheless, since much of the analysis of nineteenth-century politics dwells on hypotheses concerning the relationship between the social and political orders, and since so much is cast in class terms, some treatment must be given to this complex and difficult subject. But social class remains one of the most controversial subjects in social history, and the social history of politics, and the great research on it over the past decades, at times threatens to cast generalization on to the rocks of impossibility. As Alfred Cobban observed no little time ago, 'the new facts are becoming increasingly recalcitrant and difficult to dragoon into compliance with the old categories.'[2] The central problems, as Cobban's remark makes clear, are two: conceptual and empirical. Conceptually the issue of social class is beset with problems of definition. Empirically it is beleaguered with taxonomic problems.

As a conceptual matter, definitions of social class have been fraught with vagueness and imprecision. For example, a gentleman has been defined as a man having the capacity 'to live idly and without manual labour'.[3] A contemporary of the House of Commons of 1886 defined the gentleman 'as one to whom discourtesy is a sin and falsehood a crime'.[4] Sir George Sitwell, who sat in this House of Commons, believed the development of a nation depended not upon geographical position, natural resources, or military strength, but 'upon the discussion of classes and their relation to each other and to the soil'.[5] Musings about class, such as these, do little to organize chaos. Class: is it wealth, is it status, is it consciousness? Is it a structure or category at all? On this Mr Edward Thompson, whom all must quote on this subject, takes the line of doubt, and in a famous passage defines class 'as something which in fact happens (and can be shown to have happened) in human relationships'.[6] Here are two signals of hope. One is

---

[1] Marc Bloch, *Les Caractères originaux de l'histoire rurale française* (Paris: 1931), p. 194. Quoted in Alfred Cobban, 'The Vocabulary of Social History', *Political Science Quarterly*, 71.1 (Mar. 1956), p. 6.
[2] Cobban, 'The Vocabulary of Social History', p. 6.
[3] Quoted in Peter Roebuck, *Yorkshire Baronets, 1640–1760: Families, Estates, and Fortunes* (Oxford: 1980), p. 1.
[4] [W.R.B.], 'The English Gentleman', *The National Review*, 7 (Apr. 1886), p. 261.
[5] Sir George Sitwell, Bt., 'The English Gentleman', *The Ancestor*, 1, p. 53; quoted in Cobban, 'The Vocabulary of Social History', p. 1.
[6] Edward P. Thompson, *The Making of the English Working Class* (London: 1963), p. 9.

in Thompson's parenthetical comment. Social class, this would seem to imply, is subject to verification. The other, a larger point: social class is a relationship. Thompson puts this rather more expansively. 'We cannot have love without lovers, nor deference without squires and labourers. And class happens when some men, as a result of common experiences (inherited or shared), feel and articulate the identity of their interests as between themselves and as against other men whose interests are different from (and usually opposed to) theirs.'[7]

Wealth, class, status, the way people live—these are all intertwined, and are all a matter of degree. Moreover, taken together, they involve not only the ways others feel about individuals and groups, but also the ways those individuals and groups feel about themselves. In his famous paper on the growth of class consciousness in early Victorian England, Asa Briggs attributes it to four events: the imposition of Pitt's income tax, the impact of the Napoleonic War, the struggle for parliamentary reform, and the Corn Laws controversy.[8] Each of these events, one cannot help but note, was political. Class consciousness arose out of the particular circumstances of political conflict. Between class conditions and action, as Giovanni Sartori has observed, there are intervening variables, the working and influence of institutions, which generate class feeling.[9] Chapter 4 above has much to say on this subject for parliamentary politics in 1886.

If the concept of class is subject to verification, as Edward Thompson implies it is and as we all must believe it to be, the empirical questions are taxonomic. Only those who have tried to sift their way through the evidence on the social backgrounds of historical foot-soldiers will appreciate the degree to which social classification is fraught. Even Sir Lewis Namier, who knew more about this than anyone, appreciated these problems. 'Classification', he said 'is much more difficult than those who have never tried their hand at it would suppose.'[10] Let one example from the membership of the House of Commons in 1886 illustrate these problems. Francis Bingham Mildmay, the youngest Member of the House, was the son of a banker and the great-grandson, through his mother, of the second Earl Grey. By a complicated coding of the data it is possible to save these phenomena, and retain them all, for purposes of retrieval; but the question of establishing his social position remains. It is not without interest or importance that Mildmay included in his potted biography in Dod's *Parliamentary Companion* his connection with the Grey earldom and his father's association with a prominent banking firm. However, he ascribed to himself no personal interest in banking or business. He lists his school, Eton, his college, Trinity College, Cambridge, and his clubs, White's, the Bachelors', and St James's, but that

---

[7] Ibid., p. 9.

[8] Asa Briggs, 'Middle Class Consciousness in English Politics, 1780–1846', *Past and Present*, Apr. 1956, pp. 67–8 and *passim*. See also Briggs, 'The Language of "Class" in Early Nineteenth Century England', *Essays in Labour History*, ed. Asa Briggs and John Saville (London: 1960), pp. 43–73.

[9] Giovanni Sartori, 'From the Sociology of Politics to Political Sociology', pp. 83–5.

[10] Namier, *England in the Age of the American Revolution*, pp. 220–1.

is all. He obviously did not consider himself a business man, nor even an individual with incidental business interests. Other sources, such as the *Financial Reform Almanack*, do not indicate a connection with the world of business for him either. Moreover, the Mildmay family is listed in the 1886 edition of Burke's *Landed Gentry*. Mildmay, we learn from Bateman's *Great Landowners*, was heir to estates in Kent with an annual rental of £3,563. Therefore, by the test of self-reference, what Mildmay and his family thought of him, and by the test of what others thought of him, Mildmay can be regarded as a landed gentleman in the House of Commons of 1886. The resolution of taxonomic mares' nests such as this, and others even more difficult, relies on the patient and detailed examination of comparable evidence and the strict application of uniform criteria.

For the late nineteenth century there is comparable evidence aplenty for the social background of Members of the House of Commons. Dod's *Parliamentary Companion*, Edward Walford's *Great County Families* (1886), the various editions of Burke's *Peerage and Baronetage*, (C.G.E.), *The Complete Peerage*, the editions of Burke's *Landed Gentry* for 1871, 1879, and 1886, the *Financial Reform Almanack*, the matriculation records of the public schools and universities, and the dozens, even hundreds (sometimes one fears thousands) of autobiographies and pious biographies for the period provide a wealth of evidence on the social origins of late Victorian politicians. To determine which of the 680 Members of the House of Commons belonged to the landed classes I used these materials, and those MPs belonging to families listed in Burke's *Peerage and Baronetage*, the *Complete Peerage*, or Burke's *Landed Gentry* are so considered for purposes of this study.

The Landed Classes in the House of Commons in 1886

Irish peers	1	(.1%)
Heirs of peers	27	(3.9%)
Younger sons of peers	34	(5.0%)
Descended from peers	9	(1.3%)
Related to peerage through mothers and wives	16	(1.8%)
Baronets	54	(7.9%)
Heirs of baronets	7	(1.0%)
Younger sons of baronets	13	(1.9%)
Descended from baronets	4	(.6%)
Related to baronetage through mothers and wives	10	(1.4%)
Landed gentry (heads of families)	78	(11.5%)
Heirs of landed gentry	7	(1.0%)
Younger sons of landed gentry	14	(2.1%)
Descended from landed gentry	7	(1.0%)
Related to landed gentry through mothers and wives	26	(3.8%)
Unrelated to the peerage–baronetage–landed gentry	373	(54.8%)

Summary of Landed Classes:

Peerage–baronetage–landed gentry (male line only)	255	(37.5%)
Peerage–baronetage–landed gentry (through the female line or marriage)	52	(7.6%)
Unrelated to the PBG	373	(54.8%)

With patience most genealogical puzzles can be unsnarled. Herbert T. Knatchbull-Hugesson and Stanley Leighton are both listed in Burke's *Landed Gentry*, though both were the sons of baronets. The Knatchbull-Hugesson baronetcy dates from 1641 and the Leighton baronetcy from 1692. William Cornwallis West is listed as landed gentry, but he is plainly descended from the De la Warre earldom. These are, perhaps, efforts to single out cadet lines which would ascend in their own right, rather than through the main branches of their families. Two members of this House of Commons held foreign titles: Baron Dimsdale and Baron Henry de Worms. They are not included into this reckoning of the England landed classes. On the other hand, Baron Ferdinand James de Rothschild is. Rothschild was the second son of a father, Baron Anselm de Rothschild of Frankfurt, who held a foreign title. This Member is counted with the English landed classes because he was so connected, through marriage to his cousin, Eveline, the daughter of the first Baron Rothschild. Herbert Gardner is not considered a member of the landed élite, despite the fact he became connected to the peerage by his marriage in 1890 and was raised to the peerage himself in 1895. Finally, there are some Members of the House of Commons in 1886 who, from evidence in Bateman's *Great Landowners* and the *Financial Reform Almanack*, had some of the obvious signs of social distinction, but who are not included in Burke's *Landed Gentry* or *Peerage and Baronetage*: George Cubitt had lands to the extent of 6,789 acres valued at £8,509 p.a. in Devon, Surrey, and Sussex; John Gibson owned 5,214 acres and was the brother of Baron Ashbourn; Francis Otter was the lord of a manor with a Church living. These are not included in this estimate of the landed classes in the House of Commons of 1886. When it is said and done, however, these exclusions do not amount to very much, and exceptions of this sort affect the outlines of the evidence in only trifling ways.

It is somewhat easier to distinguish, using these materials, those MPs who had connections with the professions. What one finds is an enlargement of the numbers of Members with professions, and, in addition, an extension of the professional world. There were men of the old professions there, of course: the military and the law. To these were added men of the new professions: engineering, publishing and journalism, the civil servants, academics. What sets these men off from the landed gentlemen was their specialized training, the authority of their expertise, in contrast to a gentle style of life consisting of amateur and part-time participation in public affairs. From the world of business they were separated by the fact that they were employed, they did not employ. Experts, the professionals, were the rising men, the new men, who would reshape public life by the introduction of professional values and standards into it.[11]

Professional Men in the House of Commons in 1886

All professional men	352	(51.8%)
Army officers	70	(10.3%)
Naval officers	10	(1.5%)
Lawyers	181	(26.6%)
Physicians	16	(2.4%)
Former clergy	3	(.4%)
Newspapermen	26	(3.8%)
Academics	32	(4.7%)
Diplomatic service	7	(1.0%)
Civil service	19	(2.8%)

The collection of information on the business interests of Members of the House of Commons has proved somewhat more formidable. On one hand I wished to assemble as much information as possible relating to the business interests of these men, and on the other hand I wanted to ascertain the limitations to their business activities.

Business Men in the House of Commons in 1886

All business interests	289	(42.5%)
Bankers	38	(5.6%)
Brewers	21	(3.0%)
Colliery owners	22	(3.0%)
Merchants	65	(9.6%)
Textile manufacturers	31	(4.6%)
Manufacturers of metal products	24	(3.5%)
Railway directors	75	(11.0%)
Shipping	21	(3.0%)

The summary figure for all business interests, however, seems too inclusive, for it fails to distinguish between business interests which were substantial and those on a much smaller scale. Furthermore, it fails to distinguish between those Members whose business activities took a considerable measure of their time and those Members whose business activities were very much more incidental. In order to code the data to reflect these distinctions, I used the following general rules. Active and substantial business men were so considered if they spent considerable time engaged in large-scale business enterprises. Therefore, railway directors or directors of other

[11] Harold Perkin, *The Origins of Modern English Society, 1780–1880* (London: 1969), pp. 252–70.

companies are treated as having only incidental business interests. Then there are those MPs who had active business interests, but on a small scale. Most of these are Irish Nationalist MPs who were chemists, cattle-dealers, victuallers, fruit-brokers, hotel or public house proprietors, grocers, and drapers. These also are distinguished in the coding from Members with active and substantial business interests. Viewed in this manner, the data yielded the following results shown below.

Active and Substantial Business Interests in the House of Commons in 1886

Active and substantial business interests	224	(32.9%)
Incidental business interests only	50	(7.4%)
Active but small-scale business interests	15	(2.2%)
No business interests	391	(57.5%)
Summary:		
Active and substantial business interests	224	(32.9%)
Only incidental, small-scale, or no business interests	456	(67.1%)

This scheme does not remove all ambiguities. William Burdett-Coutts, for example, the husband of baroness Burdett-Coutts, reopened and became the owner of the Columbia Market for the sale of fish and vegetables. He also established a fishing fleet in the North Sea. These seem, however, to be more in the way of charitable activities rather than active business interests, because they were associated with Burdett-Coutt's activities as a co-operator in movements to meliorate the welfare of the working classes. Joseph Ruston was an engineer, and therefore connected to the professions, but he was the head of an engineering firm, on the employing side of the enterprise. Patrick James Foley was the 'managing' director of an assurance company, and therefore had an active and substantial business interest, as Ruston had.

While I am confident of this tabulation of active and substantial business interests, and of active and small-scale interests, I am less easy about the incidental business interests MPs had in 1886. This figure must surely be taken as a conservative reckoning. One example may illustrate my misgivings. The enumeration of railway directors in this House of Commons was initially short. The detailed research undertaken on the role of railway directors in this House of Commons by scholars working with other sources turned up nineteen additional names which I had not found in the materials I had been using.[12] They are now included, but one cannot help but wonder how many additional names lurk.

Social class, since it is based upon consciousness, an awareness of what one thinks of oneself and the regard others have for one, rests upon internalized values and standards of behaviour. As a contemporary to this

[12] Armytage, 'The Railway Rates Question and the Fall of the Third Gladstone Ministry', pp. 18–51. P. M. Williams, 'Public Opinion and the Railway Rates Question in 1886', *English Historical Review*, 67 (Jan. 1952), pp. 37–73.

House of Commons puts it in reflecting on the concept of the gentleman, if 'the brevet of a gentleman rests neither upon birth, nor wealth, nor outward manners, we seem forced to the conviction that it must somehow rest upon those inward manners which make the man, and of which the outward should be only the visible sign; in one word, upon character'.[13] Internalized qualities, whether relating to gentlemen, or to professional, business, or working classes, defy easy observation and enumeration. However, the consorting of men together, even as the consorting of crook-taloned birds, to use Namier's image, is spatial. That is to say, it occurs in definable spaces and places. By taking the places in which MPs consorted together as indicators of the internalized qualities specifying their status, it is possible to construct a status profile, and then, by comparing it with the social groups of MPs, to determine which had status and which had not. This may then be used as a device to determine how distinct from each other social groups were in the House of Commons, and whether the concept of gentility had any meaning there.

Some places, more than others, seem likely to predict who, by virtue of their being there, possessed status: the public schools, the universities, local offices in counties and boroughs, holders of Church livings, officers in the local yeomanries and militias, whether their mothers or wives were related to the peerage–baronetage–landed gentry, and the possession of lands in excess of 3,000 acres, either by their families or personally.

Preliminary List of Social Indicators

Public school educations	213	(31.3%)
University educations	318	(46.8%)
County or borough offices	376	(55.2%)
Patrons of Church livings	65	(9.6%)
Officers in the yeomanry or militia	106	(15.5%)
Mothers related to the peerage–baronetage–landed gentry	147	(21.6%)
First wives related to the peerage–baronetage–landed gentry	134	(19.7%)
Second wives related to the peerage–baronetage–landed gentry	20	(2.9%)
Held land in excess of 3,000 acres personally	110	(16.2%)
Belonged to families holding land in excess of 3,000 acres	190	(27.9%)

While the possession of each of these qualities, presumably, might be taken to signal high social status, such presumption requires a systematic test. The first part of such a test is to ascertain the extent to which these indicators of status predict each other, the extent to which they are related. That is to say, an effort to construct a measure of status requires that all elements within that measure be statistically compatible with each other. To judge for this, I constructed a matrix of Q values in which the possession of each of these indicators, or the lack of possession, was compared with the possession, or lack of possession, of all the other indicators. The formula for Q is given by the expression $Q = ad - bc / ad + bc$ in which a = the number

[13] [W.R.B.], 'The English Gentleman', p. 263.

of MPs possessing both indicators; b = the number of MPs possessing the first indicator, but not the second; c = the number of MPs possessing the second indicator, but not the first; d = the number of MPs possessing neither indicator. If the indicators being compared are related, a Q value will equal or approach unity because the a cell and the d cell will be heavily loaded and the b cell and the c cell will be lightly loaded. The Q value advances toward 1.0 when the frequencies of the indicators being compared show high numbers of Members possessing both or neither dignity. In so far as the frequencies are distributed with greater randomness and relative equality among the four cells, the value of Q declines toward 0, indicating the absence of a relationship between the two indicators under comparison. As the matrix of Q values below shows, two indicators, university education and the holding of local offices, failed to show an association with the others. The others are statistically compatible, and the matrix reveals a strong intersecting pattern of interrelationships among them.

Q Matrix of Indicators of Social Status for MPs in 1886

		1	2	3	4	5	6	7	8	9	10
1.	Public school	—	.73	.15	.75	.65	.72	.77	.77	.64	.77
2.	University		—	.06	.53	.26	.38	.49	.56	.26	.50
3.	Local office			—	.62	.47	.04	.24	.01	.64	.26
4.	Church livings				—	.63	.52	.59	.63	.90	.77
5.	Militia/										
	Yeomanry					—	.48	.57	.16	.69	.72
6.	Mother PBG						—	.70	.80	.54	.84
7.	Wife I PBG							—	.68	.71	.84
8.	Wife II PBG								—	.27	.64
9.	Personal land									—	.95
10.	Family land.										—

Even if a finer point is put on the analysis, and the holding of county offices, the position of county justice of the peace, and attendance at Oxford or Cambridge are used in making the comparisons, the values achieved are not very much better. Attendance at Oxford is associated with public school education (.86) and maternal connection to the landed classes (.73), and approaches a relationship to connection to the landed classes through marriage (.63), and patronage of Church livings (.61); it is unrelated to the other indicators of status. Attendance at Cambridge reaches an association only with connections to the landed classes through second marriages (.79). County office-holding is associated only with the patronage of Church livings (.73) and the possession of land in excess of 3,000 acres (.71), though it approaches a relationship with the holding of commissions in the yeomanry and militia (.61). Belonging to the county magistracy was unrelated to all indicators of status.

The necessity of excluding local office-holding, especially the county magistracy, from a schedule of indicators of social status is a finding which requires some pondering. The study of local élites indicates that the association of local office-holding (especially membership in the county magistracy) and status varied regionally. In Hertfordshire and Lancashire, the justices' bench was filled by recruitment practices drawing on values other than those of landed society.[14] This is a pattern, if true for the country as a whole, which may explain why, in the House of Commons of 1886, holders of local offices and county justices of the peace failed to possess other indicators of social status. For the Buckinghamshire JPs, however, the correspondence between their recruitment and the conventional ideals of gentility was considerably closer.[15] Additionally, the selection of men for local offices may have been so politicized by the late nineteenth century that those selected had no continuing association with the values of local élites. Sir James Sawyer wrote to Lord Randolph Churchill concerning appointments to the justices' bench in Birmingham: 'I think the appointment of some Tory magistrates would do us good. . . . We have had some local difficulties in carrying out a Unionist policy which a few promotions would remove.'[16]

If university attendance and local office-holding are excluded from the analysis, the two clusters of mutually consistent indicators of social status in Chapter 4 (Table 4.3) can be assembled using data drawn from the social backgrounds of Members of the House of Commons in 1886. These sets of social indicators describe two related status dimensions: one refers to external attributes, community duty, and responsibility; the second refers to personal and family attributes. Two indicators, having public school educations and membership of families possessing land exceeding 3,000 acres, fit both clusters, an indication that these were central to the notion of status in the late Victorian period.

These dimensions of status describe the barriers to social mobility and social advancement in the late nineteenth century. They were indicators of the social objectives people sought: prestige, fame, culture, citizenship, and family. They are indicators of what men thought about themselves and the lives they led, and the ways others regarded them. The import of these findings is discussed at length in Chapter 4, but it needs to be said here that the social distinction between landed gentlemen and other social groups in the House of Commons remains clear. The decline in the proportion of landed gentlemen in the House, the increase in numbers and proportions of business and professional men sitting there, and the interpenetration of landed and non-landed social groups there had not obliterated the traditional social threshold between gentlemen and non-gentlemen, and these figures provide an empirical test for this distinction among Members of the House of Commons. Gentility meant something.

---

[14] Lawrence Stone and Jeanne C. Fawtier Stone, 'Country Houses and their Owners in Hertfordshire, 1540–1879', *The Dimensions of Quantitative Research in History*, ed. William O. Aydelotte, Allan G. Bogue, and Robert William Fogel (Princeton: 1973), pp. 69, 76, 81; D. Foster, 'Class and County Government in Early Nineteenth Century Lancashire', *Northern History*, 9 (1974), pp. 48–61.

[15] Lubenow, 'Social Recruitment and Social Attitudes', pp. 247–68.

[16] Sir James Sawyer to Lord Randolph Churchill, 29 July 1886, Lord Randolph Churchill Letters 1/13/1589.

SELECT BIBLIOGRAPHY

UNPUBLISHED MANUSCRIPT COLLECTIONS

The Birmingham University Library:
  The Joseph Chamberlain Papers
The Bodleian Library, Oxford:
  The Lewis Harcourt Journal
The British Library:
  W. E. Gladstone Papers
  Herbert Gladstone Papers
  The Earl of Morley Papers
  A. J. Balfour Papers
  Sir Richard Assheton Cross Papers
  Henry Campbell-Bannerman Papers
  Sir Edward Hamilton Papers
  Sir Richard Temple, Bt. Letters
  The Earl of Carnarvon Papers
  The Earl of Iddlesleigh Papers
  The Marquess of Ripon Papers
  The Baron Avebury (Sir John Lubbock, Bt.) Papers
Churchill College, Cambridge:
  Lord Randolph Churchill Letters
  The Viscount Esher Papers
The Fitzwilliam Museum, Cambridge:
  Wilfred Scawen Blunt Manuscripts
Hatfield House, Hertfordshire:
  Third Marquess of Salisbury Manuscripts
  Fourth Marquess of Salisbury Manuscripts
Huntington Library and Art Gallery, San Marino, California:
  Grenville Correspondence, Third Duke of Buckingham and Chandos
  Papers
  George Manners Morgan Papers
Trinity College, Cambridge:
  Sir George O. Trevelyan, Bt. Papers
  William Archbishop Benson Papers

MEMOIRS, BOOKS, AND ARTICLES

Acland, Arthur H. D., *Memoirs and Letters of the Right Honourable Sir Thomas Dyke Acland, Bt.* (printed for private circulation, London: 1902).
Agg-Gardner, James, *Some Parliamentary Recollections* (London: 1927).
Allen, Edward A., 'Public School Elites in Early Victorian England: The Boys at Harrow and Merchant Taylors' School from 1825 to 1850', *Journal of British Studies*, 21.2 (Spring 1982).

Anderson, Lee F., Meredith W. Watts, Jr., and Allen R. Wilcox, *Legislative Roll-Call Analysis* (Evanston, Ill.: 1966).

Aydelotte, W. O., 'The Conservative and Radical Interpretations of Early Victorian Social Legislation', *Victorian Studies*, 11.2 (Dec. 1967).

—— 'Constituency Influence on the British House of Commons, 1841–1847', *The History of Parliamentary Behavior*, ed. W. O. Aydelotte (Princeton: 1977).

—— 'The Country Gentlemen and the Repeal of the Corn Laws', *English Historical Review*, 82 (Jan. 1967).

—— 'The Disintegration of the Conservative Party in the 1840s: A Study of Political Attitudes', *The Dimensions of Quantitative Research in History*, ed. W. O. Aydelotte, Allen G. Bogue, and Robert William Fogel (Princeton: 1974).

—— 'The House of Commons in the 1840s', *History*, 39 (Oct. 1954).

—— 'Issues and Parties in Early Victorian England', *Journal of British Studies*, 5.2 (1966).

—— *Quantification in History* (Reading, Mass., Menlo Park, California, London, and Don Mills, Ontario: 1971).

—— 'Voting Patterns in the British House of Commons in the 1840s', *Comparative Studies in Society and History*, 5.2 (Jan. 1963).

Bailey, J. (ed.), *The Diary of Lady Frederick Cavendish* (London: 1927).

Barker, Michael, *Gladstone and Radicalism: The Reconstruction of Liberal Policy in Britain, 1885–1894* (Hassocks, Sussex: 1975).

Bentley, Michael, 'Party Doctrine and Thought', *High and Low Politics in Modern Britain*, ed. Michael Bentley and John Stevenson (Oxford: 1983).

Berrington, Hugh, 'Partisanship and Dissidence in the Nineteenth Century House of Commons', *Parliamentary Affairs*, 21 (1968).

Blake, Robert, *The Conservative Party from Peel to Churchill* (London: 1970).

Blewett, Neal, *The Peers, the Parties, and the People: The General Elections of 1910* (London: 1972).

Broadhurst, Henry, *Henry Broadhurst, M.P., The Story of His Life* (London: 1901).

de Broke, Lord Willoughby, *Passing Years* (London, Bombay, and Sydney: 1924).

Bylsma, J. R., 'Party Structure in the 1852–1857 House of Commons', *Journal of Interdisciplinary History*, 7.4 (Spring 1977).

Cannadine, David, 'The Theory and Practice of the English Leisure Classes', *Historical Journal*, 21.2 (1978).

Chamberlain, Joseph, *A Political Memoir, 1880–1892*, ed. C. H. D. Howard (London: 1953).

Chapman, J. K. (ed.), *A Political Correspondence of the Gladstone Era: The Letters of Lady Sophia Palmer to Sir Arthur Gordon* (Philadelphia: 1971).

Clarke, P. F., *Lancashire and the New Liberalism* (Cambridge: 1971).

Cooke, A. B. and John Vincent, *The Governing Passion: Cabinet Government and Party Politics in Britain, 1885–1886*, (Hassocks, Sussex: 1974).

Cowling, Maurice, *The Impact of Hitler* (Cambridge: 1975).
—— *The Impact of Labour* (Cambridge: 1971).
Craig, F. W. S. (ed.), *British Electoral Facts, 1885–1965* (London: 1968).
Cromwell, Valerie, 'Mapping the Political World of 1861: A Multidimensional Analysis of House of Commons' Division Lists', *Legislative Studies Quarterly*, 7.2 (May 1982).
Crowley, D. W., 'The Crofters' "Party", 1885–1892', *Scottish Historical Review*, 35.2 (Oct. 1956).
Dewey, Clive, 'Celtic Agrarian Legislation and the Celtic Revival: Historical Implications of Gladstone's Irish and Scottish Land Acts, 1870–1886', *Past and Present*, 64 (Aug. 1974).
Dingle, A. E., *The Campaign for Prohibition in Victorian England: The United Kingdom Alliance, 1872–1895* (London: 1980).
Dod, Charles, *Parliamentary Companion* (London: 1886).
Emy, H. V., *Liberals, Radicals and Social Politics, 1892–1914* (Cambridge: 1973).
Ensor, R. C. K., 'Some Political and Economic Interactions in Later Victorian England', *Transactions of the Royal Historical Society*, 4th series, 31 (1949).
Fitzmaurice, Lord Edward, *The Life of Granville, George Leveson Gower, Second Earl Granville, K.G., 1815–1891* (London, New York, and Bombay: 1905).
Foster, Roy, *Lord Randolph Churchill, A Political Life* (Oxford: 1981).
Gathorne-Hardy, Jonathan, *The Old-School Tie: The Phenomenon of The English Public School* (New York: 1977).
Goodman, Gordon L., 'Liberal Unionism: The Revolt of the Whigs', *Victorian Studies*, 2.2 (1959).
Griffiths, P. C., 'The Caucus and the Liberal Party in 1886', *History*, 61.202 (June 1976).
Guedalla, Philip (ed.), *The Queen and Mr. Gladstone* (London: 1933).
Hamer, D. A., *Liberal Politics in the Age of Gladstone and Rosebery* (Oxford: 1972).
—— *The Politics of Electoral Pressure: A Study in the History of Victorian Reform Agitation* (Hassocks, Sussex: 1977).
Hamilton, Lord Frederic, *The Days Before Yesterday* (London: 1920).
Hamilton, James Cook, *Parties and Voting Patterns in the Parliament of 1874–1880* (unpublished Ph.D. dissertation, University of Iowa: 1968).
Hanham, H. J., *Elections and Party Management: Politics in the Time of Disraeli and Gladstone* (London: 1959).
—— 'The Problem of Highland Discontent, 1880–1885', *Transactions of the Royal Historical Society*, 4th series, 19 (1969).
—— *The Reformed Electoral System in Great Britain, 1832–1914* (London: 1968).
—— 'The Sale of Honours in Late Victorian England', *Victorian Studies*, 3 (1959–60).
Harrison, Brian, *Peaceable Kingdom: Stability and Change in Modern Britain* (Oxford: 1982).

Harrison, Brian, *Separate Spheres: The Opposition to Women's Suffrage in Britain* (London: 1978).

Healy, T. M., *Letters and Leaders of My Day* (London: 1928).

Howard, Michael, 'Empire, Race, and War in Pre-1914 Britain', *History and Imagination: Essays in Honour of H. R. Trevor-Roper*, ed. Hugh Lloyd-Jones, Valerie Pearl, and Blair Worden (London: 1981).

Howarth, Janet, 'The Liberal Revival in Northamptonshire, 1880–1895: A Case Study in Late Nineteenth Century Elections', *The Historical Journal*, 12.1 (1969).

Hosking, Geoffrey and Anthony King, 'Radicals and Whigs in the British Liberal Party, 1906–1914', *The History of Legislative Behavior*, ed. W. O. Aydelotte (Princeton: 1977).

Hunter, James, 'The Gaelic Connection: The Highlands, Ireland, and Nationalism, 1873–1922', *Scottish Historical Review*, 54.158 (Oct. 1975).

—— 'The Politics of Highland Land Reform, 1873–1895', *Scottish Historical Review*, 53.155 (Apr. 1974).

Hurst, Michael, *Joseph Chamberlain and Liberal Reunion, the Round Table Conference* (London: 1967).

Jay, Richard, *Joseph Chamberlain: A Political Study* (Oxford: 1981).

Johnson, Nancy E. (ed.), *The Diary of Gathorne-Hardy, Later Lord Cranbrook, 1886–1892: Political Selections* (Oxford: 1981).

Kellas, James G., 'The Liberal Party in Scotland, 1876–1895', *Scottish Historical Review*, 54.137 (Apr. 1965).

—— 'The Liberal Party and the Scottish Church Disestablishment Crisis', *English Historical Review*, 79 (Jan. 1964).

Kennedy, Paul, *The Realities Behind Diplomacy: Background Influences on British External Policy, 1865–1980* (London: 1981).

Kinnear, Michael, *The British Voter: An Atlas and Survey Since 1885* (Ithaca, NY: 1968).

Koss, Stephen, *Sir John Brunner, Radical Plutocrat* (Cambridge: 1970).

Leveson-Gower, George, *Years of Content, 1856–1886* (London: 1940).

Lowell, A. Lawrence, 'The Influence of Party Upon Legislation in England and America', *Annual Report of the American Historical Association* (Washington, DC: 1902).

Lubenow, W. C., 'The Class Struggle and the House of Commons: The Parliamentary Response to the London Riots of 1886', *Histoire sociale— Social History*, 18.35 (May 1985).

—— 'Ireland, the Great Depression, and the Railway Rates: Political Issues and Backbench Opinion in the House of Commons in 1886', *Proceedings of the American Philosophical Society*, 122.4 (1978).

—— 'Irish Home Rule and the Great Separation in the Liberal Party in 1886: The Dimensions of Parliamentary Liberalism', *Victorian Studies*, 26.2 (1983).

—— 'Irish Home Rule and the Social Basis of the Great Separation in the Liberal Party in 1886', *Historical Journal*, 28.1 (1985).

—— *The Politics of Government Growth: Early Victorian Attitudes Toward State Intervention, 1833–1848* (Newton Abbot: 1971).

Lucy, Henry W., *Later Peeps at Parliament from Behind the Speaker's Chair* (London: 1905).

Lyons, F. S. L., *Charles Stewart Parnell* (London: 1977).

McCalmont, Frederick H. (ed.), *The Parliamentary Poll Book of All Elections from the Reform Act of 1832 to February 1910*, 7th edn. (London: 1910).

McCarthy, Justin, *Reminiscences* (London: 1899).

McGill, Barry, 'Glittering Prizes and Party Funds in Perspective, 1882–1931', *Bulletin of the Institute for Historical Research*, 55.131 (May 1982).

MacRae, Duncan, *Dimensions of Congressional Voting* (Berkeley, California: 1958).

MacRae, Jr., Duncan, *Issues and Parties in Legislative Voting: Methods of Statistical Analysis* (New York, Evanston, and London: 1970).

Marsh, Peter, *The Discipline of Popular Government: Lord Salisbury's Domestic Statecraft, 1881–1892* (Hassocks, Sussex: 1978).

Mattheisen, Donald J., 'German Parliamentarism in 1848: Roll-Call Voting in the Frankfurt Assembly', *Social Science History*, 5.4 (Fall 1981).

—— 'Liberal Constitutionalism in the Frankfurt Parliament of 1848: An Inquiry Based on Roll-Call Analysis', *Central European History*, 12.2 (June 1979).

Matthew, H. C. G., *The Liberal Imperialists: The Ideas and Politics of a Post-Gladstonian Elite* (Oxford: 1973).

Midleton, Earl of, *Records and Recollections, 1856–1939* (London: 1939).

Morgan, Kenneth O., *Rebirth of a Nation: Wales, 1880–1980* (New York: 1981).

—— *Wales in British Politics, 1869–1922* (Cardiff: 1970).

O'Brien, Conor Cruise, *Parnell and His Party, 1880–1890* (Oxford: 1957).

O'Brien, William, *Evening Memories* (Dublin and London: 1920).

O'Connor, T. P., *Memoirs of an Old Parliamentarian* (London: 1929).

—— *The Parnell Movement, with a Sketch of Irish Parties from 1843* (London: 1886).

O'Day, Alan, *The English Face of Irish Nationalism: Parnellite Involvement in British Politics, 1880–1886* (Dublin, 1977).

Pease, Sir Alfred, *Elections and Recollections* (London: 1932).

Pedersen, Mogen N., 'The Personal Circulation of a Legislature: The Danish Folketing, 1849–1968', *The History of Legislative Behavior*, ed. W. O. Aydelotte (Princeton: 1977).

Pelling, Henry, *The Social Geography of British Elections, 1885–1910* (London, Melbourne, Toronto and New York: 1967).

Phillips, Gregory, 'The Whig Lords and Liberals, 1886–1892', *Historical Journal*, 24 (1981).

Porter, Mrs Adrian, *The Life and Letters of Sir John Henniker Heaton, Bt.* (London and New York: 1916).

Quinault, Roland, *Landlords and Parliamentary Politics* (unpublished Ph.D. dissertation, University of Oxford: 1975).

—— 'Lord Randolph Churchill and Tory Democracy, 1880–1885', *Historical Journal*, 22.1 (1979).

Rodden, Brian William, *Anatomy of the 1886 Schism in the British Liberal Party: A Study of the Ninety-Four Liberal Members of the Parliament Who Voted Against the First Home Rule Bill* (unpublished Ph.D. dissertation, Rutgers University: 1968).

Rubinstein, W. D., *Men of Property: The Very Wealthy in Britain Since the Industrial Revolution* (London: 1981).

—— 'The New Men of Wealth and the Purchase of Land in Nineteenth Century Britain', *Past and Present*, 92 (Apr. 1981).

Russell, G. W. E. (ed.), *Sir Wilfred Lawson, A Memoir* (London: 1909).

Sartori, Giovanni, 'From the Sociology of Politics to Political Sociology', *Politics and the Social Sciences*, ed. Seymour Martin Lipset (New York and Oxford: 1968).

Savage, D. C., 'Scottish Politics, 1885–6', *Scottish Historical Review*, 50.130 (Oct. 1961).

Searle, G. R., 'The Edwardian Liberal Party and Business', *English Historical Review*, 98 (Jan. 1983).

Simon, Alan, 'Church Disestablishment as a Factor in the General Election of 1885', *Historical Journal*, 18.4 (1975).

Smith, Paul, *Disraelian Conservatism and Social Reform* (London and Toronto: 1967).

Smith, Woodruff and Sharon A. Turner, 'Legislative Behavior in the German Reichstag, 1898–1906', *Central European History*, 14.1 (Mar. 1981).

Southgate, Donald, *The Passing of the Whigs, 1832–1886* (London: 1962).

Stephens, Hugh, 'The Changing Context of British Politics in the 1880s: The Reform Acts and the Formation of the Liberal Unionist Party', *Social Science History*, 6.1 (Winter 1982).

—— and David W. Brady, 'The Parliamentary Parties and the Electoral Reforms of 1884–1885 in Great Britain', *Legislative Studies Quarterly*, 1.4 (Nov. 1976).

Temple, Bt., Sir Richard, *Life in Parliament, Being the Experience of a Member in the House of Commons from 1886 to 1892 Inclusive* (London: 1893).

—— *The Story of My Life* (London, Paris, and Melbourne: 1896).

Thompson, F. M. L., *English Landed Society in the Nineteenth Century* (London: 1963).

Thompson, Paul, *Socialists, Liberals, and Labour: The Struggle for London, 1885–1914* (London: 1967).

Urwin, Derek, 'Territorial Structures and Political Developments in the United Kingdom', *The Politics of Territorial Integrity*, ed. Stein Rokkan and Derek Urwin (London, Beverly Hills, and New Delhi: 1982).

Vincent, John R., *The Formation of the Liberal Party, 1857–1868* (London: 1966).

—— (ed.), *The Later Derby Diaries: Home Rule, Liberal Unionism, and Aristocratic Life in Late Victorian England* (printed and published by the editor at the University of Bristol: 1981).

Wald, Kenneth, *Crosses on the Ballot: Patterns of British Voter Alignment Since 1885* (Princeton: 1983).

Whiteley, William Henry, *The Social Composition of the House of Commons, 1868–1885* (unpublished Ph.D. dissertation, Cornell University: 1960).

Select Bibliography

Wordsley, William, *Reasons for So and So*, in a
pamphlet... [illegible continuation of bibliographic entries]

INDEX

The party affiliations and the constituencies of Members of the House of Commons in 1886 are found in parentheses. Those marked thus * are Liberals who became Liberal Unionists by opposing Gladstone's Home Rule Bill.